D0138925

BUSINESS DATA NETWORKS AND SECURITY

Tenth Edition

BUSINESS DATA NETWORKS AND SECURITY

Raymond R. Panko
University of Hawai`i at Mānoa

Julia L. Panko
Weber State University

Boston   Columbus   Hoboken   Indianapolis   New York   San Francisco
Amsterdam   Cape Town   Dubai   London   Madrid   Milan   Munich   Paris   Montreal   Toronto
Delhi   Mexico City   Sao Paulo   Sydney   Hong Kong   Seoul   Singapore   Taipei   Tokyo

Editor-in-Chief: Stephanie Wall
Director of Marketing: Maggie Moylan
Executive Marketing Manager: Anne Fahlgren
Project Manager: Tom Benfatti
Acquisitions Editor: Nicole Sam
Program Manager: Denise Vaughn
Program Manager Team Lead: Ashley Santora
Project Manager Team Lead: Judy Leale

Cover Designer: Jon Boylan, Lumina
Cover Image: margouillat/fotolia.com
Full Service Project Management: Allan Rayer
Composition: Integra Software Solutions
Printer/Binder: Edwards Brothers Malloy
Cover Printer: Edwards Brothers Malloy
Text Font: 10/12 Palatino LT Std

Library of Congress Cataloging-in-Publication Data On File

10 9 8 7 6 5

ISBN 10:   0-13-354401-X
ISBN 13: 978-0-13-354401-5

To Sal Aurigemma. A great partner in crime in research and teaching.

BRIEF CONTENTS

Online Modules

(available at www.pearsonhighered.com/panko)

CONTENTS

Chapter 11 NETWORKED APPLICATIONS   373

Online Modules

(available at www.pearsonhighered.com/panko)

PREFACE FOR STUDENTS

Networking and security are the most exciting careers in information technology. Heck, they are the most exciting careers in the world. Professionals in these fields do not spend their careers just doing the same thing over and over again. Their work is constantly evolving, and personal growth is guaranteed.

HOW TO STUDY NETWORKING

Networking and Security Are Different

Some students find networking and security difficult. The problem seems to be that they require a different learning approach than programming and database management. In programming and database, you learn a little, apply it, learn a little more, apply it, shampoo, rinse, repeat. If there is something you don't know, there is probably another way to do it. (Except on exams and homework, of course.)

In networking, you need to know everything to do anything, and it is what you don't know that hurts you. For example, suppose that you want to connect a server to an Ethernet switch. This sounds simple enough. However, should you choose copper wire or optical fiber? If copper wire, what grade of copper wire? If fiber, which OM standard should you choose? Or should you connect the server wirelessly? In your choice, you must include speed, distance, delay, reliability, and cost. Especially cost. Budgets are eternally tight, and networking people never say "cost doesn't matter."

Security is different again. In security, you are not just dealing with design issues and the reliability of technology. You are dealing with human opponents that are engaged with you in a perpetual arms race of protections and new attack methods to get beyond those protections. It is a lot like playing a video game at a high level, but with real-world consequences.

Will employers expect you to know everything when you apply for a job? Of course not. However, they will expect you to know a *lot*. They will sit you down and ask you how to connect a server to an Ethernet switch or something else that requires you to be able to integrate what you have learned. In fact, they will do this for the material in most courses you have taken to get an understanding of how serious you are about work.

You will certainly get questions that require you to troubleshoot a problem. Troubleshooting is hard, and most people intuitively do it wrong. This book will give you a methodology for doing it right and plenty of practice in applying it.

Employers will expect applicants to be up in the field. For Wi-Fi, they may ask you about security, and they don't expect you to stop at 802.11i. Mentioning Ethernet busses and hubs in a design may end the interview. Employers expect applicants to have some knowledge of IPv6 and cloud computing. They will be interested if you know even a little about SDN.

Learning with this Book

Organization of the Book   We have tried to write this book to help you learn the material. Most basically, we present the material in short sections with Test Your Understanding (TYU) questions immediately after each section, to help you know if you have understood the section.

Pay special attention to keyterms that are boldfaced. These are the core concepts in the field. And yes, there are a lot of them. Important or frequently misunderstood concepts are broken out like this for special attention:

A rogue access point is an unauthorized access point set up within a firm by an employee or department.

Figures cover almost all important concepts in the book. There are special study figures that summarize the flow and key points in most sections that are not amenable to illustrations. The PowerPoint presentations are based on these figures. For complex illustrations, the PowerPoint presentations have builds, presenting only part of the figure at each step.

If you see a term that you learned previously but have forgotten, go to the Glossary. In Glossary entries, some page numbers are boldfaced. These are the pages on which the term was defined or characterized. Some terms are introduced more than once and may have two or more page numbers boldfaced.

Studying for Exams   Exams are the least popular elements in any course. And yes, you will have dreams about waking up late for an exam for several years after you graduate. However, there are things you can do to make your life easier.

First, study the material. Read a section. Do the TYU questions. In fact, download the homework file, which has all the questions. Put your answers into the file. The multiple choice questions in the test bank are taken from the material in the TYU questions and thought questions. A good idea is to read the material over before exams instead of just relying on your initial answers, which might not have been exactly perfect, having been based on your first reading.

Late in your study, describe the figures as if you were giving a lecture. If there is something you do not understand, note it and follow up. Take notes on your problems and insights.

At each step, ask yourself why each question and answer is important. This will give you insights and will solidify the material in your memory.

Upper-Division Learning   Initial college education focuses on learning isolated facts. Networking and security, like other advanced courses, requires something more. First, it requires the ability to compare and contrast concepts you have learned. In networking and security, there are alternative ways to do almost everything. Understanding individual alternatives is not enough. To select the best alternative, you must understand trade-offs between them. You must also see them in the broader context of the chapter. For 802.11 Wi-Fi, 802.11i provides a lot of protection; but there are other things you must also do to be secure. Life is about trade-offs. Your studying must reflect that.

Another pain point is learning multi-step procedures. It is important to learn the overall flow, understand how each step relates to the flow, understand each step, and do this all over again until you have both the flow and the details. Processes are difficult to learn because you do not have a framework clearly in mind for fitting individual facts into the bigger picture. In learning processes, it takes several cycles of studying at multiple levels to get both the overall flow and the individual steps.

ABOUT THE AUTHORS

Ray Panko is a professor of IT management and a Shidler Fellow at the University of Hawai'i's Shidler College of Business. His main courses are networking and security. Before coming to the university, he was a project manager at Stanford Research Institute (now SRI International), where he worked for Doug Englebart, the inventor of the mouse and creator of the first operational hypertext system. He received his B.S. in physics and his M.B.A. from Seattle University. He received his doctorate from Stanford University, where his dissertation was conducted under contract to the Office of the President of the United States. He has been awarded the Shidler College of Business's Dennis Ching award as the outstanding teacher among senior faculty. His e-mail is Ray@Panko.com.

Julia Panko is an assistant professor on the faculty at Weber State University. She received her doctorate from the University of California, Santa Barbara. Her research interests include the twentieth- and twenty-first-century novel, the history and theory of information technology, and the digital humanities. Her dissertation focused on the relationship between information culture and modern and contemporary novels.

Chapter 1

Welcome to the Cloud

LEARNING OBJECTIVES

By the end of this chapter, you should be able to:

- Describe basic networking, including why networks are drawn as clouds, hosts, addresses, the Internet, Internet service providers, transmission speed, and service level agreements.

- Explain how the Internet works, how Netflix uses Amazon Web Services IaaS (Infrastructure as a Service) with virtual machines, and a Google SaaS (Software as a Service).

- Describe messages, fragmentation, multiplexing, and frames versus packets.

- Describe how single point-to-point, wireless, switched, and hybrid wireless-switched networks operate—especially how switches forward incoming frames.

- Describe how internets and routers make it possible for hosts on different networks to work together.

- List the five standards layers commonly encountered in networking, describe what each layer does, describe concepts and terms in each layer, identify at which layer a given process is operating, and identify which standards agencies and standards architecture are relevant to that process.

BOX 1

By the Numbers

The Internet is enormous, growing, and changing.

- By 2003, there were already more devices connected to the Internet (computers, phones, etc.) than there were human users.[1]
- In 2010, 21% of the world's population used the Internet. In 2013, it was 39%.[2]
- In 2012, online video viewing overtook DVD and Blu-Ray viewing.[3]
- From 2011 to 2016, global IP traffic will triple, and the number of connected devices will nearly double.[4]
- In 2016, Cisco expects the Internet to carry one zettabyte of data.[5] A zettabyte is 1,000,000,000,000,000,000,000 (one sextillion) bytes.
- By 2020, there will be 50 billion devices connected to the Internet—ten times the number of human users. The great majority of these will be devices talking to other devices, without human involvement.[6]

NETFLIX DIVES INTO THE AMAZON[7]

Figure 1-1 shows that the Internet is often depicted as a cloud. This symbolizes that just as you cannot see inside a cloud, users should be oblivious to what happens inside the Internet. To them, the Internet simply works, like the electrical, water, and telephone systems.

In this course, as you might suspect, you will not be spared the burden of understanding the internals of the Internet and other networks. This knowledge will prepare you to help your employer use networks effectively. Along the way, you will learn a good deal about security, too. Networking is a vast superhighway with great potential for benefits. However, it has some rough neighborhoods.

---

[1] Suzanne Choney, "US Has More Internet-Connected Gadgets Than People," *nbcnews.com*, January 2, 2003. http://www.nbcnews.com/technology/us-has-more-internet-connected-gadgets-people-1C7782791.

[2] Geneva, "Key ICT Indicators for Developed and Developing Countries and the World (Totals and Penetration Rates)," *International Telecommunications Unions (ITU)*, February 27, 2013.

[3] Jared Newman, "Online Video Expected to Overtake DVD, Blu-ray Viewing this Year," *Techhive*, May 27, 2012. http://www.techhive.com/article/252650/online_video_expected_to_overtake_dvd_blu_ray_viewing_this_year.html.

[4] Larry Hettick, "Cisco: Networked Devices Will Outnumber People 3 to 1 in 2016," *Network World*, June 1, 2012. http://www.networkworld.com/newsletters/converg/2012/060412convergence1.html

[5] Grant Gross, "Cisco: Global 'Net Traffic to Surpass 1 Zettabyte by 2016, Cisco Says," *Network World*, May 31, 2012. http://www.pcworld.com/article/256522/cisco_global_net_traffic_to_surpass_1_zettabyte_in_2016.html

[6] Ericsson, "CEO to Shareholders: 50 Billion Connections 2020," press release, April 2010.

[7] Sources for this section include the following. Brandon Butler, "Three Lessons from Netflix on How to Live in a Cloud," *NetworkWorld*, October 9, 2013. http://www.networkworld.com/news/2013/100913-netflix-cloud-274647.html. Matt Petronzio, "Meet the Man Who Keeps Netflix Afloat in the Cloud," *mashable.com*, May 13, 2013. http://mashable.com/2013/05/13/netflix-dream-job/. Kevin Purdy, "How Netflix is Revolutionizing Cloud Computing Just So You Can Watch 'Teen Mom' on Your Phone," *www.itworld.com*, May 10, 2013. http://www.itworld.com/cloud-computing/355844/netflix-revolutionizing-computer-just-serve-you-movies. Ashlee Vance, "Netflix, Reed Hastings Survive Missteps to Join Silicon Valley's Elite," *Business Week*, May 9, 2013. http://www.businessweek.com/articles/2013-05-09/netflix-reed-hastings-survive-missteps-to-join-silicon-valleys-elite.

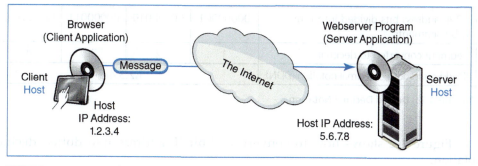

FIGURE 1-1 Internet Communication

Test Your Understanding

1. a) Why is the Internet usually depicted as a cloud? b) What is the significance of this depiction for users?

Hosts, Messages, and Addresses

Hosts   Figure 1-1 introduces some basic networking terms. First, any computer attached to a network is a **host**. Hosts include large servers that work with hundreds of users simultaneously. Hosts also include desktop PCs, laptops, tablets, smartphones, smart glasses, and smart watches. In the future, hosts will include interactive walls, tables, and appliances that will turn your entire home into an immersive interactive environment. In a trend called the **Internet of things**, even coffee makers, toasters, medical implants, and many other small and large devices around us will be hosts that communicate through networks to work better. In fact, machine-to-machine communication will eventually dominate traffic on the Internet. The term *host* is not an obvious name for computers that attach to networks, but it is the common name for them in networking.

Any computer attached to a network is a host.

Messages and Addresses   Figure 1-1 shows that application programs on different hosts communicate by sending messages to one another. Messages require addresses. For example if you want to send the first author a message, you would send it to his e-mail address, Ray@Panko.com. Hosts also need addresses. On the Internet, these are **Internet Protocol addresses** or **IP addresses**. In Figure 1-1, the IP addresses are 1.2.3.4 for the source host and 5.6.7.8 for the destination host.

Dotted Decimal Notation (DDN)   When an IP address is expressed as four numbers separated by dots (periods), this is called **dotted decimal notation (DDN)**. In reality, IP addresses are 32-bit strings of 1s and 0s. Computers have no problem working with long bit strings. Human memory and writing, however, need a crutch to deal with long bit strings. Dotted decimal notation is precisely that—a crutch for inferior biological entities like ourselves. Computers do not use DDN.

32 IP address bits divided into four 8-bit segments	00000001	00000010	00000011	00000100
Segment converted to decimal	1	2	3	4
IP address in dotted decimal notation (DDN)	1.2.3.4			

FIGURE 1-2 Dotted Decimal Notation

Figure 1-2 shows how to convert a 32-bit IP address into dotted decimal notation.

- First, divide the 32 bits into four 8-bit segments.
- Second, treat each segment as a binary number and convert this binary number into a decimal number. For example, the first segment, 00000001 in binary, is 1 in decimal.
- Third, combine the four decimal field values, separating them by dots. This gives 1.2.3.4.

How do you convert a binary number into a decimal number? The fastest way is to go to an Internet search engine and find a binary-to-digital converter. You then type each 8-bit binary segment's bits into the indicated binary box and hit the convert button. The decimal value appears in the decimal box.

We have been looking at a 32-bit IP address. However, this is not the only type of IP address. It is an **IP Version 4 (IPv4)** address. IPv4 is the dominant IP protocol on the Internet today. However, we are beginning to see significant use of **IP Version 6 (IPv6)**. As we will see in Chapter 8, IPv6 addresses are 128 bits long and are represented for human consumption in a very different way.

Test Your Understanding

2. a) What is the term we use in networking for any computer attached to a network? b) Is your smartphone a host when you use it to surf the 'Web? c) Are you as a person a host when you use a network? d) How do application programs on different hosts communicate?

3. a) What kind of addresses do hosts have on the Internet? b) What kind of address is 128.171.17.13? c) What name do we use for the format 128.171.17.13? d) Who uses this format—humans or computers? e) Convert the following 32-bit binary IP address into DDN (spaces are added for easier reading): 10000000 10101011 00010001 00001101. (Check Figure: 10000000 = 128) f) Convert 5.6.7.138 into a 32-bit IP address. (Check Figure: 5 = 00000101) Show a space between each 8-bit segment. g) What type of IP address is 32 bits long? h) What other type of IP address exists, and how long are its addresses?

The Internet

Figure 1-3 illustrates that the global Internet is not a single network. Instead, the **Internet** is a collection of thousands of single networks and smaller internets. All of these single networks and smaller internets interconnect to form a single transmission system that in

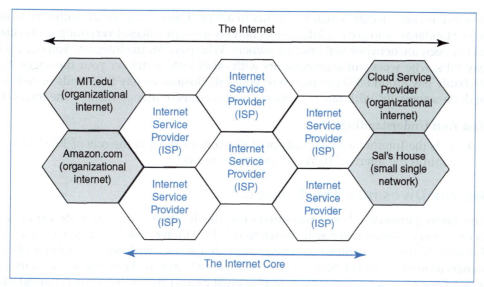

FIGURE 1-3   The Internet's Networks and Smaller Internets

principle allows any Internet host to reach any other.[8] Some of these single networks and smaller internets are owned by organizations such as Amazon.com or MIT. Smaller networks are owned by families and even individuals. In addition, some internets link these smaller networks and smaller internets together. We call these linking internets **Internet service providers (ISPs)**. ISPs collectively form the **core** of the Internet, which is also called the Internet's backbone.[9] To use the Internet, a customer must connect to an ISP.

The Internet is a collection of single networks and smaller internets. All of these networks and smaller internets interconnect to form a single transmission system.

At this point, we need to break the narrative to mention in two pieces of terminology we will use in this book.

- First, saying "single networks and internets" is cumbersome. We use the term *network* for both.
- Second, in this book, we spell internet in lowercase for internets in general and internets that are not the global Internet. We capitalize the global Internet.

Who owns the Internet? The surprising answer is, "Nobody." The ISPs and other organizations own their pieces of the Internet. Who controls the Internet? Again, nobody does. Although the **Internet Engineering Task Force (IETF)** creates standards,

---

[8] The original term for *internet* was *catanet*. When things are connected together in computer science, they are said to be concatenated. Fortunately, "catanet" never caught on, saving the Internet from a flood of bad feline jokes.

[9] For simplicity, the figure shows ISPs as if they served nonoverlapping geographic regions. Actually, ISPs often overlap geographically. National and international ISPs may connect at several geographical locations to exchange messages.

network owners decide which standards to adopt. There is no overall authority to enforce standards or to govern interconnection business practices. Everything is negotiated between the network and internet owners. Who pays for the Internet? You do. Users pay ISPs, who work out arrangements with other ISPs to deliver your messages. You probably pay around $30 per month to your ISP. Businesses pay thousands or millions of dollars annually. With rare exceptions, no government money sustains the Internet.

Test Your Understanding

4. a) Is the Internet a single network? Explain. b) What is the role of ISPs? c) Who controls the Internet? d) Who funds the Internet?

Netflix Dives into the Amazon

You know personally how individuals use the Internet. The corporate experience is often very different. We will illustrate this by talking about how Netflix uses the Internet. Netflix is a commercial streaming video service with tens of millions of customers around the world. Streaming video places a heavy load on network capacity. For a two-hour high-definition movie, Netflix must deliver five million bits (1s or 0s) each second. This is a total of nine gigabytes for that one movie. On any given night, Netflix accounts for roughly a third of the Internet traffic going into U.S. homes.

Requirements Users expect high video quality, and they will not tolerate delay or unreliability. The Internet was not designed for these requirements. The Internet is a "best effort" delivery system that often has insufficient speed and reliability and that often has too much delay for Netflix users. Netflix had to overcome these limitations.

The Internet is a "best effort" delivery system.

Video streaming also requires vast amounts of server processing capacity beyond the demands of actual streaming. Each movie must be **transcoded** into many streaming formats, and when a customer requests a movie, streaming servers have to select the best transcoded format for that particular customer.

In addition, at the heart of Netflix's business plan is an application that creates personalized viewing suggestions for individual customers. This requires the analysis of extensive data about the customer's viewing habits and the choices of other customers with similar viewing profiles.

Outsourcing In 2008, when Netflix was only delivering movies through mailed DVDs, the company suffered a crippling server outage that stopped shipments for several days. That was a wake up call for Netflix. Management realized that reliability would be critical for the online delivery it would soon introduce. It also realized that while Internet delivery would become its core business, managing servers would not. Rather than developing the expertise needed for the complex server technologies the company needed, Netflix decided to outsource server operation to a company that could meet Netflix's high requirements for capacity, reliability, and agility in responding to sudden demand changes.

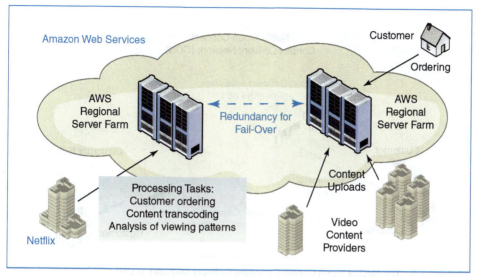

FIGURE 1-4   Netflix and Amazon Web Services (AWS)

Netflix chose **Amazon Web Services (AWS)**. Amazon had leveraged its expertise in managing vast server farms for its e-commerce needs into a cloud service that customers like Netflix could use without worrying about how the servers are operated. Figure 1-4 shows that AWS's enormous server farms had the capacity that Netflix needed for customer ordering, transcoding, and the analysis of viewing patterns. In addition, Amazon had multiple regional server farms with high fail-over capabilities. Even the loss of an entire server farm would not disrupt service for more than minutes. This brought the reliability that Netflix customers demanded. Netflix customers today log into an AWS server to order videos and to take care of other business transactions with Netflix. There are many login servers, and AWS automatically routes the user to one of them. Movie content providers upload their video directly to AWS. Netflix then transcodes the contents into many versions optimized for particular combinations of network speed and customer equipment.

Content Delivery   Netflix uses AWS to store more than one petabyte of movie content in multiple locations. However, Netflix handles content delivery itself. Figure 1-5 shows how Netflix delivers video content to individual customers. Netflix calls this **content delivery network (CDN)** *Open Connect*.

To stream movies to users, Netflix created its own webserver appliances. Each is a relatively small box that can fit into a standard 19-inch (48-cm) wide equipment rack. The Open Connect appliance is seven inches (18 cm) high and two feet (61 cm) deep. Although small in size, it holds about 100 terabytes of data on 36 hard disk drives. The processor is fast enough to stream movies simultaneously to between 10,000 and 20,000 customers. Netflix updates these CDN servers about once a year with newer hardware to increase their capabilities.

Figure 1-5 shows that *Open Connect* is a network on the Internet. It can peer with (connect to) the ISP of a customer. The CDN boxes are placed at the peering point, so

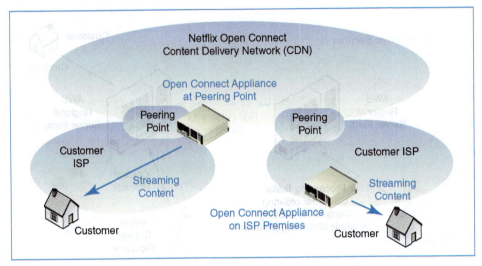

FIGURE 1-5   The Netflix Open Connect Content Delivery Network (CDN)

that traffic only travels the relatively small span of the customer's Internet service provider network. In many cases, ISPs reduce delays further by placing the appliance on their own premises, at a location near the final customer. ISPs tend to like this approach because it reduces traffic flowing across their network. The streaming traffic only goes the short distance from the nearest ISP physical location to the customer.

With only 100 TB of data storage, Open Connect appliances can only handle a portion of Netflix's 1 petabyte of content. Consequently, Netflix uses sophisticated analysis to identify the 100 TB of content most likely to be demanded by customers. It installs this content on the individual CDN servers. Of course, customer interests change rapidly, so this content has to be refreshed daily. During quiet periods in demand each day, Netflix deletes content declining in popularity and installs content of increasing demand.

Test Your Understanding

5. a) List Netflix's content delivery requirements. b) What is transcoding? c) Why does Netflix make many transcoded versions of each movie? d) How does Netflix use AWS? e) How do content delivery networks reduce streaming delays to customers?

Virtualization and Agility

Figure 1-6 shows that AWS uses virtualization to turn each physical server into several **virtual machines (VMs)**. Each VM is a software process running on the physical server. However, it acts like a real server in its connections with the outside world. It has its own IP address as well as its own data. It is even managed like a real server.

Using virtual machines gives an organization **agility**, which is the ability to make changes quickly—even very large changes. For example, Amazon can move VMs quickly from one physical server to another simply by transferring their files. It can even move VMs to servers quickly to different regions of the world. In addition, new VM **instances** (specific virtual machines) can be added in seconds. In fact, a company can **spawn (instantiate)**

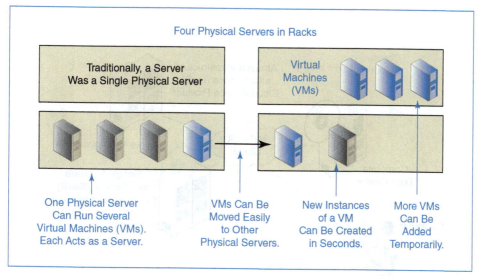

FIGURE 1-6   Server Virtualization through Virtual Machines

many copies of the same virtual machine at once, in no more time it takes to spawn a single VM instance. Physical servers offer nothing like this degree of agility. To make virtualization even more attractive to customers like Netflix, AWS provides a simple self-service application for customers to use to add new instances and do many other things themselves.

➧ Content delivery is not the only way Netflix uses Amazon Web Services. Transcoding each movie into a hundred or more versions for delivery is an enormous task. Whenever Netflix needs to transcode a movie, it spins up (spawns) a large number of VMs, splits the work up among them, processes the data in parallel, and then spins them down. Providing customized viewing recommendations to subscribers also requires an enormous amount of processing power because it uses an extremely sophisticated analysis of individual user viewing practices and the viewing practices of people who have viewed similar movies. This recommendation system also requires Netflix to spin up large numbers of servers for short periods of time. Even in content delivery, the ability to spawn and kill VMs quickly is critical. During peak evening viewing time in the United States, Netflix spins up many additional VMs for content delivery. It spins them down later to save money.

Test Your Understanding

6. a) Distinguish between physical servers and virtual machines. b) What can be done with virtual machines that would be difficult to do with physical servers? c) What is VM instantiation? d) How does Netflix use the agility offered by Amazon Web Services?

Infrastructure as a Service (IaaS) and Software as a Service (SaaS)

Amazon is a **cloud service provider (CSP)**. Figure 1-7 illustrates this concept. We saw earlier that the Internet and other networks are depicted as clouds. The figure shows that CSPs also operate their services opaquely, forming a second layer of cloud.

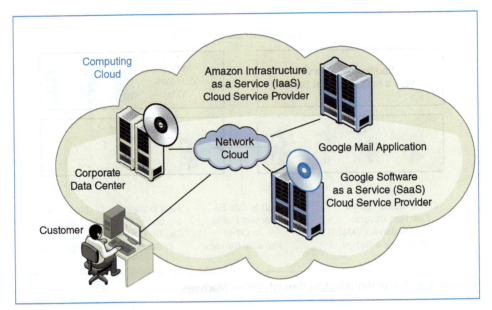

FIGURE 1-7   Cloud Service Providers, IaaS, and SaaS

Infrastructure as a Service   The AWS service that Netflix uses is referred to, generically, as **Infrastructure as a Service (IaaS)**. This ungainly name refers to the fact that AWS provides the **computing infrastructure**, which consists of server operation, database management systems, and so forth.

Netflix creates and manages its own applications for user ordering, transcoding, personalized viewing suggestions, and other matters. By outsourcing server operation to AWS, Netflix can focus its efforts more fully on developing and extending its applications.

In addition, although Netflix does not manage the servers in AWS, it tests its server/application setups constantly. Netflix has developed a family of programs called the *simian army*,[10] which it uses to selectively turn off parts of the AWS system to test how well the system responds to outages. When a change is made in an application that runs on many virtual machines, Netflix tries it out on just a few at first, then migrates it to the rest in a smooth manner.

Software as a Service   Amazon is not the only CSP that Netflix uses. Another is Google. Netflix uses Google Mail for its internal communication. In contrast to just offering IaaS, Google offers application software as well. This is called **Software as a Service (SaaS)**. Here, "software" refers to application software. SaaS actually has been popular for some time. For example, many companies use salesforce.com application software for salesforce management and customer relationship management.

Product versus Service   *As a Service* in IaaS and SaaS refers to pricing. Normally, a company buys servers as products. However, cloud services are sold like

---

[10] This name reflects the fact that individual programs have names like Chaos Monkey and Chaos Gorilla.

electrical service. You pay for the amount of service you use, and you pay only when you use it. This allows customers to avoid the capital expense (CapEx) of purchasing servers. They also avoid the risk of buying too much capacity that would go unused. IaaS appears as an operating expense (OpEx), which can be managed so that money is spent only when it must be. SaaS, in turn, changes application programs from products to services.

Test Your Understanding

7. a) What is a CSP? (Do not just spell out the acronym). b) Distinguish between IaaS CSPs and SaaS CSPs. c) Is AWS an IaaS or an SaaS for Netflix? d) Is Google an IaaS or an SaaS for Netflix? e) Who owns and manages the servers in IaaSs and SaaSs? f) Who owns and manages the applications in IaaSs and SaaSs? g) In AWS, what does Netflix manage and not manage?

Clients Move into the Cloud

Figure 1-7 shows that companies traditionally operated their own servers and applications. IaaS allows them to outsource the computing infrastructure "into the cloud." SaaS allows them to do the same with some applications.

Although servers are critical, companies also need to support **client hosts** used by individual people to receive service. Figure 1-8 shows that client hosts are also using the cloud. Most users today have multiple devices. They typically may have a desktop or laptop PC plus a tablet or two and a smartphone. They would like a consistent experience, at least to the degree possible, across these client hosts. As the figure shows, there is a **virtual client** host in the cloud, complete with application software and a virtual hard drive.

When the user turns on a laptop computer and logs into the virtual client, he or she has access to all of the virtual client's application programs and data files. In addition, the virtual client remembers its configuration, so all of the user's shortcuts and other customizations appear on the laptop application window. The user works on documents or other files and saves them. Saving sends them back to the cloud client's virtual hard drive.

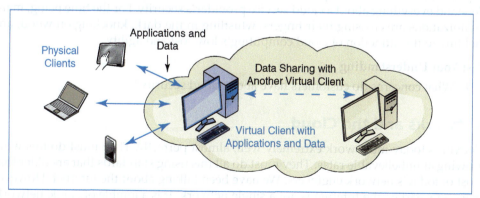

FIGURE 1-8 Client Computing in the Cloud

When the user moves to another device, he or she can continue working on the same documents with the same program, picking up exactly where he or she left off. Although screen sizes may differ and the user interface may change somewhat to suit the device, the user's experience will be similar across devices.

The fact that the hard drive is virtual also means that it can be shared in ways that laptop and desktop hard drives cannot. The user can designate certain folders or individual files sharable and grant specific people specific access rights to the data. This allows multiple users to work on word processing documents and other files collaboratively. This is revolutionizing the way that project teams create documents.

Instead of buying application software, the user typically pays an annual fee. Again, there is a shift from application software *products* to application software *services*. As new versions of the software appear, the software vendor usually updates to the newest version of the software without charging an additional fee.

Test Your Understanding

8. a) When a cloud virtual client is used, describe what happens when a user moves from one physical client device to another. b) How does the use of virtual clients facilitate file sharing among customers of the system? c) What are the advantages of using cloud application programs as a service, compared to traditional application purchasing?

➜Rain Clouds: Security

A central issue for every cloud customer is security. In cloud computing, companies are putting critical corporate data on computers owned by other organizations. In the case of Netflix, Amazon is actually a competitor in the streaming media market. If cloud service providers fail to protect data from hackers, the potential consequences are enormous. Today, cloud customers wonder if government agencies are demanding access to their data under gag orders that prevent customers from learning that this is happening. Edward Snowden's exfiltration of information from NSA servers in 2013 illustrated how even single employees can get access to masses of critical sensitive data.

To deal with security, companies must do extensive due diligence, looking in depth at how cloud service providers handle security. However, there is no way to understand everything about a cloud service provider's security. For the time being, many organizations are crossing their fingers, whistling in the dark, knocking on wood, and yielding to the attraction of cloud computing's low cost and agility.

Test Your Understanding

9. What concerns do customers have about cloud security?

Networks and the Cloud

Networks today must work extremely well, almost perfectly. They must do this while growing at unbelievable rates. They must do all this using standards that are older than most of today's network engineers. We have been talking about the Internet. However, as we saw earlier, the Internet is not a single network. It is a jumble of single networks and smaller internets ranging in size from a couple of devices in a dorm room to corporate internets for globe-spanning corporations.

The demands of cloud computing are creating enormous stresses on networks. Cloud service providers themselves create massive and fast-changing network transmission loads. Customers of cloud services also find themselves with massive increases in Internet and local network traffic. In addition to growing rapidly, networks are also facing increasing demands for reliability because a company that loses contact with its cloud service providers for even brief periods of time will suffer heavy losses.

Test Your Understanding

10. How is cloud computing impacting networking?

Service Level Agreements (SLAs): Speed

To alleviate customer concerns about service quality, cloud service providers usually offer **service level agreements (SLAs)**, which are guarantees that the CSP will meet specified service parameters or pay a penalty. (We will see in Chapter 4 that network providers in general offer SLAs.)

The most basic parameter in SLA agreements is speed. The first question people ask about a newborn baby is whether it is a boy or a girl. The first question people ask about a network is whether it is fast enough to meet their requirements.

Speed is normally measured in bits (1s or 0s) per second. This is abbreviated *bps*. Speeds are given with metric prefixes for the bps base unit. In increasing order of a thousand, these are *kbps*, *Mbps*, *Gbps*, and *Tbps*. If you are a little rusty on the metric system, see the box "Writing Speeds in Metric Notation."[11]

How much speed do you need? Figure 1-9 looks at things from the individual point of view, showing how long it will take to download various types of information at various transmission speeds. Note that e-mail is instantaneous at any common speed today. Streaming video requires a very fast connection, and for disk backup, even gigabit speed may not be enough.

Corporate networks, in turn, must carry the combined transmissions of all users and all machine-to-machine background processes. This creates an enormous aggregate need for speed. In Chapter 4, we will look at aggregating the speeds of different traffic. We will also look at SLA parameters beyond speed.

Application / Speed	100 kbps	1 Mbps	10 Mbps	100 Mbs	1 Gbps
E-mail Message (250 words)	0.02 sec	—	—	—	—
Photograph (2 MB)	3 min	16 sec	2 sec	—	—
1-Hour HDTV Program (7 Mbps)	3 days	7 hr	42 min	4 min	25 sec
Backup 500 GB hard drive	16 years	1.9 mo	5.8 da	14 hr	2 hr

FIGURE 1-9 Application Download Times

---

[11] Note that speeds are normally *not* measured in *bytes* per second. In some cases, such as file downloading, programs may report download speeds in bytes per second. If so, the abbreviation should be bps. If speed is given in bytes per second, multiply by eight to get bits per second.

Test Your Understanding

11. a) What are service level agreements? b) What happens if a service provider fails to meet its SLA? c) Is network speed usually measured in bytes per second (Bps) or bits per second (bps)? d) How many bits per second is 56 kbps without a metric prefix? e) Express 47,303,000 bps with a metric prefix. f) Why do you need to know what application you are using to know what connection speed you need? g) Distinguish between speed to individuals and corporate network speeds.

BOX 2

Writing Speeds in Metric Notation

Numbers, Base Units, and Metric Prefixes

Most network parameters are expressed using the metric system. Suppose that you see the speed 45 Mbps. Here, 45 is the number and bps is the base unit (bits per second). The metric prefix in front of the base unit is a multiplication factor. So bps is straight bits per second, kbps is 1,000 bps, Mbps is 1,000,000 bps, and Gbps is 1,000,000,000 bps. The rare Tbps is 1,000,000,000,000 bps. Note that kilo is written with a lowercase k.[12] Figure 1-10 shows this information graphically.

Removing Metric Prefixes

Sometimes, you need to change the way a number is expressed. For instance, suppose that you want to express 33 kbps without a metric prefix. The k stands for a thousand, so 33 kbps is 33 times 1,000 bps—33,000 bps. In the second row of the figure, 3.4 Mbps is 3.4 times 1,000,000 bps—3,400,000 bps.

Adding Metric Prefixes

What if you need to go in the other direction—to add metric prefixes? In the first row, we have 43,700 bps. This is 43.7 kbps. How did we get this? We divided the original number by 1,000 and added the prefix k. So we have 43,700 / 1000 * 1000 * bps. We divided the number by a thousand and multiplied the metric prefix by 1000, leaving the value the same.

Metric Prefix	Meaning	Unabbreviated	Example
kbps	1,000 bps	kilobits per second	33 kbps is 33,000 bps 43,700 bps is 43.7 kbps
Mbps	1,000 kbps	megabits per second	3.4 Mbps is 3,400,000 bps or 3,400 kbps 523,750,000 bps is 523.75 Mbps
Gbps	1,000 Mbps	gigabits per second	62 Gbps is 62,000,000,000 bps or 62,000 Mbps or 62,000,000 kbps
Tbps	1,000 Gbps	terabits per second	1.5 Tbps is 1,500,000,000,000 bps

FIGURE 1-10 Transmission Speeds in Bits per Second (bps) with Metric Prefixes

(continued)

---

[12] The uppercase metric prefix, K, stands for Kelvins. This is a measure of temperature.

For 3,400,000 bps, we divide the number by a million and add the metric prefix mega (M). So 3,400,000 bps gives 3.4 Mbps. Note that you always multiply or divide by a factor of a thousand (1,000, 1,000,000, 1,000,000,000, etc.).

Writing Numbers with Metric Prefixes Properly

How many times should you divide the number by a thousand? The answer is that you do it until you get one to three digits before the decimal point. So 7.89 Mbps (1 place) is good. So are 23.426 kbps (2 places) and 178 Gbps (3 places). However, 4,300 kbps is not good (4 places). Neither is 0.45 bps (no places before the decimal point because leading zeroes do not count).

What if you add a metric prefix to a number less than one? Then instead of dividing by a thousand, and increasing the metric prefix, you *multiply* by a thousand and *decrease* the metric prefix accordingly. If you have 0.045 Gbps, you multiply 0.045 by a thousand. This gives you 45. To compensate, you divide the metric prefix by 1,000, giving M. So you have 45 Mbps instead of 0.045 Gbps.

There is one more rule in writing numbers in metric notation. You place a space between the number and the metric prefix but not between the metric prefix and the base unit. So 45 kbps is good, but 45kbps and 45k bps are not.

Test Your Understanding

12. a) How would you write four thousand bits per second in metric notation? b) How would you write 45,250,000 bps in metric notation? c) How would you write 23.78 Mbps without a metric prefix? d) How would you write 0.047 Mbps without a metric prefix?

13. a) Write 45.6355 kbps properly. b) Write 37,400 Mbps properly. c) Write 0.032 Mbps properly. d) Write 37kbps properly. e) Write 89k bps properly.

MESSAGES

We saw earlier that application programs on hosts communicate by sending messages back and forth. Now we will look at important types of messages in networking.

Application Messages

The World Wide Web uses the **Hypertext Transfer Protocol (HTTP)** standard to standardize message exchange between browsers and webserver programs. Figure 1-11 shows that an *HTTP request message* asks for a file. The subsequent *HTTP response message* delivers the file or an error message. This exchange is called an **HTTP request/response cycle**. Browsers and webserver programs are application programs, so the messages they exchange are application messages.

Message Fragmentation, Frames, and Packets

As Figure 1-12 shows, application message can be very large. For example, a movie transfer requires the transmission of about six gigabytes of data, and even high-quality photographs take a few megabytes. Forwarding long application messages through a network would be like sending a fleet of 18-wheeler trucks through a narrow English village.

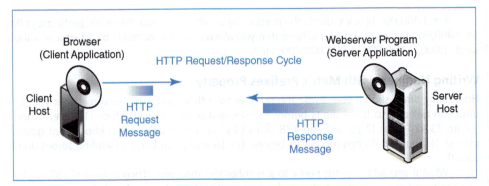

FIGURE 1-11 Application Request-Response Cycle in HTTP

Fragmentation In addition to application software, hosts also have **network software**, which handles network transmission for the operating system. As Figure 1-12 illustrates, network software does three things with application messages.

- First, if the application message is large, the network software **fragments** the long application message into many smaller message **segments**.
- Second, the network software places each segment in an electronic envelope. This "envelope" is merely a set of added bits in front of the segment (the header) and perhaps another set of added bits after the segment (the trailer). These bits contain delivery information for the segment in the envelope. Importantly, the envelope contains the address of the receiving host. The network uses this information to deliver the envelope to the destination host.
- Third, the network software on the source host transmits each segment plus envelope over the network.

The envelope and its contents are called either a *frame* or a *packet* depending on the circumstances. Later in this chapter, we will see when to use the term *frame* and when to use the term *packet*.

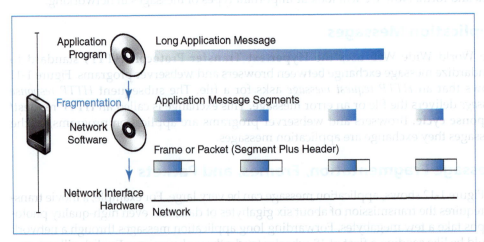

FIGURE 1-12 Fragmentation, Frames, and Packets

Application message segments are carried inside frames or packets that have delivery information.

On the destination host, the network software receives all the frames or packets delivering the application message. It removes the segments, puts them in order, and reassembles the application message. The network software passes this application message up to the application program. Note that neither application program knows that fragmentation has been done. The source application simply passes the whole application message down to the network software. The destination application receives the whole message from its network software.

Error Correction   Why do fragmentation? One reason is error correction. Suppose there is a transmission error somewhere within the network and a few bits are lost, damaging the message. The incorrect message must be retransmitted. Figure 1-13 shows retransmission with and without fragmentation.

Without fragmentation, the sender must retransmit the entire message. This adds quite a bit to the network's traffic load. In addition, if a message is long, a transmission error has a high probability of occurring each time it is sent. The message may have to be resent multiple times before it arrives correctly. Transferring a moderate-size file from home to school over a cranky telephone line and without fragmentation once took the first author three hours.

With fragmentation, the sender only needs to retransmit the single damaged frame or packet. An error will therefore increase the transfer time only slightly. The bottom line is that fragmentation increases an application message's effective speed.

Multiplexing   Figure 1-14 shows a second reason for fragmentation. Consider this analogy. Would it be nice to drive into school or work in your own personal highway lane? There would be no traffic congestion at all. That would certainly be nice, but having thousands of traffic lanes on a freeway would entail astronomical construction costs. In the real world, we have to drive on shared highways that carry many cars in each lane. The individual cars and trucks "share" the cost of the highway lane.

In networking, packets share the cost of **multiplexed** (shared) transmission lines. In the figure, two client PCs are sending messages to different servers. Their

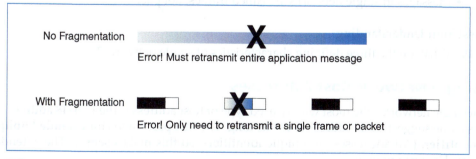

FIGURE 1-13   Fragmentation and Error Correction

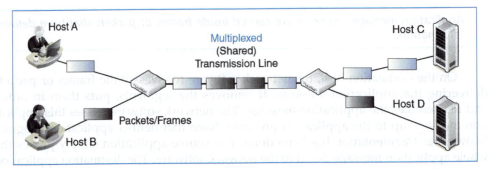

FIGURE 1-14   Fragmentation and Multiplexing

frames/packets share the capacity of the multiplexed line. Multiplexing reduces transmission costs.

It is technically possible to multiplex using large application messages. However, filling a line efficiently with large messages is impossible. To see why, consider another analogy. Hourglasses work far better with sand than with rocks. Small frames and packets can fill a transmission line very efficiently.

Test Your Understanding

14. a) What is fragmentation? b) What are frames or packets? c) How does fragmentation improve transmission speed? d) What is multiplexing? e) How does fragmentation reduce transmission cost through multiplexing?

SINGLE NETWORKS

An internet is a collection of single networks and smaller internets. We will begin with the most basic unit of networking, the single network. **Single networks** are networks that have three defining characteristics. If you do not understand these characteristics immediately, things should be clear after some examples.

- A single network uses a single technology for transmission. All devices must comply with that technology's standards.
- There is a controlled address space such that each host address is unique, like a telephone number.
- Messages in single networks are called frames, not packets.

Test Your Understanding

15. What are the three defining characteristics of single networks?

Single-Network Host Addresses

In single networks, the most widely used type of host address is the **EUI-48 address**. As its name suggests, this address is 48 bits long. The EUI part stands for **extended unique identifier**. (All addresses are unique identifiers, so this makes sense.) The extended part? Uh, just ignore it.

Different single-network standards use different types of addresses

A common type of single-network address is the EUI-48 address
    EUI stands for extended unique identifier
    It is 48 bits long
    Used in Ethernet 802.3, Wi-Fi 802.11, and Bluetooth
    However, not all single-network addresses are EUI-48 addresses

Formerly called a media access control (MAC) address
    Still commonly referred to as MAC addresses

Written as six pairs of number or letter symbols separated by dashes
    Example A1-B2-CC-92-FF-00

FIGURE 1-15 EUI-48 Addresses [Study Figure]

If you have some networking background, you might be asking, "Hey, isn't that a **Media Access Control (MAC)** address?" Actually, it is the Institute of Electrical and Electronics Engineers' (IEEE's) new name for MAC addresses. You need to know that they mean the same thing because the term "MAC address" is still widely used. However, the IEEE has deprecated the MAC name in favor of EUI-48.

EUI-48 address is the new name for Media Access Control (MAC) address.

An EUI-48 address is written as six pairs of number or letter symbols separated by dashes. For example, an EUI-48 address might be A1-B2-CC-92-FF-00. In Chapter 5, we will look at EUI-48 addresses in detail.

EUI-48 addresses are very common because they are used in 802.3 Ethernet wired networks, 802.11 Wi-Fi wireless networks, and Bluetooth. However, they are not the only kind of single-network address. Do not confuse their common use with universality.

➔*EUI-48 (MAC) addresses are very common because they are used in 802.3 Ethernet wired networks, 802.11 wireless networks, and Bluetooth. However, they are not the only kind of single-network address. Do not confuse their common use with universality.*

Test Your Understanding

16. a) What is the most widely used single-network address? b) What else is it called? c) Why is the following NOT an EUI-48 address: A9-00-FF-93-BD? d) Are all single-network addresses EUI-48 addresses?

Point-to-Point Single Networks, Physical Links, and Data links

We will now look at types of single-network technologies. Figure 1-16 shows the simplest single network technology—a point-to-point connection between two hosts. That's a network? It's like two cans connected by a string! Yes, a **point-to-point network** is not very complex, but we will see later in this chapter that it is important when we move beyond single networks to internets.

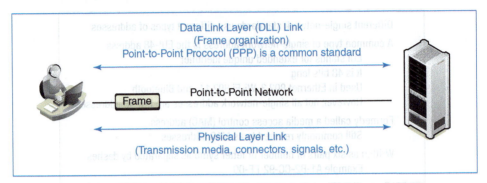

FIGURE 1-16   Point-to-Point Single Network

Physical Layer   Although this is an almost trivial network, it allows us to introduce the concept of physical layer and data link layer standards. **Physical layer** standards govern transmission media such as wires, connectors, and signaling (how 1s and 0s are represented as physical signals such as voltage changes or radio waves). Both hosts must connect to the network using the proper plug and send signals in appropriate ways.

> Physical layer standards govern transmission media such as wires, connectors, and signaling (how 1s and 0s are represented as physical signals such as voltage changes or radio waves).

Data Link Layer   A point-to-point network also allows us to introduce the concept of **data link layer (DLL)** standards. Data link layer standards determine how frames are organized. Although they are not present in a point-to-point network, networks often have forwarding devices to deliver frames in a series of hops. How these devices, including switches and access points, forward frames in a single network is also governed by DLL standards. DLL standards also govern addresses. For point-to-point networks, the most common data link layer standard is the **Point-to-Point Protocol (PPP)**. The PPP standard governs how the frame is organized.

> Data link layer standards determine how frames are organized, addresses, and other things we will see later.

Layers   We have seen the physical and data link layers briefly. We will soon see other standards layers. Layering is an important concept in network standards. In transportation, the soil layer supports the road layer. Moving up through layers, the road supports the tires, the tires support the car, the car supports the driver, and the driver supports the company he or she is working for in commercial operations. Layering allows specialization. In transportation, someone who is an expert on road construction does not have to know much about car design. In networking, someone who knows electrical signaling does not have to know much about applications—or vice versa.

Layered Standards

Often, standards are created in layers, with each layer supporting the next higher layer

For example, in driving

> The soil layer supports the road layer
> The road layer supports the tire layer
> The tire layer supports the body layer
> The body layer supports the driver layer

Layering allows specialization

Road engineers do not have to understand tire standards or body standards in detail

Physical Layer Standards

The physical connection between adjacent devices in a network is a physical link

Govern transmission media and connectors

Govern signaling to transmit ones and zeroes

Layer 1 (L1) standards

Data Link Layer (DLL) Standards

The end-to-end path of a frame between the source and destination host is a data link

Govern frame organization

Govern how forwarding devices (access points, switches) forward frames over multiple hops

Govern DLL addresses

Layer 2 (L2) standards

Point-to-Point Protocol (PPP)

The dominant data link layer standard for point-to-point networks

---

FIGURE 1-17   Physical and Data Link Layer Standards (Study Figure)

Layering allows specialization.

Layers 1 and 2 (L1 and L2)   Networking professionals often refer to network layers by number. The physical layer is the lowest layer, and it is numbered **Layer 1** or **L1**. The data link layer is the next-lowest layer, and it is numbered **Layer 2** or **L2**.

All single-network technologies require standards at both Layer 1 and Layer 2. This means that they all must standardize physical link technology and data link layer matters such as DLL addresses and DLL frame organizations.

Test Your Understanding

17. a) In what type of single-network technology is the Point-to-Point (PPP) protocol used? b) What do physical layer standards govern? c) What do data link layer (DLL) standards govern? d) At what layer do you find EUI-addresses? (The answer is not directly in the text. It requires you to integrate the information you have learned.) e) At what layer are frames defined?

18. a) Why is layering important for creating standards? b) What is the name and number of the lowest network standards layer? c) What is the name and number of the second-lowest network standards layer? d) Which layer's standards govern single-network technologies? e) At which layer or layers is PPP a standard?

Wireless Single Networks

Wireless transmission is becoming the most common way to access the Internet, a home network, or a corporate network. Figure 1-18 illustrates an **802.11 wireless network**. 802.11 is the collective name for the standards that govern wireless local area networks. These are also called **Wi-Fi networks**.

In 802.11 networks, the source and destination hosts normally do not communicate directly. In the figure, the wireless source host is transmitting a frame to a wireless access point. The wireless access point will relay the frame to the destination host. The wireless access point, in other words, forwards frames between wireless hosts.

As we just saw, physical layer standards govern a single physical connection. In Figure 1-16, which illustrated a point-to-point network, there was a single physical link. For the simple wireless network in Figure 1-18, there are *two* physical links.

In turn, we saw that data link layer standards govern frame organization and other things necessary for end-to-end connections between the source and destination hosts in a single network. In Figure 1-18, there is a single data link. There is *always* a single data link between the source and destination host in a single network, regardless of how many physical links are involved.

There is always a single data link in a single network, regardless of how many physical links the frame passes through.

Test Your Understanding

19. a) In 802.11 Wi-Fi networks, what device relays frames between the source and destination hosts? b) What two things do 802.11 data link layer standards govern? c) Is there always a single data link for a frame in a single network?

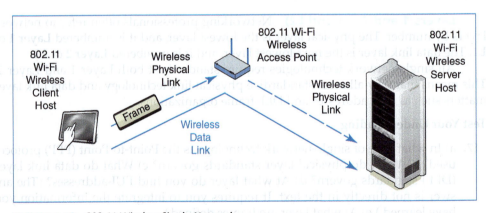

FIGURE 1-18   802.11 Wireless Single Network

Switched Single Networks

Figure 1-19 finally takes us into a larger single network, a switched network. In a **switched single network**, the frame is forwarded over a number of transmission links connected by forwarding devices called **switches**. There may be many switches between the source host and the destination host. In the figure, the frame passes through four switches along its data link.

Physical Links   The hosts and switches are connected by physical links. Typically, these physical links use copper wire or optical fiber (which carries signals as light pulses propagating through thin glass tubes). There are five physical links along the path the frame takes through the network. There often are many physical links along the path the frame travels.

Data Links   Again, the path that the frame takes all the way through the switched network is the frame's data link. There is always a single data link for a frame traveling through a single network.

Switch Operation   When the Source Host X transmits a frame, the frame goes to Switch A. That switch must decide whether to **switch** (forward) the frame to Switch B or Switch C. This is a **switching decision**.

If Switch A forwards the frame to Switch B, Switch B must decide whether to switch the frame to Switch D or Switch E. This switch-by-switch decision making will continue until the final switch along the path forwards the frame to the destination host.

How does Switch A know whether to forward the arriving frame to Switch B or Switch C? The answer, shown in Figure 1-20, is that Switch A has a **switching table** with two columns. The first is the destination address in the frame. The second is the switch or host that Switch A should send the frame to next.

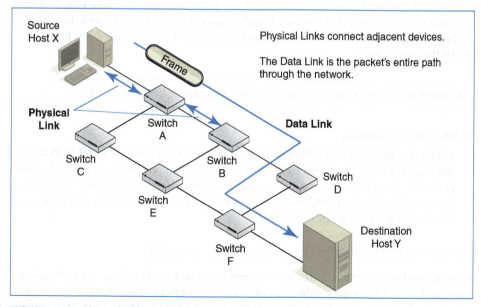

FIGURE 1-19   Physical Links and Data Links in a Switched Single Network

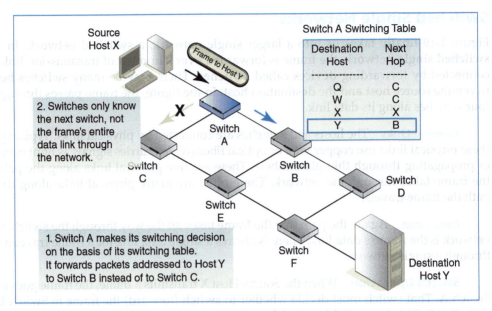

FIGURE 1-20 Address-Based Switch Decision Making

When a frame arrives addressed to Destination Host Y, Switch A looks at its switching table. The table indicates that the switch should forward the frame to Switch B. Switch A does so.

Note that Switch A only has local knowledge about what to do with incoming frames. It receives the frame from one physical link and transmits it over another physical link. It does not know the frame's entire path through the network. If Switch A passes the frame to Switch B, Switch B will also only have local knowledge. In fact, all switches along the way from the source host to the destination host only know what to do with the next frame.

A switch does not know the frame's entire path through the network.

Test Your Understanding

20. a) What decision do switches have to make when a frame arrives? b) What is this decision called? c) How do they make this decision? d) Does an individual switch know the frame's entire path through a switched single network? e) Are frames addressed to the DLL addresses of a switch or the DLL addresses of a destination host? (The answer is not in the text.)

Hybrid Switched/Wireless Single Networks

Single networks require all devices to use the same technology and therefore the same standards. Like many things in networks, however, there are a few exceptions. Figure 1-21 shows the most common exception, a **hybrid switched/wireless network**.

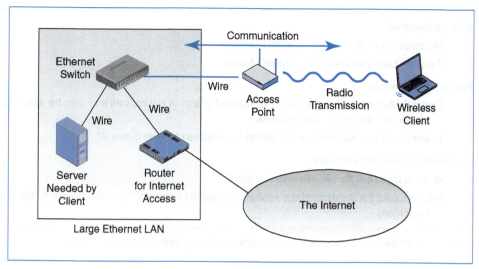

FIGURE 1-21   Hybrid Switched/Wireless Single Network

In the figure, there is a full switched Ethernet network. (Ethernet is the dominant switching technology for local area networks.) Although the figure does not show it, many hosts connect directly to a switch. In addition, some hosts connect wirelessly to 802.11 (Wi-Fi) access points. These access points connect wireless hosts to the switched networks.

Why connect wireless hosts to wired networks? When bank robber Willie Sutton was asked why he robbed banks, he allegedly said, "Because that's where the money is." In hybrid networks, wireless clients need to connect to the wired network because that is where the resources they need are. The servers they need are on the wired network. So are the routers (which we will discuss later) that connect the single network to the Internet.

When counting physical links, the wireless connection between the wireless client and the access point counts as one physical link. The wired connection between the access point and the Ethernet switch is another physical link.

Test Your Understanding

21. a) Can you have a mixed wired and wireless network? b) In a hybrid single switched network, why do wireless clients need to connect to the wired network? c) What role do access points have in hybrid switched/wireless networks?

INTERNET TRANSMISSION

Hosts on Different Single Networks

What if hosts on different single networks wish to communicate? There are three problems that must be overcome to make this possible.

• First, the single networks may have different standards. Each has its own frame organization. They would not be able to make sense of each other's frames.

Different Standards

> The single networks may have different standards
>
> If so, they cannot understand each other's frames

Overlapping Addresses

> Even if the two networks follow the *same* standard, a host on one network may have the same DLL address as a host on the other network.
>
> To which host with the same number should the combined network deliver it?

Link to Connect the Single Network

> How would you link the two networks together?
>
> If the link used the standards of one network, it would not connect to the other network for the first two reasons

---

FIGURE 1-22   Problems Connecting Hosts on Different Single Networks (Study Figure)

- Second, even if the two networks follow the *same* standard, this does not mean that they can interoperate. Most fundamentally, a host on one network may have the same DLL address as a host on the other network. For example, both networks may number their hosts 1, 2, 3, 4, and so forth. In a combined network, there would be many hosts with the same number. If a message is sent to an address, to which host should the combined network deliver it?
- Third, how would you link the two networks together? If the link used the standards of one network, it would not connect to the other network for the first two reasons.

Test Your Understanding

22. If two hosts are on two different single networks, what three problems must be overcome if they are to be able to communicate?

→ Creating the Internet

The problem of connecting hosts on different single networks was not an academic exercise for Bon Kahn at the Advanced Research Projects Agency (ARPA) in the late 1960s. He was funding several research projects on several different research networks. One was the switch-based ARPANET, which was the precursor to today's Internet. Two others were a short-distance radio network and a satellite data network. He needed researchers on these and other research network to be able to share resources. Kahn also realized that he was not the only person to face this problem. Kahn worked with Vint Cerf at UCLA and later Stanford to solve the problem. The solution they came up with was remarkably simple, at least in principle.

Routers   Figure 1-23 illustrates part of their solution. It shows that they introduced a new device that they called a *gateway*. Today, we call this device a **router**. Routers do the work of connecting networks together.

Of course, single networks have no idea what a router is. They only know how to deliver frames to hosts. Routers circumvent this problem by pretending to be hosts. In the figure, Host A on Network 1 wishes to send an application message to Host B on

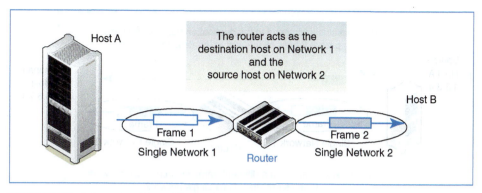

Host A

The router acts as the destination host on Network 1 and the source host on Network 2

Host B

Frame 1

Single Network 1

Router

Frame 2

Single Network 2

FIGURE 1-23 Internetworking with a Router

Network 2. On Network 1, the router acts as a destination host, accepting a frame from Host A. The router then creates a new frame acceptable on Network 2. Acting like a host on Network 2, the router sends this frame to Host B. On the two single networks, operation is completely normal.

IP Addresses   As just noted, data link layer addresses are not necessarily unique across different single networks. The way Kahn and Cerf addressed this problem was to create an entirely new type of address, the Internet Protocol address or IP address, which we saw earlier. Like telephone numbers, IP addresses are given out in a way that guarantees that all host IP addresses would be unique. We will see how this is done in Chapter 8.

IP Packets   Kahn and Cerf also created a new type of message. Unlike frames, which can only travel in single networks, **IP packets** travel all the way from the source host to the destination host. An IP packet delivers an application segment from the source host to the destination host.

There is no need to change the way single networks handle frames. In Figure 1-24, the IP packet "pretends" to be an application segment, and the frame simply carries the packet instead of the actual application segment.

How can the packet pretend that it is an application message segment? The answer is that the hosts and routers act as accomplices. Single networks do not create frames. They merely deliver them. Nor do they look inside frames at the messages these frames carry.

Hosts and routers, however, have software that does know about IP packets and how to use them. Host 1.2.3.4 creates an IP packet for Host 5.6.7.8. It places this packet in Frame 1 and sends the frame to the interface (port) of the router on Single Network 1.

The router also has an interface that connects it to Single Network 2. The router removes the packet from Frame 1, places the packet in Frame 2, which is suitable for Single Network 2, and sends the frame out that interfaces to Host 5.6.7.8.

Host 5.6.7.8 removes the packet from the frame. The packet has now finished its journey from Host 1.2.3.4 to Host 5.6.7.8. The switches and other devices on the single network along the way do not know that they were duped, and the hosts and routers do not gloat about their complicity in Cerf and Kahn's stratagem. It just works for everybody.

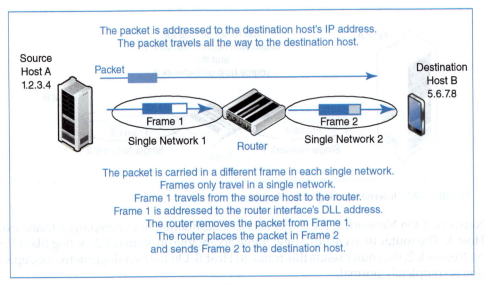

FIGURE 1-24   IP Packet and Data Link Layer Frame

Encapsulation   Putting something inside something else is called **encapsulation**. Figure 1-25 shows encapsulation in internets. Traditionally, a frame in a single network carried an application message segment. In internets, an IP packet is encapsulated in a frame. The IP packet, in turn, encapsulates an application message segment. So a frame in an internet consists of a frame header, followed by an IP packet header, followed by an application message segment. (There may also be a frame trailer if the standard at the DLL has a trailer.)

Today, hosts assume that they are on an internet. Consequently, all frames now consist of a frame header, an IP packet header, and an application message segment. On a single network, there is no router, of course. The destination host's network program understands that and acts appropriately.

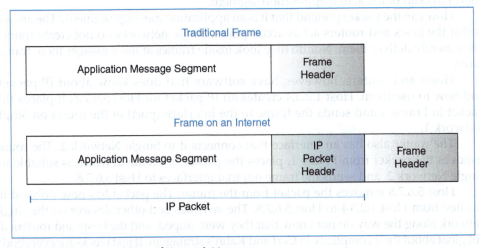

FIGURE 1-25   Encapsulation of Network Messages

Test Your Understanding

23. a) What device connects different single networks together into an internet? b) Do single networks know that they are delivering frames to a router? c) To what type of device do single networks think they are delivering frames? d) What devices understand what is really happening?

24. Why was a new type of address needed for the Internet?

25. a) On the Internet, what new type of message travels between the source and destination host? b) How are these messages carried in single networks? c) Describe what happens to a packet between the source and destination host. d) Draw a frame in terms of encapsulation (what message is inside what other message).

Routes and Layer 3

Routes   We saw that at Layer 1, devices are connected by physical links. At Layer 2, the path a frame travels through a single network is a data link. We need a name for the path a packet takes from the source host to the destination host across an internet. The name for this is the packet's **route**. Figure 1-26 shows a packet that travels across three single networks from Host A to Host B. The path a frame takes through each network is called its data link.

A route is the path that a packet takes from the source host to the destination host across an internet.

Note that there is always a single route for a packet through an internet and that the number of data links is the number of single networks separating the source and destination host (in this case, three). The number of physical links is entirely dependent on the single network technologies, sizes, and other factors.

Note that there is always a single route for a packet through an internet and that the number of data links is the number of single networks separating the source and destination host.

Note also that Network Y is a point-to-point network. It probably follows the PPP standard. Linking routers is the main use of point-to-point networks today, so PPP really is an important protocol in networking.

Layer 3 and the Internet Protocol   Effectively, Kahn and Cerf added a third layer of networking, **Layer 3**. L3 is the **internet layer**. Note that we write internet in lower case when referring to the layer. The main standard at the internet layer is the **Internet Protocol (IP)**. IP governs the transmission of packets by routers across an internet between the source and destination hosts. It specifically governs IP addresses, packet syntax, router operation, and internets themselves. Although adding another layer with addresses, paths and forwarding devices works, it creates two layers of addresses, messages, and forwarding devices. Figure 1-27 compares the two layers across these dimensions.

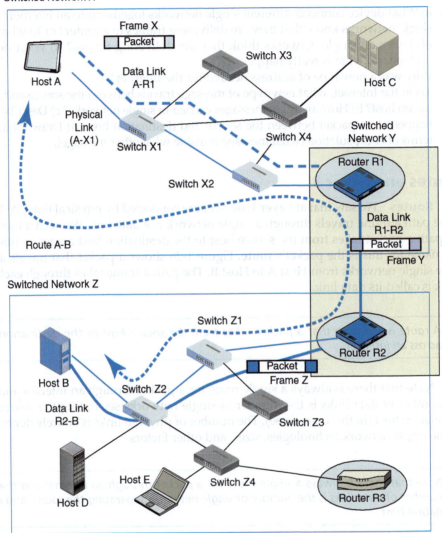

FIGURE 1-26 Physical Links, Data Links, and a Route

Test Your Understanding

26. a) What is a route? b) Distinguish between a data link and a route. c) When a packet travels through an internet, are there usually more data links or routes along the way? d) How many routes are there when a packet is transmitted? e) When a packet is transmitted from a source host to a destination host separated by four single networks, how many packets will there be? (Answer: 1) f) How many frames will there be? (Answer: 4) g) When a packet is transmitted from a source host to a destination host separated by 17 single networks, how many packets will there be? h) How many frames will there be?

Concept	Data Link Layer	Internet Layer
Layer Name (Number)	Layer 2 (L2)	Layer 3 (L3)
Name	Data Link Layer	Internet Layer
Main Standard	Various (Ethernet 802.3, Wi-Fi 802.11, PPP, etc.)	IP
Addresses	Data Link Layer addresses (e.g., EUI-48 addresses)	IP addresses
Messages	Frames	Packets
Forwarding Devices	Switches, Access Points, etc.	Routers
Paths	Data Links	Routes

FIGURE 1-27   Repeated Concepts at the Data Link and Internet Layers

27. a) Distinguish between physical links, data links, and routes. b) When Host A in Figure 1-26 transmits a packet to Host D, how many physical links, data links, and routes will there be? c) How many packets will there be? d) How many frames? (Answers: 7 physical links, 3 data links, 1 route, 1 packet, 3 frames.)
28. a) When Host A in Figure 1-26 transmits a packet to Host C, how many physical links, data links, and routes will there be? b) How many packets will there be? c) How many frames?
29. a) At what layer do you find: a) IP addresses, b) EUI-48 addresses, c) packets, d) frames, e) wireless connections, f) wire connections, g) switches, and h) routers?

BOX 3

"Packet Switching"

The idea of fragmenting large application messages and sending the segments in small individual messages is known generically as **packet switching**. However, from the discussion we have just seen, packets are never switched. Rather, *frames are switched* in single networks and *packets are routed* in internets. Networking terminology needs a consistency police.

> "Packet switching" is a generic name for fragmentation and envelopes
>
> However, the term "packet switching" is never used on single networks or internets
>
> In switched networks, frames are switched
>
> In internets, packets are routed

FIGURE 1-28   "Packet Switching" (Study Figure)

Test Your Understanding

30. Both single switched networks and routed networks are said to use packet switching. Why is this term confusing?

STANDARDS LAYERS

Companies do not want to limit themselves by buying all of their hardware and software from a single vendor. They want to pit vendors against each other so that vendors have to compete for their dollars. Competition brings lower prices. It encourages vendors to keep adding new features to prevent their products from degenerating into commodities. From a risk viewpoint, standards mean that if your vendor goes out of business, your company is not SOL (strictly out of luck).

Competition requires hardware and software from different vendors to be able to **interoperate** (work together effectively). This requires standards. **Standards** are detailed rules of operation that specify how two hardware or software processes work together. Standards govern such things as connectors, wiring, wireless operation, switching, routing, frames, packets, and application program messages. We will not look at standards much in this chapter. This is not because they are unimportant. It is because standards are so important that they require an entire chapter (Chapter 2). However, it is important to understand one general concept about standards at this point, namely layers.

Standards are detailed rules of operation that specify how two hardware or software processes work together.

Five Layers

As discussed earlier, network standards are created in layers. Each layer supports the layer above it. Figure 1-29 shows that there are five general standards layers.

Layers 1 through 3 (Physical, Data Link, and Internet Layers)

We saw that physical links connect adjacent devices, data links are paths that frames take through single networks, and routes are paths that packets take through an

Number	Name	Role
5	Application	Standardizing communication between two application programs of a certain type.
4	Transport	Fragmentation and other functions.
3	Internet	Transmit a packet across an internet. Packet organization, router operation, other things needed to transmit a packet across a route in an internet.
2	Data Link	Transmit a frame across a single network. Frame organization, switch and access point operation, and other things needed to transmit a frame across a data link in a single network.
1	Physical	Transmission media, plugs and connectors, signaling.

FIGURE 1-29 General Standards Layers

internet. They are defined at standard layers 1 through 3. These are the physical, data link, and internet layers.

- Physical link standards describe transmission media and signaling.
- Data link layer standards describe the structure of frames, DLL addresses, and how to deliver frames across a single network.
- Internet layer standards describe the structure of IP packets, IP addresses, and how to deliver packets across a series of routers in an internet.

Layers 4 and 5 (Transport and Application Layers)

We have also seen the top two layers, although we did not name them earlier. The **application layer** standardizes communication between application programs. This includes application messages. HTTP operates at the application layer, standardizing communication between the browser and the webserver application programs. Thanks to layering, application designers do not have to worry about transmission through single networks and internets. They concern themselves strictly with application layer matters.

The application layer standardizes communication between application programs.

The **transport layer** does fragmentation on the source host, as we saw in Figure 1-12. The transport layer also does reassembly on the destination host. This frees application programs from the need to worry about fragmentation. In Chapter 2, we will see that the transport layer has several other functions, including error correction.

The transport layer does fragmentation of the application message on the source host and reassembly on the destination host.

Test Your Understanding

31. a) What is required for competition among vendors? b) What benefits do standards bring? c) Name the five layers from bottom to top. d) Give the number for each layer name. e) What does Layer 1 standardize? f) Layer 2? g) Layer 3? h) Layer 4? i) Layer 5?

Standards Agencies and Architectures

Standards are created by organizations called **standards agencies**. Figure 1-30 shows the most important standards agencies. It also shows their **standards architectures**, which are the broad frameworks within which they create individual standards.

OSI: ISO and ITU-T   Standards at the physical and data link layers are governed by two organizations working together. **ITU-T** creates standards for telecommunications networks that provide voice, video, and data transmission services. **ISO** creates

Architecture	OSI	TCP/IP
Standards agency/agencies	ISO and ITU-T	Internet Engineering Task Force (IETF)
Architecture name	OSI	TCP/IP
Examples of standards	802.3 Ethernet, 802.11 Wi-Fi, optical fiber	TCP, IP, DNS
Layers at which dominant	Physical (1) and Data Link (2)	Internet (3) and Transport (4)

FIGURE 1-30 Networking Standards Agencies and Architectures

many computer standards. Networking involves both computers and transmission services, so this pair of organizations is a natural partnership for creating network standards that combine computers and transmission. ITU-T and ISO develop their standards within a standards architecture called **OSI**. This is an acronym for Reference Model for Open Systems Interconnection. Mercifully, this is never spelled out. This choice of acronyms is unfortunate because it is easy to confuse ISO (a standards agency) with OSI (a standards framework).

ISO is the standards agency, while OSI is a standards framework.

TCP/IP: The IETF and RFCs Neither ISO nor ITU-T considered internetworking in detail until internets were well established. Consequently, another organization took the lead in internet standards. This was the **Internet Engineering Task Force (IETF)**. It calls its architecture **TCP/IP**, after two of its standards, TCP and IP. TCP is the standard for fragmenting application messages. IP is the standard for moving packets across routers through the Internet. Again, terminology is a bit confusing. TCP/IP is a standards architecture, while TCP and IP are individual standards.

The Internet Engineering Task Force (IETF) is the standards agency for the Internet.

TCP/IP is a standards architecture, while TCP and IP are individual standards.

Relative Dominance Overall, ISO and ITU-T dominate standards development at the physical and data link layers (Layers 1 and 2). In turn, the IETF dominates standards development at the internet and transport layers (Layers 3 and 4). Although there are exceptions, these patterns of domination are very strong.

ISO and ITU-T dominate standards development at the physical and data link layers (Layers 1 and 2).

The IETF dominates standards development at the internet and transport layers (Layers 3 and 4).

The Application Layer   At the application layer, there is no dominance. There are many standards created by many standards agencies. For example, many World Wide Web standards are developed by the **World Wide Web Consortium (W3C)**. IETF created the SMTP e-mail protocol used almost universally to deliver mail from a sender's mail server to the receiver's mail server. The IETF is even working collaboratively with ISO to develop standards for voice over IP and other applications.

Test Your Understanding

32. a) Distinguish among ISO, OSI, and ITU-T. b) In what two layers do OSI standards dominate? c) What is the standards agency for the Internet? d) In what two layers do its standards dominate?

TCP/IP Supervisory Applications: The Domain Name System (DNS)

TCP and IP (along with the UDP standard we will see in the next chapter) are sufficient for delivering packets over an internet. However, the TCP/IP family of standards also has a large family of **supervisory standards** that govern matters beyond packet transmission. We will look at only one of them in this chapter. You will see many more throughout this book.

If you want to call someone, you need to know the other party's telephone number. If you only know the party's name, you can call directory service and get their number. Similarly, each Internet host has an IP address. Some also have **host names**, such as Amazon.com and boisestate.edu. IP addresses, not host names, are the official addresses of Internet hosts. You cannot send packets to a host name—only to an IP

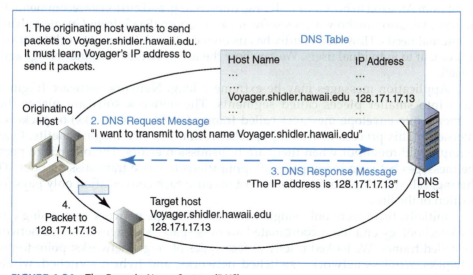

FIGURE 1-31   The Domain Name System (DNS)

address. Suppose that you want to shop at Amazon.com. You type its host name in your browser. Your browser, knowing that it needs Amazon.com's IP address, contacts a **domain name system (DNS)** server, which is like a directory service for host names and IP addresses. The DNS server looks up the IP address for Amazon.com and sends it back to your browser. Your browser will then send packets to Amazon.com's IP address.

Test Your Understanding

33. a) To send packets to a target host, what must the source host know? b) If the source host knows the host name of the target host, how can it get the target host's IP address?

CONCLUSION

Synopsis

The Internet is not the only network. It is, however, like the 500-pound gorilla in the room. The Internet is enormous, and it is still growing and evolving at a fierce pace. The Internet is not a single network. Rather, it is a mix of single networks and smaller internets. They work together to deliver messages between any two computers attached to the Internet. We saw that a computer attached to the Internet is a host. The core of the Internet consists of Internet service providers (ISPs), who deliver messages, which we later saw are called IP packets, between customer networks. No organization owns or controls the Internet, and customers pay fees for its upkeep.

"The cloud" is the biggest buzzword in networking today. Unlike many marketing-driven terms, cloud computing is actually important. In fact, it is the major driving force in networking today. We saw how Netflix uses infrastructure as a service (IaaS) from Amazon to host user ordering, transcoding, and customer recommendation analysis. We also saw how it uses software as a service (SaaS) from Google to handle its internal needs. However, Netflix has its own content delivery network for streaming content to individual users. We saw how the use of virtual machines brings agility to IaaS.

Application messages may be extremely long. Network software fragments them into smaller pieces called segments. The network software places these segments into envelope messages called frames (in single networks) or packets (in internets). This process of framing/packetization has two major benefits. One is to improve throughput when there are transmission errors. The other is to permit the messages between many pairs of applications to share transmission lines. This sharing, called multiplexing, reduces cost because each conversation only pays for a fraction of the line.

Initially, there were only single networks. A single network uses a single network technology and has a coordinated address space. Messages in single networks are called frames. We looked briefly at four types of single networks: point-to-point networks, wireless networks, switched networks, and hybrid switched/wireless networks.

In single networks, there are two layers of standards. Physical layer standards govern the physical connection between adjacent devices. Data link layer (DLL) standards specify how frames are organized and delivered over the single network. DLL standards also govern addresses. There is a separate physical link between each pair of devices that are connected. There is only a single data link, which is the path the frame takes in a single network all the way from the source host to the destination host.

In switched networks, frames travel through multiple switches on their data links from the source host to the destination host. Each switch decides how to forward the frame to the next switch, based on the destination address in the frame. Note that each switch only worries about the next switch along the data link. Individual switches do not know the frame's entire path through the data link.

What if you were using one single network and the server you wanted to reach was on a different single network? There was no way to do this for many years. Even if the two single networks used the same technology—which was far from certain—addresses on the different networks might not be unique.

Internets solve this conundrum. They do this by adding a third layer of networking, the internet layer. The internet layer defines a new type of message, which is called a packet. Internet layer addresses are assigned globally, so that no two hosts around the world will have the same internet layer addresses. The internet layer also defines a new type of network forwarding device, a router, to connect different single networks. The global Internet uses the Internet Protocol (IP), and so do most private internets, even if they are not connected to the worldwide Internet.

Internets cannot work independently of single networks. As the packet travels from the source host to the destination host across the internet, it travels through multiple single networks. In each single network, the packet is encapsulated inside a frame specific to that network. Except in the last single network, the receiving router removes the packet from the arriving frame, puts it in a new frame, and sends the frame over a single network to a next-hop router. This continues until the final single network, which contains the destination host. The final router places the packet into a frame and transmits the frame directly to the destination host. The packet's passage through the internet is complete. The path that a packet takes all the way across an internet is its route.

Standards are critical to networking because they allow vendors to compete for the customer's business. To simplify standards (and product) development, the standardization task is divided into five layers. We have already talked about the physical layer, the data link layer, and the internet layer. The transport layer is responsible for dividing application messages into segments and for other functions we will see in the next chapter. The highest layer, the application layer, governs how application programs understand each other. We looked briefly at an important application layer standard, HTTP.

Standards are set by organizations called standards agencies. At the physical and data link layers, nearly all standards are set jointly by two standards agencies, the ITU-T and ISO. Confusingly, their standards architecture is called OSI. At the internet and transport layers, the Internet Engineering Task Force (IETF) dominates standards. Its standards are named TCP/IP standards, after two of its many individual standards, TCP and IP.

The Internet Protocol (IP) governs the delivery of packets across many routers in an internet. We saw that the domain name system (DNS) standard allows a host that knows the host name of a host it wants to communicate with to discover the official address (the IP address) of the target host. You will see many more supervisory standards as you go through this course.

END-OF-CHAPTER QUESTIONS

Thought Questions

1-1. a) When Host D in Figure 1-26 transmits a packet to Host C, how many physical links, data links, and routes will there be? b) How many packets will there be? c) How many frames? (Check answers are 7, 3, 1, 1, and 3).

1-2. a) When Host A in Figure 1-26 transmits a packet to Host C, how many physical links, data links, and routes will there be? b) How many packets will there be? c) How many frames?

1-3. A frame is addressed to the *data link layer (DLL)* address of the device at the end of the frame's data link. The packet is addressed to the *IP address* of the host at the end of the packet's route. a) When Host C in Figure 1-26 transmits a packet to Host D, to which address is the first *frame* addressed (be specific)? b) To which address is the *packet* addressed? c) When router R1 sends the packet along in a Frame to Router R2,

to which address is the frame addressed? d) To which address is the packet addressed?

1-4. a) What type of single network is Network X in Figure 1-26? b) What type of single network is Network Y? c) What protocol does Network Y follow at the data link layer?

1-5. What is the difference between the Internet and the World Wide Web? The answer is not in the text.

1-6. Use Excel's dec2bin() function to convert from dotted decimal notation to binary. The IP address in dotted decimal notation is 128.171.17.13. What is it in binary?

1-7. Use the Excel bin2dec() function to convert the following 32-bit IP addresses into dotted decimal notation: 10101010 10101011 00001111 11111000. (Spaces added for ease of reading.) Hint: 10101010 is 170 dotted decimal notation.

Troubleshooting Questions

Troubleshooting is an important skill to have when networks go wrong. The job is to find the root cause of the problem from observed symptoms through logical and empirical tests.

- First, understand the symptoms in detail. Often, a small point is the key to identifying the problem.
- Second, know all the system's components and decide analytically which ones might be the cause of the problem. This almost always requires you to draw the network just to identify the elements that need to be considered.

- Third, list all of the possible causes of the problem. You do not start testing them one at a time. To think of one thing and consider it, then do this again and again, is chaotic, unprofessional, and usually futile. Use this approach to answer the following troubleshooting questions.
- Fourth, exclude as many possibilities as possible logically because they do not fit the details of the situation.
- Fifth and last, prioritize the alternatives you cannot eliminate logically. Begin with the most likely ones and perhaps the easiest to test.

1-9. A server that you use daily is unusually slow. So are other servers you try. Troubleshoot the problem using the five-step method described above. List the steps in order. Draw the picture.

1-10. You type a URL, and your browser tells you that the host you are trying to reach does not exist.

This message probably comes from a DNS server. Troubleshoot the problem using the five-step method described above. List the steps in order. Be sure to draw a picture of the situation.

Perspective Questions

1-11. What was the most surprising thing you learned in this chapter?

1-12. What was the most difficult material for you in this chapter?

Chapter 1a

Hands On: A Few Internet Tools

LEARNING OBJECTIVES

By the end of this chapter, you should be able to:

- Test your Internet connection speed.
- Look up a host's IP address by querying a DNS server.
- Use ping and traceroute to diagnose an Internet connection.

Hands-On Exercises

1. How fast is your Internet connection? See with one of the following websites. If you are asked to download a program for the test or run a program to see why your computer is running slowly, do not do so. Sites offering speed testing include www.zdnet.com/broadband-speedtest/, testmy.net, testinternetspeed. org, www.speedtest.net, and www.speakeasy.net/speedtest/. Report download speed, your upload speed, and your access technology (home DSL connection, school lab, 3G mobile phone, 4G mobile phone, etc.). Use two of these tools on one device or a single tool on two different devices.

2. Look up the IP address for panko.com. Tools for doing DNS lookups include ping. eu and networktools.com. If you are asked to download a program for the test or run a program to check your computer, do not do so. What result do you get?

3. Ping looks up whether an IP address or host name represents an active host and what delay there is in reaching the host. Traceroute is similar but shows all routers along the way. Tools for pinging and traceroute include ping.eu and networktools. com. If you are asked to download a program for the test or run a program to check your computer, do not do so. Try ping and traceroute for panko.com. If ping fails or if traceroute cannot get all the way to the host, a firewall may be prohibiting ping and traceroute. What results do you get?

4. Repeat the previous question for yahoo.com.

Chapter 1b

Design Exercise: A Small Home Network

LEARNING OBJECTIVES

By the end of this chapter, you should be able to:

- Design a small home network.

A SMALL HOME NETWORK

We have looked at networking principles so far. This design exercise looks at a real, although very small network—a network in a residential home. This is a network on the family's premises, so by definition, it is a local area network. Although this is a small network, it has most of the elements you have studied in this chapter.

Components

Figure 1b-1 illustrates the basic hardware devices in a typical home computer network.

- The heart of the network is a wireless access router. We will look at this device in more detail a little later.
- A broadband modem connects the home network to an Internet service provider via a wired connection or a wireless connection. We will look at wired ISP connections in Chapter 10.
- There are two client hosts. One is connected to the wireless access router using a 4-pair unshielded twisted pair (UTP) cable. Figure 1b-2 shows that 4-pair UTP consists of eight copper wires arranged in pairs, with each pair twisted around each other several times per inch. Four-pair UTP looks like a fat home telephone wire. It terminates in an RJ-45 connector. We will see more about 4-pair UTP in Chapter 5.

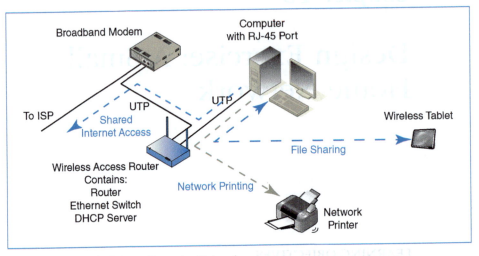

FIGURE 1B-1   Typical Home Computer Network

- The other client is a tablet with wireless capability. It connects to the wireless access point via radio signals. With wireless connections, there is no need to buy UTP cables and run them to each computer. However, as we will see in Chapter 6, wireless transmission is not always reliable or as fast as UTP transmission. We will also see in Chapter 6 that the main standard for wireless LAN (WLAN) transmission is 802.11.
- The final element is a wireless network printer. This printer also communicates with the wireless access router via 802.11. An increasing number of printers are network printers, which communicate with the access router via UTP, 802.11, or both.

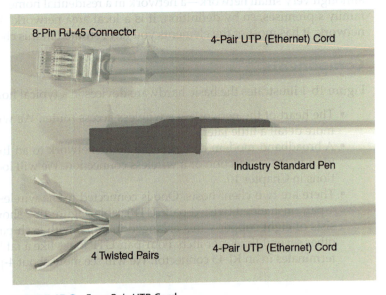

FIGURE 1B-2   Four-Pair UTP Cord

The Wireless Access Router

The wireless access router deserves special attention because it contains several important hardware functions.

- First, although it is more than just a router, the access router really is a router. Routers connect two networks. The access router connects the home network to the network of the ISP that provides Internet access.
- Second, the router has a built-in Ethernet switch. Most home access routers have at least four RJ-45 ports for UTP connections. The router in the figure has another RJ-45 port to connect to the broadband modem.
- The router has a wireless access point to connect by radio to wireless hosts within the house. Not all routers have built-in wireless access points.
- In this chapter, we saw that client PCs get their IP addresses from DHCP servers. Somewhat amazingly, the wireless access router has a built-in DHCP server. Figure 1b-3 shows that the DHCP server gives IP addresses to the two clients (192.168.0.5 and 192.168.0.6) and to the network printer (192.168.0.7). The wireless access router's DHCP server also gives the wireless access router its own IP address (192.168.0.1).
- The wireless access router also provides network address translation (NAT), which translates between the internal IP addresses and the single IP address the ISP gives to the household (60.47.243.112). As Figure 1b-4 illustrates, the ISP's DHCP server only gives the household a single IP address. When an internal device transmits, NAT converts the IP source addresses in its packets to the ISP's single allocated IP address. It then sends the packet on to the ISP. When packets arrive from the ISP, all have the IP address provided by the ISP as their destination addresses. The NAT function in the wireless access router places the internal IP address of the internal PC or the network printer into the packet's destination IP address field.

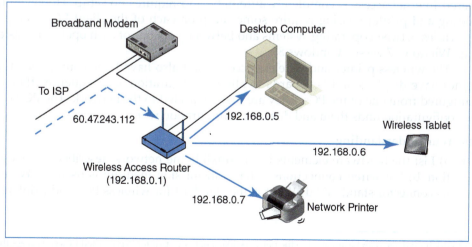

FIGURE 1B-3 DHCP in a Small Home Network

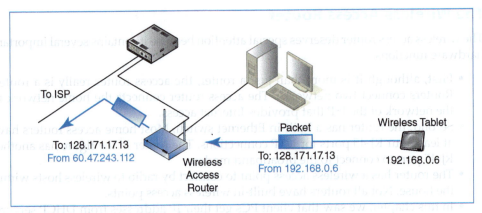

FIGURE 1B-4 Network Address Translation (NAT) in a Small Home Network

Services

Once the network is set up, the users can focus on the services their home network provides. Three of these services dominate today:

- Shared Internet access allows the two client PCs to use the Internet simultaneously, as if each was plugged directly into the broadband modem.
- File sharing allows the two client PCs to share files on each other's hard drives. For example, one PC may have the family budget. A user at the other PC can access the budget file at any time.[1] Printer sharing allows either client PC to print to the printer. Both can even print at the same time. If they do, the printer will store one job in the print queue until it finishes printing the other.

Configuration

Shared Internet access is completely automatic and requires no setup. However, file sharing and printer sharing require some setup on each of the client PCs. The process varies between operating systems and between versions of each operating system (e.g., Windows 7 versus Windows 8).

The wireless printer and wireless access point also have to be configured. They do not have displays and keyboards to allow configuration. Consequently, they are configured from one of the PCs. They are first connected to the network. The PC doing the configuration finds them and does the configuration work.

Test Your Understanding

1. a) List the hardware elements in the small home network described in this section. b) For wired connections, what transmission medium is used? c) What is its connector standard? d) What is the standard for wireless PCs and printers to

---

[1] Network hard drives can be attached to the network like a network printer. Networked PCs can access them directly.

communicate with a wireless access point? e) What are the five hardware functions in a wireless access router? f) Why is the DHCP function necessary? g) Why is NAT necessary? h) What three services does this network provide to the desktop PC and the wireless tablet? i) Which devices need to be configured? (List them.)

DESIGN EXERCISE

Design Question

1. Design a network for your home, dorm room, or some other small area. Write a one-paragraph description. Draw a picture. Cost out wireless access routers that support the 802.11ac standard. Cost out a UTP patch cord (a pre-made UTP cord) that is at least 10 feet long. You may get your costs online, but be specific about the equipment name, model, and so forth.

Chapter 2

Network Standards

LEARNING OBJECTIVES

By the end of this chapter, you should be able to:

- Explain how Internet standards are made and why this approach is valuable.
- Provide the definitions of network standards and protocols, message syntax, semantics, and order.
- Discuss message ordering in general and in HTTP and TCP.
- Discuss message syntax in general and in Ethernet frames, IP packets, TCP segments, UDP datagrams, and HTTP request and response messages.
- Explain how to encode application messages into bits (1s and 0s).
- Explain vertical communication on hosts.

HOW INTERNET STANDARDS CAME TO BE

Those who love sausage and revere the law should never see either being made.

Attributed to German Chancellor Otto von Bismarck

Standards are detailed and precise. You might expect standards creation to be logical and
rational. For some standards agencies, this is true. The International Telecommunication
Union–Telecommunications Standards Sector (the ITU-T in OSI) is part of the ITU, which
is an agency of the United Nations. The secretaries of state of individual countries are the

nominal participants, although they rarely participate directly. ITU-T has a methodical process for developing new standards. The International Organization for Standards (ISO)[1] also has strict formal processes.

With the Internet, standards setting is different. The Internet grew out of the ARPANET research network funded by the Advanced Research Projects Agency (ARPA).[2] ARPA funded it to explore the then-new technology of packet switching (what we would now call frame switching). Figure 2-1 shows that when the ARPANET began in 1969, it had four sites: UCLA, the Stanford Research Institute Augmentation Research Center, UCSB, and the University of Utah. Each site had a switch called an interface message processor (IMP). IMPs exchanged packets (actually frames) through 50 kbps lines, which seemed blazingly fast at the time.

Bolt, Beranek, and Newman (BBN) built the IMPs and designed protocols for IMPs to exchange messages. That was all they did. The first four sites were chosen because they had the technical savvy to get their large host computers to work with the IMPs.

At meetings during the ARPANET's development phase, researchers from the four sites met with BBN to discuss the network. They realized that the ARPANET would be useless without many additional standards. There had to be standards for hosts to

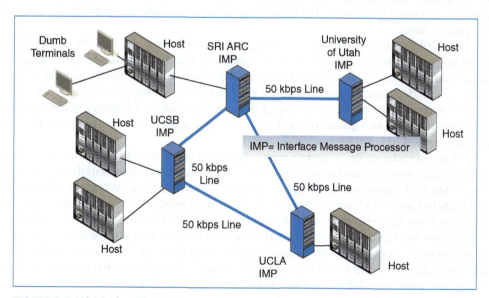

FIGURE 2-1 The Early ARPANET

---

[1] No, the acronyms do not work well with the names, but these are the standard names and acronyms. ISO, by the way, is not an acronym for International Organization for Standardization in any language. It was chosen because *iso* means "true" in Greek.

[2] Is it ARPA or DARPA? It depends on the year. It was born ARPA in 1958. In 1972, it became DARPA to emphasize its status as a Department of Defense agency. In 1993, it went back to ARPA. Then it went back to DARPA in 1996. DARPA, "ARPA-DARPA: The Name Chronicles," undated. http://www.darpa.gov/arpa-darpa.html. Last viewed August 2009.

communicate with their IMPs. Far more fundamentally, there had to be application standards if the network was to be useful. There was nobody to set these standards, so the participants decided to do it themselves. They called their small team the Network Working Group and asked others to join them. When they came up with a standard, they did not call it a standard because they felt that they lacked the authority to do so. Steve Crocker, who led the group and wrote the first document, called it a Request for Comments (RFC). Today, new standards are still RFCs.

Group members developed important application standards. In 1971, Ray Tomlinson saw that e-mail could work across sites. He was already working on e-mail for users of a single host. Mail systems on single hosts used usernames as addresses for delivering mail. Tomlinson saw that an ARPANET address would have to include both a host name and a username on the host. Looking at his keyboard, he saw that the @ sign did not seem to be used very much.[3] He assigned it to separate the username from the host name. It took him a weekend to write the software. E-mail quickly dominated use of the ARPANET.

Born in the late 1960s, the Network Working Group reflected its times. There was a strong focus on egalitarian participation and the recognition of technical merit. A few years later, the Internet Engineering Task Force (IETF) took over Internet standards development. Like the Network Working Group, the IETF has no formal membership. Anyone can participate in the IETF Working Groups that develop individual standards in specific areas.

Describing the way the IETF works, Dave Clark wrote, in 1992, "We reject: kings, presidents, and voting. We believe in: rough consensus and running code."[4] Rejecting kings and presidents refers to the IETF's strong egalitarian culture. In general, anyone with a good idea stands a fair chance of being heard. By not suppressing new ideas, this culture accounts for much of the rapid development pace of Internet standards. The rejection of voting and going forward if there was rough consensus also made the IETF action-oriented.

The importance of "running code" is not as obvious. Most standards agencies develop full complex standards in committee. When vendors implement these standards, they often find unforeseen ambiguities and even contradictions. When they build their products to these standards, they often find that their products do not interoperate with products from different vendors who supposedly follow the same standard. In addition, committees tend to design standards that are so complex that products take extensive resources to develop and are therefore expensive and slow to develop. In the IETF, almost all standards are created based on running demonstration systems. Experience identifies unforeseen problems and solves them before standards are made.

More subtly, demonstration code is simple. This leads to simple standards. Many IETF RFCs even have "simple" in their name; for instance, the Simple Mail Transfer Protocol standardizes communication among mail servers. Simple products emerge quickly, so while OSI development plodded along slowly, simple TCP/IP products

---

[3] Personal communication with Ray Tomlinson, May 1986.

[4] Dave Clark, "A Cloudy Crystal Ball—Visions of the Future," *Proceedings of the Twenty-Fourth Internet Engineering Task Force*, Massachusetts Institute of Technology NEARnet, Cambridge, MA, July 13–17, 1992, pp. 539–543.

BOX 1

April 1 and RFCs

The IETF has always had a sense of whimsy. In the United States and some other countries, April 1 is April Fool's Day—a day to play jokes on people by telling them something completely false. A robust tradition in the IETF is the publishing of a facetious RFC or two on April Fool's Day. One of the most popular is RFC 2549, *IP over Avian Carriers*. Written in 1990, this RFC describes how to transmit IP packets using carrier pigeons. This RFC was updated twice, in 1999 (to add quality of service) and 2011 (so that the protocol will work with the new IPv6 protocol). Another April 1 RFC warned of a serious authentication problem at IETF meetings. There were so many heavily bearded guys that it was impossible to tell them apart. RFC 3093 introduced the Firewall Enhancement Protocol, which allows all traffic to pass through firewalls while leaving the firewall in place (and useless). An April 1 RFC from 1998, the *Hyper Text Coffee Pot Protocol*, has the promise of growing into a real protocol as the Internet of things unfolds. One limitation in the protocol is that decaf coffee was explicitly excluded. The explanation was, "Why bother?"

---

appeared fast, at low prices. As something of an insult (although it was not intended to be), the IETF sometimes took bloated OSI standards and created simpler versions of them. These simplified versions often became dominant. Over time, simple IETF standards usually evolve to become full-featured, but each step along the way is based on real-world experience.

Test Your Understanding

1. a) Why are Internet standards called RFCs? (Do not just spell out the name.) b) What factors in the Internet's informal development process lead to rapid standards development and low-cost products?

INTRODUCTION

We looked at network standards briefly in Chapter 1. In this chapter, we will look at standards at a more conceptual level, developing taxonomies of standards types. Much of the rest of this book focuses on specific standards; you will need to understand standards broadly to know where those specific standards fit into the overall standards picture. This chapter also looks in some detail at the most important standards on the Internet and in corporate networks. These include Ethernet, IP, TCP, UDP, and HTTP.

Standard = Protocol

In this text, we use the terms *standard* and *protocol* to mean the same thing. In fact, standards often have *protocol* in their names. Examples are the Hypertext Transfer Protocol, the Internet Protocol, the Transmission Control Protocol, and the User Datagram Protocol.

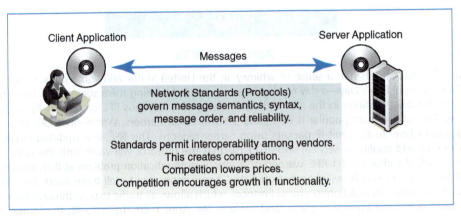

FIGURE 2-2   Network Standards

Network Standards

What Are Network Standards?   As Figure 2-2 illustrates, **network standards** are rules of operation that govern the exchange of messages between two hardware or software processes. To give a human analogy, in the first author's classes, the standard language is American English. Not all of his students are native English speakers, but we are able to communicate because we use a standard language.

In this chapter, we will see that network standards govern a number of message characteristics, including semantics, syntax, message order, reliability, and connection orientation.

Network standards are rules of operation that govern the exchange of messages between two hardware or software processes. This includes message semantics, syntax, message order, reliability, and connection orientation.

Standards Bring Competition   Standards are important because they allow products from different vendors to **interoperate** (work together). In Figure 2-2, the client program might be a Chrome browser from Google, and the server program might be Microsoft's IIS webserver program. Although these companies may actively dislike each other, their products work together because they exchange messages using the Hypertext Transfer Protocol (HTTP) network standard.

With network standards, it is impossible for any company to maintain a monopoly by refusing to allow others to use its proprietary communication protocols. Competition drives down prices. It also spurs companies to add new features so that their products will not be pure commodities that can only compete on price. These new features often appear in the next version of the standard.

Network standards are not only the key to competition. They are also the key to networking in general. To work in networking, you need to understand individual standards so that you can design networks, set up network components, and troubleshoot problems. Learning networking is heavily about learning standards. In this chapter, we will look broadly at the general characteristics of standards and will also look at some key network standards.

Recap of Chapter 1 Standards Concepts

In Chapter 1, we saw that standards can be described in terms of their layer of operation.

Delivery Layers   As Figure 2-3 shows, three layers are involved in the transmission of packets between source hosts and destination hosts.

- *Physical links* are connections between adjacent devices, such as a host and a switch, two switches, two routers, a router and a switch, and so forth. Physical layer standards are not concerned with messages. Their job is to turn the bits of data link layer messages (frames) into signals.
- Data link layer standards govern the transmission of frames between two hosts, two routers, or a host and a router *across a single point-to-point, switched, wireless, or hybrid switched/wireless network*. The path that a frame takes is called its *data link*. This layer governs switch operation and frame organization.
- Internet layer standards govern the transmission of packets from the source host to the destination host, across multiple networks in an internet. The path that a packet takes between the two hosts is called its *route*. This layer governs router operation and packet organization.

A common source of confusion is that concepts are repeated at the data link and internet layers but with different terminology. This occurs because internetworking required the adding of a second layer of standards to those needed for transmission through single networks.

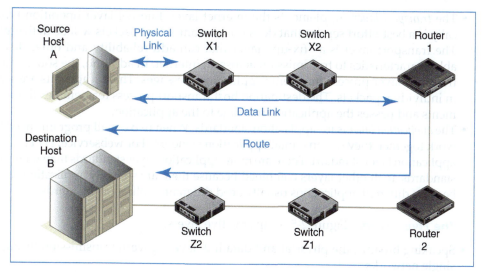

FIGURE 2-3   The Physical, Data Link, and Internet Layers

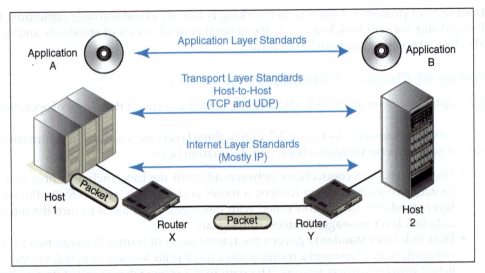

FIGURE 2-4 Transport and Application Processes

Also, recall that packets are carried inside frames. When a source host sends a packet to a destination host, the packet travels within a frame in each network along the way. If there are 19 single networks on the route between the source and destination hosts, a single packet will travel in 19 different frames.

The Transport and Application Layers The physical, data link, and internet layers are for standards that move packets along their way between the source host and the destination host. In contrast, Figure 2-4 shows that transport and application processes govern processes that exist only on the two communicating hosts.

- The *transport layer* supplements the internet layer. Internet layer operation typically is a best-effort service that does not guarantee that packets will be delivered. The transport layer is a "fix-up" layer that can add reliability and other desirable characteristics to transmission across an internet. In addition, the source host transport layer process fragments application messages. These fragments are sent in individual packets. The destination host transport process reassembles the segments and passes the application message to the application.
- The *application layer* is for application standards. When two e-mail programs need to work together, they use an e-mail application standard. For webservice, HTTP is an application layer standard. There are more application layer standards than there are standards at all other layers combined because there are so many applications and because different applications usually need different application standards.

The Five Layers Figure 2-5 recaps the five layers.

- Speaking broadly, the physical and data link layers govern transmission through single networks.
- Also speaking broadly, the internet and transport layers together govern transmission through an internet. The internet layer governs packet organization

Broad Function	Layer	Name	Specific Function
Interoperability of application programs	5	Application	Application layer standards govern how two applications work with each other, even if they are from different vendors.
Transmission across an internet	4	Transport	Transport layer standards govern aspects of end-to-end communication between two end hosts that are not handled by the internet layer. These standards also allow hosts to work together even if the two computers are from different vendors or have different internal designs.
	3	Internet	Internet link layer standards govern the transmission of packets across an internet—typically by sending them through several routers along the route. Internet layer standards govern packet syntax and router operation.
Transmission across a single network	2	Data Link	Data link layer standards govern the transmission of frames across a single network—typically by sending them through several switches along the data link. Data link layer standards govern frame syntax and switch operation.
	1	Physical	Physical layer standards govern transmission between adjacent devices connected by a transmission medium.

FIGURE 2-5 Layers Recap

and raw packet delivery. The transport layer fixes up problems and does fragmentation and assembly.

- Finally, the application layer governs how two applications work together.

Test Your Understanding

2. a) Give the definition of network standards that this chapter introduced. b) In this book, do *standards* and *protocols* mean the same thing?

Network Standard Characteristics

Network standards govern communication. Figure 2-6 notes, more specifically, that standards govern four specific things about message exchanges: semantics, syntax, order, and reliability. In this section, we will focus on message order, semantics, and syntax, but we will also introduce the concept of reliability.

Message Ordering In medicine and many other fields, a *protocol* is a prescribed series of actions to be performed in a particular order. In cooking, if you do not process the ingredients of a cake in the right order, the cake is not likely to turn out very well.

In this same way, network standards govern **message ordering**. For the Hypertext Transfer Protocol standard that we saw in Chapter 1, message ordering is very simple.

Network Standards

Network standards are rules that govern the exchange of messages between hardware or software processes on different hosts, including message ordering, message syntax, message semantics, and reliability.

Message Order

Turn taking, order of messages in a complex transaction, who must initiate communication, etc.

In the World Wide Web, the client program sends an HTTP request message

The webserver program sends back an HTTP response message

The client must initiate the interaction

Other network standards have more complex turn-taking; for instance TCP

Human turn taking is loose and flexible

Message order for network standards must be rigid because computers are not intelligent

Message Semantics

Semantics = the meaning of a message

HTTP request message semantics: "Please give me this file"

HTTP response message semantics: Here is the file. (Or, I could not comply for the following reason)

Network standards normally have a very limited set of possible message meanings

For example, HTTP requests have only a few possible meanings

GET: Please give me a file

PUT: Upload and store this file (not often used)

A few more

Message Syntax (Organization)

Like human grammar, but more rigid

Header, data field, and trailer (Figure 2-9)

Not all messages have all three parts

Field lengths are measured in bits or bytes

Bytes are also called octets

FIGURE 2-6 Network Standards Concepts

The client sends an HTTP request message, and the server sends back an HTTP response message. Many protocols, including the Transmission Control Protocol (TCP) standard, which we will see in this chapter and in Chapter 8, involve many messages being sent in precise order.

Human beings are intelligent, so message ordering in human conversations tends to be informal and even chaotic. Software is not intelligent, so message ordering in protocols has to be very rigid and exact.

Semantics To limit the complexity of software, protocols usually define only a few message types, and these types usually have only a few options. Put another way, network protocols greatly limit the **semantics** (meaning) of their messages. For example, the most common HTTP request message is a GET message, which requests a file. There is also a POST request message, which uploads a file to the webserver. Similarly, the semantics of an HTTP response message are, "Here is the file," or "Sorry, I can't deliver the file."

Semantics is the meaning of a message.

Syntax   In addition, while human grammar is very flexible, network messages have very rigid **syntax**, that is, message organization. A little later in this chapter, we will look at the syntaxes of several important protocol messages.

Syntax is how a message is organized.

Test Your Understanding

3. a) What three aspects of message exchanges did we see in this section? b) Give an example not involving networking in which the order in which you do things can make a big difference. c) Distinguish between syntax and semantics.

EXAMPLES OF MESSAGE ORDERING

We will look at two examples of message ordering. We will look first at the very simple message ordering in HTTP. We will then look at the more complex message ordering in TCP.

Message Ordering in HTTP

Figure 2-7 illustrates an HTTP request–response cycle. As we have just noted, the client sends a request, and the server sends a response. Note that the cycle is always initiated by the client, not by the server. The server cannot transmit unless the client has sent it an HTTP request message. This is a very simple type of message ordering.

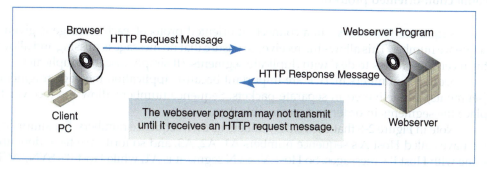

FIGURE 2-7   An HTTP Request–Response Cycle

Message Ordering and Reliability in TCP at the Transport Layer

Many protocols have much more complex rules for message ordering. We will look at the Transmission Control Protocol at the transport layer to see an example of this complexity.

The Situation   Figure 2-8 shows the transport layer processes on Host A and Host B. They are communicating via HTTP at the application layer. The Hypertext Transfer Protocol requires the use of TCP at the transport layer. The figure shows a sample communication session, which is called a connection.

Segments   In TCP, messages are called **TCP segments** because each carries a segment (fragment) of a fragmented application message (or is a control segment that does not carry application data).

The Three-Step Handshake Opening   The communication begins with a **three-step handshake**.

- Host A, which is the client in the HTTP exchanges, initiates the communication. It transmits a TCP SYN segment to Host B. This indicates that Host A wishes to communicate.
- Host B sends back a TCP SYN/ACK segment. The SYN indicates that it also is willing to begin the communication. The ACK part is an acknowledgment of Host A's SYN message. In TCP, all segments are acknowledged, with the primary exception of pure ACKs. (If pure ACKs had to be acknowledged, there would be an endless series of ACKs.)
- Host A sends back a pure TCP ACK segment. This acknowledges Host B's SYN/ACK.

In TCP, all segments are acknowledged, with the primary exception of pure ACKs.

Connections   TCP creates connections with distinct openings and closings. This is like a telephone call, in which you informally make sure that the other person can talk at the start of a call and mutually agree to end the call. In technical jargon, TCP is a **connection-oriented** protocol.

Sequence Numbers   In a connection-oriented protocol, each message is given a sequence number. This allows the receiver to ensure that no message is missing and allows the receiving process to deal with duplicate segments. (It simply discards duplicates.)

Sequence numbers in TCP are important because application message fragments (segments) are delivered in separate packets. Sequence numbers allow the receiver to place the segments in order and reassemble them.

Note in Figure 2-8 that each side numbers its own sequence numbers. For simplicity, we have called Host A's sequence numbers A1, A2, A3, and so forth. We have done the same with Host B's messages. So Host A's SYN segment is A1, while Host B's SYN/ACK is B1, and Host A's acknowledgment of the SYN/ACK is A2.

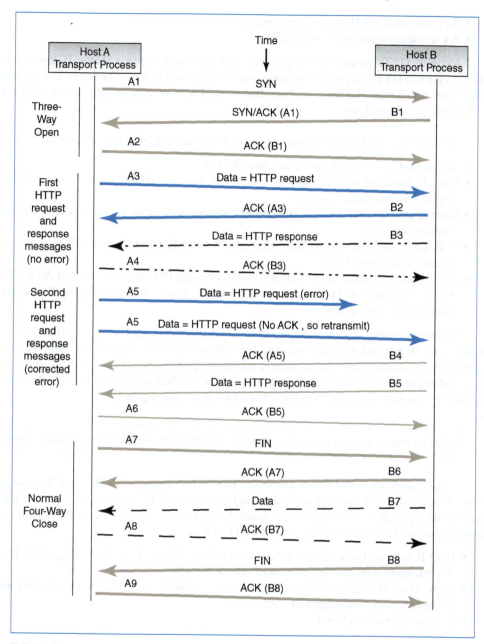

FIGURE 2-8 A TCP Session

Carrying Application Data The next four segments (A3, B2, B3, and A4) constitute a request–response cycle.

- A3 carries an HTTP request.
- B2 is an ACK of A3.

- B3 carries the HTTP response message.
- A4 acknowledges the receipt of B3.

Usually, HTTP request messages are small enough to fit in a single TCP segment. However, most HTTP responses are long and must be sent in a number of TCP segments. This does not change the basic picture, however. There would simply be several more exchanges like B3 and A4.

Reliability   TCP is a **reliable** protocol. This means that it corrects errors.

- Segment A5 is sent but never reaches Host B.
- Host B does not send an acknowledgment, because ACKs are only sent when a segment is received correctly.
- Host A realizes that A5 has not been acknowledged. After a certain period of time, it retransmits A5.
- This time, the segment arrives correctly at Host B. Host B sends B4, which is an acknowledgment of A5.
- Finally, Host B sends an HTTP response message (B5) and receives an ACK (A6). Again, sending an HTTP response message tends to take several TCP data/ acknowledgment cycles.

In this example, Segment A5 never reached the receiving transport process. What would have happened if A5 had reached the transport process but was damaged during transmission? In this case, the receiving transport process would discard the segment. It would not send an ACK. So there is a simple rule for ACKs. Unless a transport process receives a segment correctly, it does not send an acknowledgment.

Unless a transport process receives a segment correctly, it does not send an acknowledgment.

The Four-Step Handshake Closing   Host A has no more HTTP request messages to send, so it closes the connection. It does so by sending a FIN segment (A7), which Host B acknowledges (B6). This means that Host A will not send new data. However, it will continue to send ACKs to segments sent by Host B.

- Host B has one more data segment to send, B7. When it sends this segment, Host A's transport process responds with an ACK (A8).
- Now, Host B is finished sending data. It sends its own FIN segment (B8) and receives an acknowledgment (A9).
- The connection is closed.

Perspective   TCP is a fairly complex protocol. It uses connections so that it can apply sequence numbers to segments. This allows it to fragment long application messages and deliver the segments with an indication of their order. It also uses connections so that it can provide reliable data to the application layer program above it.

We will see that almost all other protocols are unreliable. Many standards check for errors, but if they find an error, they simply discard the message. Discarded messages never get to the transport process on the other host, so they are never acknowledged. Receiving no acknowledgment, the sender resends them.

Why make only TCP reliable? There are two answers. First, TCP sits just below the application layer. This allows it to send clean data to the application program regardless of errors at lower levels, which are corrected by TCP resends.

Second, although all routers along the way do internet layer processing, only the two hosts have transport layer processes, so error correction is done only once, on the two hosts. It is not done at each packet hop between routers or in each frame hop between switches. Error correction is a resource-consuming process, so it should be done as little as possible. Doing error correction at the transport layer processes on the two hosts accomplishes this.

Test Your Understanding

4. a) Describe the simple message ordering in HTTP. b) In HTTP, can the server transmit if it has not received a request message from the client? c) Describe the three-step handshake in TCP connection openings. d) What kind of message does the destination host send if it does not receive a segment during a TCP connection? e) What kind of message does the destination host send if it receives a segment that has an error during a TCP connection? f) Under what conditions will a source host TCP process retransmit a segment? g) Describe the four-step handshake in TCP connection closes. h) After a side initiates the close of a connection by sending a FIN segment, will it send any more segments? Explain. i) In Figure 2-8, suppose Host A had already sent A6 before it realized that it would need to resend A5. When it then resent A5, A6 would arrive before A5. How would Host B be able to put the information in the two segments back in order?

EXAMPLES OF MESSAGE SYNTAX

We have just looked at message ordering. Now we will turn to message syntax. In this book, we will be looking at the syntax of many different types of messages. To give you a feeling for message syntax, we will look at the syntax of five important message types.

Syntax: General Message Organization

Figure 2-9 shows that message syntax in general can have three parts—a header, a data field, and a trailer.

Data Field   The **data field** is the heart of the message. It contains the content being delivered by the message. In an HTTP response message, the data field contains the file that the response message is delivering.

The data field contains the content being delivered by a message.

Header   The message **header**, quite simply, is everything that comes before the data field.

The message header is everything that comes before the data field.

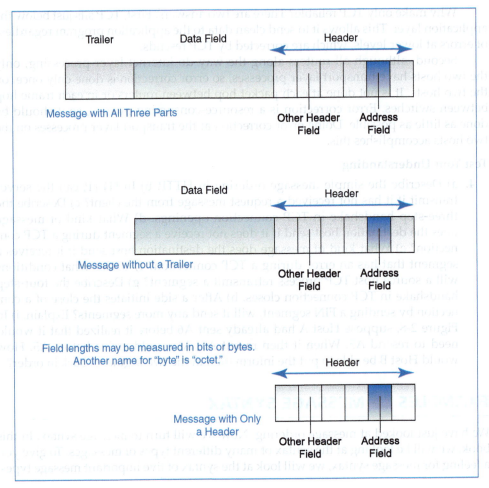

FIGURE 2-9 General Message Organization

Trailer   Some messages also have **trailers**, which consist of everything coming *after* the data field.

The message trailer is everything that comes after the data field.

Not All Messages Have All Three Parts   HTTP messages demonstrate that only a header is present in all messages. Data fields are not always present but are very common. Trailers are not common.

Fields in Headers and Trailers   The header and trailer usually contain smaller syntactic sections called **fields**. For example, a frame or packet has a destination address header field, which allows switches or routers along the way to pass on the frame or packet they receive. When we look at network standard messages in this chapter and in later chapters, we will be concerned primarily with header fields and trailer fields.

The header and trailer usually contain smaller syntactic sections called fields.

Octets   Field lengths can be measured in bits. Another common measure for field lengths in networking is the octet. An **octet** is a group of 8 bits. Hey, isn't that a byte? Yes, exactly. *Octet* is just another name for *byte*. The term is widely used in networking, however, so you need to become familiar with it. *Octet* actually makes more sense than *byte*, because *oct* means "eight." We have octopuses, octagons, and octogenarians.[5]

An octet is a group of 8 bits.

Test Your Understanding

5. a) What are the three general parts of messages? b) What does the data field contain? c) What is the definition of a header? d) Is there always a data field in a message? e) What is the definition of a trailer? f) Are trailers common? g) Distinguish between headers and header fields. h) Distinguish between octets and bytes.

The Ethernet Frame Syntax

Messages at the data link layer are frames. In wired local area networks (LANs), the dominant network standard is Ethernet. Actually, Ethernet, like most "standards," is really a family of standards. Ethernet has many different physical layer protocols from which a company can choose. However, generally speaking, it has a single data link layer frame standard, which Figure 2-10 illustrates.

The fields in the frame are delimited by their lengths in octets or bits. The destination host or switch first receives the first bit of the destination address field. It then counts bits until, 48 bits later, it gets to the next field, then to the field after it, and so forth. Then it can process the frame.

Ethernet has a complex frame syntax. We will look at its components in more detail in Chapter 5. There are only four fields that we need to emphasize at this time: the source and destination address fields, the data field packet, and the Frame Check Sequence field.

Source and Destination Address Fields   Ethernet has data link layer source and destination address fields. Each address is 48 bits long. Traditionally, these have been called **MAC addresses**. However, they are now called **Extended Unique Identifier 48-bit (EUI-48) addresses**.

---

[5] What is the eighth month? (Careful!)

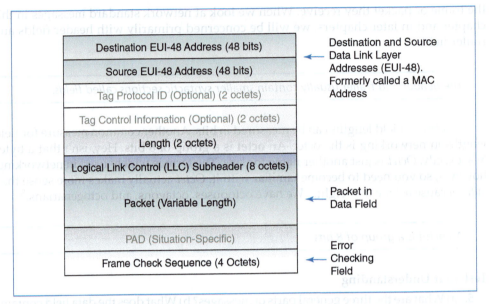

FIGURE 2-10   Ethernet Frame

Packet in the Data Field   We saw in Chapter 1 that frames carry packets in their data fields. The figure illustrates how this occurs in Ethernet.

Frame Check Sequence Field   The four-octet Frame Check Sequence field is used for error detection. The sending data link layer process computes a number based on other bits in the frame. It places this number in the Frame Check Sequence field. The receiver recomputes this 32-bit number. If the recomputed number is the same as the number transmitted in the Frame Check Sequence field, then there have been no errors during transmission, and the receiver accepts the frame. If the numbers are different, there was a propagation error and the frame is corrupted. If so, the receiving data link layer process simply discards the frame. This is error detection but not full error correction. Ethernet is not a reliable protocol.

Test Your Understanding

6. a) How long are Ethernet EUI-48 addresses? b) What were they called tradition-ally? c) What devices read Ethernet destination EUI-48 addresses? d) If the receiver detects an error on the basis of the value in the Frame Check Sequence field, what does it do? e) Ethernet does error detection but not error correction. Is Ethernet a reliable protocol? Explain.

The Internet Protocol (IP) Packet Syntax

32 Bits per Row   Figure 2-11 illustrates the syntax of Internet Protocol (IP) version 4 (IPv4) packets. Later, we will look at the syntax of IP version 6 (IPv6) packets.

Internet Protocol Version 4 (IPv4)				
Bit 0				Bit 31
Version Number (4 bits)	Header Length (4 bits)	Diff-Serv (8 bits)	Total Length (16 bits)	
Identification (16 bits)			Flags (3 bits)	Fragment Offset (13 bits)
Time to Live (8 bits)		Protocol (8 bits)	Header Checksum (16 bits)	
Source IP Address (32 bits)				
Destination IP Address (32 bits)				
Options (if any)			Padding	
Data Field (dozens, hundreds, or thousands of bits) often contains a TCP segment or UDP datagram				

FIGURE 2-11 The Internet Protocol (IP) Packet Syntax in IPv4

An IP packet, like an Ethernet frame, is a long string of bits (1s and 0s). Of course, drawing the packet this way would require a page several meters wide. Instead, Figure 2-11 shows that we usually depict an IP packet as a series of rows with 32 bits per row. In binary counting, the first bit is zero. Consequently, the first row shows bits 0 through 31. The next row shows bits 32 through 63. This is a different way of showing syntax than we saw with the Ethernet frame, but it is a common way of showing syntax in TCP/IP standards, so you need to be familiar with it.

Source and Destination IP Address Fields　Each IPv4 packet has source and destination IP addresses. Each is 32 bits long, so each has its own row in the header. Routers use destination IP addresses to decide how to forward packets so that they will get closer to their destination.

Unreliability　The IPv4 **Header Checksum** field is like the Frame Check Sequence field in the Ethernet frame. It also is used for error detection. As in the case of Ethernet frames, incorrect IP packets are simply discarded. There is no retransmission. So like Ethernet, IP is not a reliable protocol.

Test Your Understanding

7. a) How many octets long is an IPv4 header if there are no options? (Look at Figure 2-11.) b) List the first bit number on each IPv4 header row in Figure 2-11, not including options. Remember that the first bit in Row 1 is Bit 0. c) What is the bit number of the first bit in the destination address field in IPv4? (Remember that the first bit in binary counting is Bit 0.) d) How long are IPv4 addresses? e) What device in an internet besides the destination host reads the destination IP address? f) What is this device's purpose in doing so? g) Is IP reliable or unreliable? Explain.

Transmission Control Protocol Segment Syntax

Earlier, we saw message ordering in the transmission of TCP segments. Now we will look at the syntax of TCP segments.

Fields in TCP/IP Segments   When IP was created, it was designed to be a very simple "best effort" protocol (although its routing tables are complex). The IETF left more complex internetwork transmission control tasks to TCP. Consequently, network professionals need to understand TCP very well. Figure 2-12 shows the organization of TCP messages, which are called TCP segments.

TCP Segment

Bit 0				Bit 31
Source Port Number (16 bits)			Destination Port Number (16 bits)	
Sequence Number (32 bits)				
Acknowledgment Number (32 bits)				
Data Offset (4 bits)	Reserved (3 bits) 0 0 0	Flag Fields* (9 bits)	Window Size (16 bits)	
Checksum (16 bits)			Urgent Pointer (16 bits)	
Options (if any)				Padding
Data Field				

*Flag fields are 1-bit fields. They include SYN, ACK, and FIN bits

UDP Datagram

Bit 0	Bit 31
Source Port Number (16 bits)	Destination Port Number (16 bits)
UDP Length (16 bits)	UDP Checksum (16 bits)
Data Field	

FIGURE 2-12   TCP Segment and UDP Datagram

Flag Fields   TCP has nine single-bit fields. Single-bit fields in general are called **flag fields**. If a flag field has the value 1, it is said to be **set**. (If it has the value 0, it is said to be **not set**.) In TCP, flag fields allow the receiving transport process to identify the kind of segment it is receiving. We will look at three of these flag bits:

- If the ACK (acknowledgment) bit is set, then the segment acknowledges another segment. When the ACK bit is set, the acknowledgment field also must be filled in to indicate which message is being acknowledged.
- If the SYN (synchronization) bit is set (has the value 1), then the segment requests a connection opening.
- If the FIN (finish) bit is set, then the segment requests a normal connection closing.

Single-bit fields are called flag fields. If a flag field has the value 1, it is said to be set. (If it has the value 0, it is said to be not set.)

Earlier, we talked about TCP SYN segments, ACK segments, and FIN segments. These are simply segments in which the SYN, ACK, or FIN bits are set, respectively.

Sequence Numbers   Each TCP segment has a unique 32-bit **sequence number**. This sequence number increases with each segment. Sequence numbers allow the receiving transport process to put arriving TCP segments in order if IP delivers them out of order.

Acknowledgment Numbers   Earlier in this chapter, we saw that TCP uses acknowledgments (ACKs) to achieve reliability. If a transport process receives a TCP segment correctly, it sends back a TCP segment acknowledging the reception. We saw earlier that if the sending transport process does not receive an acknowledgment, it transmits the TCP segment again.

The **acknowledgment number** field indicates which segment is being acknowledged. One might expect that if a segment has sequence number X, then the acknowledgment number in the segment that acknowledges it would have acknowledgment number X. Later in this book, we will see that the situation actually is more complex.

The acknowledgment number indicates which segment is being acknowledged.

Test Your Understanding

8. a) Why was TCP designed to be complex? b) Why is it important for networking professionals to understand TCP? c) What are TCP messages called?
9. a) Why are sequence numbers good? b) What are 1-bit fields called? c) If someone says that a flag field is set, what does this mean? d) If the ACK bit is set, what other field must have a value? e) What is the purpose of the acknowledgment number field?

User Datagram Protocol (UDP) Datagram Syntax

Applications that cannot use the high functionality of TCP or that do not need this functionality can use the **User Datagram Protocol (UDP)** at the transport layer instead of TCP. UDP does not have openings, closings, or acknowledgments, and so it produces substantially less traffic than TCP. UDP messages are called datagrams. Because of UDP's simple operation, the syntax of the UDP datagram shown in Figure 2-12 is very simple. Besides two port number fields, which we will see next in this chapter, there are only two header fields.

- There is a **UDP length** field so that the receiving transport process can know how long the datagram is. The packet in the datagram's data field has variable length, so the UDP datagram has variable length.
- There also is a **UDP checksum** field that allows the receiver to check for errors in this UDP datagram.[6] If an error is found, however, the UDP datagram is discarded. In contrast to TCP, UDP has no mechanism for retransmission.

Test Your Understanding

10. a) What are the four fields in a UDP header? b) Describe the third. c) Describe the fourth. d) Is UDP reliable? Explain.

Port Numbers

Both TCP and UDP headers begin with two port number fields, one specifying the sender's port number and one specifying the receiver's port number. Servers and clients use these port number fields differently.

Server Port Numbers   Computers are multitasking machines, which means that they can run several programs at the same time. Figure 2-13 shows a server running *SMTP* (the Simple Mail Transfer Protocol), *HTTP*, and *FTP* (the File Transfer Protocol)

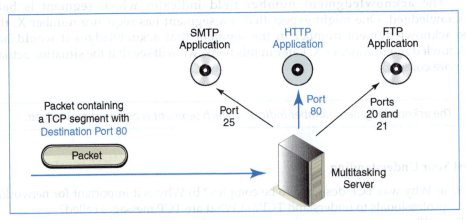

FIGURE 2-13   Server Port Numbers

---

[6] If the UDP checksum field has 16 zeroes, error checking is not to be done at all.

programs. If a packet arrives, how does the TCP or UDP process know which of the application programs running on the server should receive the message?

The answer is that the TCP or UDP process uses a port number. A server's **port number** specifies a particular application running on the server. Port 20 or 21 specifies the FTP (file transfer protocol) program, while Port 25 specifies the SMTP (e-mail) program, and Port 80 specifies the HTTP (World Wide Web) application.

A server administrator can choose any port number for a program, but there are **well-known port numbers** that are normally used to specify particular server application programs. For example, most webservers use Port 80 for the web-server program. The well-known port numbers have a port number range reserved for their use—port numbers 0 through 1023. To send a TCP or UCP message to the application program on a server, the sender puts the appropriate port number in the destination port number field.

Client Port Numbers   Clients use port numbers differently. For every conversation a client initiates, it randomly generates an **ephemeral port number**. On Windows computers, this is the range from Port 1024 to Port 4999. These port numbers are ephemeral, in the sense that they are discarded when a conversation between the client and a particular webserver ends. If the client communicates with the same server program later, the client will generate a new ephemeral port number.

Figure 2-14 shows a client host (60.171.18.22) communicating with a blue server host (1.33.17.13). The server port number is Port 80, indicating that the client is communicating with the HTTP program on the server. The client has generated ephemeral Port 2707. When the client transmits to the server, the source port number field has the value 2707 and the destination port number 80. When the server replies, the source port number is 80 and the destination port number is 2707.

The client is simultaneously connected to an SMTP application on a server (123.30.17.120), which uses the well-known port number 25. For this conversation, the

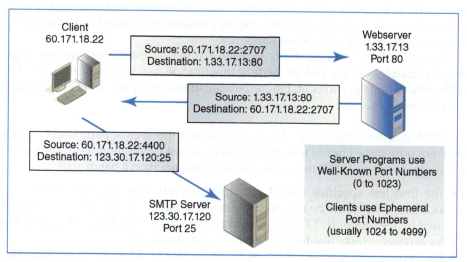

FIGURE 2-14 Client Port Numbers and Sockets

client randomly generates ephemeral Port 4400. When the client transmits, the source port number is 4400 and the destination port number is 25.

Sockets Figure 2-14 shows that a conversation always involves a source IP address and a source port number, plus a destination IP address and a destination port number. It is common to represent each IP address and port number as a **socket** which is simply the IP address, a colon, and the port number. When the client transmits to the webserver, the source socket is 60.171.18.22:2707 and the destination socket is 1.33.17.13:80. When the webserver replies, the source socket is 1.33.17.13:80, and the destination socket is 60.171.18.22:2707.

Test Your Understanding

11. a) What type of port numbers do servers use for common server programs? b) What type of port numbers do clients use when they communicate with server programs? c) What is the range of port numbers for each type of port? d) How are ephemeral port numbers generated? e) Why are they called *ephemeral*?

12. a) What is the syntax of a socket? b) In Figure 2-14, when the client transmits to the mail server, what is the source port number? c) What is the destination port number? d) What is the source socket? e) What is the destination socket? f) When the SMTP server transmits to the client host, what is the source port number? g) What is the destination port number? h) What is the source socket? i) What is the destination socket?

HTTP Request and Response Message Syntax

The highest layer is the application layer (Layer 5). Standards at this layer govern how application programs talk to one another. We have used HTTP in most of our examples so far. However, there are many application layer standards—more than there are standards at any other layer. There are application layer standards for e-mail, database queries, and every other application. After network professionals master the network and internet work standards that this course presents, they spend much of the rest of their careers mastering application standards.

Unfortunately, some students become fixated on examples and lose sight of general principles. At the risk of feeding this fixation, we will look at the syntax for the Hypertext Transfer Protocol. Figure 2-15 illustrates the syntax of HTTP request and response messages.

HTTP Request Message The HTTP request message is particularly simple. It consists of only three lines of text. Some HTTP request messages have additional lines, but it is rare to see an HTTP request message with more than a handful of lines.

- The first line specifies the GET method (which requests a file retrieval), the location of the file to be retrieved (/panko/home.htm), and the version of HTTP used by the sender (HTTP 1.1). This and other lines end with [CRLF]. This stands for carriage return/line feed. It means to start a new line.
- The second line specifies the host to which this HTTP request message should be sent.

HTTP

    The application layer is the highest layer

    It has more standards than any other layer

    HTTP is not the only application layer standard; it is one of many

    Many application layer protocols, such as SMTP for e-mail, are much more complex than HTTP

HTTP Request Message

    GET /panko/home.htm HTTP/1.1[CRLF]

    Host: voyager.shidler.hawaii.edu[CRLF]

    Connection: Keep-Alive

HTTP Response Message

    HTTP/1.1 200 OK[CRLF]

    Date: Tuesday, 20-MAR-2014 18:32:15 GMT[CRLF]

    Server: name of server software[CRLF]

    MIME-version: 1.0[CRLF]

    Content-type: text/plain[CRLF]

    [CRLF]

    File to be downloaded. A string of bytes that may be text, graphics, sound, video, or other content.

Notes

    A relatively old feeling protocol

    Fields ended by CRLF, which starts a new line

    Based on e-mail (an old protocol) for rapid development

FIGURE 2-15   Hypertext Transfer Protocol Message Syntax

- The third line specifies that the TCP connections should be kept active over multiple request–response cycles. Without this, the TCP connection would end after each request–response cycle and would have to be reestablished before each request–response cycle.

After the first line, fields in the header have a very specific syntax. There is a *keyword*, a *colon*, and then a *value* for the keyword, then a carriage return/line feed.

These three lines form the header of the message. The sender is transmitting no data, so there is no data field. Nor is there anything after a data field, so there is no trailer.

HTTP Response Message   Figure 2-15 also shows the syntax of a relatively simple HTTP *response* message that responds to the HTTP request message we have just seen.

First, there is a header. The header is everything that comes before the data field, which is the file being delivered.

- The first line begins with HTTP/1.1 to show that it is willing to speak in this version of the standard. The 200 is a code that describes the response. The 200 code states that the message is delivering the requested file. The browser uses the code to know how to react. What about the final OK? The browser ignores it. HTTP is humanly readable, and the "OK" is designed to tell humans reading the message what the 200 code means, that everything is alright.

- After the first line, other fields in the header have a keyword, a colon, a value for the keyword, and then a carriage return/line feed.
- The Date keyword is followed by a colon and the date and time the HTTP response message was sent.
- The Server keyword, in turn, describes the webserver software sending the response. Browsers know that different webserver programs respond somewhat differently. Knowing the webserver program helps the browser adjust.
- The final line containing the [CRLF] is a blank line. It indicates the end of the header.

Following the header is the file being sent to the browser. This is a long byte stream that constitutes the text document, photograph, video clip, or other type of file being delivered.

As usual, there is no trailer.

A Text Protocol   In contrast to the other protocols we have looked at, HTTP is a fairly primitive protocol. It delimits fields with carriage return/line feeds instead of having fields that end at a certain number of bits. Separating the header from the data field with a blank line also seems rather crude. Most application protocols are much more complex than HTTP.

Tim Berners-Lee, who created HTTP, based this standard on e-mail standards. An e-mail header has a number of keywords (e.g., To and From) followed by a colon, the value for the keyword, and a new line. E-mail standards were already very old when HTTP was created, but they got the job done. HTTP also got the job done. In particular, new keywords can be added very easily, given the robust way HTTP has of ending a field and starting a new field.

Test Your Understanding

13. a) Is the application layer standard always HTTP? b) Which layer has the most standards? c) At which layer would you find standards for voice over IP? (The answer is not explicitly in this section.) d) Are all application layer standards simple like HTTP? e) In HTTP response headers, what is the syntax of most lines (which are header fields)? f) In HTTP request and response message, how is the end of a field indicated? g) Do HTTP request messages have headers, data fields, and trailers? h) Do HTTP response messages that deliver files have headers, data fields, and trailers?

CONVERTING APPLICATION MESSAGES INTO BITS

Encoding

One function of application layer programs is to convert messages into bits. This conversion is called **encoding**. At the transport layer and lower layers, all messages consist of bits. Original application layer messages, in contrast, may have text, numbers, graphics images, video clips, and other types of information. It is the application layer's job to convert all of these into bits before putting them in the application layer message.

Test Your Understanding

14. a) What is encoding? b) At what layer is encoding done?

Encoding Text as ASCII

To convert text data to binary, applications use the **ASCII code**, whose individual symbols are each 7 bits long. Seven bits give 128 possibilities. This is enough for all keys on the keyboard plus some extra control codes.

Figure 2-16 shows some ASCII codes. It shows that uppercase letters and lowercase letters have different ASCII codes. This is necessary because the receiver may need to know whether a character is an uppercase or lowercase letter. ASCII can also encode the digits from 0 through 9, as well as punctuation and other characters. There are even ASCII control codes that tell the receiver what to do. For example, when we looked at HTTP, we saw carriage returns and line feeds. A carriage return is 0001101, and a line feed is 0001010.

For transmission, the 7 bits of each ASCII character are placed in a byte. The eighth bit in the byte is not used today.[7]

Test Your Understanding

15. a) Explain how many bytes it will take to transmit "Hello World!" without the quotation marks. (Check Figure: 12.) b) If you go to a search engine, you can easily find converters to represent characters in ASCII. What are the 7-bit ASCII codes for "Hello world" without the quotation marks? (Check: H is 1001000.)

Category	Meaning	7-Bit ASCII Code	8th bit in Transmitted Byte
Upper-Case Letters	A	1000001	Unused
Lower-Case Letters	a	1100001	Unused
Digits (0 through 9)	3	0110011	Unused
Punctuation	Period	0101110	Unused
Punctuation	Space	0100000	Unused
Control Codes	Carriage Return	0001101	Unused
Control Codes	Line Feed	0001010	Unused

FIGURE 2-16 Encoding Text as ASCII

---

[7] Early systems used the eighth bit in each byte as a "parity bit" to detect errors in transmission. The total number of bits in a byte was made a whole odd (or even) number by the value of the parity bit. This could detect a change in a single bit in the byte. At today's high transmission speeds, however, transmission errors normally generate multibit errors rather than single-bit errors. Consequently, parity is useless and is ignored.

Converting Integers into Binary Numbers (1s and 0s)

Some application data consists of **integers**, which are whole numbers (0, 1, 2, 3, ... 345, etc.). The sending application program encodes integers as binary numbers. Figure 2-17 shows how this is done.

Normal arithmetic uses Base 10 representation. A number such as 503 has three decimal positions. Each position has a value that is a power of 10. The position to the farthest right has a value of 10^0 (1). The next has the value 10^1 (10). The third has the value 10^2 (100). Consequently, the number 503 means $5*100 + 0*10 + 3*1$. This comes so naturally that we do not notice we are treating numbers this way.

Computers use binary (Base 2) arithmetic. Figure 2-17 shows that the positions in binary numbers represent 2^0, 2^1, 2^2, 2^3, 2^4, 2^5, and so forth. These positions have the values 1, 2, 4, 8, 16, 32, and so forth. Consequently, 1010 in binary has the value $1*8 + 0*4 + 1*2 + 0*1 = 10$ in decimal. Given this process, you can convert any binary number into its decimal equivalent. In this case, we converted 1010 in binary to 10 in decimal.

Of course, encoding requires conversion in the opposite direction—from decimal to binary. Figure 2-18 shows how to do this conversion. Here, we wish to convert the decimal number 11 into binary.

- The highest value that will go into 11 is 8, which is 1000. This gives a remainder of 3 (11 – 8).
- In the next step, the highest decimal value that will fit into 3 is 2, or 10 in binary. So now we have 1010 (1000 + 10). The remainder is 1 (3 – 2).
- Finally, the largest decimal value that will fit into 1 is 1. This gives us 1011. The remainder is now 0, so we are finished converting the decimal number 11 into binary.

Representing Decimal (Base 10) Numbers

	10^4	10^3	10^2	10^1	10^0
Position Exponent	10^4	10^3	10^2	10^1	10^0
Position Value in decimal	10,000	1,000	100	10	1
Decimal Number			5	0	3
Decimal Representation	$503 = 5*100 + 0*10 + 3*1$				

Representing Binary (Base 2) Numbers

	2^4	2^3	2^2	2^1	2^0
Position Exponent	2^4	2^3	2^2	2^1	2^0
Position Value in decimal	16	8	4	2	1
Binary Number	0	1	0	1	0
Decimal Equivalents	0	8	0	2	0
Decimal Representation	$1010 = 1*8 + 1*2 = 10$				

FIGURE 2-17 Converting Binary Numbers to Decimal

Position / Value / Step					Remainder
Binary Position	4	3	2	1	
Binary Value	8	4	2	1	
Step 0: Decimal number = 11	--	--	--	--	11
Step 1: 8 is the largest digit that will fit into 11	1	0	0	0	11−8 = 3
Step 2: 2 is the largest digit that will fit into 3	1	0	1	0	3−2 = 1
Step 3: 1 is the largest digit that will fit into 1	1	0	1	1	1−1 = 0 (finished)
Final binary number	1	0	1	1	

FIGURE 2-18   Encoding a Decimal Number into Binary

Test Your Understanding

16. Answer the following without a calculator. a) What is an integer? b) Is 4,307 an integer? c) Is 45.7 an integer? d) Convert the binary number 100 to decimal. (Check Figure: 4.) e) Convert the binary number 1111 to decimal. f) Convert the binary number 10110 to decimal. g) Convert the binary number 100100 to decimal. h) Convert the decimal number 8 to binary. (Check Figure: 1000.) i) Convert 6 to binary. j) Convert 15 to binary. k) Convert 67 to binary.

Encoding Alternatives

Some application data can be expressed as alternatives, such as North, South, East, or West. The application layer process will create a field in the application layer message and represent each alternative as a group of bits. For instance, the four cardinal compass points can be represented by a 2-bit field within the application message. North, South, East, and West can be represented as 00, 01, 10, and 11, respectively. (These are the binary numbers for 0, 1, 2, and 3.) There is no order to the alternatives, so any choice can be represented by any pair of bits.

We just saw that having four alternatives requires a 2-bit field. More generally, if a field has b bits, it can represent 2^b alternatives. This gives us the following equation:

Equation 1: $a = 2^b$, where a is the number of alternatives and b is the number of bits

We have just seen that a 2-bit field can represent 2^2 alternatives, or 4. Here, b is 2, so a is 4. What if you need to represent six alternatives? Two bits will not be enough, because 2^2 is only 4 and we need 6. A three-bit field will give us 2^3 alternatives, or 8. This gives us enough alternatives. Two alternatives will go unused.

If a field has N bits, it can represent 2^N alternatives.

Bits in Field	Number of Alternatives That Can Be Encoded	Possible Bit Sequences	Examples
1	$2^1 = 2$	0, 1	Yes or No, Male or Female, etc.
2	$2^2 = 4$	00, 01,10, 11	North, South, East, West; Red, Green, Blue, Black
4	$2^4 = 16$	0000, 0001, 0010, …	Top 10 security threats. Three bits would only give 8 alternatives. (With 4 bits, 6 values go unused)
8	$2^8 = 256$	00000000, 00000001, …	One byte per color gives 256 possible colors levels.
16	$2^{16} = 65,536$	0000000000000000, 0000000000000001, '…	Two bytes per color gives 65,536 color levels.
32	$2^{32} = 4,294,967,296$	000000000000000 0000000000000000, etc.	Number of Internet Protocol Version 4 addresses

If a field has b bits, it can represent $a = 2^b$ alternatives.

FIGURE 2-19 Binary Encoding to Represent a Certain Number of Alternatives

Figure 2-19 illustrates how alternatives encoding is done for fields that have 1, 2, 4, 8, 16, and 32 bits. It shows that with one bit, you can encode yes or no, male or female, or any other dichotomy. Two bits, as we just saw, are good for the four cardinal compass points. With 4 bits, you can have 16 alternatives. You need 4 bits to represent the top 10 security threats, because 3 bits will encode only eight alternatives. Using 4 bits to represent 10 threats will waste six alternatives, but this is necessary. With 8 bits, you can represent 256 alternatives.

The $a = 2^b$ rule is not only used at the application layer. In many layer messages, fields represent alternatives. A one-octet field has 8 bits, so it can represent 2^8 possible alternatives (256).

You should memorize the number of alternatives that can be represented by 4, 8, and 16 bits, because these are common field sizes. Each added bit doubles the number of alternatives, while each bit subtracted cuts the number of alternatives in half. So if 8 bits can represent 256 alternatives, 7 bits can represent 128 alternatives (half as many), while 9 bits can represent 512 alternatives (twice as many). How many alternatives can 6 and 10 bits represent?

Test Your Understanding

17. a) What does the equation $a = 2^b$ mean? b) How many alternatives can you represent with a 4-bit field? (Check Figure: 16.) c) For each bit you add to an alternatives field, how many additional alternatives can you represent? d) How many alternatives can you represent with a 10-bit field? (With 8 bits, you can represent 256 alternatives.) e) If you need to represent 128 alternatives in a field, how many bits long must the field be? (Check Figure: 7.) f) If you need to represent 18 alternatives in a field, how many bits long must the field be? g) Come up with three examples of things that can be encoded with 3 bits.

Encoding Voice

Increasingly, applications involve voice and even video. Figure 2-20 illustrates how voice encoding is done. Video encoding is done similarly. When you speak into a landline or mobile telephone, your voice loudness rises and falls thousands of times per second at different frequencies. This sends pressure waves into your phone's microphone. The microphone converts this into increases and decreases in electricity. The resultant electrical signal rises and falls when your voice loudness rises and falls. To put it another way, the electrical signal is analogous to the voice signal. Therefore, we call this electrical signal an **analog signal**.

The analog signal must be converted into 1s and 0s. This is done by an electrical circuit called a **codec**. Converting outgoing analog signals into digital signals is called *encoding*. Converting incoming digital signals into analog signals to cause the earpiece to vibrate is called *decoding*. Codec is a merciful shortening of these two terms. There are several codec standards. Some specify a higher traffic burden in terms of bits per second; these have higher voice quality. Others are more parsimonious about bandwidth but give lower voice quality.

A codec converts between analog microphone signals and digital transmitted signals.

Test Your Understanding

18. a) Why is the electrical signal generated by a microphone called an analog signal? b) What two things does a codec do? c) Is there a single codec standard?

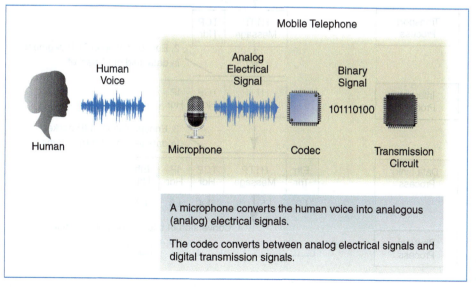

FIGURE 2-20 Encoding Voice

VERTICAL COMMUNICATION ON HOSTS

So far, we have talked about what happens at individual layers. For instance, the transport process on the sending host sends TCP segments or UDP datagrams to the transport process on the receiving host.

Obviously, however, there is no direct connection between the two hosts at the transport layer. Barring software telepathy, all communication must somehow travel through the physical layer.

In Chapter 1, we saw that Layer 3 packets are carried in the data fields of Layer 2 frames in single networks. Networking people say that the packet is encapsulated (placed) in the data field of the frame. In general, **encapsulation** is placing a message in the data field of another message.

Encapsulation is placing a message in the data field of another message.

Figure 2-21 shows that encapsulation actually is a process that occurs repeatedly.

- In the figure, the source host's application layer process sends an HTTP message to the application layer process on the destination host. The source host's application

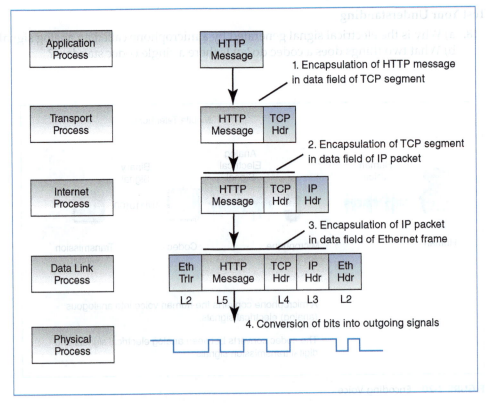

FIGURE 2-21 Layered Communication on the Source Host

process cannot deliver the HTTP message, so it passes the HTTP message down to the transport layer process on the source host.

- The transport layer process encapsulates the HTTP message in the data field of a TCP segment. The transport layer then passes the TCP segment down to the internet layer process.
- The internet layer process encapsulates the TCP segment in the data field of an IP packet. It then passes the packet down to the data link layer.
- The data link layer process encapsulates the IP packet in a data link layer frame. If the single network standard is Ethernet, this is an Ethernet frame. If the single network standard is the Point to Point Protocol (PPP), this is a PPP frame. The data link layer process may also add a trailer.

The whole process is like a set of Russian nesting dolls. So the frame consists of the following:

- The data link layer header
- The IP header
- The TCP header
- The application message segment
- The data link layer trailer (If the single network standard has a trailer in its frame standard).

At the physical layer, something very different occurs. When the physical layer process receives the frame from the data link layer process, it does not do encapsulation. It merely converts the bits of the frame into signals and transmits these signals out on the physical link connecting it to a switch, router, or host.

Test Your Understanding

19. a) What is encapsulation? b) Why is encapsulation necessary for there to be communication between processes operating at the same layer but on different hosts, routers, or switches? c) After the internet layer process in Figure 2-21 receives the TCP segment from the transport layer process, what two things does it do? d) After the data link layer process in Figure 2-21 receives the IP packet from the internet layer process, what two things does it do? e) After the physical layer process receives a frame from the data link layer process, what does the physical layer process do? f) If encapsulation occurs on the source host, what analogous process do you think will occur on the destination host? (The answer is not in the text.)

CONCLUSION

Synopsis

In this chapter, we looked broadly at standards. Most of this book (and the networking profession in general) will focus on standards, which are also called protocols. Standards govern message exchanges. More specifically, they place constraints on message semantics (meaning), message syntax (format), message order, and reliability.

Standards are connection-oriented or connectionless. In connection-oriented protocols, there is a distinct opening before content messages are sent and a distinct closing afterward. There also are sequence numbers, which allow fragmentation and are used in supervisory messages (e.g., acknowledgments) to refer to specific messages. In connectionless protocols, there are no such openings and closings. Connectionless protocols are simpler than connection-oriented protocols, but they lose the advantages of sequence numbers.

In turn, reliable protocols do error correction, while unreliable protocols do not. Although unreliable protocols may do error detection without error correction, this does not make them reliable. In general, standards below the transport layer are unreliable in order to reduce costs. The transport standard usually is reliable; this allows error correction processes on just the two hosts to correct errors at the transport layer and at lower layers, giving the application clean data. Figure 2-22 compares the main protocols we have seen in this chapter in terms of connection orientation and reliability.

To discuss message ordering in more detail, we looked at HTTP and TCP. Message ordering in HTTP is trivial. The browser must initiate the communication by sending an HTTP request message; afterward the webserver program may transmit. TCP, in contrast, has complex message ordering. Correctly received TCP messages (called TCP segments) are acknowledged by the receiver. If the sender does not receive an acknowledgment promptly, it retransmits the unacknowledged segment. This gives reliability.

To discuss message syntax in more detail, we looked briefly at the syntax of Ethernet frames, IP packets, TCP segments, UDP datagrams, and HTTP request and response messages. We saw that they represent syntax in three different ways. We will be looking at the syntax of many messages in this course, so you should be familiar with all methods for representing syntax. In the discussion, we saw that octet is another name for byte. We also saw that application programs on multitasking servers are usually represented by well-known port numbers, while clients use ephemeral port numbers to represent conversations with server programs. A socket consists of an IP address, a colon, and a port number. It represents a particular program (or conversation) on a particular host.

The application layer process must convert text, graphics, video, and other application layer content into bits (1s and 0s). In this chapter, we looked at how application programs encode ASCII text, integers, a number of alternatives, and voice and video streams into strings of bits.

We looked at how layer processes work together on the source host. After each layer creates its message, it immediately passes the message down to the next-lower-layer process. The data link, internet, and transport processes take every message they are given and encapsulate it in a message suitable for that layer.

Layer	Protocol	Connection-Oriented or Connectionless?	Reliable or Unreliable?
5 (Application)	HTTP	Connectionless	Unreliable
4 (Transport)	TCP	Connection-oriented	Reliable
4 (Transport)	UDP	Connectionless	Unreliable
3 (Internet)	IP	Connectionless	Unreliable
2 (Data Link)	Ethernet	Connectionless	Unreliable

FIGURE 2-22 Protocols in This Chapter

END-OF-CHAPTER QUESTIONS

Thought Questions

2-1. How do you think TCP would handle the problem if an acknowledgment were lost, so that the sender retransmitted the unacknowledged TCP segment, therefore causing the receiving transport process to receive the same segment twice?

2-2. a) In Figure 2-14, what will be the value in the destination port number field if a packet arrives for the e-mail application? b) When the HTTP program on a webserver sends an HTTP response message to a client PC, in what field of what message will it place the value 80?

2-3. Do the following without using a calculator or computer, but check your answers with a calculator or computer. a) Convert 110100 to decimal. (Check Figure: 52.) b). Convert 001100 to decimal. c) Convert 7 to binary. (Check Figure: 111.) d) Convert 47 to binary. e) Convert 327 to binary.

2-4. Do the following without using a calculator or computer, but check your answers with a calculator or computer. You need to represent 1,026 different city names. How many bits will this take if you give each city a different binary number? Explain your answer.

Brainteaser Questions

2-5. How can you make a connectionless protocol reliable? (You may not be able to answer this question, but try.)

2-6. Spacecraft exploring the outer planets need reliable data transmission. However, the acknowledgments would take hours to arrive. This makes an ACK-based reliability approach unattractive. Can you think of another way to provide more reliable data transmission to spacecraft without using acknowledgments? (You may not be able to answer this question, but try.)

Perspective Questions

2-7. What was the most surprising thing you learned in this chapter?

2-8. What was the most difficult material for you in this chapter?

Chapter 2a

Hands-On: Wireshark Packet Capture

LEARNING OBJECTIVES

By the end of this chapter, you should be able to:

- Use the Wireshark packet capture program at a novice level.
- Capture packets in real time.
- Analyze the packets at a novice level.

INTRODUCTION

A good way to practice what you have learned in this chapter is to look at individual packets. Packet capture programs record packets going into and out of your computer. If you capture a brief webserver interaction, you can look at header fields, TCP three-step connection starts, and other information. There are several good packet capture programs. We will look at Wireshark, which is simple to use, popular, and free to download. (At least at the time of this writing.)

GETTING WIRESHARK

To get Wireshark, go to wireshark.org. Do *not* go to wireshark.com. Follow the instructions and download the program on your computer.

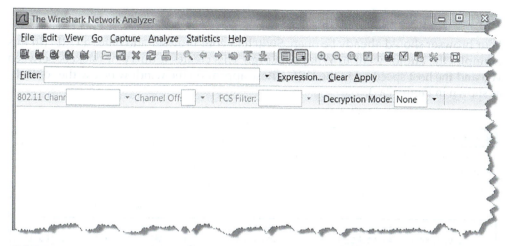

FIGURE 2A-1   Initial Wireshark Screen

USING WIRESHARK

Getting Started

After installation, open the Wireshark program. You will see the opening screen. It will look like the screen in Figure 2a-1. There will be controls at the top with a blank area below them. You will soon fill this area with your packet capture.

Starting a Packet Capture

To start a packet capture, click on the Go menu item. Then, when the Wireshark: Capture Interfaces dialog appears, as Figure 2a-2 illustrates, select a network interface and click on Start.

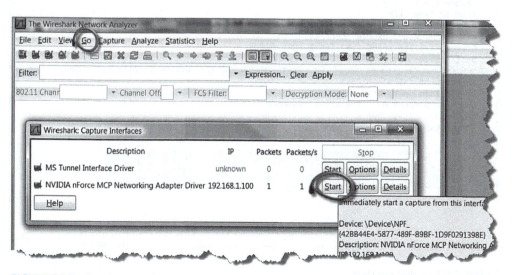

FIGURE 2A-2   Starting a Packet Capture in Wireshark

Getting Data

Your browser should already be open. Switch to your browser and enter a URL. (In this example, the author went to Wikipedia.org.) This creates a flurry of packets between you and the host specified in the URL. These appear on the window below the controls, as shown in Figure 2a-3.

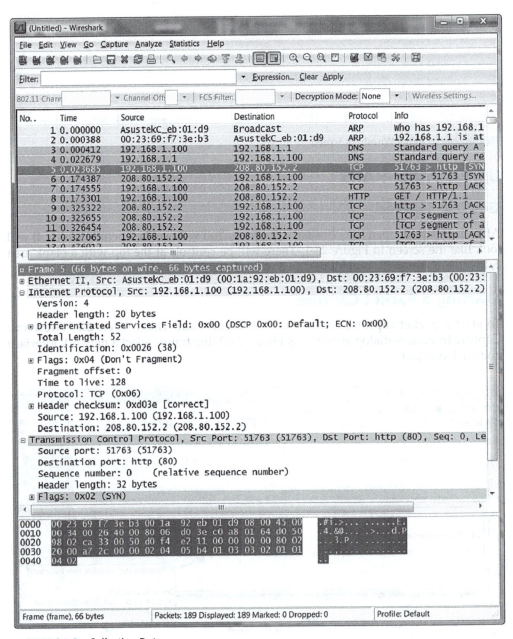

FIGURE 2A-3   Collecting Data

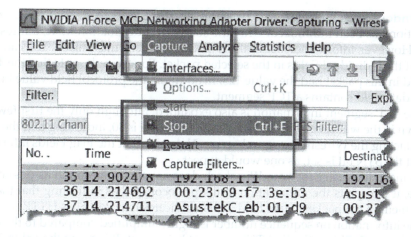

FIGURE 2A-4 Stopping the Data Collection

Stopping Data Collection

To stop the data collection, click on the Capture menu item, as Figure 2a-4 shows. When the dropdown menu appears, select *Stop*. You now have a packet stream to analyze.

Looking at Individual Packets

Now you can begin looking at individual packets. To see how to do this, look again at Figure 2a-3.

Packet Summary Window In the upper window in the display area, you can see the packets one at a time. The capture begins with two ARP packets, which we will discuss when we get to the TCP/IP chapters.

Then comes two DNS packets. In the example, the author typed the host name Wikipedia.org in the URL. The author's computer (192.168.1.100) sent a DNS request message to its DNS server to get the IP address for Wikipedia.org. The DNS sent back the requested IP address.

Now, the author's computer opened a connection to 208.80.152.2, which is Wireshark.org's IP address.[1] It first sent a TCP SYN segment to 208.80.152.2. This is Frame 5. In Figure 2a-3, the frame has been selected.

Information about the contents of this particular frame is shown in a window below the window showing each frame on a single line. First, the window shows information on the Ethernet header and trailer. Next comes information about the IP packet, followed by information about the TCP SYN segment contained in the packet.

---

[1] If you try this, you may get a different IP address. Many firms have multiple physical webservers that they associate with a host name. A DNS response message returns the IP address of one of these physical servers.

Window with Detailed Information on the Selected Packet   The Ethernet information has been minimized. Only the source and destination MAC addresses are shown. However, information about the IP packet has been maximized. You can see the values of the individual fields in the selected packet. For example, note that the Time to Live field in this packet had the value 128. In addition, the protocol field value indicates that the data field contains a TCP segment.

The TCP segment information is also expanded, although only the first few fields are shown in the window. Note that the destination port is 80, indicating that the author was contacting the Wireshark.org webserver. Note also that the Flag Fields information says that the SYN bit is set, as one would expect.

To make life easier for you, Wireshark does as much translation as possible. For example, it interprets the information in the protocol field as indicating that there is a TCP segment in the packet's data field. It also indicates that Port 80 is HTTP.

The information on sequence number is highly simplified compared to the discussion in Chapter 2. This is the first TCP segment being sent. It is given the value 0 rather than its complex real value.

Hex Window   The lowest window shows the contents of the packet in hexadecimal (Base 16) format. Hex is difficult for new analysts to interpret, but it is very compact compared to the information in the middle window. Experienced packet analysts quickly learn the positions of important fields and learn to read the hex symbols for that field.

FIGURE 2A-5   Wireshark Options

Options

Figure 2a-5 shows that Wireshark capture options allow you to control what packets are captured. If you are connected to multiple external servers simultaneously, this can allow you to capture only packets for a particular connection.

Exercises

1. Do the following:
   - Download Wireshark.
   - Start Wireshark.
   - Turn on Wireshark capture.
   - Type a URL in your browser window (not Wikipedia.org).
   - After a few seconds, stop the capture.
   - Answer the following questions:
     1a. What URL did you use? What was the IP address of the webserver?
     1b. Find the frame in which your PC sent the SYN packet. List the source and destination IP address, the source and destination port numbers, and the header checksum.
     1c. Select the SYN/ACK packet. List the source and destination IP address, the source and destination port numbers, and the header checksum.
     1d. Select the packet that acknowledges the SYN/ACK segment. List the source and destination IP address, the source and destination port numbers, and the header checksum.

2. Change the options so that only packets you send are recorded. Do a capture. Click on the window containing Wireshark and hit Alt-Enter. This captures the window to your clipboard. Paste it into your homework.

Chapter 3

Network Security

LEARNING OBJECTIVES

By the end of this chapter, you should be able to:

- Describe the threat environment, including types of attacks and types of attackers.
- Explain in detail the protection of dialogues by cryptography, including symmetric key encryption for confidentiality and electronic signatures.
- Evaluate alternative authentication mechanisms, including passwords, smart cards, biometrics, digital certificate authentication, and two-factor authentication.
- Describe firewall protection, including stateful packet inspection, intrusion prevention systems, and next-generation firewalls.
- Describe the role of antivirus protection.

THE TARGET BREACH

Near the end of the 2013 holiday season, Target announced that thieves had stolen data from 40 million credit cards scanned at Target stores in preceding weeks.[1] The attackers had downloaded malware to nearly all point-of-sale (POS) systems in American Target stores. This malware captured magnetic stripe information and sent it to data thieves.[2] Target did not reveal in its first announcement that thieves were already committing

---

[1] Alastair Jamieson and Erin McClam, "Millions of Target Customers' Credit, Debit card Accounts May Be Hit by Data Breach," NBC News, December 19, 2013. http://www.nbcnews.com/business/consumer/millions-target-customers-credit-debit-card-accounts-may-be-hit-f2D11775203.

[2] Jaikumar Vijayan, "Security Firm IDs Malware Used in Target Attack," Computerworld.com. http://www.computerworld.com/s/article/9245491/Security_firm_IDs_malware_used_in_Target_attack.

fraud with the stolen card data. A month later, Target announced that a separate but related theft had occurred during roughly the same period. Attackers had stolen personal information on roughly 70 million Target customers.[3] Consumers were shocked and worried by these thefts. Many cancelled their charge cards and demanded new cards from their banks. Within weeks, a barrage of lawsuits began. Based on past mega-breaches, such as the TJX breach described in Chapter 7, the final cost to Target will be hundreds of millions of dollars.

The POS Attack

Target released little information about either compromise, but analysts gradually constructed a likely picture of how the attacks had occurred. News reports naturally focused on the POS systems, but the theft involved a complex series of steps inside and outside Target. Figure 3-1 shows the most important of these steps.

The theft did not begin with a direct attack on Target. Rather, it began with an attack on Fazio Mechanical Services, which did work for Target in the Mid-Atlantic region.[4] Fazio had credentials on a vendor server that handled electronic billing and other matters. The attackers probably sent an employee a spear phishing e-mail that tricked the employee into loading malware onto his or her machine. The malware captured the Fazio credentials on the vendor server and sent it back to the attackers. The attackers then used these credentials to get access to the vendor server. From this initial foothold, they were able to move more deeply into the Target network.

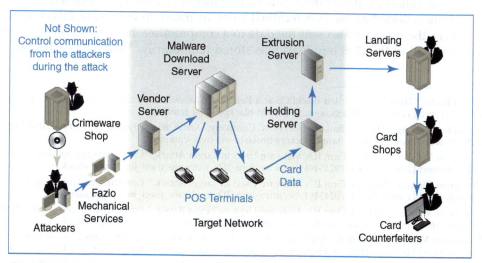

FIGURE 3-1   The Target Breach

---

[3] Target, "Target Provides Update on Data Breach and Financial Performance," January 10, 2014. http://pressroom.target.com/news/target-provides-update-on-data-breach-and-financial-performance.

[4] Fazio Mechanical Services, "Statement on Target Data Breach," date viewed April 26, 2014. http://faziomechanical.com/Target-Breach-Statement.pdf. Brian Krebs, "Target Hackers Broke in Via HVAC Company," KrebsOnSecurity.com, February 5, 2014. http://krebsonsecurity.com/2014/02/target-hackers-broke-in-via-hvac-company.

Now inside the Target network, thieves uploaded point-of-sale (POS) malware, which they had purchased from an online crimeware shop, to a malware download server within Target. There is suspicion that the thieves actually took over Target's internal server that downloaded updates to the point-of-sale systems.[5] In any case, the malware was downloaded to a few POS systems initially and then to nearly all Target point-of-sale systems in the United States.[6]

The malware was a variant of the BlackPOS malware that had been in existence for almost a year.[7] It was readily available at online crimeware shops for a price of about $2,000.[8] The attackers probably modified the software to attack Target's specific POS terminals.[9] They probably also modified it so that existing antivirus programs would not detect it.[10] It is common for hackers to maintain small server farms to test malware against popular antivirus products.

The malware collected magnetic stripe data from every card swiped at the terminal. This occurred before the information was encrypted and sent over the Target network. Most sources called the malware a *RAM scraper*, indicating that it sent everything in the POS terminal's memory to the attackers.[11] Actually, it was more selective, stealing only data on the magnetic stripes of swiped cards.[12] This included the primary account number, the expiration date, the name of the card owner, and optional information. Stolen data did not include the card security code, which is a 3-digit or 4-digit number printed on a credit card. Companies ask you for this number when you cannot present your card physically. For credit cards, there was sufficient information on the magnetic stripe to create counterfeit credit cards. For debit cards, the theft included encrypted PINs, but there is no indication at the time of this writing that these PINs were decoded.[13]

Data collected at the POS terminal went, as usual, to legitimate Target servers. However, the malware also sent the data to a compromised holding server where the data from all of the POS terminals was stored temporarily.[14] For data extrusion, the

---

[5] Brian Krebs, "These Guys Battled BlackPOS at a Retailer," *KrebsonSecurity.com*, February 14, 2014. http://krebsonsecurity.com/2014/02/these-guys-battled-blackpos-at-a-retailer/.

[6] Brian Krebs, "Target Hackers Broke in Via HVAC Company," *KrebsOnSecurity.com*, February 5, 2014. http://krebsonsecurity.com/2014/02/target-hackers-broke-in-via-hvac-company/.

[7] Jaikumar Vijayan, "Security Firm IDs Malware Used in Target Attack," *Computerworld.com*. http://www.computerworld.com/s/article/9245491/Security_firm_IDs_malware_used_in_Target_attack.

[8] Jaikumar Vijayan, "Security Firm IDs Malware Used in Target Attack," *Computerworld.com*. http://www.computerworld.com/s/article/9245491/Security_firm_IDs_malware_used_in_Target_attack.

[9] Jaikumar Vijayan, "Security Firm IDs Malware Used in Target Attack," *Computerworld.com*. http://www.computerworld.com/s/article/9245491/Security_firm_IDs_malware_used_in_Target_attack.

[10] Jaikumar Vijayan, "Security Firm IDs Malware Used in Target Attack," *Computerworld.com*. http://www.computerworld.com/s/article/9245491/Security_firm_IDs_malware_used_in_Target_attack.

[11] Target, "Target Provides Update on Data Breach and Financial Performance," January 10, 2014. http://pressroom.target.com/news/target-provides-update-on-data-breach-and-financial-performance.

[12] Brian Krebs, "These Guys Battled BlackPOS at a Retailer," *KrebsonSecurity.com*, February 14, 2014. http://krebsonsecurity.com/2014/02/these-guys-battled-blackpos-at-a-retailer.

[13] Adam Greenberg, "Hackers Seek to Decrypt PIN Codes Likely Stolen in Target Breach," *SC Magazine*, January 8, 2014. http://www.scmagazine.com/hackers-seek-to-decrypt-pin-codes-likely-stolen-in-target-breach/article/328529/.

[14] Keith Jarvis and Jason Milletary, "Inside a Targeted Point-of-Sale Data Breach," *Dell SecureWorks*, January 24, 2014. http://krebsonsecurity.com/wp-content/uploads/2014/01/Inside-a-Targeted-Point-of-Sale-Data-Breach.pdf.

attackers compromised another server that would deliver the data to the attackers outside the Target network.[15] This extrusion server pulled batches of card data sets from the holding server and transmitted them to landing servers in Russia, Brazil, Miami, and other locations.[16] The thieves could not conceal the IP addresses of the landing servers, so they probably moved the data quickly to other servers.

Now the attackers monetized their stolen data. They wholesaled batches of data to online *card shops* that then sold the data to counterfeiters. Data on individual cards was stored in a searchable database. For example, thieves know that using a credit card in a city that is not the owner's may result in a credit freeze. Consequently, card shops allowed customers to search by zip code. Counterfeiters also refined their purchases in other ways, based on such factors as whether the card had a high debt limit. Based on the characteristics of each card, counterfeiters paid from $20 to more than $100 per card. The first customers received a money-back guarantee that 100% of the card data was useable.[17] Over time, the guaranteed percentage fell, and prices declined.

The counterfeiters used the card data to create fake credit cards that looked legitimate down to the graphics used by individual banks. They then copied data from a single legitimate card onto the magnetic stripe on each counterfeit card. This allowed them to purchase high-end merchandise and then sell the merchandise to traditional fences.

The attacks needed to transmit control messages frequently into the Target network, in order to compromise servers and take actions to direct actions on these servers during the attack. All of these messages had to go through Target's firewalls. Showing this information in Figure 3-1 would create an unintelligible spider web of arrows. However, it was critical for the attackers to maintain a hole in the victim's firewalls during the entire attack process.

Test Your Understanding

1. a) List the steps taken by the attackers. b) How did the attackers gain access to Target's network? c) List the internal Target servers the attackers compromised. d) How did the attackers exfiltrate the card data? e) List the criminal groups, besides the main attackers, who were involved in the overall process. f) What benefit did the attackers seek to obtain from their actions? g) Comment on the fact that Target knew that fraud was already occurring with the stolen card data but did not reveal this when it announced the breach.

Damages

It will take months and perhaps years before we will understand the damage from the Target breach fully. However, it is easy to identify victims in the case. One was Target itself. In the period from the breach revelation to February 2014, Target sales

---

[15] Keith Jarvis and Jason Milletary, "Inside a Targeted Point-of-Sale Data Breach," Dell SecureWorks, January 24, 2014. http://krebsonsecurity.com/wp-content/uploads/2014/01/Inside-a-Targeted-Point-of-Sale-Data-Breach.pdf.

[16] Brian Krebs, "Non-US Cards Used at Target Fetch Premium," *KrebsonSecurity.com*, December 13, 2014, http://krebsonsecurity.com/2013/12/non-us-cards-used-at-target-fetch-premium/.

[17] Brian Krebs, "Cards Stolen in Target Breach Flood Underground Markets," *KrebsonSecurity.com*, December 20, 2014. http://krebsonsecurity.com/2013/12/cards-stolen-in-target-breach-flood-underground-markets/.

fell 5.3% from the previous year, and profits fell 46%.[18] This profit decline was roughly $500 million. In addition, Target will probably pay out several hundred million dollars due to lawsuits brought by commercial and governmental organizations. The company's Chief Technical Officer resigned fairly soon after the breach.[19] The company's CEO resigned in May 2014.[20]

Consumers are protected against fraudulent credit card purchases—but only if they notify their credit card company quickly of fraudulent charges on their bills. Credit card companies will drop these transactions from bills. However, this process entails time loss and frustration. It sometimes even involves disagreements about whether charges are truly fraudulent. There is even more time lost if the consumer cancels the credit card and gets a new card to get better peace of mind. Finally, the prospects of credit card fraud and identity fraud created psychological costs for many cardholders.

Banks and credit card processors will not lose money in the case of reported fraudulent purchases. Just as the customer does not pay them, banks and credit card processors do not pay the retail stores in which the fraudulent purchases were made. These financial services companies will face substantial costs in the replacement of compromised cards. However, they are likely to recover these costs successfully in lawsuits against Target based on precedents set in the TJX breach discussed in Chapter 7.

Fraud will hit retailers the hardest. They rarely recover merchandise purchased fraudulently. However, there is one thing that physical retailers can do. Counterfeiters normally only create a single card master from which all counterfeit cards in a batch are made. All counterfeit cards in the batch have the same printed name, credit card number, expiration date, and other information. The magnetic stripe data, however, will be specific to a single compromised credit card. This is why store clerks look at the last four digits on the card number on the physical credit card. If this is different from information on the magnetic stripe, the card is fraudulent.

Test Your Understanding

2. a) How was Target damaged by the breach? b) Were banks and credit card bureaus damaged by the breach? c) How were consumers damaged by the breach? d) How were retailers damaged by the breach? e) What can retailers do to defend themselves against counterfeit credit cards? f) How can criminals get around this precaution? (The answer is not in the text.)

Perspective

The Target breach was not an isolated incident. Surveys have found that most firms suffer at least one compromise each year. Successful attacks are becoming ever more frequent, sophisticated, and damaging. In 2012, the director of the Federal Bureau of

---

[18] "Target Profits Plunge 46% after Holiday Security Breach," *BBC.com*, February 26, 2014. http://www.bbc.com/news/business-26358556.

[19] Anne D'Innocenzio, "Target's Chief Information Officer Resigns," *The Associated Press*, March 5, 2014. http://www.nytimes.com/2014/03/06/business/targets-chief-information-officer-resigns.html?_r=0.

[20] Clare O'Connor, "Target CEO Gregg Steinhafel Resigns in Data Breach Fallout," *Forbes*, May 5, 2014. http://www.forbes.com/sites/clareoconnor/2014/05/05/target-ceo-gregg-steinhafel-resigns-in-wake-of-data-breach-fallout/.

Investigation Robert Mueller made the following statement: "Terrorism remains the FBI's top priority. But in the not too distant future, we anticipate that the cyber threat will pose the number one threat to our country."[21] In 2014, the Center for Strategic and International Studies, estimated global damage from cybercrime.[22] It concluded that cybercrime reduced the entire world's gross domestic product by almost 1%. Cybercrime is not a distant threat.

INTRODUCTION

Networks give us access to almost anything, anytime, anywhere. Unfortunately, they give the same access to criminals, national governments, terrorists, and just plain jerks. Wherever there has been opportunity, there has been crime and vandalism. Networks are no exception. Security is the snake in the network garden.

Network thinking focuses on adequate planning, software bugs, and mechanical breakdowns. In contrast, security thinking must anticipate the actions of intelligent adversaries who will try many things to succeed and adapt to the defenses you put in place.

Giving you even a broad view of security is too much for one chapter. The next chapter looks at how to manage security as part of overall network management. As security expert Bruce Schneier has said in many of his writings, "Security is a process, not a product."

Test Your Understanding

3. How does security thinking differ from network thinking?

TYPES OF ATTACKS

We will begin by looking at the threat environment that corporations face. The **threat environment** consists of the types of attacks that companies face and the types of attackers who engage in these attacks. We will begin by looking at *types of attacks*.

Malware Attacks

Malware is a generic name for evil software. It includes viruses, worms, Trojan horses, and other dangerous attack software. Malware attacks are the most frequent attacks that companies face. Nearly every firm has one or more significant malware compromises each year.

Malware is any evil software.

---

[21] Federal Bureau of Investigation Press release. Speech by Robert S. Mueller III, Director, Federal Bureau of Investigation, RSA Cyber Security Conference, San Francisco, California, March 1, 2012.

[22] Center for Strategic and International Studies, "Net Losses: Estimating the Global Cost of Crime," June 2014. http://www.mcafee.com/us/resources/reports/rp-economic-impact-cybercrime2-summary.pdf.

> **Malware**
>
> A general name for evil software
>
> **Vulnerabilities**
>
> Vulnerabilities are security flaws in specific programs
>
> Vulnerabilities enable specific attacks against these programs
>
> Vendors release patches to close vulnerabilities
>
> However, users do not always install patches promptly or at all, so continue to be vulnerable
>
> Also, zero-day attacks occur before the patch is released for the vulnerability

FIGURE 3-2 Malware and Vulnerabilities (Study Figure)

Test Your Understanding

4. a) What is malware? b) What are the most frequent attacks on companies?

Vulnerabilities and Patches

Most types of malware can only succeed if a program under attack has a security vulnerability. A **vulnerability** is a flaw in a program that permits a specific attack or set of attacks to succeed against the program. Vulnerabilities are found in popular application programs frequently.[23]

A vulnerability is a flaw in a program that permits a specific attack or set of attacks against this program to succeed.

When a software vendor discovers a vulnerability, the company issues a **patch**, which is a small program designed to fix the security vulnerability. After patch installation, the program is safe from attacks based on that particular vulnerability. Too often, however, users fail to install patches, and their programs continue to be vulnerable. Even if they do install patches, furthermore, they may delay, giving the attacker a long window of opportunity.

Of course, if attacks begin before the program vendor creates a patch (or even learns about the attack), then all attacks against vulnerable computers will succeed. A vulnerability-specific attack that occurs before a patch is available is called a **zero-day attack**. In such cases, there would be no signature yet to check for. On the security black market, well-funded adversaries can often purchase information that allows them to create zero-day attacks.

---

[23] A 2014 study by Cenzic found that 96% of all applications it tested had at least one vulnerability. The median number of flaws per application was 14. Andy Patrizio, "Nearly All Apps Are Vulnerable in Some Way," *NetworkWorld*, March 3, 2014. http://www.networkworld.com/article/2226448/microsoft-subnet/nearly-all-apps-are-vulnerable-in-some-way--report-says.html.

A vulnerability-specific attack that occurs before a patch is available is called a zero-day attack.

Test Your Understanding

5. a) What is a vulnerability? b) How can users eliminate vulnerabilities in their programs? c) What name do we give to attacks that occur before a patch is available?

Viruses and Worms

The earliest pieces of malware were viruses and worms. A **virus** attaches itself to another program, much as a human virus attaches itself to your cells. **Worms**, in turn, are stand-alone programs.

Typical **propagation vectors** (computer-to-computer transmission methods) include e-mail attachments, peer-to-peer file transfer networks, social networks, and websites that ask the visitor to download a special program to experience their contents. They propagate through USB RAM sticks. In Afghanistan, the Taliban left infected USB RAM sticks in public places. When U.S. forces found these drives and inserted them into their USB ports, they spread the infection throughout their networks.

Some worms also have another trick up their sleeves. Most ways in which viruses and worms spread involve human gullibility at least to some extent. Human gullibility is widespread, but it is slow. **Directly propagating** worms are able to jump by themselves from an infected computer to another target computer that has a particular vulnerability. Directly propagating worms can spread with amazing speed. In 2003, the

---

Viruses

> Pieces of code that attach themselves to other programs

Worms

> Stand-alone programs that do not need to attach to other programs

Typical Propagation Vectors

> E-mail attachments
>
> Visits to websites (even legitimate ones)
>
> Social networking sites
>
> Many others (USB RAM sticks, peer-to-peer file sharing, etc.)
>
> These require human gullibility, which is slow

Directly propagating worms

> Jump to victim hosts directly
>
> No action is necessary on the part of the victim
>
> Target hosts must have a specific vulnerability for this to succeed
>
> Directly propagating worms can spread with amazing speed

FIGURE 3-3 Viruses and Worms (Study Figure)

Slammer worm infected 90% of all vulnerable computers attached to the Internet within 10 minutes. Fortunately, only a small fraction of all Internet hosts had the vulnerability that Slammer used. Also, fortunately, most worms are not directly propagating.

Test Your Understanding

6. a) How do viruses and worms differ? b) What is a propagation vector? c) What are common propagation vectors for viruses and worms? d) What other propagation do some worms use? e) Why is it especially dangerous?

Other Types of Malware

Viruses and worms are arguably the most common types of malware, but they are certainly not the only types of evil software.

Mobile Code on Webpages   An HTML webpage can contain a **script**, which is a group of commands written in a simplified programming language, usually JavaScript. Scripts execute when the webpage loads or when the user takes a particular action. Scripts can enhance the user's experience, and many webpages will not work unless script execution is enabled, which is usually done by default. Furthermore, nearly all are safe. A few, however, can cause problems. Scripts are called **mobile code** because they travel with the downloaded webpage from the webserver to the browser.

Trojan Horses   In *The Iliad*, the Trojan horse was supposed to be a gift offering. It was really a trap. In malware, a Trojan horse has two characteristics.

- First, it disguises itself as a legitimate system file. This makes it difficult to detect.
- Second, in contrast to viruses, worms, and mobile code, a Trojan horse cannot propagate to another computer on its own initiative. It must be placed there by another piece of malware, by a human hacker, or by a user downloading the program voluntarily.

Mobile Code on Webpages
    HTML webpages can contain scripts
    Scripts are called mobile code because they are downloaded with the webpage
    Scripts are normally benign but may be damaging if the browser has a vulnerability
    The script may do damage or download a program to do damage

Trojan Horses
    Trojan horses are programs that disguise themselves as system files
    Spyware Trojans collect sensitive data and send the data it to an attacker

Downloaders
    Malware that downloads a larger malware program onto the infected computer

Spam
    Unsolicited commercial e-mail

FIGURE 3-4 Other Types of Malware (Study Figure)

A Trojan horse cannot spread from one computer to another by itself.

An especially problematic category of Trojan horses is **spyware**—a name given to Trojan horses that **surreptitiously** (without your knowledge) collect information about you and send this information to the attacker. Spyware programs can monitor your keystrokes looking for passwords and other sensitive information. They can also search through your data files looking for Social Security Numbers, bank account numbers, and other information. In either case, they send the results to the attacker.

Downloaders   Some malware exists to download other malware onto the victim's computer. These **downloaders** can be small, making insertion relatively simple and difficult to detect. When the downloader gains a foothold, however, it can download a very large program.

Spam   Perhaps the most annoying type of malware on a day-in, day-out basis is **spam**,[24] which is unsolicited commercial e-mail. Spammers send the same solicitation e-mail message to millions of e-mail addresses in the hope that a small percentage of all recipients will respond. The danger of spam is that the receiver will unwittingly fall for a fraud.

Spam is unsolicited commercial e-mail.

Test Your Understanding

7. a) Are scripts normally bad? b) Under what circumstances are scripts likely to be dangerous? c) Why are scripts on webpages called mobile code? d) What are Trojan horses? e) How do Trojan horses propagate to computers? f) What is spyware? g) What do downloaders do? h) Why are they used? i) What is the definition of spam?

Payloads

In war, when a bomber aircraft reaches its target, it releases its payload of bombs. Similarly, after they spread, viruses, worms, and other types of malware may execute pieces of code called **payloads**. Malicious payloads can completely erase hard disks and do other significant damage. In some cases, they can take the victim to a pornography site whenever the victim mistypes a URL. In other cases, they can turn the user's computer into a spam generator or a pornography download site. Not all malware has malicious payloads or payloads at all, but even malware without a payload can cause the victim's computer to crash or run slowly.

---

[24] Except at the beginnings of sentences, e-mail spam is spelled in lowercase. This distinguishes unsolicited commercial e-mail from the Hormel Corporation's meat product, Spam, which should always be capitalized. In addition, Spam is not an acronym for "spongy pink animal matter."

After propagation, viruses and worms execute their payloads

    Malicious payloads do damage

    Payloads can erase hard disks

    Payloads can send users to pornography sites if they mistype URLs

Even malware without payloads can do damage

    Not all malware has payloads—malicious or otherwise

    Can still cause computer to run slowly or crash

FIGURE 3-5 Payloads (Study Figure)

Test Your Understanding

    8. What are payloads?

Attacks on Human Judgment

In many cases, malware will only succeed if the victim uses poor judgment, say by allowing a program to install itself on the user's PC or smartphone. In some cases, the victim knows that he or she is taking a risk, say by visiting an unsavory website. However, in many cases, the adversary must make it seem like taking the wrong action is the correct thing to do.

Social Engineering Attacks   As technical defenses have improved, malware writers have focused more heavily on **social engineering**, which is a euphemism for tricking the victim into doing something against personal or organizational security

Social Engineering

    Tricking the victim into doing something against personal or organizational security interests

    Open e-mail attachments, visit websites, etc.

Phishing Attacks

    A sophisticated social engineering attack in which an authentic-looking e-mail or website entices the user to enter his or her username, password, or other sensitive information

    Spear phishing attacks have messages customized for a particular target individual

Credit Card Number Theft

    Uses stolen credit card numbers to make unauthorized transactions

Identity Theft

    Involves collecting enough data to impersonate the victim in large financial transactions

    Can result in much greater financial harm to the victim than credit card theft

    May take a long time to restore the victim's credit rating

FIGURE 3-6 Attacks on Human Judgment (Study Figure)

interests. Viruses and worms have long tried to do this with e-mail attachments—for example, by telling the user that he or she has won a lottery and needs to open the attachment for the details. Social engineering attacks include e-mail messages with enticing subject fields, links to attractive websites, and many other ruses. The range of social engineering attacks has expanded greatly in the last few years.

Social engineering is tricking the victim into doing something against personal or organizational security interests.

Phishing Attacks   Most social engineering attacks try to entice all *recipients* to fall for the ruse. However, a growing number of social engineering attacks involve **phishing**,[25] which is the use of authentic-looking e-mail or websites to entice the user to send his or her username, password, or other sensitive information to the attacker. One typical example of phishing is an e-mail message that appears to be from the person's bank. The message asks the person to "confirm" his or her username and password in a return message. Another typical example is an e-mail message with a link to what appears to be the victim's bank website but that is, in fact, an authentic-looking fake website. The critical thing in phishing is to make the user believe in the authenticity of the trick because it is visually plausible. Phishing success rates can be high.

Phishing is the use of authentic-looking e-mail or websites to entice the user to send his or her username, password, or other sensitive information to the attacker.

Spear Phishing Attacks   Phishing attacks are designed to be attractive to certain groups of victims. **Spear phishing attacks**, in turn, are directed at a *particular individual*, such as a company's purchasing manager. The attacker learns a great deal about the person and crafts a message with specific details that will cause the victim to believe that this *must* be a legitimate message. For example, if the person's boss is traveling, the message may purport to come from the boss and contain details about the boss's trip and recent events in the department. The Target compromise probably began with a spear phishing attack against Fazio Mechanical Services.

In spear phishing, attacks are directed at a particular individual, such as a company's purchasing manager.

---

[25] IT attackers often replace f with ph. For example, phone freaking (dialing long-distance numbers illegally) became phone phreaking and later just phreaking.

Credit Card Number Theft   A common goal of attacks on human judgment is to steal credit card numbers. A message may convince the user to type a credit card number to purchase goods. Ideally, the thief will also obtain the three-digit security code on the back of the card, the person's full name, and their mailing address for billing. The thief can use this information to make unauthorized purchases.[26]

Identity Theft   In some cases, thieves collect enough data about a victim (name, address, Social Security Number, driver's license number, date of birth, etc.) to impersonate the victim in complex crimes. This impersonation is called **identity theft**. Thieves commit identity theft in order to purchase expensive goods, take out major loans using the victim's assets as collateral, obtain prescription drugs, get a job, enter the country illegally, and do many other things. Identity theft is more damaging than credit card theft because it can involve large monetary losses that are not reimbursed by anyone. In addition, correcting the victim's credit rating can take months. Some victims have even been arrested for crimes committed by the identity thief.

In identity theft, thieves collect enough data about a victim to impersonate the victim during complex crimes.

Test Your Understanding

9. a) What is social engineering? b) Distinguish between social engineering in general and phishing in particular. c) Distinguish between phishing and spear phishing. d) Distinguish between credit card number theft and identity theft. e) Which tends to produce more damage? Explain.

Human Break-Ins (Hacking)

A virus or worm typically has a single attack method. If that method fails, the attack fails. However, human adversaries can attack a company with a variety of different approaches until one succeeds. This flexibility makes human break-ins much more likely to succeed than malware break-ins.

What is Hacking?   **Hacking** is defined as *intentionally* using a computer resource *without authorization* or *in excess of authorization*. The key issue is authorization.[27] If you see a password written on a note attached to a computer screen, this does not mean that you have authorization to use it. Also, note that it is hacking even if a person has legitimate access to an account but uses the account for unauthorized purposes.

---

[26] Credit card firms will refund money spent by the carder, but this can be a painful process, and the victim must notify the credit card firm promptly to be eligible for a refund. Debit cards often have no such protection.

[27] Note also that the unauthorized access must be intentional. Proving intentionality is almost always necessary in criminal prosecution, and hacking is no exception.

Humans Can Use Many Attack Methods

> This makes them more dangerous than malware, which usually has only one or two attack methods

Hacking

> *Intentionally* using a computer resource without authorization or in excess of authorization.

If use fits the definition, it is hacking

> For example, if you find a username and password on a piece of paper negligently left around, you are still not authorized to use the account, so it is hacking if you do use it

Irrelevant Considerations

> Not properly protected: does not excuse hacking

> Just testing the resource's security does not excuse hacking

Penalties Depend on the Amount of Damage Done

> Easy to do damage accidentally

FIGURE 3-7   Human Break-Ins (Hacking) (Study Figure)

Hacking is intentionally using a computer resource without authorization or in excess of authorization.

All hacking is illegal. Penalties differ by the type of asset that is hacked and by the amount of damage done, but it is very easy to do enough harm accidentally to merit a jail term, and "intentionally" only applies to intending to use the asset, not intending to damage.

Test Your Understanding

10. a) What is the definition of hacking? b) If you see a username and password on a Post-It note on a monitor, is it hacking if you use this information to log in? Explain in terms of the definition. c) You discover that you can get into other e-mail accounts after you have logged in under your account. You spend just a few minutes looking at another user's mail. Is that hacking? Explain in terms of the definition. d) If you click on a link expecting to go to a legitimate website but are directed to a website containing information you are not authorized to see. Is that hacking? Explain in terms of the definition.

Stages in the Attack

Attacks typically take place in two stages.

The Break-In   To hack a computer, the attacker must have an **exploit** for the server being attacked. This may be a piece of software. It may also be a procedure or a combination of the two. He or she uses this exploit to take over the host by sending exploit packets. Confusingly, the act of breaking into a computer is also called an **exploit**, as is the program the attacker uses during the break-in.

> **Exploit**
>
> The actual break-in
>
> The tool used is also called an exploit
>
> **After the Break-In**
>
> Manually exploits the resource
>
> Leaves a Trojan horse behind for continuous automated exploitation

FIGURE 3-8 Stages in an Attack (Study Figure)

After the Break-In   After the break-in, the damage begins. The attacker can then exploit the victim manually, looking through files, deleting them, and transferring them outside the network. The attack can also add continuing exploitation software, such as a Trojan horse that turns the victim computer into a porno site.

Test Your Understanding

11. a) What is an exploit? b) What may the attacker do after compromising a system?

Denial-of-Service (DoS) Attacks Using Bots

The goal of **denial-of-service (DoS) attacks** is to make a computer or entire network unavailable to its legitimate users.

> *The goal of denial-of-service (DoS) attacks is to make a computer or entire network unavailable to its legitimate users.*

Distributed Denial-of-Service (DDoS) Attack   As Figure 3-9 shows, most DoS attacks involve flooding the victim computer with attack packets. The victim computer becomes so busy processing this flood of attack packets that it cannot process legitimate packets. The overloaded host may even fail.

More specifically, the attack shown in the figure is a **distributed DoS (DDoS) attack**. In this type of DoS attack, the attacker first installs programs called *bots* on hundreds or thousands of PCs or servers. This collection of compromised computers is called a **botnet**. When the user sends these bots an attack command, they all begin to flood the victim with packets.

Typically, the adversary does not communicate with bots directly. Rather, he or she sends orders to a **command and control server**, which then sends attack commands to the bots. In effect, the attacker is two levels removed from the attack, making the botmaster difficult to identify.

Bot Versatility   Bots are not limited to DDoS attacks. **Bots** are general-purpose exploitation programs that the botmaster can remotely update after installation. As Figure 3-9 shows, the adversary can have the command and control computer push

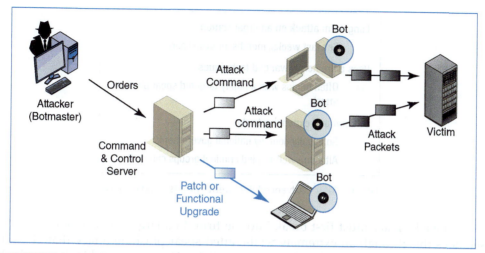

FIGURE 3-9 Distributed Denial-of-Service (DDoS) Attack Using Bots

updates out to all of the bots. Some upgrades are bug fixes. Others change the bots' core functionality. For example, the bots may be programmed to send out spam initially. As spam blockers succeed in shunting aside traffic for these bots, the bots can be reprogrammed as DDoS attack machines or for other attack purposes.

> *Bots are general-purpose exploitation programs that the botmaster can remotely control after installation and that can even be upgraded remotely with new capabilities.*

Bot masters may sell their botnets to other attackers. They may also rent a subset of their bots to a specific attacker for a specific purpose. In either case, botmasters give the buyer or renter access to the command and control server. (Given the importance of command and control servers, most botnets have several in case one is disabled.)

Test Your Understanding

12. a) What is the purpose of a denial-of-service attack? b) Which programs directly attack the victim in a distributed denial-of-service attack? c) What is a collection of compromised computers called? d) What is the person who controls them called? e) To what computer does the attacker send messages? f) What gives bots flexibility? g) Explain the steps of a distributed DoS attack.

Advanced Persistent Threats

In the past, criminal attacks were brief and limited—the electronic equivalent of smash-and-grab thefts in jewelry stores. Increasingly, however, we are experiencing **advanced persistent threats (APTs)** in which the adversary has multiple objectives that he or she continues to pursue for a period of months or even years. These are true nightmares for corporations.

Long-term attack on an organization
Can last weeks, months, or even years
Uses extremely advanced techniques
Often begins with a highly targeted spear phishing attack
Difficult and expensive to do
So usually done by national governments
Although well-funded criminal groups can do it

FIGURE 3-10 Advanced Persistent Threats (Study Figure)

The adversary must first break into the firm. In a large majority of cases, he or she does this through an extremely well-crafted spear phishing attack that gives the attacker access to critical authentication credentials. (This was probably the case in the Target breach case at the beginning of this chapter.) "Advanced" refers to the degree of skill exhibited by APT adversaries in everything they do.

The adversary uses the initial foothold to explore and break into other parts of the firm's IT infrastructure. The attacker may also install Trojan horses and other exploitation programs.

Persistent means that the adversary continues to conduct surveillance on the network, learning more about its operations and finding additional weaknesses. Gradually, over a period of months or even years, the adversary can exploit much of the network. Persistent presence without detection requires great skill. It also requires ample resources over a long period. Not surprisingly, most APTs are undertaken by government agencies, although well-funded criminal groups have done them.

Test Your Understanding

13. a) Explain "advanced" in the term *advanced persistent threat*. b) Explain "persistence" in the context of APTs. c) Why are APTs expensive to carry out? d) Why are they particularly dangerous?

TYPES OF ATTACKERS

The threat environment consists of types of attacks and types of attackers. As Figure 3-11 shows, there are many different types of attackers facing organizations today.

Hackers

When most people think of attackers, they normally have two pictures in their minds. The first is the "old-school hacker" driven by curiosity, the thrill of the break-in, and the desire to increase one's reputation among other old-school hackers. They were seen as annoying but not too damaging.

Today, the situation is very different. Hackers today are overwhelmingly **career criminal hackers**. This has been true since the beginning of this century. Criminal hackers attack to make money. They steal credit cards to engage in illicit credit card purchases, they steal trade secrets to sell them to competitors (or to blackmail firms,

---

Hackers

> Old-school hackers driven by curiosity, a desire for power, and peer reputation
>
> Today, most hackers are career criminals who hack for money
>
> Criminal attackers are well-funded and have an online criminal infrastructure

Malware Attackers

Employees, Ex-Employees, and Other Insiders

> Current employees: revenge or theft
>
> IT and security employees are the most dangerous
>
>> Already have access
>>
>> Know the systems
>>
>> Know how to avoid detection
>>
>> Are trusted by the organization
>
> Ex-employees are dangerous, so all access must be terminated before leaving
>
> Contractors with access permissions are also "insiders"

Cyberwar and Cyberterror

> Cyberterror attacks by terrorists
>
> Cyberwar by nations
>
> Dangerous because tend to be sophisticated
>
> Dangerous because focus on doing widespread damage instead of committing isolated crimes

---

FIGURE 3-11 Types of Attackers

warning that they will release the trade secrets if they are not paid), they encrypt hard drives then demand payment for a key to decrypt them again, they turn corporate servers into pornography websites, and do anything else they can to make money at the expense of their victims. Many old-school hackers have become career criminals or hire out their services to criminal hackers.

Today, most hackers are career criminals.

Career criminal attackers often work in loosely structured gangs. Funded by their crimes, many criminals can afford to hire the best hackers and to enhance their own security-breaking skills. Consequently, criminal attacks are not just growing in numbers; they also are growing very rapidly in technical sophistication.

Criminal attackers have access to a vast online community that gives them access to exploit programs with slick user interfaces and prepaid annual updates. There are markets for them to buy and sell credit card numbers and identity information. Many elements of this black market are in countries where regulation is minimal at best.

Test Your Understanding

14. a) What type of adversary are most hackers today? b) Why is this type of attacker extremely dangerous? c) What resources can they purchase and sell over the Internet?

Malware Attackers

In the United States and most other countries, it is not illegal to write malware. It is, however, illegal to release malware to do damage or to sell malware that will be used that way. In practice, finding malware releasers after an attack is extremely difficult.

Test Your Understanding

15. a) Is it generally illegal to write malware in the United States? b) What actions regarding malware *are* illegal?

Employees, Ex-Employees, and Other Insiders

A large number of attacks are undertaken not by outsiders but by employees. Often, they are disgruntled employees who attack for revenge. However, they can also be employees who simply want to steal.

The most dangerous employees are IT staff members and especially IT security staff members. They typically have far more access than other employees, have much better knowledge of corporate systems, have extensive knowledge of how to avoid detection, and are trusted to be defenders. An ancient Roman question, "Quis custodiet ipsos custodes?" means "Who guards the guardians?" It is a serious question in security.

Ex-employees also attack firms. Again, revenge is a common motive. Another is stealing trade secrets that the employee worked on and believes are "his" or "hers." It is important to terminate all ex-employee access to internal resources after they leave. In fact, before an employee leaves, it is important to monitor them for signs that they are infiltrating company intellectual property.

Often, contractors and service providers are given access credentials. This makes them "insiders." When Edward Snowden stole files from the National Security Agency in early 2013, he was an employee of contractor Booz Allen Hamilton in Hawaii. In the Target breach, the account that thieves used to break into Target's computers was that of an air conditioning service company performing services for Target.

Test Your Understanding

16. a) Why may employees attack? b) Who are the most dangerous employees? c) For what four reasons are these employees especially dangerous? d) Why may ex-employees attack? e) What should be done when an employee leaves the firm? f) Why are contractor firms more dangerous than other outside firms?

Cyberterrorists and National Governments

On the horizon is the danger of far more massive **cyberterror** attacks by terrorists and even worse **cyberwar** attacks by national governments. These could produce unprecedented damages in the hundreds of billions of dollars.

The United States has acknowledged that it has long had cyberwar capabilities, and it established a consolidated Cyberwar Command in 2009. It is clear that several other countries have these capabilities as well (especially China). Countries could use IT to do espionage to gather intelligence, conduct attacks on opponents' financial and power infrastructures, or destroy enemy command and control facilities during physical attacks.[28]

Cyberterror attacks by terrorists are also likely. During physical attacks, terrorists might disable communication systems to thwart first responders and to spread confusion and terror among the population. Cyberterrorists could also conduct purely IT-based attacks. While the United States was afraid of side effects from cyberwar attacks on Iraq, terrorists would have no such qualms.

Cyberwar and cyberterror are particularly dangerous for three reasons. First, funding allows them to be extremely sophisticated. Second, they focus on doing damage instead of committing thefts. Third, they are dangerous because they are likely to be directed against many targets simultaneously for massive damage.

Espionage has more limited objectives than destructive attacks. In spying, the goal is to learn an enemy's secrets. Several countries are doing this on a massive scale. In many cases, they are also targeting commercial enterprises to steal trade secrets useable to firms in their countries. The Chinese have been very effective in penetrating classified U.S. defense resources in recent years.

Test Your Understanding

17. a) What are cyberterror and cyberwar attacks? b) Why are cyberwar and cyberterror attacks especially dangerous?

PROTECTING DIALOGUES CRYPTOGRAPHY

Having looked at the threat environment, we will now begin to look at the tools that companies use to attempt to thwart attackers. One of these is cryptography. Formally, **cryptography** is the use of mathematics to protect information.

Cryptography is the use of mathematics to protect information.

Cryptography is important in and of itself. We begin with "crypto," however, because it is part of many other protections that companies use to thwart attackers. A knowledge of cryptography is necessary to understand how they work.

---

[28] A 2009 article in the *New York Times* reported that before the 2003 invasion of Iraq, the United States considered an attack that would shut down Iraq's entire financial infrastructure (John Markoff and Thom Shanker, " '03 Plan Displays Cyberwar Risk," *New York Times*, August 1, 2009. www.msnbc.msn.com/id/3032619/%2328368424). This attack was not approved, but not because it was infeasible. It was held back because its impact might have spread beyond Iraq and might even have damaged the U.S. financial system. More recently, attacks by the United States and Israel used the Stuxnet worm to damage a specific group of nuclear centrifuges in a specific factory in Iran. The researchers who discovered Stuxnet were amazed by its complexity and by the scope of the operation that produced and tested it. It even involved forged digital certificates for important firms.

Symmetric Key Encryption for Confidentiality

Encryption for Confidentiality When most people think of cryptography, they think of **encryption for confidentiality**, which Figure 3-12 illustrates. **Confidentiality** means that even if an eavesdropper intercepts a message, he or she will not be able to read it. The sender uses an encryption method, called a **cipher**, to create a message that an eavesdropper cannot read. However, the receiver can **decrypt** the message in order to read it.

Symmetric Key Encryption Most encryption for confidentiality uses **symmetric key encryption** ciphers, in which the two sides share a single key to encrypt messages to each other and to decrypt incoming messages. Figure 3-12 shows how symmetric key encryption works.

- When Party A sends to Party B, Party A encrypts with the single key, Party B decrypts with the key.
- When Party B sends to Party A, in turn, Party B uses the single key to encrypt, while Party A uses the single key to decrypt.

The process is symmetric because the same key is used in both directions. The dominant symmetric key encryption cipher today is the **Advanced Encryption Standard (AES)**.

Key Length Earlier, we looked at brute force password guessing. Symmetric keys also can be guessed by the attacker's trying all possible keys. In cryptanalysis (the cracking of cyphers and keys), it is called **exhaustive search**. The way to defeat exhaustive

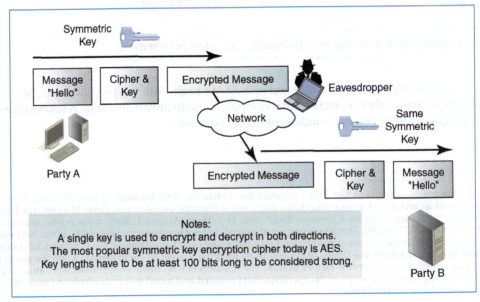

Notes:
A single key is used to encrypt and decrypt in both directions.
The most popular symmetric key encryption cipher today is AES.
Key lengths have to be at least 100 bits long to be considered strong.

FIGURE 3-12 Symmetric Key Encryption for Confidentiality

key searches is to use long keys, which are merely binary strings. For symmetric key ciphers, symmetric key lengths of 100 bits or greater are considered to be strong. AES supports multiple strong key lengths up to 256 bits.

Keys are long strings of bits.

Test Your Understanding

18. a) What is a cipher? b) What protection does confidentiality provide? c) In two-way dialogues, how many keys are used in symmetric key encryption? d) What is the minimum size for symmetric keys to be considered strong?

Electronic Signatures: Message Authentication and Integrity

In addition to encrypting each packet for confidentiality, cryptographic systems normally add **electronic signatures** to each packet. This is illustrated in Figure 3-13. Electronic signatures are small bit strings that provide message-by-message authentication, much as people use signatures to authenticate individual written letters. Authentication means proving a sender's identity. An electronic signature allows the receiver to detect a message added to the dialogue by an impostor.

Authentication means proving a sender's identity.

Electronic signatures also provide **message integrity**, meaning that the receiver will be able to detect if the packet is altered by an attacker while the packet is in transit. Consequently, cryptographic systems provide three protections to every packet. Encryption for confidentiality provides message-by-message confidentiality, while electronic signatures provide message-by-message authentication and message integrity.[29]

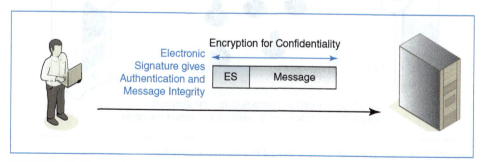

FIGURE 3-13   Electronic Signature for Authentication

---

[29] Another common protection is anti-replay. In some cases, an attacker may be able to do damage by capturing an encrypted message. Although the attacker cannot read the encrypted message, he or she may be able to accomplish objectives by simply retransmitting the message later. Anti-replay protections prevent this.

Test Your Understanding

19. a) What two protections do electronic signatures provide? b) What three protections are typically given to each packet?

Host-to-Host Virtual Private Networks (VPNs)

Sometimes, transmission through untrusted networks is necessary. One of these is the Internet, which has no built-in security and is full of attackers. Another untrusted network is a wireless network because anyone can intercept your transmissions. The way to address a lack of security is to communicate with cryptographic protections. This is said to give you a host-to-host **virtual private network (VPN)**. Figure 3-14 illustrates this concept. Of course, transmissions actually pass through a real network. In terms of security, however, the hosts are effectively communicating via a private network that connected just them.

Multiple cryptographic protections must be applied within a VPN conversation, including initial authentication and message-by-message protection for authentication, integrity, and confidentiality. Users do not have to worry about this. VPNs always use a **cryptographic system**, which is a bundle of protections that work automatically.

The most common cryptographic system for browser–webserver VPNs is SSL/TLS. SSL/TLS was created as Secure Sockets Layer (SSL) by Netscape. The Internet Engineering Task Force then took over the standard, renaming it Transport Layer Security (TLS). It is called by both names today, so we call it **SSL/TLS**.[30]

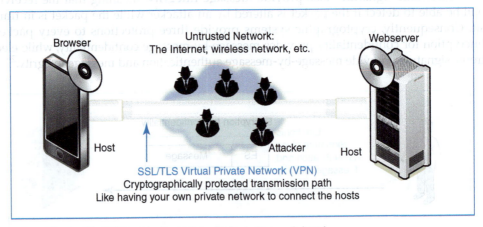

FIGURE 3-14 SSL/TLS Host-to-Host Virtual Private Network (VPN)

---

[30] When you use SSL/TLS, the URL begins with https://. Although you will not notice it, the port number in TCP changes from 80 to 443, which indicates HTTP over SSL/TLS.

SSL/TLS is an attractive cryptographic system for Web applications because SSL/TLS is built into every webserver and browser today, so the cost of adding SSL/TLS protection is negligible. Given security threats on the Internet, SSL/TLS should be used whenever possible.

Test Your Understanding

20. a) Distinguish between private networks and virtual private networks. b) Why do users not have to worry about the details of cryptographic processes when they are using a VPN? c) For what application was SSL/TLS most widely used? d) Why is it attractive for this application?

OTHER FORMS OF AUTHENTICATION

Electronic signatures provide message-by-message authentication. However, there are many types of authentication in use today, each with strengths and weaknesses. Authentication is crucial to controlling access to resources so that adversaries can be prevented from reaching them.

Terminology and Concepts

Figure 3-15 illustrates the main terminology and concepts in authentication. The user trying to prove his or her identity is the **supplicant**. The party requiring the supplicant to prove his or her identity is the **verifier**. The supplicant tries to prove his or her identity by providing **credentials** (proofs of identity) to the verifier.

The type of authentication tool that is used with each resource must be *appropriate for the risks to that particular resource*. Sensitive personnel information should be protected by very strong authentication methods. However, strong authentication is expensive and often inconvenient. For relatively nonsensitive data, weaker but less expensive authentication methods may be sufficient.

Test Your Understanding

21. a) What is authentication? b) Distinguish between the supplicant and the verifier. c) What are credentials? d) Why must authentication be appropriate for risks to an asset?

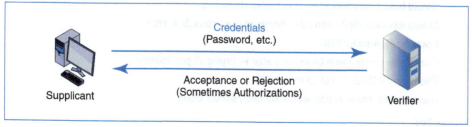

FIGURE 3-15 General Authentication Concepts

Reusable Passwords

The most common authentication credential is the **reusable password**, which is a string of characters that a user types to gain access to the resources associated with a certain **username** (account) on a computer. These are called *reusable* passwords because the user types the same password each time he or she needs access to the resource. Unfortunately, the reusable password is the weakest form of authentication, and it is appropriate only for the least sensitive assets.

The reusable password is the weakest form of authentication, and it is appropriate only for the least sensitive assets.

Ease of Use and Low Cost The popularity of password authentication is hardly surprising. For users, passwords are familiar and relatively easy to use. For corporate IT departments, passwords add no cost because operating systems and many applications have built-in password authentication.

Reusable Passwords

   Passwords are strings of characters

   They are typed to authenticate the use of a username (account) on a computer

   They are used repeatedly and so are called reusable passwords

Benefits

   Ease of use for users (familiar)

   Inexpensive because they are built into operating systems

Often Weak (Easy to Crack)

   Hackers use password dictionaries that include common passwords, names, and simple variations such as capitalizing the first letter and adding a number at the end

   Dictionary attacks can crack almost all passwords in seconds or minutes

Passwords Should Be Long and Complex

   Should have a minimum of eight to twelve characters

   Should mix case, digits, and other keyboard characters ($, #, etc.)

   Example: r8pWm#4D*&2B

   Can only be cracked with brute force attacks (trying all possibilities)

   This is very difficult and often impossible

   However, long, complex passwords are often written down

Perspective

   Overall, can only be used for the least sensitive assets

FIGURE 3-16 Reusable Password Authentication (Study Figure)

Dictionary Attacks   The main problem with passwords is that most users pick very weak passwords.[31] To break into a host by guessing and trying passwords, hackers often use **password dictionaries**. These are lists of passwords likely to succeed. Running through a password dictionary to see if a password is accepted for a username is called a **dictionary attack**. Password dictionaries typically have three types of entries: a list of common passwords, the words in standard dictionaries, and hybrid versions of words such as capitalizing the first letter and adding a digit at the end.[32]

If a password is in one of these dictionaries, the attacker may have to try a few thousand passwords, but this will only take seconds. No password that is in a cracker dictionary is adequately strong, no matter how long it is.

Long Complex Passwords and Brute-Force Attacks   Fortunately, good passwords cannot be broken by dictionary attacks. Good passwords have two characteristics. First, they are complex. It is essential to have a mix of upper and lower case letters that does not have a regular pattern such as alternating uppercase letters and lowercase letters. It is also good—and some would say necessary—to include non-letter keyboard characters such as the digits (0 through 9) and other special characters (&, #, /, ?, etc.).

If a password is complex, it can only be cracked by a **brute-force attack**, in which the cracker first tries all combinations of one-character passwords, then all combinations of two-character passwords, an so forth, until the attacker finds one that works.

Complexity is not enough, however. Complex passwords must also be long. For short complex passwords, brute force attacks will still succeed. Beyond about 10 or 12 characters, however, there are too many combinations to try in a reasonable period of time.

Scope of Usefulness   Overall, while long complex passwords can defeat determined attacks, most users select passwords that can be cracked with dictionary attacks. Reusable passwords are no longer appropriate in an era when password cracking programs can reveal most passwords in seconds or minutes. Passwords are only useful for nonsensitive assets.

Test Your Understanding

22. a) Why are passwords widely used? b) What types of passwords are susceptible to dictionary attacks? c) Can a password that can be broken by a dictionary attack be adequately strong if it is very long? d) What types of passwords can be broken only by brute-force attacks? e) What are the characteristics of passwords that are safe from even brute-force attacks? f) Why is it undesirable to use reusable passwords for anything but the least sensitive assets?

---

[31] In a study of 10,000 passwords, Mark Burnett at xato.net found that almost 10% were "password," "123456," or "12345678." Also in the top 20 were "111111," "abc123," "1234," "12345," "football," and "letmein." Trying just the top 100 passwords would allow a hacker to get into 40% of accounts. Trying the top 1,000 would get into 91%. One weakness in this study is that password case was not considered. However, given the lax attitude of most users toward passwords, separating different strings with different case patterns probably would not have made a difference.

[32] Another variation is to replace the letter 0 with a zero, s with $, and to do other look-similar replacements. An example would be *pa$$w0rd*. Yet another example is to repeat the password, for example *pizzapizza*.

23. Create a table. The first column should have the following passwords. The second should list the type of attack that a cracker will use against it. The third should say whether it is adequately strong and justify the assessment. a) M&12dGm/8#56, b) password, c) r3B*tRx, d) HonoluluHonolulu, e) BrOwNsToNe, f) TiGErShArK, g) woostershire.

Other Forms of Authentication

Companies are beginning to look for stronger types of authentication for most of their resources. This will allow them to replace most or all of their reusable password access systems. We have space to mention only the few types of authentication shown in Figure 3-17.

Access Cards To get into your hotel room, you may have to swipe an **access card** through a card reader. If you have a debit card, this also is a type of access card because it identifies you, allowing you to make purchases. Many bus systems let riders purchase access cards to pay for their travel. Many companies use access cards for door access control. In addition, simple access card readers can be plugged into USB ports on computers for computer access.

Perspective

    Goal is to replace reusable passwords

Access Cards

    Permit door access

    Can be used for computer access

    Proximity access cards do not require physical contact

Biometrics

    Biometrics uses body measurements to authenticate you

    Vary in cost, precision, and susceptibility to deception

    Fingerprint recognition

        Inexpensive but poor precision, deceivable

        Sufficient for low-risk uses

        On a notebook, may be better than requiring a reusable password

    Iris recognition

        Based on patterns in the colored part of your eye

        Expensive but precise and difficult to deceive

    Facial recognition

        Based on facial features

        Controversial because can be done surreptitiously—without the supplicant's knowledge

---

FIGURE 3-17 Other Forms of Authentication

Biometrics   In biometric authentication, access control is granted based on something you always have with you—your body. **Biometrics** is the use of body measurements to authenticate you.

Biometrics is the use of body measurements to authenticate you.

There are several types of biometrics. They differ in cost, precision, and susceptibility to deception by someone wishing to impersonate a legitimate user.

- At the low end on price, precision, and the ability to reject deception is **fingerprint recognition**, which looks at the loops, whorls, and ridges in a finger. Although fingerprint recognition is not a strong form of authentication, its price makes it acceptable for low-risk resources such as laptop computers with little sensitive information, tablets, and smart phones. For such devices, fingerprint recognition may be preferred to reusable passwords, given the tendency of people to pick poor passwords and forget them.

- At the high end of the scale on price, precision, and the ability to reject deception is **iris recognition**,[33] which looks at the pattern in the colored part of your eye. Although extremely precise, iris scanners are too expensive to use for computer access. They are normally used for access to sensitive rooms. However, as the processing power on small devices like tablets and smartphones improves, we may begin to see iris scanning on them.

- A controversial form of biometrics is **facial recognition**, in which an individual is identified by his or her facial features. This is controversial because facial recognition can be done **surreptitiously**—without the knowledge of the person being scanned. This raises privacy issues. We are beginning to see facial recognition scanning on tablets and smartphones.

Digital Certificate Authentication   The strongest form of authentication is **digital certificate authentication**.[34] Figure 3-18 illustrates this form of authentication.

- In this form of authentication, each party has a secret **private key** that only he or she knows.

- Each party also has a **public key**, which anyone can know. It is not kept secret.

- A trusted organization called a **certificate authority (CA)** distributes the public key of a person in a document called a **digital certificate**. A digital certificate is cryptographically protected for message integrity, so that it cannot be changed without this change being obvious in a way that causes the verifier to reject it.

---

[33] In science fiction movies, eye scanners are depicted as shining light into the supplicant's eye. This does not happen. Iris scanners merely require the supplicant to look into a camera. In addition, science fiction movies use the term retinal scanning. The retina is the back part of the eye; it has distinctive vein patterns. Retinal scanning is not used frequently because the supplicant must press his or her face against the scanner.

[34] It is also good for authenticating software processes, which have no heads or fingers and have a difficult time swiping access cards.

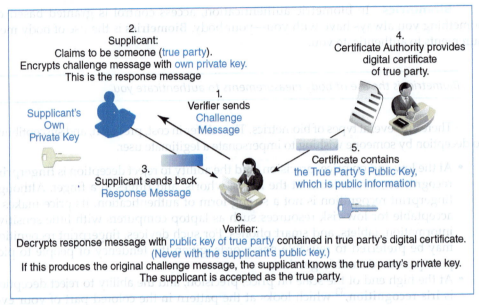

FIGURE 3-18 Digital Certificate Authentication

First, the supplicant claims to be someone we will call the **true party**. To test this claim, the verifier sends the subject a **challenge message**. This is just a random stream of bits. It is not even encrypted for confidentiality.

Second, to prove its claim to being the true party, the supplicant encrypts the challenge message *with his or her private key*[35] and sends this **response message** to the verifier. Again, there is no encryption for confidentiality.

Third, the verifier gets the true party's digital certificate, which contains the true party's public key. The verifier tests the response message by decrypting it with the *public key of the true party*, which is contained in the digital certificate. If the decryption produces the original challenge message, then the supplicant knows the private key of the true party. Only the true party should know this key. Therefore, it is reasonable to authenticate the supplicant as the true party.

Note that the verifier uses the public key of the true party—not the supplicant's public key. If the verifier used the supplicant's public key, the test would always succeed. The supplicant's public key would decrypt the message correctly. Impostors would *always* be authenticated.

Note that the verifier uses the public key of the true party—not the supplicant's public key.

---

[35] You should never say *the* private key or *the* public key. In a conversation each side has a public key and a private key. So always say the sender's public or private key, the receiver's public or private key, the supplicant's public or private key, the verifier's public or private key, or the true party's public or private key.

Two-Factor Authentication   Debit cards are potentially dangerous because if someone finds a lost debit card, the finder might be able to use it to make purchases. Consequently possession of the debit card is not enough to use it. To use a debit card, the user must type a **personal identification number (PIN)**, which usually is four or six digits long. Requiring two credentials for authentication is called **two-factor authentication**. Two-factor authentication increases the strength of authentication.[36]

Two-factor authentication requires two forms of authentication.

Test Your Understanding

24. a) How do you authenticate yourself with an access card? b) What is biometrics? c) Why may fingerprint recognition be acceptable for user authentication to a laptop? d) Why is iris recognition desirable? e) Why is face recognition controversial?

25. a) In digital certificate authentication, what does the supplicant do? b) What does the verifier do? c) Does the verifier decrypt with the true party's public key or the supplicant's public key? Why is this important? d) What electronic document contains the true party's public key? e) From what type of organization does the verifier get the digital certificate?

26. Why is two-factor authentication desirable?

FIREWALLS

In hostile military environments, travelers must pass through checkpoints. At each checkpoint, guards will examine their credentials. If the guards find the credentials insufficient, the guard will stop the traveler from proceeding and note the violation in a checkpoint log.

Supplicant needs two forms of credentials

Example: debit card and PIN

Strengthens authentication

Fails if attacker controls user's computer

Fails if an attacker can intercept authentication communication

---

FIGURE 3-19   Two-Factor Authentication (Study Figure)

---

[36] However, if a user's computer is compromised, the attacker typically controls both credentials, so two-factor authentication gives no security. Two-factor authentication may also fail if an eavesdropper can intercept authentication communication between the supplicant and the verifier. Two-factor authentication is desirable, but factors that limit its use must be understood.

Dropping and Logging Provable Attack Packets

Figure 3-20 shows that firewalls operate the same way. When a packet arrives, the **firewall** examines it. If the firewall identifies a packet as a **provable attack packet,** the firewall discards it.[37] (Synonyms for provable are definite, certain, etc.) On the other hand, if the packet is not a provable attack packet, the firewall allows it to pass.

If a firewall identifies a packet as a provable attack packet, the firewall discards it.

The firewall copies information about each discarded packet into a **firewall log file**. Firewall managers should read their firewall log files every day to understand the types of attacks coming against the resources that the firewall is protecting.

Note that firewalls pass *all* packets that are not provable attack packets, even if they are suspicious. By analogy, police cannot arrest someone unless they have probable cause, which is a reasonably high standard of proof. They cannot arrest someone for being suspicious.

Consequently, firewalls never stop all attack packets. It is important to harden all internal hosts against attacks by adding firewalls, adding antivirus programs, installing all patches promptly, and taking other precautions. This chapter focuses on network security, rather than host security, so we will not consider host hardening.

When most people think of firewalls, they think of filtering packets arriving at a network *from the outside*. Figure 3-20 illustrates this **ingress filtering**. Most firms also do

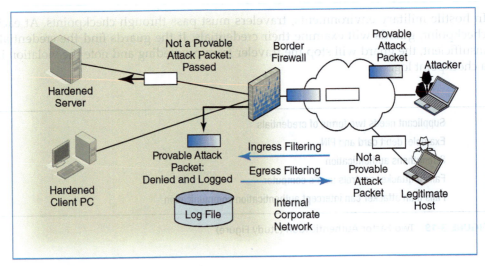

FIGURE 3-20 General Firewall Operation

---

[37] Synonyms for provable are certain, etc. The point is that there is no doubt.

egress filtering, that is, they filter packets going from the network *to the outside*. Egress filtering also attempts to prevent sensitive corporate information from being transmitted out of the firm.

Test Your Understanding

27. a) What does a firewall do when a provable attack packet arrives? b) Does a firewall drop a packet if it probably is an attack packet? c) Why is it important to read firewall logs daily? d) Distinguish between ingress and egress filtering.

Stateful Packet Inspection (SPI) Firewalls

How do firewalls examine packets to see if they are attack packets? Actually, there are several **firewall filtering mechanisms**. We will only look at two—stateful packet inspection (SPI) and application-aware firewalls.

The most widely used firewall filtering method is **stateful packet inspection (SPI)**, which treats different types of packets differently, spending the most resources on the riskiest packets, which are relatively few, and spending less time on the more numerous, less risky packets.

States and Filtering Intensity   When you talk with someone on the telephone, there are two basic stages to your conversation.

- At the beginning of a call, you need to identify the other party and to decide whether you are both willing to have a conversation.
- If you do decide to talk, you seldom have to consider whether the conversation should go on with this person.

The key point here is that you do different things in different stages of a conversation. In the first stage, you have to pay careful attention to identifying the caller and making a decision about whether it is wise to talk to him or her. After that, you simply talk and normally do not have to spend much time thinking about whether to talk to the person or who the person is.

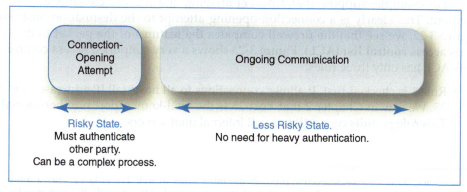

FIGURE 3-21   States in a Conversation (Study Figure)

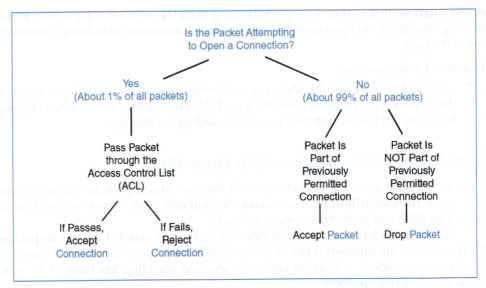

FIGURE 3-22 Stateful Packet Inspection (SPI)

Most firewalls today use stateful packet inspection (SPI) filtering, which uses the insight that there are also stages in network conversations and that not all stages require the same amount of firewall attention. At the simplest level, Figure 3-22 shows that there are two stages, which SPI firewalls call **states**: opening a connection (conversation) and ongoing communication afterward.[38]

SPI Filtering in the Connection-Opening State SPI firewalls focus heavily on the opening state. They have complex rules to tell them whether to allow the conversation (connection). If they decide to allow a connection, however, they give minimal attention to packets in the ongoing communication state. This makes sense because the decision to allow a connection is the most complex and dangerous stage in the connection.

For example, suppose that a packet arriving at a firewall contains a TCP SYN segment. This clearly is a connection-opening attempt to the destination host. From Figure 3-22, we see that the firewall compares the features of the packet to the rules in its **access control list (ACL)**. Figure 3-23 shows a very simplified access control list. This ACL has only three rules.

- Rule 1 is checked first. It allows connections to all hosts (all IP addresses) on Port 25. We saw in Chapter 2 that Port 25 is the well-known port number for SMTP. This rule permits connections to all internal mail servers.

---

[38] Sometimes, stateful packet inspection firewalls use other states as well. For instance, after a connection begins, there may be a stage in which a new port must be opened in the firewall. In voice over IP, there typically is one port to connect the VoIP programs. The actual call must use a new port designated for that purpose. The SPI firewall will conduct appropriate inspections during this process.

Rule	Destination IP Address or Range	Service	Action
1	ALL	25	Allow connection
2	10.47.122.79	80	Allow connection
5	ALL	ALL	Do not allow connection

Note: ACLs are only applied to packets that attempt to open a connection.

FIGURE 3-23   Access Control List (ACL) for Attempts to Open a Connection

- If Rule 1 does not match the packet, the firewall looks at Rule 2 in the ACL. This rule permits connections to a single internal host, 10.47.122.79, on Port 80. This rule allows access to a single internal webserver—the webserver at IP address 10.47.122.79. This is safer than Rule 1 because Rule 1 opens the firewall to *every* internal mail server, while Rule 2 opens the firewall only to connections to *a single* server.
- If Rule 2 does not match the packet, the firewall looks at the third (and final) rule. This rule is called the **default rule** for incoming packets that try to open a connection. (The default is what you get if you do not explicitly specify something else.) This last rule ensures that unless a packet is explicitly allowed by an earlier rule, it is dropped and logged.

What happens if a packet containing a TCP SYN segment arrives with the destination address 10.20.12.220 and the destination port number 80? This is an attempt to open a connection. Consequently, the SPI firewall takes the left fork in Figure 3-22. It passes the connection information to the access control list.

- First, the firewall tests the packet against the first rule in the ACL. The rule does not apply because the port number in the rule is 25 instead of 80.
- The firewall goes on to the next rule. This rule also does not apply, because the IP address does not match the IP address in the connection.
- The third and final rule matches, of course. Consequently, the firewall decides to reject the connection and logs the decision.

Note that the decision is to accept or reject a *connection*, not just an *individual packet*. This is an important decision, so doing all of the processing to pass the packet through the ACL is justified.

What if the SPI firewall decides instead to permit a connection? Then it adds the connection to its **approved connections table**. As shown in Figure 3-24, each connection is a row containing the IP address and port number of the internal host and the IP address and port number of the external host. In other words, the row has the internal and external sockets for each connection.

Although ACL rules generally are not complex, there tend to be many rules in real access control lists. Comparing a single connection-opening attempt against the ACL can be time consuming. Fortunately, only a very small percentage of all packets arriving at a firewall are connection-opening attempts—probably under 1%. Only these have to be passed through the ACL.

	Internal Host		External Host	
Connection	IP Address	Port Number	IP Address	Port Number
1	128.171.17.13	3270	10.74.118.4	80
2	128.171.34.5	4747	60.3.5.75	25
...	...	...	...	...

FIGURE 3-24 Approved Connections Table for a Stateful Packet Inspection (SPI) Firewall

Handling Packets During Ongoing Communication If a packet does not attempt to open a connection, then either the packet is part of an approved connection in the approved connections table (Figure 3-24) or the packet is spurious. When any packet that does not attempt to open a connection arrives, then the stateful firewall does the following (see Figure 3-22).

- If the packet is part of an established connection, it is passed without further inspection. (However, these packets can be further filtered if desired.) An example would be a packet with an internal socket of 128.171.34.5:4747 and an external socket of 60.3.5.75:25:25. This matches Connection 2 in Figure 3-24. The packet should be passed.
- If the packet is not part of an approved connection, then it must be spurious. It is dropped and logged. An example would be a packet with an internal socket of 128.171.34.5:4747 and an external socket of 60.3.5.75:80. This is not a match to either row. The packet is dropped and logged.

What kind of packet does not attempt to open a connection? The answer is simple for TCP. Only packets with SYN segments attempt to open a connection. For UDP, the answer is somewhat more complex. Essentially, if an arriving packet containing a UDP datagram arrives and the connection is in the table, the packet is allowed through. If the packet does not match the approved connection table, however, it is not immediately dropped. Instead, it is considered to be a possible attempt to open a connection and is passed through the ACL. If it is allowed, a row will be added to the approved connections table. Although UDP does not have connections, subsequent UDP exchanges between two sockets are treated as if they were parts of a single connection.

Note that the SPI firewall only makes a decision whether or not to pass a single *packet* for non-connection opening attempts. It does not have to make a decision about the entire *connection* as it must do in connection-opening attempts.

If processing a packet that does not attempt to open a connection sounds simple, it is. Nearly all packets—perhaps 99%—are not part of connection-opening attempts. Consequently, most packets are handled with very little processing power. This makes stateful firewalls very inexpensive overall.

Perspective Although the simple operation of stateful packet inspection makes it inexpensive, stateful filtering provides a great deal of protection against attacks. This combination of low cost and strong security is responsible for the dominance of SPI today in main border firewalls.

Test Your Understanding

28. a) Why are states important? b) What packets are compared to the ACL in an SPI firewall? c) When a packet that is part of an ongoing connection arrives at a stateful packet inspection firewall, what does the firewall do? d) When a packet that is not part of an ongoing connection and that does not attempt to open a connection arrives at an SPI firewall, what does the firewall do? e) Why are stateful firewalls attractive? f) What type of firewalls do most corporations use for their main border firewalls?

29. a) How will an SPI firewall handle a packet containing a TCP segment that is a pure acknowledgment? b) How will an SPI firewall handle a packet containing a TCP SYN segment? c) How will an SPI firewall handle a packet containing a TCP FIN segment? d) How will a firewall handle a packet containing a UDP datagram? (The answer is not in the text.) e) How will the access control list (ACL) in Figure 3-23 handle a packet that attempts to open a connection to an FTP server? Explain.

Next-Generation Firewalls (NGFWs)

A problem with stateful packet inspection firewalls is that they only look at IP addresses and port numbers in their rules. They do not look at everything in a packet, much less at application messages that are delivered in multiple packets. To detect and prevent more attacks, companies are now implementing **Next-Generation Firewalls (NGFWs)** that go far beyond what traditional SPI firewalls do.

Deep Inspection Most fundamentally, NGFWs do deep inspection. This means that they look at everything in a packet, including the application message segment and all fields in the IP header and the TCP or UDP header. In addition, because application messages may be split across multiple packets, deep inspection reassembles packet streams to read application messages.

Application Awareness Deep inspection gives next-generation firewalls the ability to identify the type of application that created a particular stream of messages. This permits the firewall to execute pass/drop rules based on application policies. For example, a company may have a policy to ban Netflix or limit YouTube to no more than 5% of all traffic. Application awareness is necessary because so many applications now run over Port 80. Port-based policies are no longer sufficient.

Intrusion Detection System (IDS) Functionality It would be naïve to expect firewalls to stop all attack packets. Most obviously, they do not drop suspicious packets—only definite attack packets. Intrusion detection systems (IDSs) focus specifically on identifying suspicious transmissions. When they find suspicious packet streams, they log them for firewall administrators to examine. If a threat appears to be very serious, the IDS sends an alarm to firewall administrators. IDSs can detect many sophisticated attacks because they use deep inspection to examine tell-tale signs at all three layers and over streams of packets. Consequently, IDS functionality is found in NGFWs.

However, intrusion detection systems generate many false alarms. Companies must invest sufficient human resources into handling alarms and reading log files. Even

---

Limitations of Stateful Packet Inspection (SPI) Firewalls

    Limited primarily to examining socket data

    Cannot detect what applications are actually using Port 80

    Cannot identify problems in streams of packets

Next-Generation Firewall (NGFW) Operation

    Uses deep inspection

    Examines all fields in the internet and transport layer

    Examines application layer content

    Requires reassembling application messages from multiple segments

Capabilities

    Application Awareness

        Can identify which application created traffic

        Can base rules on application policies

    Intrusion Detection System (IDS) Functionality

        Can detect suspicious traffic

        Log suspicious traffic

        Notify the security administrator of high-threat suspicious traffic

        Produce many false alarms that can dull vigilance

    Intrusion Prevention Systems (IPS) Functionality

        IDSs that drop packets that are suspicious but for which there is high confidence that they are attacks

    Reputation Management

        Whitelists and blacklists in external reputation management databases

        Used to inform decisions about packets to and from these sites

    NAT and VPN Traversal

        Traditional firewall functionality

        VPN traversal passes encrypted traffic without inspection

Wire-Speed Operation

    Processing requirements per packet are heavy

    Yet must be able to process at the highest speed of incoming transmission lines

    Traditional firewalls are general-purpose computers that do processing with step-by-step software

    NGFWs use purpose-built hardware that can do processing in hardware

---

FIGURE 3-25 Next-Generation Firewalls (NGFWs) (Study Figure)

then, finding the one or two true attacks in a long stream of false alarms leads to frustration and flagging vigilance. In the case of the Target security breach, the FireEye IDS detected the attack, but Target security personnel did not follow up on the alarm.

Although IDSs create many problems, firms now realize that firewalls alone will never stop attacks. Too many attack packets get through all firewalls. Unless a compromise is detected after it succeeds, the damage can become enormous. However, the average business receives about 10,000 security alerts per day, only a handful of which are real threats. Finding these real attacks is literally like finding a needle in a haystack.[39]

Intrusion Prevention System (IPS) Functionality   The statement that IDSs do not drop suspicious packets is not entirely true. In some cases, suspicion rises to the level of high confidence, although not certainty. Denial-of-service attacks are a good example of this. In such cases, the IDS administrator may be able to program the IDS to actually drop such packets. Marketers in companies that built these IDSs relabeled them **intrusion prevention systems (IPSs)**. Next-generation firewalls also have the ability to drop packets based on high confidence that the packet is an attack packet.

Reputation Management   Many companies now use external services that compile lists of websites and other resources with very good reputations or very bad reputations. These are called **whitelists** and **blacklists**, respectively. NGFWs use **reputation management** databases to enhance their ability to identify potentially bad content and to give fast-track approval to other content.

NAT and VPN Traversal   All firewalls today implement NAT functionality. They also universally allow approved VPN traffic to traverse them without filtering. It can be argued that the VPN traversal is the opposite of a security feature because it permits encrypted traffic to pass through unfiltered. However, this is a necessary tradeoff between encryption security and filtering security.

Wire-Speed Operation   The challenge of creating next-generation firewalls is that they require an extremely large amount of processing power. At the same time, they must not delay traffic. Avoiding delay is becoming ever more difficult as transmission line speeds increase. NGFW vendors acknowledge the requirement for **wire-speed operation**, meaning that they can receive and process traffic at the full speed of the lines coming into them. They do this by relying on **application-specific integrated circuits**, which are purpose-built computer chips that can process NGFW functions far more quickly than traditional firewalls built from general-purpose computer chips that do their firewall-specific processing in step-by-step software.

Test Your Understanding

30. a) Why are SPI firewalls limited in their ability to detect attack packets? b) What is deep inspection? c) Why is the ability to create firewall policies for individual applications important? d) Distinguish between IDS and IPS functionality. e) In reputation management, distinguish between white lists and black lists. f) What is VPN traversal? g) What is firewall VPN traversal's implication for security? h) Why is wire-speed operation important in firewalls? i) What allows wire-speed operation despite the heavy processing power required for NGFW filtering and the increasing speed of transmission lines?

---

[39] John E. Dunn, "Average US Business Fields 10,000 Security Alerts per Day, Damballa Analysis Finds," *Techworld.com,* May 13, 2014. http://news.techworld.com/security/3516426/average-us-business-fields-10000-security-alerts-per-day-damballa-analysis-finds/.

BOX: ANTIVIRUS PROTECTION

Both firewalls and antivirus programs attempt to stop attacks. However, they work at different levels. Firewalls work at the level of packets and groups of packets. Antivirus (AV) programs, in contrast, examine entire files. When an e-mail message arrives at a mail server, the server may pass any attachment the message carries to an AV program for vetting.

Firewalls work at the level of packets and groups of packets. Antivirus (AV) programs, in contrast, examine entire files.

Antivirus programs do not simply check for viruses. They also examine the attached file for worms, Trojan horses, and other forms of malware. These programs were named antivirus programs when "malware" was roughly synonymous with "virus." Although the scope of detection has broadened, the name antivirus has stuck.

Traditionally, AV programs only looked for malware signatures, which are snippets of code that let the antivirus program identify particular malware programs. Signature detection is still widely used, but it is no longer sufficient. First, the number of malware programs is now so large that the processing power to detect all known malware via signature detection would drive any computer to its knees. More fundamentally, many malware programs now mutate constantly, rewriting their code in a way that maintains functionality while making the matching of strings of characters useless.

Today, AV programs also look for behavioral patterns—things the attachment file is attempting to do. To give an extreme example, if the file is a program that will try to

---

Firewalls versus Antivirus Filtering

　Firewalls work on packets and groups of packets

　Antivirus filtering works on files

Antivirus Filtering

　Not limited to viruses

　Looks for all forms of malware

Signature Detection

　Looks for byte patterns that characterize individual malware programs

　There are now too many malware programs to test for all malware program signatures

　Also, many malware programs mutate, changing their signatures

Behavioral Detection

　Analysis of what the program is attempting to do

　Reformat the hard drive, etc.

　May run programs in a sandbox (environment it cannot escape from) to study it

---

FIGURE 3-26 Antivirus Protection (Study Figure)

reformat a computer's hard drive, that is an undeniable indication that the program is malware. Some AV programs even run the suspect program in a sandbox (environment it cannot escape from) to watch it operate.

Test Your Understanding

31. a) Distinguish between what firewalls look at and what antivirus programs look at. b) Are AV programs used to detect more than viruses? Explain. c) Distinguish between signature detection and behavioral pattern detection. d) Why is signature detection not enough?

CONCLUSION

Synopsis

Security is now an integral part of every network project from requirements to ongoing operations. It is important to design security into networks up front instead of trying to add it later at far higher cost and at a substantially lower rate of success. We discuss network security throughout the book. In this chapter and the next, we look at security in depth.

We began with a discussion of the threat environment—the types of people and organizations that attack you and the types of attacks they use. Attackers include hackers, malware writers, insiders, terrorists, and national governments. Hackers today are mainly career criminals, who are dangerous because they are well-funded, work in gangs, and can buy attack software on the Internet. Insider attacks are common and tend to be damaging because insiders have access to systems, know systems well, know how to avoid detection, and tend to be trusted. Attacks by cyberterrorists and national governments tend to be very dangerous because they can afford to engage in highly sophisticated attacks, focus on doing damage instead of committing isolated crimes, and execute their attacks against many targets all at once. Cyberwar attacks by national governments would overwhelm normal corporate defenses. Governments have the resources to engage in advanced persistent threats, which are highly sophisticated attacks that take place over months or years and give the attacker broad access to the organization's system.

Attack methods are also diverse. Malware is a generic name for evil software—viruses, worms (especially directly propagating worms), Trojan horses, and spam, to name only a few. Malware often propagates between computers and then executes a payload, which is a program that does damage to the victim's computer.

Hackers break into a computer resource and then can do a wide range of damage. We discussed how they perform an exploit (break-in), do damage manually, and plant malware in the system to keep doing damage. We discussed the specific definition of hacking, which is intentionally using a computer resource without authorization or in excess of authorization.

In a distributed denial-of-service attack, a botmaster builds an army of bot programs on compromised computers. The botmaster then overwhelms a selected victim with a flood of attack packets. Bots can be upgraded to fix bugs or to equip them to do a different kind of attack.

Many attacks attempt to bypass technical security through social engineering, which is a euphemism for tricking people into taking actions that compromise personal or organizational security. In phishing, the adversary crafts an e-mail message or website that looks official and reputable. In spear phishing, the enticing content is customized to a particular *individual*. Advanced persistent threats typically begin with a successful spear-phishing attack.

Companies defend against attacks in many ways. One is cryptography, which is the use of mathematics to provide security. For example, a company may encrypt all transmissions for confidentiality, so that an attacker cannot read them. This normally uses symmetric key encryption. Messages can also be given electronic signatures so that their authenticity can be checked and to provide message integrity—assurance that the message has not been tampered with en route.

Knowing whom you are communicating with can reduce risks. In authentication, a supplicant presents credentials to prove its identity to a verifier. Traditionally, authentication meant reusable passwords, and passwords are widely used today. However, companies are trying to move away from them because they are not very secure. Dictionary attacks can break most passwords in seconds or minutes. Long complex passwords can defeat dictionary attacks, but they are typically written down or forgotten. Today, companies increasingly are using physical access cards, biometrics (such as fingerprint, iris, and face recognition), and cryptographic methods using digital certificate authentication. Using two forms of authentication—two-factor authentication—provides stronger authentication in most circumstances.

Firewalls stop definite attack packets from entering or leaving the firm. They do not stop suspicious packets, so they are not a panacea for stopping attacks. Most firewalls today use stateful packet inspection (SPI), in which the intensity of packet examination depends on the state of the conversation. Packets attempting to open a new connection are particularly dangerous and are given extensive scrutiny. The packet's characteristics are compared to a long list of rules in the firewall's access control list (ACL). In contrast, packets that do not attempt to open a new connection are given only cursory scrutiny. If they are part of an approved connection, they are passed. If not, they are dropped. By focusing expensive filtering resources on comparatively rare but risky connection-opening packets, SPI firewalls can provide very good security at reasonable cost. To overcome the limitations of stateful packet inspection, however, companies are beginning to adopt next-generation firewalls, which can base accept/deny rules on the specific application used in the connection, not simply IP addresses and port numbers.

SPI firewalls are now being superseded by these next-generation firewalls. NGFWs use deep inspection to look beyond IP addresses and port numbers. Deep inspection looks at all fields in packet headers and at application messages. This allows them to implement policies for individual applications. It also permits intrusion detection and intrusion prevention functionality. NGFWs also use reputation management. Custom-built computer chips provide the speed needed for the heavy processing required by NGFW filtering methods, allowing these firewalls to operate at wire speed despite rapid increases in transmission speed.

Firewalls look at packets and groups of packets. In contrast, antivirus programs look at entire files. Despite the name "antivirus," they check for all forms of malware. Traditionally, they used signature detection based on byte patterns that characterize specific malware programs. Malware has become good at evading signature detection, so antivirus programs now use behavioral analysis to see what a program is attempting to do.

In this chapter, we discussed security threats and defenses. In Chapter 4, we will discuss how to manage security. As security expert Bruce Schneier has often warned, "Security is a process, not a product." Unless companies manage security consistently and well, the best technical tools will be useless. Chapter 4's purpose is actually broader—to discuss network management in general. Security management is only part of network management.

END-OF-CHAPTER QUESTIONS

Thought Questions

3-1. a) What form of authentication would you recommend for relatively unimportant resources? Justify your answer. b) What form of authentication would you recommend for your most sensitive resources?

3-2. What is the promise of newer authentication systems?

3-3. Keys and passwords must be long. Yet most personal identification numbers (PINs) that you type when you use a debit card are only four or six characters long. Yet this is safe. Why?

3-4. Rewrite the ACL in Figure 3-23. Add access to an FTP server with IP address 10.32.67.112. Do not just state the rule.

3-5. In digital certificate authentication, the supplicant could impersonate the true party by doing the calculation with the true party's private key. What prevents impostors from doing this?

3-6. What are the implications for digital certificate authentication if the true party's private key is stolen?

Perspective Questions

3-7. What was the most surprising thing you learned in this chapter?

3-8. What was the most difficult part of this chapter for you?

Chapter 4

Network and Security Management

LEARNING OBJECTIVES

By the end of this chapter, you should be able to:

- Describe growth trends in network demand and budgets.
- Discuss network quality of service (QoS) and be able to specify service level agreement (SLA) guarantees.
- Design a network layout based on required traffic volumes between sites, considering redundancy.
- Describe options for dealing with momentary traffic peaks.
- Describe and apply strategic security planning principles.
- Describe the importance of centralized network and security management and discuss tools for centralizing network and security management. Explain how software-defined networking (SDN) may revolutionize the way that networks are managed and what benefits SDN may bring.

FAILURES IN THE TARGET BREACH

After every breach, companies should pause to take lessons from the experience. This type of reflection, if it leads to appropriate changes, will reduce the odds of similar breaches in the future.

One lesson from the Target breach is that you cannot trust external businesses you deal with to have good security. In the case of Fazio Mechanical Services, an employee fell for a spear phishing attack. This could happen in any company. However, Fazio made it more likely. It used the free consumer version of an antivirus program, Malwarebytes

Anti-Malware.[1] This free version did not do real-time assessment for arriving e-mail messages and attachments. If Fazio had used a commercial antivirus program for their e-mail, the employee probably would have seen a warning that opening an attachment was a bad idea or even that a specific threat existed in the attachment.

The breach also taught a number of lessons about Target's security. After the attackers gained a foothold on the vendors' server, they were able to move into more sensitive parts of the network in order to download malware onto the POS terminals, compromise a server to create a holding server, and compromise another server to act as an extrusion server. The low-security and highly sensitive parts of the network should have been segregated. They were not, or at least not enough.

Another issue is that Target received explicit warnings when the attackers were setting up the extrusion server. The thieves had to download malware onto the extrusion server in order to take it over and to manage subsequent FTP transmission. Target used the FireEye intrusion detection program. Target's intrusion detection team notified the Minneapolis security staff that a high-priority event had occurred on November 30, 2013.[2] In addition, the thieves had trouble with the initial malware. They had to make additional updates on December 1 and December 3. These resulted in additional FireEye warnings being sent to Target's Minneapolis security group. Had Target followed up on these warnings, they could have stopped or at least reduced the data extrusion, which began on December 2.[3]

Target may have been lax in understanding the danger of POS attacks. In April and August in 2013, VISA had sent Target and other companies warnings about new dangers regarding POS data theft.[4] It appears that Target's own security staff expressed concern for the company's exposure to charge card data theft.[5] If Target did not respond to this risk aggressively, this would have been another serious lapse.

Overall, Figure 3-1 showed that the thieves had to succeed at every step in a complex series of actions. Lockheed Martin's Computer Incident Response Team[6] staff called this a *kill chain*, which is a term borrowed from the military. The kill chain concept was designed to visualize all of the manufacturing, handling, and tactical steps needed for a weapon to destroy its target. Failure in a single step in a kill chain will

---

[1] Brian Krebs, Email Attack on Vendor Set Up Breach at Target, February 14, 2014. http://krebsonsecurity.com/2014/02/email-attack-on-vendor-set-up-breach-at-target/.

[2] Michael Riley, Ben Elgin, Dune Lawrence, and Carol Matlack, *Missed Alarms and 40 Million Stolen Credit Card Numbers: How Target Blew It, Bloomberg Businessweek*, March 13, 2014. http://www.businessweek.com/articles/2014-03-13/target-missed-alarms-in-epic-hack-of-credit-card-data.

[3] Aviv Raff, *PoS Malware Targeted Target*, Seculert, January 16, 2014. http://www.seculert.com/blog/2014/01/pos-malware-targeted-target.html.

[4] Jim Finkle and Mark Hosenball, *Exclusive: More Well-Known U.S. Retailers Victims of Cyber Attacks – Sources, Reuters*, January 12, 2014. http://www.reuters.com/article/2014/01/12/us-target-databreach-retailers-idUSBREA0B01720140112.

[5] Danny Yadron, Paul Ziobro, Devlin Barrett, *Target Warned of Vulnerabilities Before Data Breach, The Wall Street Journal*, February 14, 2014. http://online.wsj.com/news/articles/SB10001424052702304703804579381520736715690.

[6] Eric M. Hutchins, Michael J. Cloppert, and Rohan M. Amin, *Intelligence-Driven Computer Network Defense Informed by Analysis of Adversary Campaigns and Intrusion Kill Chains*, Lockheed Martin, 2011. http://www.lockheedmartin.com/content/dam/lockheed/data/corporate/documents/LM-White-Paper-Intel-Driven-Defense.pdf.

create overall failure. Lockheed has suggested that companies should actively consider security kill chains and look for evidence that one of the steps is occurring. Success in identifying an operating kill chain may allow the company to stop it or at least disrupt or degrade it. The warnings when malware was put on the extrusion server could have done exactly that.

Until one understands likely kill chains in depth, however, it is impossible to understand that events are part of each kill chain. Conversely, understanding the kill chain can allow the company to act before a kill chain fitting that pattern begins. For example, even cursory thinking about charge card data theft would lead the company to realize that thieves would probably use FTP transfers to unusual servers, that command communication would probably use certain ports in firewalls, and so forth.

Even well-defended companies suffer security compromises. However, when strategic planning is not done, if protections are not put into place, or if the security staff is not aggressive in doing the work required for the protections to work, the risk of compromises becomes a near certainty. Security expert Ben Schneier said "Security is a process, not a product."[7] Boxes and software are not magic talismans.

Test Your Understanding

1. a) What security mistake did Fazio Mechanical Services make? b) Why do you think it did this? (This requires you to give an opinion.) c) How might segregation of the network have stopped the breach? d) Why do you think the Minneapolis security staff did not heed the FireEye warning? (This requires you to give an opinion.) e) What warnings had Target not responded to adequately? f) What happens in a kill chain if a single action fails anywhere in the chain? g) How can kill chain analysis allow companies to identify security actions it should take? h) Explain why security is a process, not a product.

INTRODUCTION

In the first three chapters, we looked at general network concepts and security. However, technology means nothing unless a company manages it well. In this chapter, we will look at network and security planning. Although the concepts are broad, they apply to everything networking professionals do at every level.

Management is critical. Today, we can build much larger networks than we can manage easily. For example, even a mid-size bank is likely to have 500 Ethernet switches and a similar number of routers. Furthermore, network devices and their users are often scattered over large regions—sometimes internationally. While network technology is exciting to talk about and concrete conceptually, it is chaos without good management.

A pervasive issue in network management is cost. In networking, you never say, "Cost doesn't matter." Figure 4-1 illustrates that network demand is likely to grow rapidly

---

[7] Ben Schneier, "Computer Security: Will We Ever Learn?" *Crypto-Gram Newsletter*, May 15, 2000. https://www.schneier.com/crypto-gram-0005.html.

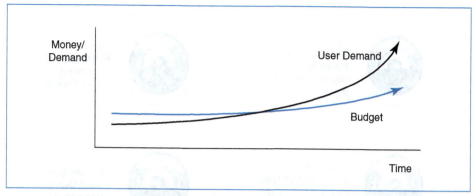

FIGURE 4-1 Network Demand and Budgets

in the future, just as it has in the past. The figure also illustrates that network budgets are growing slowly if they are growing at all.[8]

Taken together, these curves mean that network budgets are always stretched thin. If the network staff spends too much money on one project, it will not have enough left to do another important project. Although there are many concerns beyond costs, cost underlies everything in network management.

Test Your Understanding

2. a) Compare trends in network demand and network budgets. b) What are the implications of these trends?

NETWORK QUALITY OF SERVICE (QoS)

In the early days of the Internet, networked applications amazed new users. However, new users soon added, "Too bad it doesn't work better." Today, networks are mission-critical for corporations. If the network breaks down, much of the organization comes to a grinding and expensive halt. Networks must not only work. They must work *well*. Companies are increasingly concerned with network **quality-of-service (QoS) metrics**, that is, quantitative measures of network performance. Figure 4-2 shows that companies use a number of QoS metrics. Collectively, these metrics track the service quality that users receive.

Test Your Understanding

3. a) What are QoS metrics? (Do not just spell out the acronym.) b) Why are QoS metrics important?

---

[8] In fact, costs for equipment and transmission lines are falling. This is especially true in cellular transmission. The chief technology officer of Ericsson has said that network efficiencies reduced the price per bit transmitted 50 percent per year from 2008 to 2013. During this time, the cost per megabit fell from 46 cents to 1 to 3 cents. However, transmission volume has doubled each year, so customer bills did not go down. Stephen Lawson, "5G Will Have to Do More than Just Speed Up Your Phone, Ericsson Says," *PC World*, October 17, 2013. http://www.pcworld.com/article/2055880/5g-will-have-to-do-more-than-just-speed-up-your-phone-ericsson-says.html?tk=rel_news.

FIGURE 4-2 Quality-of-Service (QoS) Metrics

Transmission Speed

There are many ways to measure how well a network is working. The most fundamental metric, as we saw in Chapter 1, is speed. While low speeds are fine for text messages, the need for speed becomes very high as large volumes of data must be delivered, and video transmission requires increasingly higher transmission speeds.

Rated Speed versus Throughput and Aggregate Throughput

NOTE: Some students find the distinction between rated speed and throughput difficult to learn. However, we must use this distinction throughout this book, so be sure to take the time to understand it.

Rated Speed versus Throughput The term *transmission speed* is somewhat ambiguous. A transmission link's **rated speed** is the speed it *should* provide based on vendor claims or on the standard that defines the technology. For a number of reasons, transmission links almost always fail to deliver data at their full rated speeds. In contrast to rated speed, a network's **throughput** is the data transmission speed the network *actually* provides to users.

A transmission link's rated speed is the speed it should provide based on vendor claims or on the standard that defines the technology.
Throughput is the transmission speed a network actually provides to users.

Aggregate versus Individual Throughput Sometimes transmission links are shared. For example, if you are using a Wi-Fi computer in a classroom, you share the wireless access point's throughput with other users of that access point. In shared

> **Rated Speed**
>
> The speed a system should achieve according to vendor claims or to the standard that defines the technology
>
> **Throughput**
>
> The data transmission speed a system *actually* provides to users
>
> **Aggregate versus Rated Throughput on Shared Lines**
>
> The aggregate throughput is the total throughput available to all users in part of a network
>
> **Individual Throughput**
>
> The individual throughput is an individual's share of the aggregate throughput

FIGURE 4-3 Rated Speed, Throughput, Aggregate Throughput, and Individual Throughput (Study Figure)

situations, it is important to distinguish between a link's **aggregate throughput**, which is the total it provides to all users who share it in a part of a network, and the link's **individual throughput** that single users receive as their shares of the aggregate throughput. Individual throughput is always lower than aggregate throughput. As you learned as a child, despite what your mother said, sharing is bad.

Test Your Understanding

4. a) Distinguish between rated speed and throughput. b) Distinguish between individual and aggregate throughput. c) You are working at an access point with 20 other people. Three are doing a download at the same time you are. The rest are looking at their screens or sipping coffee. The access point channel you share has a rated speed of 150 Mbps and a throughput of 100 Mbps. How much speed can you expect for your download? (Check figure: 25 Mbps). d) In a coffee shop, there are 10 people sharing an access point with a rated speed of 20 Mbps. The throughput is half the rated speed. Several people are downloading. Each is getting five Mbps. How many people are using the Internet at that moment?

Other Quality-of-Service Metrics

Although network speed is important, it is not enough to provide good quality of service. Figure 4-2 showed that there are other QoS categories. We will look briefly at three of them.

Availability One is **availability**, which is the percentage of time that the network is available for use. Ideally, networks would be available 100% of the time, but that is impossible in reality. On the Public Switched Telephone Network, the availability target usually is 99.999%. Availability on data networks is usually lower, although by carefully adding redundancy, Netflix and some other companies can reach telephone availability levels.

Error Rates Ideally, all packets would arrive intact, but a small fraction do not. The **error rate** is the percentage of bits or packets that are lost or damaged during delivery. (At the physical layer, it is common to measure bit error rates. At the internet layer, it is common to measure packet error rates.)

When the network is overloaded, error rates can soar because the network has to drop the packets it cannot handle. Consequently, companies must measure error rates when traffic levels are high in order to have a good understanding of error rate risks.

The impact of even small error rates can be surprisingly large. TCP tries to avoid network congestion by sending TCP segments slowly at the beginning of a connection. If these segments get through without errors, TCP sends the following segments more quickly. However, if there is a single error, the TCP process assumes that the network is overloaded. It falls back to its initial slow start rate for sending TCP segments. This can produce a major drop in throughput for applications.

Latency When packets move through a network, they will encounter some delays. The amount of delay is called **latency**. Latency is measured in **milliseconds (ms)**. A millisecond is a thousandth of a second. When latency reaches about 125 milliseconds, turn taking in telephone conversations becomes difficult. You think the other person has finished speaking, so you begin to speak—only to realize that the other party is still speaking.

Jitter A related concept is **jitter**, which Figure 4-4 illustrates. Jitter occurs when the latency between successive packets varies. Some packets will come farther apart in time, others closer in time. While jitter does not bother most applications, VoIP and streaming media are highly sensitive to jitter. If the sound is played back without adjustment, it will speed up and slow down. These variations often occur over millisecond times. As the name suggests, variable latency tends to make voice sound jittery.

Jitter is the average variability in arrival times (latency) divided by the average latency.

Engineering for Latency and Jitter Most networks were engineered to carry traditional data such as e-mail and database transmissions. In traditional applications, latency was only slightly important, and jitter was not important at all.

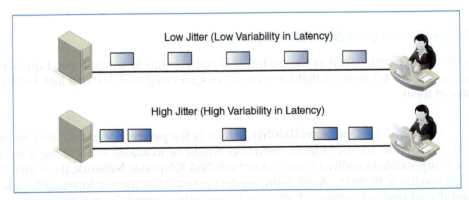

FIGURE 4-4 Jitter

However, as voice over IP (VoIP), video, and interactive applications have grown in importance, companies have begun to worry more about latency and jitter. They are finding that extensive network redesign may be needed to give good control over latency and jitter. This may include forklift upgrades for many of its switches and routers.

Test Your Understanding

5. a) What is availability? b) How does network availability usually compare to availability on the telephone network? c) When should you measure error rates? Why? d) When an application uses TCP at the transport layer, why is error rate a problem for throughput? e) What is latency? f) Give an example not listed in the text of an application for which latency is bad. g) What is jitter? h) Name an application not listed in the text for which jitter is a problem. i) Why may adding applications that cannot tolerate latency and jitter be expensive?

Service Level Agreements (SLAs)

When you buy some products, you receive a guarantee that promises that they will work and that specifies what the company will do if they do not work as promised. In networks, service providers often provide **service level agreements (SLAs)**, which are contracts that guarantee levels of performance for various metrics such as speed and availability. If a service does not meet its SLA guarantees, the service provider must pay a penalty to its customers.

Worst-Case Specification   SLA guarantees are expressed as **worst cases**. For example, an SLA for speed would guarantee that speed will be *no lower* than a certain amount. If you are downloading webpages, you want at least a certain level of speed.

Service Level Agreements (SLAs)

   Guarantees for performance

   Penalties if the network does not meet its service metrics guarantees

Guarantees specify worst cases (no worse than)

   Lowest speed (e.g., no worse than 1 Mbps)

   Maximum latency (e.g., no more than 125 ms)

   SLAs are like insurance policies

Often written on a percentage basis

   No worse than 100 Mbps 99.5% of the time

   Because as the percentage increases, additional engineering raises network costs

   100% compliance would be prohibitively expensive

Residential services are rarely sold with SLA guarantees

   It would be too expensive

FIGURE 4-5   Service Level Agreements (SLAs) (Study Figure)

You certainly would not want a speed SLA to specify a *maximum* speed. More speed is good. Why would you want to impose penalties on the network provider for exceeding some maximum speed? That would give them a strong incentive not to increase speed! Making things better is not the SLA's job.

SLA guarantees are expressed as worst cases. Service will be no worse than a specific number.

For latency, in turn, an SLA would require that latency will be *no higher* than a certain value. You might specify an SLA guarantee of a maximum of 65 ms (milliseconds). This means that you will not get worse (higher) latency.

Percentage-of-Time Elements In addition, most SLAs have percentage-of-time elements. For instance, an SLA on speed might guarantee a speed of at least 480 Mbps 99.9% of the time. This means that the speed will nearly always be at least 480 Mbps but may fall below that 0.1% of the time without incurring penalties. A smaller exception percentage might be attractive to users, but it would require a more expensive network design. Nothing can be guaranteed to work properly 100% of the time, and beyond some point, cost grows very rapidly with increasing percentage guarantees.

Corporations versus Individuals Companies that use commercial networks expect SLA guarantees in their contracts, despite the fact that engineering networks to meet these guarantees will raise costs and prices. Consumer services, however, rarely have SLAs because consumers are more price sensitive. In particular, residential Internet access service using DSL, cable modem, or cellular providers rarely offer SLAs. This means that residential service from the same ISP may vary widely across a city.

Test Your Understanding

6. a) What are service level agreements? b) Does an SLA measure the best case or the worst case? c) Would an SLA specify a highest speed or a lowest speed? d) Would an SLA specify a highest availability or a lowest availability? e) Would an SLA specify highest latency or lowest latency? f) Would an SLA guarantee specify a highest jitter or a lowest jitter? g) What happens if a carrier does not meet its SLA guarantee? h) If carrier speed falls below its guaranteed speed in an SLA, under what circumstances will the carrier *not* have to pay a penalty to the customers? i) Does residential ISP service usually have SLA guarantees? Why? j) A business has an Internet access line with a maximum speed of 100 Mbps. What two things are wrong with this SLA?

NETWORK DESIGN

Implementing a network project requires a company to go through all phases of the systems development life cycle (SDLC). In most cases, these stages are similar to those for other IT projects. One special area in the SDLC is the design of a new network or of a modified network.

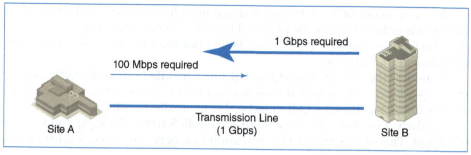

FIGURE 4-6 Two-Site Traffic Analysis

Traffic Analysis

Network design always begins with traffic requirements. **Traffic analysis** asks how much traffic must flow over each of the network's many individual transmission links. Figure 4-6 shows a trivial traffic analysis. A company only has two sites, A and B. A needs to be able to transmit to B at 100 Mbps. B needs to be able to transmit to A at 1 Gbps. Transmission links usually are symmetric, meaning that they have the same speed in both directions. Therefore, the company must install a transmission link that can handle 1 Gbps.

As soon as the number of sites grows beyond two, traffic analysis becomes difficult. Figure 4-7 shows a three-site traffic analysis. For simplicity, we will assume that transmission is symmetric between each pair of sites.

The figure shows that Site Q attaches to Site R, which attaches to Site S. Site Q is west of Site R. Site S is east of Site R. Site Q needs to be able to communicate with Site R at 45 Mbps. Site R needs to be able to communicate with Site S at 2 Gbps. Site Q needs to be able to communicate with Site S at 300 Mbps. There are two links—Link Q-R and Link R-S.

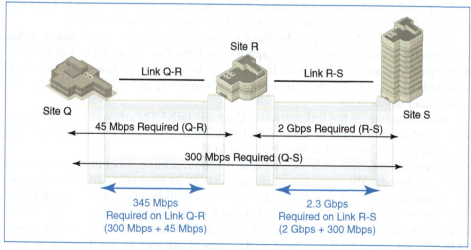

FIGURE 4-7 Three-Site Traffic Analysis

Are you overwhelmed by the last paragraph? Anyone would be! In traffic analysis, it is critical to draw the picture. Figure 4-7 shows how the three sites are laid out and what links connect them. After laying out the sites and links, you draw the three required traffic flows.

Note that the link between Q and R must handle both Q–R traffic (45 Mbps) and the Q–S traffic (300 Mbps). It does not handle any of the traffic between R and S, however. Consequently, Link Q-R must be able to handle 345 Mbps.

Similarly, Link R–S must be able to handle R–S traffic (2 Gbps) and Q–S traffic (300 Mbps). This means that the transmission link between R and S must be able to handle 2.3 Gbps.

If a company has more than two or three sites, doing traffic analysis calculations manually becomes impossible. Companies use simulation programs that try different options for using links to connect its many sites. For each case, traffic analysis is done on each link. However, you need to understand what the program is doing, and the way to do that is to work through a few examples with only a few sites.

Test Your Understanding

7. Do a three-site traffic analysis for the following scenario. Site X attaches to Site Y, which attaches to Site Z. Site X is east of Site Y. Site Z is west of Site Y. Site X needs to be able to communicate with Site Y at 3 Gbps. Site Y needs to be able to communicate with Site Z at 1 Gbps. Site X needs to be able to communicate with Site Z at 700 Mbps. Supply a picture giving the analysis. You may want to do this in Office Visio or a drawing program and then paste it into your homework. a) What traffic capacity will you need on the link between Sites X and Y? (Check Figure: 3.7 Gbps.) b) On the link between Y and Z?

Redundancy

Transmission links sometimes fail. Suppose that the transmission link between R and S in Figure 4-7 failed. Then Q would still be able to communicate with R, but Q and R would not be able to communicate with S. Obviously, this is undesirable.

The solution is to install redundant transmission capacity. **Redundant transmission capacity** is extra transmission capacity on links that is normally not needed but will be needed if another link fails. To illustrate this, Figure 4-8 again shows Sites Q, R, and S. This time, there is a direct link between between Q and S. Now, each site can talk to each other site directly.

What happens if the link between Q and R fails? The answer is that Site Q can still talk to Site S through the direct link. In addition, Q can still talk to R by sending its transmissions to S, which will send them on to R.

However, this will only be possible if the remaining links have the redundant capacity to handle the rerouted traffic as well as its normal traffic. For instance, if the link between Q and S is only 300 Mbps, this will be enough if there are no failures. However, if Link Q-R fails, the link will need another 45 Mbps. So it will need to have 345 Mbps of capacity to handle a Link Q-R failure. Link R–S will also need 45 Mbps more capacity. It will need 2.045 Gbps of capacity to handle both R–S traffic and Q–R traffic.

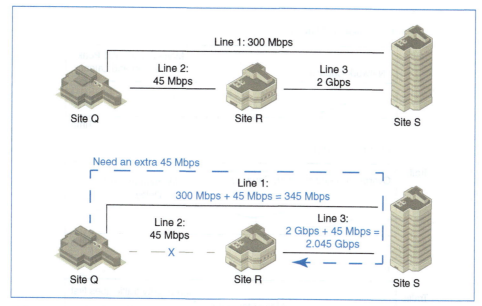

FIGURE 4-8   Three-Site Traffic Analysis with Redundancy

Test Your Understanding

8. a) What is the purpose of redundancy in transmission links? b) If the link between R and S fails in Figure 4-8, how much capacity will the other links need? (Draw the picture.) (Check Figure: Q-R will need to be able to carry 2.045 Gbps.) c) If the link between Q and S fails, how much capacity will the other links need? (Draw the picture.) d) What if both links in the previous two question parts fail? (Draw the picture.)

Momentary Traffic Peaks

Traffic volume varies constantly. Some of this is systematic. In addition, network traffic has a strong random component, and when there is randomness, there will *always* be occasional traffic spikes. These **momentary traffic peaks** typically last only a fraction of a second or a second or two, but they can be disruptive. As Figure 4-9 shows, we are concerned with momentary traffic peaks that exceed the network's transmission link capacities.

Switches and routers have small *buffers* that can hold frames or packets they cannot transmit because of the momentary congestion. They will have to wait to forward frames or packets. This produces latency. Even when buffers are present, they are limited in size. When the buffer size is exceeded, frames or packets will be lost. Applications that use TCP at the transport layer will retransmit lost segments, but retransmission will increase the traffic volume, adding to the overload.

Overprovisioning   Figure 4-9 shows three techniques for addressing momentary traffic peaks. The first is overprovisioning, which simply means installing so much more capacity than you normally need that momentary traffic peaks will be so rare and

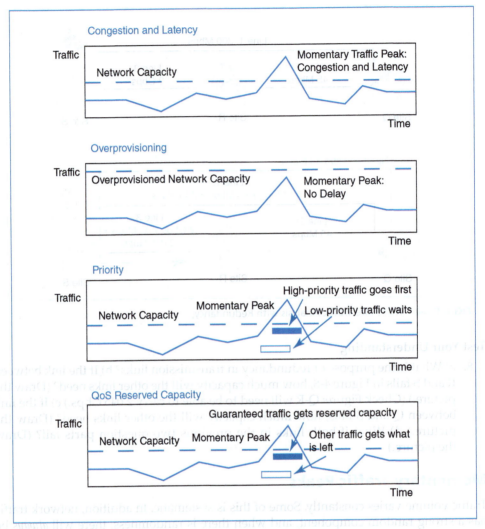

FIGURE 4-9 Addressing Momentary Traffic Peaks

so brief that they can be ignored. The advantage of overprovisioning is that it places no additional labor burden on the network staff. The disadvantage is that overprovisioning is expensive in terms of transmission link costs. Overprovisioning may make sense in LANs where additional capacity is rather inexpensive. In wide area networks, however, the high cost of transmission capacity makes this impractical.

Priority A second approach is to assign a **priority level** to frames or packets, based on their tolerance for latency and loss. Voice over IP is extremely latency intolerant. Delays in transmission make turn taking in conversations very difficult. When you hear silence, you begin talking, but as soon as you do, you realize that the other person has been talking. In addition, lost frames or packets create silences that VoIP systems must fill with artificial sound. On the other hand, e-mail can easily tolerate a delay of several seconds. Consequently, VoIP frames and packets get high priority, so that they will get through immediately. E-mail would get low priority because a delay of a few seconds is not a problem in e-mail. All switches and routers from corporations come with the ability to use priority, so priority does not increase capital expense. Priority will bring lower transmission link costs than overprovisioning, but it requires more labor in assigning priority to different traffic flows and configuring devices.

Quality of Service Guarantees   A more extreme approach is to give **QoS guarantees** to certain traffic flows such as VoIP. To provide QoS guarantees, the company must allocate **reserved capacity** on each switch and transmission line. This is great for traffic flows with QoS guarantees. However, it means that all other traffic only gets what is left over, even if the reserved capacity is not being used.

Test Your Understanding

9. a) What are momentary traffic peaks? b) How long do they last? c) What two problems do they create? d) What choices do you have for reducing the impact of delays for latency intolerant traffic? e) What is the advantage of each compared to the others? f) What is the disadvantage of each compared to the others? g) Compared to e-mail and voice over IP, what priority would you give to network control messages sent to switches and routers? (The answer is not in the text.) h) Which of the three options would work if you have chronic (frequent) traffic loads that exceed your network's capacity? (The answer is not in the text.)

STRATEGIC SECURITY PLANNING PRINCIPLES

Security Is a Management Issue

People tend to think of security as a technology issue, but security professionals know that security is primarily a management issue. Unless a firm does excellent planning, implementation, and day-to-day execution, the best security technology will be wasted. As noted security expert Bruce Schneier has often said, "Security is a process, not a product."[9] Unless firms have good security processes in place, the most technologically advanced security products will do little good.

Security is primarily a management issue, not a technology issue.

One thing that sets security management apart from other aspects of network management and IT management in general is that the security team must battle against *intelligent adversaries*, not simply against human mistakes and technical unreliability. Companies today are engaged in an escalating arms race with attackers, and security threats and defenses are evolving at a frightening rate.

---

[9] Bruce Schneier, *Crypto-Gram Newsletter*, May 15, 2000. http://www.schneier.com/crypto-gram-0005.html.

Test Your Understanding

10. a) Why is security primarily a management issue, not a technology issue? b) What sets security management apart from other aspects of network management and IT management in general?

The Plan–Protect–Respond Cycle

Figure 4-10 shows the overall process that companies follow to deal with threats. On the left is the threat environment, which consists of the attackers and attacks the company faces. We looked at the threat environment in Chapter 3.

The rest of the figure illustrates how companies mount their defenses against the threats they face. The figure shows that companies constantly cycle through three phases of security management. This is the **plan–protect–respond cycle**.

Planning   In the **plan phase**, companies assess the threat environment and decide how they will meet these threats. In strategic network management, we talk about the need to close network performance gaps by creating a project portfolio that creates the maximum benefits for the company's limited budget. Companies must do the same for security. In our discussion of the planning stage, we will focus on core principles that companies adopt to make their planning effective.

Protecting   In the **protect phase**, companies provide actual protections on a day-to-day basis. We looked at protections such as firewalls in Chapter 3. In Figure 4-10, the protect phase bubble is larger than the other three. This emphasizes the fact that the protect phase is much larger than the other two phases in terms of time

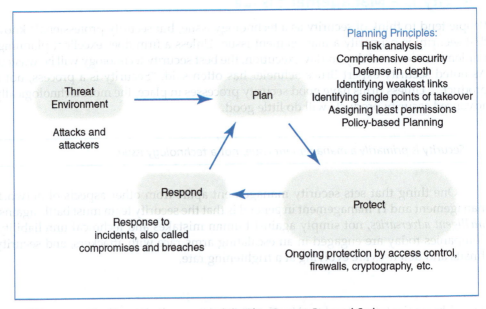

FIGURE 4-10   The Threat Environment and the Plan–Protect–Respond Cycle

spent and resource expenditure. However, without extensive and insightful planning, it is possible to spend a great deal of time and effort mounting protections without being very effective.

Responding   In the **response phase**, the company must respond when it suffers a successful security attack. We call successful attacks **compromises, incidents,** or **breaches**. It would be nice if compromises never occurred. In fact, they will. Like fire departments, security teams must respond immediately and effectively. This requires careful planning and rehearsal because every second counts in reducing the cost of breaches.

Test Your Understanding

11. a) What happens in each stage of the Plan–Protect–Respond cycle? b) Which stage consumes the most time?

Security Planning Principles

Perhaps more than any other aspect of IT, effective security depends on effective planning. Security planning is a complex process that we can discuss only briefly. We will focus on some key planning principles that must be observed in all security thinking.

Risk Analysis   Many would say that the goal of security is to stop all threats to the corporation. Surprisingly, that is not true. Stopping all attacks is impossible. Despite strong security efforts, there will still be some risk of a compromise. There has always been crime in society, and there always will be. The same is true of security incidents. No matter how much money a company spends on security, it cannot stop all threats. It could go bankrupt trying. Rather, the goal of security is to reduce the risk of attacks to the extent that is **economically feasible**.

The goal of security is to reduce the risk of attacks to the extent that is economically feasible.

Security Is a Management Issue, Not a Technology Issue

    Without good management, technology cannot be effective

    A company must have good security processes

Security Planning Principles

    Risk analysis

    Comprehensive security

    Defense in depth

    Weakest link analysis

    Single points of takeover

    Least permissions in access control

FIGURE 4-11   Security Planning Principles

Risk analysis is the process of balancing risks and protection costs. Corporate security planners have to ask whether investing in a countermeasure against a particular threat is economically justified. For example, if the probable annual loss from a threat is $10,000 but the security measures needed to thwart the threat will cost $200,000 per year, the firm obviously should *not* spend the money. Instead, it should accept the probable loss.

Risk analysis is the process of balancing risks and protection costs.

Figure 4-12 gives an example of a risk analysis for a hypothetical situation. Without a countermeasure, the damage per successful attack is expected to be $1,000,000, and the annual probability of a successful attack is 20%. Therefore, the annual probable damage is $200,000 without a countermeasure. The probable net annual outlay therefore is $200,000 if no action is taken.

Countermeasure A is designed to cut the damage of a successful attack in half. So the damage per successful attack is expected to be $500,000 instead of a million dollars. The countermeasure will not reduce the probability of a successful attack, so that continues to be 20%. With Countermeasure A, then, the annual probable damage will be $100,000. However, the countermeasure is not free. It will cost $20,000 per year. Therefore, the net annual probable outlay is $120,000 with the countermeasure.

Countermeasure A, then, will reduce the net annual probable outlay from $200,000 to $120,000. The countermeasure has a value of $80,000 per year. This is positive, so Countermeasure A is justified.

There is also a second candidate countermeasure, Countermeasure B. This countermeasure will reduce the probability of a successful attack by 25%, from 20% to 15%. The loss would not be reduced at all. This countermeasure would cost $60,000 annually, giving a net annual probable outlay of $210,000. This exceeds the no-countermeasure's figure of $200,000. The annual probable outlay is negative $10,000 if the countermeasure is used. This countermeasure would not make sense even if it was the only candidate countermeasure.

Security professionals may be tempted to think of costs in terms of hardware and software spending. However, most countermeasures require extensive security labor. In fact, labor is often the biggest cost. More broadly, security often increases labor costs

Countermeasure	None	A	B
Damage per successful attack	$1,000,000	$500,000	$1,000,000
Annual probability of a successful attack	20%	20%	15%
Annual probable damage	$200,000	$100,000	$150,000
Annual cost of countermeasure	$0	$20,000	$60,000
Net annual probable outlay	$200,000	$120,000	$210,000
Annual value of countermeasure	$0	$80,000	($10,000)

FIGURE 4-12 Risk Analysis Calculation

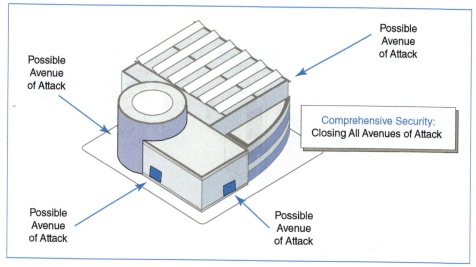

FIGURE 4-13   Comprehensive Security

for users. If users spend even a few extra minutes each time they must use a particular resource, this can lead to substantial cost. It could tip the scales against installing the countermeasure.

Comprehensive Security   To be safe from attack, a company must close off *all* avenues of attack. Figure 4-13 illustrates this principle. In contrast, an attacker only needs to find one unprotected avenue to succeed. Although it is difficult to achieve **comprehensive security**, it is essential to come as close as possible.

Comprehensive security is closing off all avenues of attack.

Defense in Depth   Another critical planning principle is defense in depth. Every protection will break down occasionally. If attackers have to break through only one line of defense, they will succeed during these vulnerable periods. However, if an attacker has to break through two, three, or more lines of defense, the breakdown of a single defense technology will not be enough to allow the attacker to succeed. Having successive lines of defense that must *all* be breached for an attacker to succeed is called **defense in depth**. Figure 4-14 illustrates the principle.

Having several lines of defense that must all *be breached for an attacker to succeed is called defense in depth.*

In the figure, there are four protections in succession. The first is a border firewall at the connection between the company site and the Internet. The second is a host firewall on a particular server. The third is the use of good practice in patching

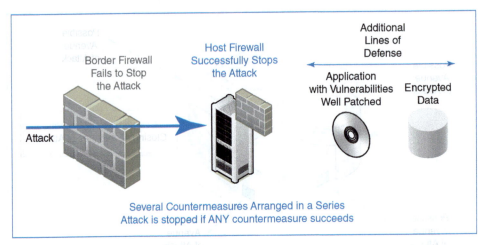

FIGURE 4-14 Defense in Depth

application vulnerabilities. The fourth is encrypting all data for confidentiality so that the attacker cannot read sensitive information even if all other defenses fail.

The figure shows what happens if the border firewall does not stop an attack. In this case, the host firewall catches the attack and stops it. The company should fix the border firewall quickly, so that it becomes part of the effective defense, but attack packets will not get through to the target data while the border firewall is being fixed.

Identify and Manage Weakest Links   Defense in depth is a way to increase security by having a series of protections so a single failure will not compromise security. In contrast, many individual protections consist of a series of internal steps that must *all* work if the protection is to succeed. If one fails, the countermeasure fails. For example, an antivirus program may protect a user by identifying a malicious attachment. However, if the user fails to use good judgment and opens the attachment anyway, there is no protection.

Figure 4-15 shows how weakest links can compromise a countermeasure. Here the countermeasure is a firewall. The firewall has five components, all of which must be effective for the firewall to be effective. These are the firewall hardware, firewall software, a firewall access control list (ACL), the firewall log file, and the practice of reading the log file frequently. In the figure, the ACL is defective. Even if all the other elements are fully effective, the firewall will fail to stop an attack. Similarly, if the company fails to read the firewall log file regularly, it will fail to keep the ACL up to date, and this will cause the firewall to fail.

It is easy to confuse defense in depth and weakest link analysis because a series of elements is present in both.

- Typically, defense in depth involves a series of different countermeasures, while weakest link analysis involves a single countermeasure with multiple components.
- In defense in depth, ANY element must be effective to stop an attack. In weakest link analysis, ALL elements must be effective to stop an attack.

FIGURE 4-15 Weakest Link Analysis

Identify and Manage Single Points of Takeover Another principle is to focus on **potential single points of takeover**. Later in this chapter, we will see that companies often control many individual firewalls through a single firewall policy server (see Figure 4-16). If an attacker takes over the firewall policy server, there is no end to the damage that he or she can do. The central firewall policy server is a **potential single point of takeover**, which means that if an attacker can take it over, they gain control over a significant portion of your network.

Companies usually cannot and do not want to eliminate potential single points of failure. Having a central firewall policy server greatly improves a company's control over its firewalls, eliminating inconsistencies and reducing management costs. Eliminating this single point of failure by going back to configuring firewalls individually is not an answer to the threat. Rather, it is critical for companies to identify all single points of takeover and harden them very well against attacks.

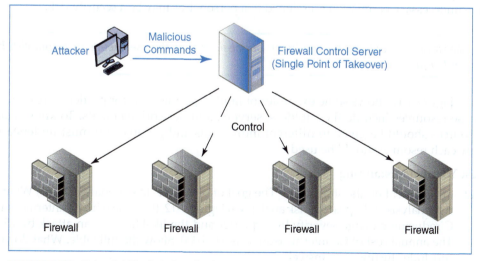

FIGURE 4-16 Potential Single Point of Takeover

Assigning Least Permissions in Access Control   Security planners constantly worry about access to resources. People who get access to resources can do damage to those resources. Not surprisingly, companies work very hard to control access to their resources. **Access control** is limiting who may have access to each resource and limiting his or her permissions when using the resource.

Access control is limiting who may have access to each resource and limiting his or her permissions when using the resource.

One aspect of access control that we saw in the previous chapter is authentication, which is requiring users requesting access to prove their identities. However, just because you know who someone is does not mean that he or she should have unfettered access to your resources. (There undoubtedly are several people you know whom you would not let drive your car.)

Authorizations or **permissions** are the actions that an authenticated user is allowed to take on the resource. For example, although everyone is permitted to view the U.S. Declaration of Independence, no one is allowed to add his or her own signature at the bottom.

Authorizations or permissions are the actions that an authenticated user is allowed to take on the resource.

An important principle in assigning permissions is to give each person **least permissions**—the minimum permissions that the user needs to accomplish his or her job. In the case of access to team documents, for example, most team members may be given read-only access, in which the user can read team documents but not change them. It is far less work to give the user extensive or full permissions so that he or she does not have to be given additional permissions later. However, it is a terrible security practice. If even one unnecessary permission is assigned to a person, this may be a security risk.

Least permissions are the minimum permissions that the user needs to accomplish his or her job.

Figure 4-17 shows some examples of limited permissions for particular resources. These resources include files, folders, servers, and network elements. To know what resources should be given to different individuals and groups, you must understand how each resource should be used.

Test Your Understanding

12. a) Comment on the statement, "The goal of security is to eliminate risk." b) What is risk analysis? c) Repeat the risk analysis in Figure 4-12, this time with Countermeasure C reducing damage severity by a quarter and the likelihood of an attack by 75%. The annual cost of Countermeasure C is $175,000. Show the full table. What do you conclude? Justify your answer.

Access Control

> If attackers cannot get access to a resource, they cannot exploit it
>
> Access control is limiting who may have access to each resource
>
> and limiting his or her permissions when using the resource

Authentication versus Authorizations (Permissions)

> Authentication: Proof of identity
>
> Authorizations: Permissions a particular authorized user is given with a resource
>
> Just because a user is authenticated does not mean that he or she will be permitted to do everything

Principle of Least Permissions

> Give each authenticated user only the minimum permissions he or she needs to do his or her job
>
> Cannot do unauthorized things that will compromise security

Examples of Limited Permissions

> Create files but not delete files
>
> Cannot access files above a specified level of sensitivity
>
> Read files but not write (edit) them
>
> See files in own folders but not all folders
>
> Connect to the person's department server but not to the Finance server
>
> Do certain things but cannot give others permission to do them

---

FIGURE 4-17 Least Permissions in Access Control

13. a) What is comprehensive security? b) Why is it important? c) What is defense in depth? d) Why is defense in depth necessary? e) Distinguish between defense in depth and weakest link analysis. f) What must companies do about potential single points of takeover? g) Distinguish between authentication and authorizations. h) What is another term for authorizations? i) What is the principle of least permissions? j) Why is it important?

Policy-Based Security

We have discussed the importance of security planning and major security principles. Now we will look at how plans are implemented in well-run organizations.

Policies The heart of security management is the creation and implementation of security policies. Figure 4-18 illustrates how policies should be used. **Policies** are broad statements that specify *what should be accomplished*. For example, a policy might be, "All information on USB RAM sticks must be encrypted." Policymakers have the overview knowledge that operational people do not have. For instance, policymakers may know that new laws create serious liabilities unless USB RAM sticks are encrypted. Operation-level people may not realize this.

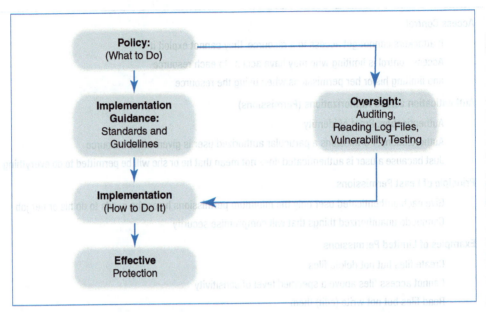

FIGURE 4-18 Policy-Based Security

Policy versus Implementation Note that the policy does not specify which encryption technology should be used or other implementation details. Put another way, policies describe *what* should be done, not *how* to do it.

This separation of policy from implementation permits the implementers to carry out the policy in the best way possible for particular situations. Policymakers should have superior overview knowledge. However, implementers know about specific technologies and the local situation. They have the specific knowledge that policymakers do not, including technical knowledge. Unless they are given the latitude to use this knowledge, weak implementation is likely to doom the policy's effectiveness. Separating policies from implementation prevents senior security professionals from micromanaging operating-level people inappropriately. The separation of policies from implementation uses the strengths of both policy makers and implementers.

> *Policymakers have the overview knowledge that operational people do not have. Implementers know about specific technologies and the local situation that policymakers do not. Separating policies from implementation uses the strengths of both.*

The separation of policy from implementation certainly does not mean that policy is irrelevant to implementation. It is easy to get lost in implementation details. Having a clear policy permits everybody involved in implementation to stay synchronized by checking whether what he or she is doing will lead to the successful implementation of the policy.

Implementation Guidance   In many cases, the policymaker will only specify the policy. However, in some cases, the policymakers will also create some implementation guidance. **Implementation guidance** consists of instructions that are more specific than policies but less specific than implementation.

Implementation guidance consists of instructions that are more specific than policies but less specific than implementation.

For example, after establishing a policy that USB RAM sticks must be encrypted, implementation guidance might be added in the form of a directive that the encryption must use keys at least 128 bits long. This ensures that implementers will not have the latitude to choose weak encryption that can be defeated by an attacker.

There are two general forms of implementation guidance: standards and guidelines. **Standards** are *mandatory* directives that *must* be followed. Requiring 128-bit encryption is a standard. It is mandatory for implementers to follow the directive.

Standards are mandatory directives that must be followed.

In contrast, **guidelines** are directives that *should* be followed. This gives the implementer not only guidance but also some leeway in deciding whether to follow the guidance. This does not mean that implementers can ignore guidelines. They *must* consider them carefully. However, for good reason, they can elect not to follow them.[10] For example, a guideline that security staff members should have three years of security work experience indicates that someone hiring a security staff member must consider that having at least three years of experience is a reasonable expectation. If the person doing the hiring selects someone with only two years of work experience, he or she should have a very good reason for doing so. Following guidelines is optional, but seriously considering guidelines is mandatory.

Guidelines are implementation guidance directives that should be followed but that need not be followed, depending on the context.

When do firms use guidelines instead of standards for implementation guidance? The answer is that they use guidelines for situations that are not amenable to black-and-white rules. Encryption strength is relatively easy to specify. The quality of work experience requires human judgment.

---

[10] In the *Pirates of the Caribbean* movies, there was a running joke that the Pirate Code is "more of a guideline, really."

Oversight Figure 4-18 also shows that policymakers cannot merely toss policies and implementation guidance out and ignore how implementation is done. It is essential for management to exercise **oversight**, which refers to a collection of methods for ensuring that policies have been implemented appropriately in a particular implementation.

Oversight is a collection of methods for ensuring that policies have been implemented appropriately in a particular implementation.

One form of oversight is an audit. An **audit** samples actions taken within the firm to ensure that policies are being implemented properly. Note that an audit only *samples* actions. It does not look at everything, which would be impossible to do. However, if the sampling is done well, the auditor can issue an opinion on whether a policy is being carried out appropriately based on well-considered data.

An audit samples actions taken within the firm to ensure that policies are being implemented properly.

Another form of oversight is reading **log files**. Whenever users take actions, their actions should be recorded in log files. Reading log files can reveal improper behavior. Of course, if these log files are not read, they are useless. Log files should be read daily or even several times each day. Few people enjoy reading log files to look for problems, so enforcement must be carefully tracked.

Reading log files can reveal improper behavior.

Yet another important oversight mechanism is vulnerability testing. Simply put, **vulnerability testing** is attacking your own systems before attackers do, so that you can identify weaknesses and fix them before they are exploited by attackers. It is important to set up vulnerability tests cautiously, however. Before doing a vulnerability test, the tester must have explicit written permissions for each test based on a detailed description of what will be done and what damage might be done accidentally. Vulnerability testers who do not take these precautions have been accused of making malicious attacks. This has resulted in firings and even jail terms.

Vulnerability testing is attacking your own systems before attackers do, so that you can identify weaknesses and fix them before they are exploited by attackers.

Note that the policy drives both implementation and oversight. Implementers who attempt to implement the policy must interpret the policy. Auditors and other oversight professionals must also interpret the policy. If the implementers are lax, the auditors should be able to identify this. However, if oversight practitioners and implementers disagree, this may simply mean that they are interpreting the policy differently. Policymakers may find that one or the other has made a poor choice in interpreting the policy. They may also find that the policy itself is ambiguous or simply wrong. The important thing is to identify problems and then resolve them.

Policies drive both implementation and oversight.

Effective Protection   Policies certainly do not give protection by themselves. Neither may unexamined implementations. Protection is most likely to be effective when excellent implementation is subject to strong oversight.

Test Your Understanding

14. a) What is a policy? b) Distinguish between policy and implementation. c) What is the benefit of separating policies from implementation? d) Why is oversight important? e) Compare the specificity of policies, implementation guidance, and implementation. f) Distinguish between standards and guidelines. g) Which *must* be followed? h) Must guidelines be considered? i) List the three types of oversight listed in the text. j) What is vulnerability testing, and why is it done? k) Why is it important for policy to drive both implementation and oversight?

CENTRALIZED NETWORK MANAGEMENT

Given the complexity of networks, network managers need to turn to network management software to support much of their work. Many of these are network visibility tools, which help managers comprehend what is going on in their networks.

Ping

The oldest network visibility tool is the basic ping command available in all operating systems. If a network is having problems, a network administrator can simply **ping** a wide range of IP addresses in the company. When a host receives a ping, it should send back a reply. If it replies, it is obviously in operation. If it does not, it may not be. In Figure 4-19, host 10.1.2.5 does not respond to its ping. This signals a potential problem.

By analyzing which hosts and routers respond or do not respond, then drawing the unreachable devices on a map, the administrator is likely to be able to see a pattern that indicates the root cause of the problem. Of course, manually pinging a wide range of IP addresses could take a prohibitive amount of time. Fortunately, there are many programs that ping a range of IP addresses and portray the results.

Test Your Understanding

15. If you ping a host and it does not respond, what can you conclude?

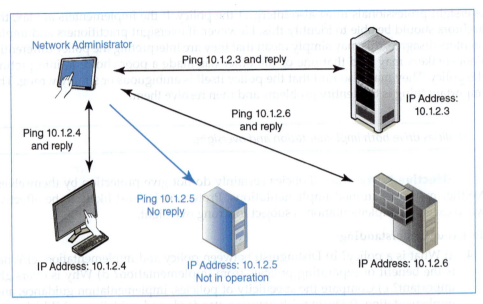

Network Administrator

Ping 10.1.2.3 and reply

IP Address:
10.1.2.3

Ping 10.1.2.6
and reply

Ping 10.1.2.4
and reply

Ping 10.1.2.5
No reply

IP Address: 10.1.2.4

IP Address: 10.1.2.5
Not in operation

IP Address: 10.1.2.6

FIGURE 4-19   Ping

The Simple Network Management Protocol (SNMP)

Ping can tell you if a host is available. It can also tell you the latency in reaching that host. For remote device management, most network operation centers use more powerful network visualization products based on the **simple network management protocol (SNMP)**, which is illustrated in Figure 4-20. In the network operations center (NOC), there is a computer that runs a program called the **manager**. This manager manages a large number of **managed devices**, such as switches, routers, servers, and PCs.

Agents   Actually, the manager does not talk directly with the managed devices. Rather, each managed device has an **agent**, which is hardware, software, or both. The manager talks to the agent, which in response talks to the managed device. To give an analogy, recording stars have agents who negotiate contracts with studios and performance events. Agents provide a similar service for devices.

Get Commands and the Management Information Base (MIB)   The network operations center constantly collects data from the managed devices using SNMP **Get** commands. It places this data in a **management information base (MIB)**. Data in the MIB allows the NOC managers to understand the traffic flowing through the network. This can include failure points, links that are approaching their capacity, or unusual traffic patterns that may indicate attacks on the network.

Set   In addition, the manager can send **Set** commands to the switches and other devices within the network. Set commands can reroute traffic around failed equipment or transmission links, reroute traffic around points of congestion, or turn off expensive transmission links during periods when less expensive links can carry the traffic adequately.

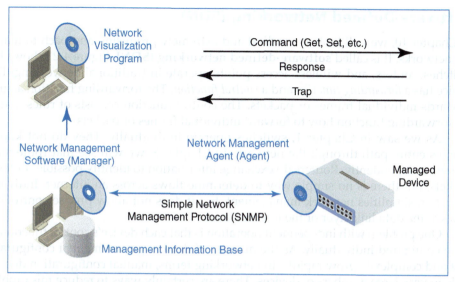

FIGURE 4-20 Simple Network Management Protocol (SNMP)

Trap Normally, the manager sends a command and the agent responds. However, if the agent senses a problem, it can send a **Trap** command on its own initiative. The trap command gives details of the problem.

Network Visualization Program There is one more program in the figure—a **network visualization program**. This program takes results from the MIB and interprets the data to display results in maps, find root causes for problems, and do other tasks. Note that this functionality is *not* included in the simple network management protocol. SNMP simply collects the data in a way that network visualization programs can use. This lack of specification allows network visualization program vendors to innovate without being constrained by standards.

Automation Many other network management chores can be automated to reduce the amount of work that network managers need to spend on minutia. For example, many routers are given a standard corporate configuration when they are installed. Doing this manually can take an hour or more per router. However, it may be possible to create a standard configuration, store it, and simply download it onto new routers. In addition, if corporate standard configurations change or a patch must be installed on all routers, it may be possible simply to "push out" these changes to all routers.

Test Your Understanding

16. a) List the main elements in SNMP. b) Does the manager communicate directly with the managed device? Explain. c) Distinguish between Get and Set commands. d) Where does the manager store the information it receives from Get commands? e) What kind of message can agents initiate? f) Why is network automation important? g) What do network visualization programs do? h) Why is the ability to push changes out to devices beneficial?

Software-Defined Networking (SDN)

In Chapter 10, we will look at a radical and extremely promising approach to managing networks. It is called **software-defined networking (SDN)**. Figure 4-21 shows how switches, routers, and wireless access points operate in traditional networking. Each device has a *forwarding function* and a *control function*. The forwarding function actually forwards individual frames or packets. The control function consists of rules that tell the forwarding function how to forward individual frames or packets.

As we saw in Chapter 1, switches operate individually. They do not know a frame's entire path through the network. In Chapter 8, we will see that routers also operate independently. Routers do exchange information to identify possible routes for packets, but there is no simple way to determine flows across an internet. Individual operation simplifies network management, but it does not allow precise control over flows at the data link layer or the internet layer.

One problem with independent operation is that each device's control function has to be configured individually. As the number of devices grows, manual configuration cost and complexity grow rapidly. In networking terms, manual configuration does not scale to very large numbers of devices. There are certainly ways to reduce this problem. For instance, standard configurations for routers can be stored and downloaded rapidly to new routers. However, the need for some manual configuration still remains on a per-router basis.

Although this approach has worked for many years, its limitations are rapidly growing more serious. These were first noticed in cloud server farms. In a multitenant server farm, it is important to ensure that virtual machines for different customers cannot talk to each other through the site's local area network. This means that forwarding rules may have to change each time the cloud service provider spawns a new VM. Given the rate of VM spawning in cloud server farms, manual reconfiguration of the server farm network has become extremely difficult, especially when many routers and switches have to be reconfigured after each VM spawn.

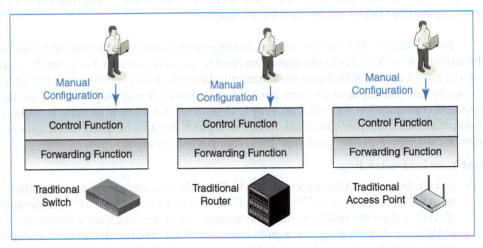

FIGURE 4-21 Traditional Device Control in Networking

In 2008, researchers created a new approach, which they called software-defined networking (SDN). As Figure 4-22 shows, the forwarding function of each switch or router operates as it always has, to forward frames or packets. However, the control function does not stay the same. Instead, the control function accepts commands from an **SDN controller**. Formally, **software-defined networking (SDN)** separates the network forwarding function from the control function and places the control function in an SDN controller.

Software-defined networking (SDN) separates the network device forwarding function from the control function and places the control function in an SDN controller.

SDN controllers permit centralized control of all network devices, including switches, routers, wireless access points, and other possible forwarding devices. The researchers created software-defined networking to study experimental forwarding algorithms in working network environments. In CSP server farms, however, operators soon discovered that this approach was exactly what they needed to manage their own networks as agilely as they managed their VM instances. As we will see in Chapter 10, software-defined networking is beginning to spread not only within data centers but also across local and wide area networks. If SDN does become widespread, it will completely change the way firms manage their networks, and it will do so in a very positive way. Nothing in networking is so potentially disruptive for the field.

Figure 4-22 shows the SDN controller communicating with switches and routers through the OpenFlow Protocol. **OpenFlow** is an open (nonproprietary) protocol for communication between an SDN controller and SDN-compatible switches, routers, and access points. Strictly speaking, using OpenFlow is not necessary for SDN.

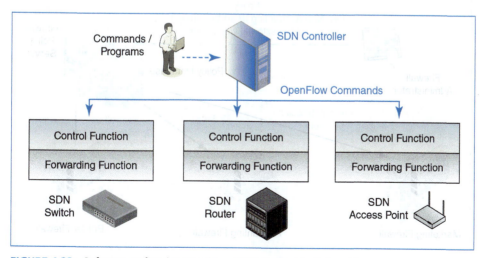

FIGURE 4-22   Software-Defined Networking (SDN) Control in Networking

However, if OpenFlow becomes dominant, today's difficult problem of controlling networks made from the products of multiple vendors will be solved.

OpenFlow is an open (nonproprietary) protocol for communication between an SDN controller and SDN-compatible switches, routers, and access points.

Test Your Understanding

17. a) What are the two functions in network forwarding devices? b) Traditionally, how is the control function in each device managed? c) What problems does this create? d) In a server farm, what may have to be changed if a new VM is spawned? e) How are device control functions managed in software-defined networking? f) What device manages the control functions on forwarding devices? g) What are the benefits of SDN?

CENTRALIZED SECURITY MANAGEMENT

Centralized management is also important in security management. For example, a company may have dozens or even hundreds of firewalls on its network. It would be easy to accidentally misconfigure a few of these firewalls to ignore individual access control rules. Figure 4-23 shows a central firewall management system designed to prevent such oversights. The firewall administrator creates high-level access policies for firewalls to implement. In the figure, the **firewall policy** being implemented is that any IP address not in the accounting department may access any external

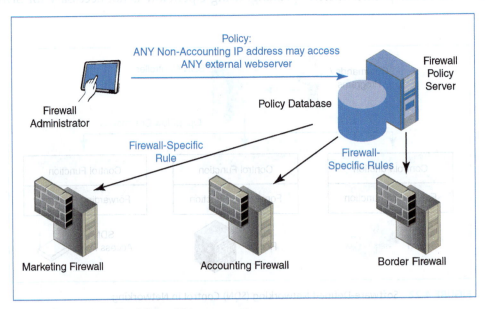

FIGURE 4-23 Centralized Firewall Management

webserver. Many companies allow access to all external webservers from all internal clients. This security administrator has decided that open access is good but that it should not extend to hosts within the accounting department. The firewall administrator sends this policy to the **firewall policy server**, which places the policy in its policy database.

The firewall policy server then creates detailed **firewall rules** to implement this new policy (such as ACL rules in stateful inspection firewalls). It then pushes these rules out to all of the company's many firewalls. These rules are firewall-specific. The Accounting firewall, for example, may get a different firewall rule to implement this policy than the main border firewall or the Marketing firewall.

Separating firewall policies from firewall rules (which implement firewall policies) is an example of policy-based security. The firewall administrator sets high-level policies. The firewall policy server does the work needed to convert this policy into individual firewall rules. The firewall policy server will not make human mistakes like forgetting to configure a particular firewall. If there is a question about a particular firewall rule on a particular firewall, furthermore, the firewall administrator can ask what policy it implements. Policies are usually easier to understand than specific firewall rules.

Test Your Understanding

18. a) Distinguish between firewall policies and firewall rules. b) When a firewall administrator sends a policy to the policy server, what does the policy server do? c) Which is easier to understand—a firewall policy or a firewall rule?

CONCLUSION

Synopsis

This is the last of four introductory chapters. In this chapter, we looked at network and security management. Technology is never enough. How well people manage the firm's networks and security makes all the difference in the world.

Networks today must work well. Networks must meet goals for quality-of-service (QoS) metrics. We looked at speed, availability, error rates, latency, and jitter. After discussing individual QoS metrics, we looked at service level agreements (SLAs), which guarantee performance levels for certain QoS metrics, usually for a certain percentage of time. Many find it confusing that QoS metrics specify that service will be *no worse* than certain values. For example, SLAs will specify a minimum speed, not a maximum speed.

Designing networks is a complex process. We looked at basic principles of traffic analysis, which identifies the traffic that various transmission links must sustain, including redundancy in case of link failures. Traffic analysis forms the core of network design. We also looked at ways to manage momentary traffic peaks, including overprovisioning, priority, and QoS guarantees with reserved capacity.

Security management follows the plan–protect–respond cycle. Planning prepares the company for day-to-day protection both now and in the future. Response happens when protections break down, as they inevitably do. Of course, experience in managing protections and responses feeds back into the planning process.

Strategic security planning uses the following six planning principles that must be considered in every project plan:

- *Risk analysis*. Many people believe that the purpose of security is to eliminate risk. Unfortunately, all countermeasures cost money. It is always critical to balance potential damage against the cost to prevent it. The purpose of security is to reduce risk to a degree that is economically justified.
- *Comprehensive security*. Attackers only have to find one avenue of attack into a firm or into a specific asset. In contrast, the security staff must discover and close off all avenues of attack. This comprehensive security cannot always be achieved, but firms must constantly look for unprotected avenues of approach.
- *Defense in depth*. Every security protection sometimes breaks down. Defense in depth means creating a *series of protections* that the attacker must break through to succeed. Unless *all* fail, the attacker will not succeed.
- *Avoiding weakest links*. Some *individual protections* have multiple parts that *must all work effectively* if the protection is to work. If one component is quite likely to be defective, then the protection's value will be suspect. For example, if someone is likely to fall for spear phishing and opens an attachment with a virus, the best technical protections will break down.
- *Avoiding potential single points of failure*. The centralization of functions can provide efficiency and control. However, when functions are centralized, this often creates a potential single point of takeover that could lead to serious problems if an attacker were to take control. Potential single points of failure usually cannot be eliminated. Instead, they must be identified and given intense attention.
- *Assigning least permissions*. Even if you authenticate someone, this does not mean that you will let him or her do anything to your resources. It is important to give authenticated users the minimum permissions (authorizations) they need to do their work.

We looked at policy-based security in which a high-level policy group creates security policies and lower-level staff members implement the policy. Policies specify *what is to be done*. Implementation focuses on *how to do it*. This division of labor works because high-level policy people have a broad understanding of security risks and can create policies that will give comprehensive security. Implementation is done by lower-level staff members who know the technology and local situation in far greater detail. They are best suited for deciding how to do implementations. Sometimes, the policy group creates intermediate implementation guidance consisting of standards (which must be followed) and guidelines that must be considered, although they do not have to be followed if there is good reason not to. A separate oversight process ensures that implementations are faithful to appropriate policies.

We closed with a discussion of centralized management for networking and security. By simplifying and automating many actions, centralized management prevents labor costs from increasing as rapidly as networking and security device numbers. We began with ping, which is in the toolbox of every network administrators. Network management depends heavily on the Simple Network Management Protocol (SNMP). We will look at SNMP again in more detail in Chapter 9. In network management, software-defined networking (SDN) may revolutionize the way we manage networks by allowing us to control all network forwarding devices from an SDN server.

For centralized security management, we saw how firewall policy servers accept firewall policies and then send customized firewall rules to individual firewalls to implement the policy.

END-OF-CHAPTER QUESTIONS

Thought Questions

4-1. Your home is connected to the Internet. You get to create SLAs that the ISP must follow. Being reasonable, write SLAs you would like to have for the following things: a) Write an SLA for speed. b) Write an SLA for availability. c) Write an SLA for latency. d) Write an SLA for jitter. Do not just say what each SLA should include; actually write the SLAs as the ISP would write them.

4-2. A company has offices in Honolulu, Seattle, Ogden, and Dublin, Ireland. There are transmission links between Honolulu and Seattle, Seattle and Ogden, and Ogden and Dublin. Honolulu needs to communicate at 1 Gbps with each other site. Seattle and Dublin only need to communicate with each other at 1 Mbps. Ogden and Dublin need to communicate at 2 Gbps, and Ogden and Seattle need to communicate with each other at 10 Mbps. How much traffic will each transmission link have to carry? Show your work. (Check Figure: Ogden-Seattle needs 2.011 Gbps.)

4-3. a) Suppose that an attack would do $100,000 in damage and has a 15% annual probability of success. Spending $9,000 per year on Measure A would cut the annual probability of success by 75%. Do a risk analysis comparing benefits and costs. Show your work clearly. b) Should the company spend the money? Explain. c) Do another risk analysis if Measure A costs $20,000 per year. Again, show your work. d) Should the company spend the money? Explain.

4-4. An executive opened an e-mail attachment because the content looked like it came from a subordinate. In addition, the executive knew that the company did antivirus filtering. Actually, this was a spear phishing attempt, and the attachment contained malware. What security planning principle does this breakdown represent?

4-5. Edward Snowden, a server administrator, was able to copy many CIA secret and top secret files to a USB RAM stick. What security planning principle breakdown allowed this?

4-6. Why do you think companies create guidelines for some things instead of creating standards for them?

4-7. If oversight practitioners and implementers disagree on whether an implementation is correct, what might be wrong?

Perspective Questions

4-8. What was the most surprising thing you learned in this chapter?

4-9. What was the most difficult part of this chapter for you?

Chapter 4a

Hands-On: Microsoft Office Visio

LEARNING OBJECTIVE

By the end of this chapter, you should be able to:

- Create a simple Visio diagram.

WHAT IS VISIO?

Microsoft Office Visio is a drawing program. The professional version has special symbols for drawing network diagrams. Visio is widely used by network professionals to visualize networks they are designing.

USING VISIO

Visio is part of the Microsoft Office family. Installing Visio is like installing any other Office product.

Figure 4a-1 shows how to start a Visio drawing. Of course, this begins by selecting File and then New. In the figure, Network has been selected for the type of drawing. Detailed Network Diagram has been selected.

As Figure 4a-2 shows, this brings up a window with a canvas on which you can drag shapes. In the figure, the shape of a generic server has been dragged on to the screen. As you can see, many other network diagramming shapes can be dragged onto the screen.

After you have added the devices you need, it is time to begin showing how they are connected. As Figure 4a-3 shows, there is a connector icon at the top of the screen.

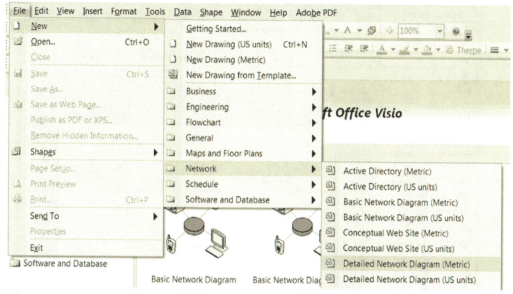

FIGURE 4A-1   Starting a Visio Drawing

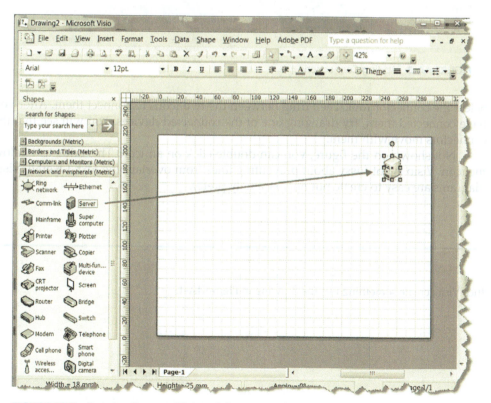

FIGURE 4A-2   Drawing Canvas with Icon Being Dragged

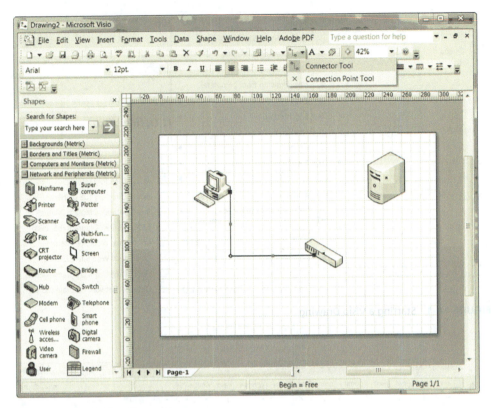

FIGURE 4A-3 Adding Connections

Select the connector tool. Then drag between the two icons to connect them. After you have connected them, try dragging one of the connected devices. You will see that the connectors move with them.

Not shown on the figure, you can double-click on an icon. This adds text below the icon. Visio is not fussy about preventing lines from overlapping text. Overall, Visio diagrams are easy to create but not extremely pretty.

Exercise

In Microsoft Office Visio, create something like the drawing in Figure 4A-1.

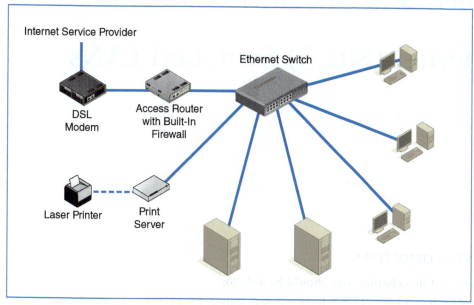

FIGURE 4A-4 Sample Drawing

Chapter 5

Ethernet (802.3) Switched LANs

LEARNING OBJECTIVES

By the end of this chapter, you should be able to:

- Explain how Ethernet LAN technology is standardized.
- Describe digital and binary signaling and why they reduce transmission errors.
- Explain the technologies of 4-pair UTP and optical fiber and compare and contrast their relative strengths and weaknesses.
- Explain full duplex transmission and the distinction between serial and parallel transmission.
- Design a physical network based on knowledge of Ethernet physical link standards, including link aggregation.
- Describe the Ethernet frame. Explain basic Ethernet data link layer switch operation.
- Explain why the Rapid Spanning Tree Protocol is necessary and how it functions. Explain priority, manageability, and power over Ethernet (POE) in Ethernet LANs.
- Describe security threats to Ethernet LANs and how they are addressed by the 802.1X and 802.1AE standards.

ETHERNET BEGINS

Bob Metcalfe, a PhD student at Harvard University, wrote his dissertation on the new ARPANET. His committee turned it down, deeming it insufficiently theoretical. Metcalfe was devastated. He had been offered a position at the Xerox Palo Alto Research Center (PARC), which was doing cutting-edge high technology research. In particular, PARC had just built the Alto, which looked like a PC but was far more powerful. It had a full-page display and a graphical user interface using the mouse, which PARC adopted from

Doug Engelbart's Augmentation Research Center at SRI. Apple later popularized this interface with the Macintosh.

When Metcalfe told Xerox that he was not graduating, PARC told him to come anyway and finish his dissertation later. Metcalfe asked for a brief delay to allow him to visit the University of Hawaii's ALOHAnet project first. ALOHAnet did packet switching using radio. Stations could transmit anytime they wished, and a central hub would retransmit correctly received packets. If two stations transmitted at the same time, their packets (actually frames) became garbled and were not retransmitted. Metcalfe was granted the delay. During his visit, he analyzed the ALOHAnet protocol and found several ways to improve turn-taking. He added the analysis to his dissertation. This time, his committee accepted it.

At Xerox, he was given the task of networking the Altos with one another and with PARC's high-speed laser printer. He realized that his improvements to the ALOHAnet protocol would permit him to run a similar network over physical transmission media. There were several possible physical technologies to consider. To keep his options open, he referred to physical media generically as the Ether, after a discredited 19th century theory about how light propagated. He hand-soldered printed circuit boards to implement his protocol, and he added them to the Altos. Before the end of the year, the Alto Ethernet was operational and running well. Although the network only ran at 2.94 Mbps, it had great potential.

Xerox decided not to commercialize Ethernet. Metcalfe generated outside interest and started his own company, 3Com. In 1982, the IEEE started the 802 Committee to set standards for networks on and near a customer site. The committee assigned Ethernet standardization to its 802.3 Working Group.

In those days, Ethernet had competition from other local area network standards. However, the brilliant simplicity of Bob Metcalfe's protocol meant that Ethernet products were substantially cheaper and faster to develop than products following competing protocols. Ethernet 802.3 quickly blew the competition out of the water. In the following years, its speed has increased to 100 Gbps, and Ethernet has continued its dominance. Metcalfe's simple but elegant protocol became the stuff of legend.

Although Ethernet was a testimony to Bob Metcalfe's technical brilliance and commercial persistence, the 802.3 Working Group had to use equal brilliance to keep increasing Ethernet's speed from one seemingly impossible number to another. As we will see in Chapter 10, Ethernet has even expanded into wide area networking. IP over Ethernet promises to be a dominant pattern in the future of networking.

INTRODUCTION

Local Area Networks

Ethernet was created for **local area networks (LANs)**, which are networks that operate on a **customer premises**, which might be a home, an office in a building, an entire building, or a university campus.

Ethernet was created for local area networks (LANs), which are networks on a customer premises.

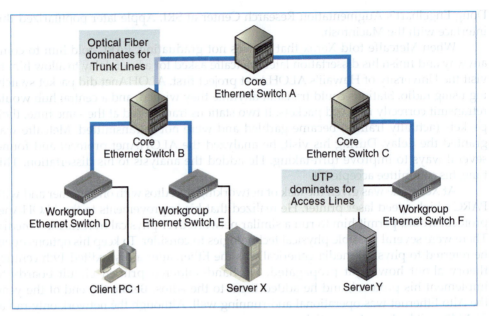

FIGURE 5-1 Simple Switched Ethernet Network

Test Your Understanding

1. What is a local area network (LAN)?

Switched Technology

Figure 5-1 illustrates a simple Ethernet network. At its heart is a collection of Ethernet switches. The switches that connect hosts to the network are called **workgroup switches**. Switches that connect switches to other switches are **core switches**. Figure 5-2 is a workgroup switch. It is 48 cm (19 inches) wide so that it can fit into a standard equipment

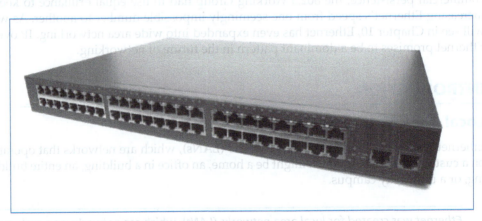

FIGURE 5-2 Ethernet Workgroup Switch with 48 Ports

rack. It is 9 cm (3.5 inches) tall. Core switches are the same width and depth but typically range from about 18 cm (7 inches) to about a meter tall.

Switches that connect hosts to the network are workgroup switches. Switches that connect switches to other switches are core switches.

UTP and Optical Fiber   To connect hosts to switches and switches to other switches, there is a transmission link. As we will see later in this chapter, there are two technologies for transmission links. One is **4-pair unshielded twisted pair (UTP)** copper wire. The other is optical fiber. UTP carries electrical signals over copper wire pairs. **Optical fiber** carries light signals through very thin glass tubes. Transmission links that connect hosts to workgroup switches are called **access links**. Transmission links that connect switches to other switches are called **trunk links**.

Transmission links that connect hosts to workgroup switches are called access links. Transmission links that connect switches to other switches are called trunk links.

Figure 5-3 shows that the main benefit of optical fiber is distance span. While UTP in buildings is normally limited to runs of 100 meters, optical fiber can span longer distances. At 1 Gbps, in fact, fiber can span a distance of several hundred meters. The penalty for greater distance span using fiber is greater cost. Fiber is more expensive to buy and lay than UTP. Many believe that fiber can carry signals faster than UTP; however, both can carry all but the highest speed signals, which few organizations use. In practice, fiber gives longer distances, not higher speeds.

Core Switch Capacity   Switches in the network core must carry the frames of many conversations, so they must have high processing speeds. Workgroup switches, in contrast, only carry the conversations of the hosts they serve directly. They can operate much more slowly and still give adequate service. Slowness per se is not a virtue, but the low cost that lower processing power brings is a definite virtue.

Characteristic	Unshielded Twisted Pair	Optical Fiber
Medium	Copper wire	Glass
Signal	Electrical	Light
Maximum Distance in LANs	Usually 100 meters	Usually far longer
Typical Maximum Speed	About the same	About the same
Cost	Lower	Higher

FIGURE 5-3   UTP versus Optical Fiber

Test Your Understanding

2. a) Distinguish between the two types of Ethernet switches in terms of what they connect. b) Distinguish between the two types of Ethernet transmission link technologies in terms of what they typically connect. c) What is the advantage of optical fiber over UTP? d) Why do core switches need more processing power than workgroup switches?

Ethernet Standards Development

Ethernet is a switched single network. Consequently, it requires standards at Layer 1 and Layer 2. OSI dominates standards at these layers. Consequently, we would expect Ethernet standards to be developed by ISO or ITU-T. In many cases, however, more specialized standards agencies develop standards; ISO and ITU-T then ratify them as official OSI standards.

In the case of LAN standards, nearly all come from the **IEEE Standards Association**, which is the standards setting arm of the Institute of Electrical and Electronics Engineers (IEEE). More specifically, LAN standards are created by the 802 LAN/MAN[1] standards committee, which is normally simply called the **802 Committee**.

The work of the 802 Committee is done in **working groups**.

- The **802.3 Working Group** creates Ethernet standards, so we will use the terms *Ethernet* and *802.3* interchangeably.
- The 802.1 Working Group develops standards used in multiple working groups, especially security standards. We will look at the 802.1X and 802.1AE security standards in this chapter.
- The 802.11 Working Group, in turn, creates the wireless LAN standards, which we will see in Chapters 6 and 7.

We will use the terms Ethernet *and 802.3* interchangeably.

IEEE Standards Association

    802 LAN/MAN Standards Committee

        802.1 Working Group

            Standards used by multiple working groups
            Security standards

        802.3 Working Group

            Ethernet standards

        802.11 Working Group

            Wi-Fi wireless LAN standards

FIGURE 5-4   IEEE LAN/MAN Standards Committee (Study Figure)

---

[1] A MAN is a metropolitan area network. It goes beyond the corporate premises and serves a city and its suburbs.

Test Your Understanding

3. a) What standards association creates most LAN standards? b) What is the name of its committee for developing LAN standards? c) Which 802 Working Group creates Ethernet standards? d) Will we use the terms *Ethernet* and *802.3* interchangeably? e) Which working group is likely to develop security standards to be used by multiple LAN/WAN technologies?

Physical and Data Link Layer Operation

Ethernet networks are single networks, so they require standards at the physical layer and the data link layer. Figure 5-5 shows Ethernet standards in the broader picture of 802 standards.

Single networks use standards at the physical layer and the data link layer.

The lowest row shows that Ethernet has many physical layer standards. Only three are shown—100BASE-TX, 1000BASE-T, and 1000BASE-SX—but there are many others. As electronics improve, the 802.3 Working Group constantly creates new faster physical layer standards.

The data link layer is both more complex and simpler. It is more complex than the physical layer because the 802 Committee subdivided the data link layer into two layers. The higher layer, the **Logical Link Control (LLC) layer**, has functionality that all 802 standards use to interact with the internet layer. There is only a single standard at the LLC layer. This is 802.2. It is largely invisible in its operation, and we will not look at it further.

The data link layer is simpler than the physical layer because each working group has a single standard at the **Media Access Control (MAC) layer**.[2] This layer has functionality specific to a particular working group's core operation. For

Internet Layer		IP				
Data Link Layer	LLC Layer	802.2				
	MAC Layer	802.3 MAC Layer Standard			802.11 MAC Layer Standard	
Physical Layer		100BASE-TX	1000BASE-T	1000BASE-SX	802.11n	802.11ac

LLC is the Logical Link Control Layer
MAC is the Media Access Control Layer

FIGURE 5-5 Ethernet (802.3) Physical and Data Link Layer Standards

---

[2] In early non-switched versions of 802.3, multiple hosts shared a single transmission link. If two transmitted at the same time, there would be a collision. Consequently, 802.3 needed media access control, which is an awkward way of saying that it needed a mechanism to control when individual stations could access the media (transmit). This was the essence of what happened in the Ethernet-specific data link layer, so that layer was called the MAC layer. Switching brought unshared links from the host to the workgroup switch, so access control was no longer needed. However, the name continued.

Ethernet, it includes governing frame design, switch operation, and other data link layer matters. The 802.11 Wi-Fi Working Group, in turn, has the 802.11 MAC Layer Standard that governs how access points deal with frames and other 802.11-specific matters.[3]

Test Your Understanding

4. a) At what layers do single networks require standards? b) Distinguish between the LLC layer and the MAC layer. c) Which data link layer do networking professionals work with? d) How many standards does Ethernet have at the MAC layer? e) Is this answer still true at the physical layer?

ETHERNET PHYSICAL LAYER STANDARDS

Physical layer standards govern connectors and transmission media. They also govern signaling. We will look at signaling first because it introduces concepts you will need when you look at UTP and optical fiber transmission media.

Test Your Understanding

5. What three things do physical layer standards govern?

Signaling

Bits and Signals   A frame is a long series of 1s and 0s. To transmit the frame over a physical medium, the sender must convert the 1s and 0s into physical signals. These signals will **propagate** (travel) down the transmission link to the device at the other end of the physical link.

Binary and Digital Signaling   Figure 5-6 illustrates two popular types of signaling, binary and digital signaling. **Binary signaling** has two **states** (conditions), which may be two voltage levels or light being turned on or off. One state represents a 0. The other state represents a 1. In the figure, a 0 is represented as a high voltage, and a 1 is represented as a low voltage. In optical signaling, a 1 might represent light being turned on, while a 0 might represent light being turned off.

In binary signaling, there are *two* possible states. This makes sense because "bi" is Latin for two. The figure also shows **digital signaling**, in which there are a *few* states (2, 4, 8, etc.).[4] How many "is few?" In some systems, there can be 32 or even 256 states, but the number of states is usually much lower. The number of states is always a multiple of two—four, eight, sixteen, and so forth.

---

[3] On hosts, Ethernet physical and data link layer processes are handled in hardware. The circuitry that implements Ethernet is called a network interface card (NIC). It received this name when it was a separate printed circuit board. Today, the NIC is built into the computer's main printed circuit board. Perhaps we should call it the network interface circuit, but the old name has endured.

[4] If "bi" means two, where does "digital" come from? It comes from the fact that we call our ten fingers *digits*. In fact, some early computer systems operated on Base 10 arithmetic, the same arithmetic that we ten-fingered people use. Very quickly, however, the advantages of building computers and transmission systems that used two or a multiple of two states brought about binary and digital computation and later signaling.

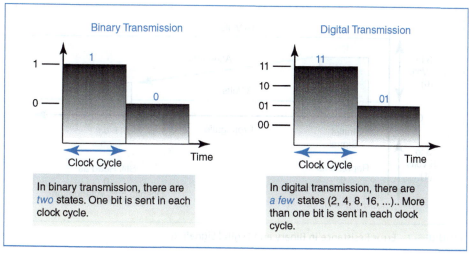

FIGURE 5-6   Binary and Digital Signaling

Note: In binary signaling, there are two possible states. In digital signaling, there are a few possible states (2, 4, 8, etc.).

Having more than two states adds to the complexity and therefore the cost of signaling. However, Figure 5-6 shows that if you have multiple states, you can send multiple bits in a single clock cycle. With two states, you can only represent a single 1 or a 0. With four states, however, the lowest state might represent 00, the next lowest state might represent 01, the next 10, and the highest 11. With four states, then, you can send two bits at a time.

We have talked about binary and digital transmission systems as if they were different. Actually, binary transmission is a subset of digital transmission. In binary transmission, *few* means two. Although binary transmission is the most common form of digital transmission and deserves its own name, all transmission in a typical network can properly be called digital.

Binary transmission is a type of digital signaling. Not all digital signaling, however, is binary signaling.

Error Resistance   Why use digital transmission? The answer is that digital transmission is fairly resistant to transmission impairments. In Figure 5-7, a 0 is represented by a signal between 3 volts and 15 volts, while a 1 is represented by a signal between minus 3 volts and minus 15 volts. This is the signaling scheme used by the serial ports found on older computers. (The signaling schemes on newer interfaces are too complex to describe simply.)

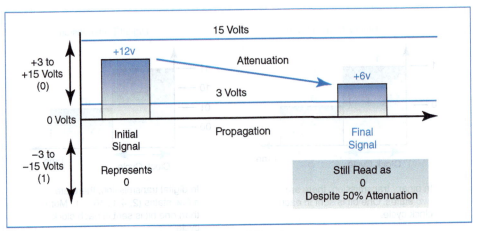

FIGURE 5-7 Error Resistance in Binary and Digital Signaling

In Figure 5-7, the sender transmits a 12-volt signal. This is a 0. However, as the signal propagates, it attenuates to 6 volts. This is 50% attenuation, a substantial loss. However, the receiver will still correctly record the signal as a 0 because 6 volts is between 3 volts and 15 volts. The attenuation does not cause an error in reading the signal. This is why binary transmission is error-resistant.

However, think about what happens to error resistance as the number of states increases. Even with four states, a much smaller propagation effect might cause 11 to be misinterpreted as 10. In general, as the number of states grows, error resistance declines proportionally. Consequently, there is a strong tendency to use binary signaling in practice. In examples in this book, we will use binary signaling almost exclusively.

Clock Cycles When a device transmits, it holds the signal constant for a brief period of time called the **clock cycle**. The receiver can read the signal at any time within the clock cycle and read it correctly. In addition, if the sender wishes to send 1111 with four-state signaling, it will transmit a highest-level signal in four consecutive clock cycles. The receiver can tell that this is four 1s instead of a single 1 because the transmission is four clock cycles long instead of one.

To transmit more bits per second, the sender uses either more states or briefer clock cycles. The latter is much easier in practice. Suppose that you are transmitting in binary and the clock cycle is 1/1000th of a second. This means that you can transmit a thousand bits per second. To transmit a gigabit per second with binary signaling, each clock cycle needs to be *one-billionth* of a second long. The limiting factor on transmission speed today is the ability of sending and receiving devices to work properly over ever shorter clock cycle times.

Test Your Understanding

6. a) What must a sender do to send the bits of a frame over a transmission medium? b) Distinguish between binary and digital signaling. c) What is a state? d) Why is binary transmission error-resistant? e) In Figure 5-7, by what percentage could the signal attenuate before it became unreadable? f) How does error resistance differ

in binary and digital signaling? g) Why are clock cycles necessary? h) If the binary transmission rate is 50 Mbps, how long will a clock cycle be? Express your answer as a fraction of a second.

4-Pair Unshielded Twisted Pair Copper Wiring

UTP Cables   Figure 5-8 shows 4-pair unshielded twisted pair wiring. A UTP cord has eight wires organized into four pairs. The two wires of each pair are twisted around each other several times per inch. Often, this wiring is inaccurately but understandably called **Ethernet cable**.[5]

RJ-45 Connectors and Jacks   Your home telephone cord terminates in a snap-in connector at each end. One connector snaps into your wall jack and the other snaps into your telephone. Figure 5-9 shows that 4-pair UTP uses a similar snap-in connector called the **RJ-45 connector**. It looks like your telephone connector, but it is a little wider because it has to terminate eight wires. It snaps into an **RJ-45 jack** in a host or a switch. The figure also shows the RJ-45 jack that the RJ-45 connector snaps into. Many vendors now use the term *Ethernet* for RJ-45 because Ethernet is the major user of these connectors and jacks.

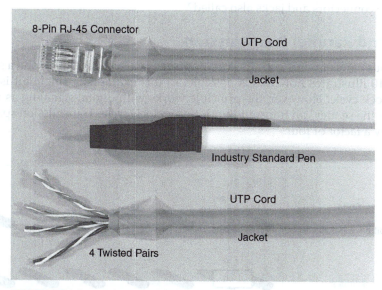

FIGURE 5-8 Four-Pair Unshielded Twisted Pair Copper Wiring

---

[5] OK, but what about the *unshielded* in the name? This is a hangover from the early days of twisted pair copper wiring. In some early cases, metal shielding was placed around each wire pair, and more metal shielding was placed around the four shielded pairs. This provided protection from something we will see a little later, electromagnetic interference. However, shielded twisted pair wiring is thick and expensive. In addition, experience showed that it was rarely necessary for electromagnetic interference shielding. Consequently, the copper wiring available in stores is *unshielded* twisted pair wiring.

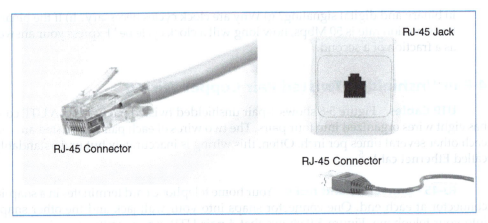

FIGURE 5-9 RJ-45 (Ethernet) Connector and Jack

Test Your Understanding

7. a) What type of copper wiring is widely used in Ethernet? b) How many wires are there in a UTP cord? c) How many pairs? d) How are the two wires in each pair organized? e) What type of connectors and jacks does 4-pair UTP use? f) What are RJ-45 connectors and jacks also called?

Serial and Parallel Transmission

Having four pairs of wires permits faster transmission speeds than having a single pair. Figure 5-10 illustrates how this is possible. In this example, a single bit is transmitted per clock cycle. However, the principle works with digital signaling as well. With four pairs, the sender can transmit four bits per clock cycle. Transmission speed would increase by a factor of four.

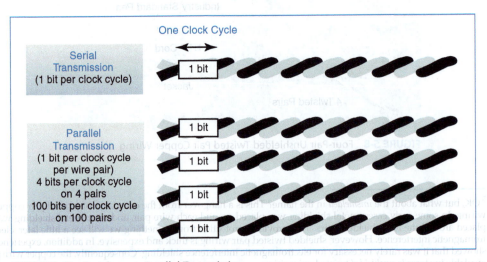

FIGURE 5-10 Serial versus Parallel Transmission

Transmitting over a single pair of wires is called **serial transmission** because the bits of successive clock cycles follow one another in series. If there is more than one pair carrying the transmission bits, this is called **parallel transmission**. All modern Ethernet signaling standards specify parallel signaling.

Test Your Understanding

8. What is the advantage of parallel transmission compared to serial transmission?

UTP Installation Limitations

The technology of UTP is extremely complex. However, observing two limitations when installing UTP ensures that transmission quality will be good.

UTP Quality Categories and Distance Limits
Not all UTP cords have the same quality. To indicate quality, UTP wiring is labeled by quality categories. Larger category numbers indicate higher quality. Nearly all UTP cabling on the market today is **Category 5e** (enhanced), **Category 6**, or **Category 6A** (advanced) UTP. These standards are informally but most commonly called Cat 5e, Cat 6, and Cat 6A.

Which quality category should you use? It depends on how fast you want to transmit. Figure 5-11 shows maximum distances for various speeds and quality categories. Speeds are governed by Ethernet signaling standards. Note that, with a single exception, Ethernet cords can be up to 100 meters long.[6]

Connectorization and Terminal Crosstalk Interference
Placing an RJ-45 connector on the end of a 4-pair UTP cable is called **connectorization**.[7] If connectorization is not done correctly, the cord will not work properly. It may not stop working entirely, but the performance degradation can be significant and will be difficult to diagnose.

Ethernet Signaling Standard	Transmission Speed	UTP Quality Category	Maximum Cord Length
100BASE-TX	100 Mbps	Category 5e, 6, 6A	100 meters
1000BASE-T	1 Gbps	Category 5e, 6, 6A	100 meters
10GBASE-T	10 Gbps	Category 6	55 meters
10GBASE-T	10 Gbps	Category 6A	100 meters

FIGURE 5-11   UTP Quality Category, Transmission Speed, and Maximum Distance

---

[6] What happens if you disregard these distance limits? The effects tend to be subtle but important. As signals travel, they grow weaker. As they do, there will be more errors because the receiver will not always be able to read them. In addition, wires always have random energy, which is called noise. As a signal gets weaker it gets closer to the average noise. In addition to the signal becoming too weak to read reliably, it will start being hit by occasional noise spikes (in random processes, there are invariably outliers) that garble the signal. Overall, pushing standards beyond their distance limits is risky. It creates intermittent problems that are nearly impossible to diagnose. Pushing UTP beyond its limits makes no economic sense.

[7] Hey, don't blame us. We don't make up these terms!

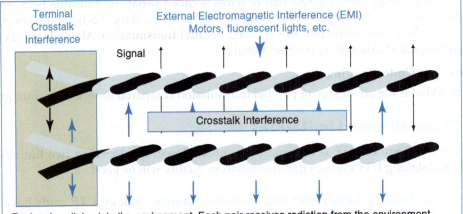

Each pair radiates into the environment. Each pair receives radiation from the environment. Signals in adjacent pairs interfere with one another (crosstalk). Twisting each pair helps reduce this crosstalk interference. Crosstalk interference is worst at the ends, where the wires are untwisted to put them into the RJ-45 connector. This is terminal crosstalk interference.

FIGURE 5-12 Terminal Crosstalk Interference

Figure 5-12 shows that wire pairs act like antennas. They receive any electromagnetic signals in the environment. This is called **electromagnetic interference (EMI)**. It is generated by nearby motors, fluorescent lights, and even other wire pairs in a wire bundle. The last is called **crosstalk interference**. If the EMI is large, the interference will make the pair's signal unreadable.

As Alexander Graham Bell discovered, twisting the wires in a pair greatly reduces problems caused by EMI. To add a connector, unfortunately, it is necessary to straighten out the ends of the wires to slide them into the RJ-45 connector. It might seem that this small distance of straight wire would not be important compared to 100 meters of twisted wire. In fact, it is very important. If wires are untwisted too far, **terminal crosstalk interference** between the untwisted wires will be crippling. Again, however, there is a simple installation rule to defeat this terminal cross-talk interference. Do not untwist the wires more than 1.25 cm (0.5 inch). Observing this installation discipline will make terminal crosstalk interference a nonissue.

Test Your Understanding

9. a) Of what wire characteristic is category a measure? b) What types of UTP wiring can carry signals 100 meters at 1 Gbps? c) What types of UTP wiring can carry signals in 10GBASE-T? d) Which can carry 10 Gbps Ethernet 100 meters? e) What is terminal crosstalk interference? f) What installation discipline can make terminal crosstalk interference a nonissue? g) State the two installation disciplines that will reduce UTP transmission problems to negligibility.

Optical Fiber

Core and Cladding   Figure 5-13 shows that optical fiber carries light signals through a thin strand of glass called the **core**. In fiber's simplest form, light is turned on for a 1 or off for a 0 during each clock cycle.

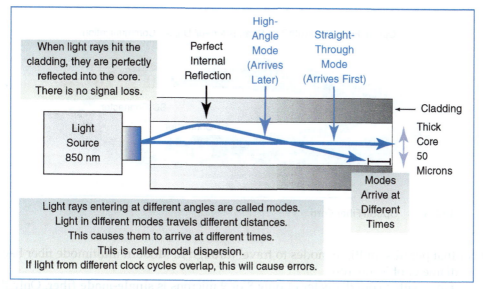

FIGURE 5-13 Optical Fiber Transmission

The figure also shows that the core is surrounded by a thin glass cylinder called the **cladding**. When a light ray hits the boundary between the core and cladding, it is reflected back into the core. The light never enters the cladding and so is never lost. Consequently, there is very low attenuation as the signal travels. Light signals can travel a very long way through the types of fiber—much farther than electrical signals can travel through UTP.[8]

Core and cladding diameters are given in **microns** (micrometers or μm). Most fiber cords being installed in LANs today have 50-micron core diameters. In comparison, an average human hair is about 75 microns thick.[9] Whatever the core diameter, the cladding diameter is 125 microns.

Modal Dispersion, Multimode Fiber, and Single-Mode Fiber   For technical reasons, light rays can only enter the core at a few angles. These rays are called **modes**. Figure 5-13 shows two modes entering the fiber. One travels directly through the center of the core. The other bounces against the core/cladding boundary repeatedly as it travels. Traveling different distances, they will arrive at slightly different times. This is called **modal dispersion**. If the cord is too long, slower modes from one clock cycle will overlap the faster modes of the next clock cycle. This will make the signal unreadable. Modal dispersion limits propagation distance in **multimode fiber**, that is,

---

[8] Figure 5-13 shows two light rays entering the fiber. One travels directly through the center of the core. The other bounces around as it travels. For technical reasons, light rays can only enter a narrow glass core at a few angles. These permitted light rays are called modes.

[9] Actually, human hair varies in thickness from about 40 microns to 120 microns. Hair less than 60 microns thick is considered to be fine hair. Hair more than 80 microns thick is called thick or coarse. See, you learned something from reading this book.

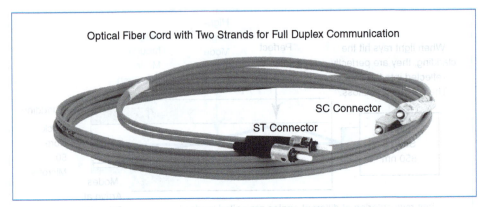

Optical Fiber Cord with Two Strands for Full Duplex Communication

SC Connector

ST Connector

FIGURE 5-14 Optical Fiber Cord

fiber that permits multiple modes to travel through it. Modern multimode fiber had a core diameter of 50 microns.

Fiber with a core diameter of only 8 or 9 microns is **single-mode fiber**. Only the mode traveling straight through can propagate through it. With no modal dispersion, single-mode fiber can carry signals several kilometers. However, single-mode fiber is more expensive to buy and install than multimode fiber, and multimode fiber distances are generally fine for LANs. Consequently, multimode fiber dominates the use of fiber in Ethernet LANs.

Optical Fiber Cords and Connectors   Figure 5-14 shows an optical fiber cord. The cord has two **strands** for **full duplex transmission**, which is the ability to transmit in two directions simultaneously. Each strand carries the signal in one direction.

Note that optical fiber does not use RJ-45 connectors. Several optical fiber connectors and jacks have been standardized. The cord in Figure 5-14, in fact, has different connectors at each end. One end has a square **SC connector**. The other has a round **ST connector**. This cord would connect a core switch with **SC jacks** with a core switch with **ST jacks**. In practice, there is no problem mixing and matching fiber connectors. Optical fiber cords can be terminated with any type of standard connector.

Light Source Wavelength   Figure 5-15 shows that light propagates as a wave. The distance between successive wave heights, troughs, starts, stops, and so forth is called the **wavelength**. The strength of the signal is called its **amplitude**. If you are familiar with ocean waves, the wavelength is the physical distance between successive waves. Amplitude is how hard the wave will hit you.

For LAN fiber, the normal wavelength is 850 nm (nanometers). The use of 850 nm light is popular because it travels far enough for typical LAN fiber distance needs and because transmitters and receivers operating at this wavelength window are relatively inexpensive. Longer-wavelength optical fiber using 1,310 or 1,550 nm light can carry signals many kilometers. Although longer wavelength light gives long transmission distances, longer-wavelength light sources are much more expensive. There is usually no need for them in LANs.

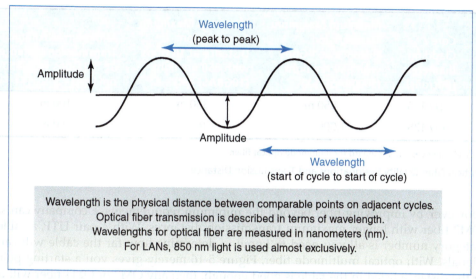

FIGURE 5-15 Light Amplitude and Wavelength

Test Your Understanding

10. a) Does the signal travel through the optical fiber core, cladding, or both? b) Why can signals travel very far through optical fiber? c) What are modes? d) What is modal dispersion? e) Why is it bad? f) What is the core diameter of multimode fiber? g) What is the core diameter of single-mode fiber? h) What is the advantage of single-mode fiber over multimode fiber? i) Why does multimode fiber dominate in Ethernet LANs anyway?

11. a) Why does an optical fiber cord have two strands? b) What is the ability to transmit in both directions simultaneously called? c) What is the definition of wavelength? d) What three wavelengths are used in optical fiber transmission? e) Which dominates in LANs? Why?

Multimode Optical Fiber Quality Standards

For UTP, we saw that there are distance limits that depend on the category (quality) of the UTP cord. Optical fiber also has distance limitations based on quality. Most LAN fiber today is multimode fiber. Figure 5-16 shows that there are two optical fiber quality standards for multimode fiber sold today, OM3 and OM4. OM is an abbreviation for **optical multimode**. **OM4** fiber cables can carry signals farther than **OM3** cables.[10] They also cost more.

Figure 5-16 shows minimum maximum transmission distances for OM3 and OM4 at speeds of 1 Gbps, 10 Gbps, and 100 Gbps. "Minimum maximum" sounds like a contradiction, but it is not. If a company wishes to label a cable as having OM3 quality, then the maximum distance at 1 Gbps must be at least 550 meters with 850 nm light.

---

[10] The OM1 and OM2 standards are no longer being used in new optical cabling. However, they are still in use in corporate LANs.

Multimode Fiber Quality Standard	Core / Cladding diameters (microns)	Minimum Maximum Transmission Distance at 1 Gbps with 850 nm light (1000BASE-SX)	Minimum Maximum Transmission Distance at 10 Gbps with 850 nm light (10GBASE-SR)	Minimum Maximum Transmission Distance at 100 Gbps with 850 nm light
OM3	50 / 125	550 m	300 m	100 m
OM4	50 / 125	1,000 m	440 m	150 m

OM stands for Optical Multimode; it is a standard for multimode optical fiber.

FIGURE 5-16 Optical Fiber Quality Designations and Transmission Distance

However, by improving fiber beyond the minimum requirements, a company can sell OM3 fiber with longer maximum transmission distances. With 4-pair UTP, a cable's category number is all you need to know to determine how far the cable will carry signals. With optical multimode fiber, Figure 5-16 merely gives you a starting point. If the distance listed in the table is good enough, then any OM3 or OM4 fiber will do. If you need to go somewhat farther, you need to check the specific maximum distances of available vendors for their OM3 and OM4 fiber offerings.

Test Your Understanding

12. a) Which optical multimode standards govern LAN fiber today? b) If you needed to transmit at 1 Gbps over a distance of 375 meters, which options in Figure 5-16 would meet your requirements? c) Which would you choose? Explain. d) If you needed to transmit at 10 Gbps over a distance of 400 meters, which options in Figure 5-16 would meet your requirements? e) Which would you choose? Explain. f) If you needed to transmit at 1 Gbps over a distance of 85 meters, what would you select as your solution? g) Using OM4 fiber, a company transmits at 10 Gbps over a distance of 500 meters. How is this possible?

Link Aggregation (Bonding)

Ethernet transmission capacity usually increases by a factor of 10. What should you do if you only need slightly more speed than a certain standard specifies? For instance, suppose that you have a pair of gigabit Ethernet switches that you need to connect at 1.5 Gbps?

Figure 5-17 illustrates that a company can use two or more UTP or fiber trunk links to connect a pair of switches. The IEEE calls this **link aggregation**. Networking professionals also call this **bonding**. Ethernet supports link aggregation with both UTP and fiber.

Link aggregation uses existing ports and usually is inexpensive compared to purchasing new faster switches. However, after two or three aggregated links, the company should compare the cost of link aggregation with the cost of a tenfold increase in capacity by moving up to the next Ethernet speed. Going to a much faster trunk link will also give more room for growth.

Test Your Understanding

13. a) What is link aggregation? b) What is it also called? c) If you need to connect two 1000BASE-SX switches at 2.5 Gbps, what are your options? d) Why may link

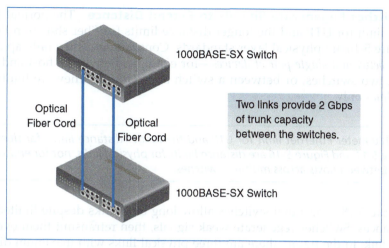

1000BASE-SX Switch

Optical
Fiber Cord   Optical
              Fiber Cord

Two links provide 2 Gbps
of trunk capacity
between the switches.

1000BASE-SX Switch

FIGURE 5-17 Link Aggregation (Bonding)

aggregation be more desirable than installing a single faster link? e) Why may link aggregation not be desirable if you will need several aggregated links to meet capacity requirements?

Ethernet Physical Layer Standards and Network Design

Using Figure 5-11, Figure 5-16, and Figure 5-17 in Network Design Note that if you know the speed you need (100 Mbps, 1 Gbps, etc.) and if you know what distance you need to span, the information in Figure 5-11, Figure 5-16, and Figure 5-17 will show you what type of transmission link you can use.

For instance, suppose that you need a speed of 2.5 Gbps between two switches that are 130 meters apart. This is over 100 meters, so you could not use UTP. You would need optical fiber to span this distance.

For speed, 1 Gbps would not be sufficient, and 10 Gbps might be expensive. Your best choice probably would be three bonded 1000BASE-SX links, although you would consider the cost of moving up to a 10 Gbps fiber standard.

Alternatively, if you are designing a network from scratch, say for a new facility, the options presented in Figure 5-11 for UTP and Figure 5-16 for optical fiber will allow you to consider alternative placements for your switches. With longer physical links, you can place your switches farther apart on average, reducing the total number of switches. This might save money. In the end, of course, you have to enumerate alternatives and crunch the cost numbers for each.

One general rule of thumb is that if a transmission link can span the distance between two switches, it will not make economic sense to use an intermediate switch. Doing so may permit the use of less expensive links between the end switches and the intermediate switch, but switches cost far more than transmission links.

One general rule of thumb is that if a transmission link can span the distance between two switches, it will not make economic sense to use an intermediate switch.

Switches Regenerate Signals to Extend Distance   The normal 100-meter Ethernet limit for UTP and the longer distance limits for fiber shown in Figure 5-11 and Figure 5-16 are physical layer standards. Consequently, they only apply to connections *between a single pair of devices*—for example, between a host and a switch, between two switches, or between a switch and a router. They are limitations for *physical links* only.

The 100-meter Ethernet limit for UTP and the longer distance limits for fiber shown in Figure 5-11 and Figure 5-16 are distance limits for physical links, not for end-to-end data links between hosts across multiple switches.

Figure 5-18 shows that switches allow long data links despite limited physical link distances. Switches regenerate weak signals, then retransmit them over another physical link. In the figure, there are three physical links with maximum distances of 100 meters, 550 meters, and 100 meters. With this configuration, the maximum data link span is 750 meters. With many switches instead of just two, 802.3 LANs with very large data link distances can be built. There is no maximum end-to-end distance between pairs of hosts in an Ethernet network.

There is no maximum end-to-end distance (data link distance) between pairs of hosts in an Ethernet network.

Test Your Understanding

14. a) In Figure 5-11 and Figure 5-16, is the maximum distance for a single physical link or for the data link between two hosts across multiple switches? b) At what layer or layers is the 802.3 100BASE-TX standard defined—physical, data link,

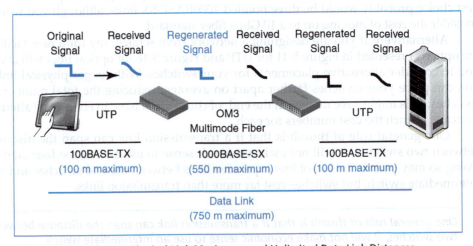

FIGURE 5-18   Ethernet Physical Link Maximums and Unlimited Data Link Distances

or internet? c) In Figure 5-18, what would the maximum data length be if both the physical link on the left and the physical length in the middle were changed to OM4 fiber? d) If you need to span 600 meters at 1 Gbps, what options do you have? (Include the possibility of using an intermediate switch.) e) How would you decide which option to choose?

ETHERNET DATA LINK LAYER STANDARDS

Single switched networks, like all single networks, require standards at the physical and data link layers. We have just seen that Ethernet has many physical layer standards. We will now turn to Ethernet's single data link layer standard. Figure 5-5 shows that despite many physical layer standards, Ethernet only has a single data link layer standard: the **802.3 MAC Layer Standard**, which governs frame organization and switch operation.

The Ethernet Frame

Figure 5-19 shows an Ethernet 802.3 frame, which we saw briefly in Chapter 2. We will now look at some elements in the Ethernet frame in more detail.[11] Recall that an *octet* is a byte.

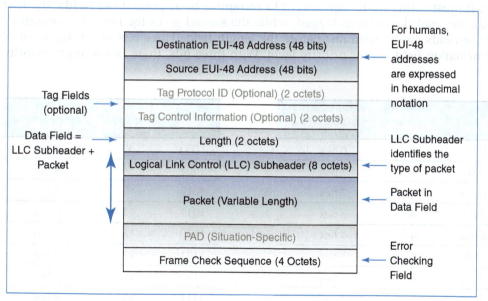

FIGURE 5-19 Ethernet 802.3 Frame

---

[11] We will not look at two fields sometimes shown in an Ethernet frame, the preamble and start of frame delimiter. These are synchronization fields that are now considered part of Ethernet's physical layer operation. Nor will we look at the PAD field, which was important in the early days of Ethernet technologies but no longer has a meaningful role to play. In any case, networking professionals do not look at the PAD field when inspecting the contents of an 802.3 frame.

Source and Destination Address Fields We saw in Chapter 2 that the source and destination Ethernet address are EUI-48 addresses. While computers work with this raw 48-bit form, humans normally express these addresses in Base 16 **hexadecimal (hex) notation**. To convert a 48-bit Ethernet address into hex notation, follow these three steps:

- First, divide the 48 bits into twelve 4-bit units, which computer scientists call nibbles.
- Second, convert each nibble into a hexadecimal symbol, using Figure 5-20. For example, 1100 is a C.
- Third, write the symbols as six pairs with a dash between each pair—for instance, B2-CC-66-0D-5E-BA. (Each pair represents 1 octet.) In this case, the first byte would be 10110010, which becomes 1011 0010, which becomes B 2, which becomes B2 (followed by a dash).

To convert a hex address back to binary, change each symbol pair back to its 8-bit pattern. For example, if a hex pair is 2E, 2 is 0010, and E is 1110, so 2E is equivalent to the octet 00101110. Note that you must keep the two leading 0s in 0010.

Tag Fields (Optional) In Chapter 4, we saw that companies may give frames priority levels so that high-priority frames for latency-intolerant applications can go first. This was not in the original 802.3 standard. If a company wishes to use priority, it must configure its equipment to recognize two optional **tag fields**: the first indicates that the frame is tagged, while the second gives the tagged information. These fields are inserted just before the length field. Three bits in the Tag Control Information field are for priority level. With three bits, there can be eight priority

4 Bits	Decimal (Base 10)	Hexadecimal (Base 16)	4 Bits	Decimal (Base 10)	Hexadecimal (Base 16)
0000	0	0 hex	1000	8	8 hex
0001	1	1 hex	1001	9	9 hex
0010	2	2 hex	1010	10	A hex
0011	3	3 hex	1011	11	B hex
0100	4	4 hex	1100	12	C hex
0101	5	5 hex	1101	13	D hex
0110	6	6 hex	1110	14	E hex
0111	7	7 hex	1111	15	F hex

Divide a 48-bit Ethernet address into 12 four-bit "nibbles." (1010, 0001, etc.)
Convert each group of 4 bits into a Hex symbol. (A, 1, etc.)
Combine two hex symbols into pairs and place a dash between pairs (A1-etc.)
For example, 10100001 becomes 1010 0001, which becomes A 1, which becomes A1 (followed by a dash)
The finished hex expression might be: A1-36-CD-7B-DF-01 hex

FIGURE 5-20 Hexadecimal Notation

levels. Note that these tag fields are optional. If priority and the other matters they handle are not used, there are no tag fields in the frame.

Length Field   The **length field** contains a binary number that gives the *length of the data field* (not of the entire frame) in octets. The maximum length of the data field is 1,522 octets. There is no minimum length for the data field.[12]

The Data Field   The **data field** contains two subfields: the LLC subheader and the packet that the frame is delivering.[13]

- The **logical link control layer (LLC) subheader** is 8 octets long. The purpose of the LLC subheader is to describe the type of packet contained in the data field. For instance, if the LLC subheader ends with the code 08-00 hex, then the data field contains an IPv4 packet. To give another example, the code 86-DD hex indicates an IPv6 packet.
- The data field also contains the packet that the MAC layer frame is delivering. The packet usually is far longer than all other fields combined.

Frame Check Sequence Field   The last field in the Ethernet frame is the **Frame Check Sequence Field**, which permits error detection. This is a 4-octet field. The sender does a calculation based on other bits in the frame and places the 32-bit result in the Frame Check Sequence Field. The receiver redoes the calculation and compares its result with the contents of the Frame Check Sequence Field. If the two are different, there is an error in the frame. If there is an error, the receiver simply discards the frame. There is no retransmission of damaged frames.

Test Your Understanding

15. a) What were Ethernet addresses originally called? b) What are they called today? c) What are the steps in converting EUI-48 addresses into hex notation? d) Convert 11000010 to hex. e) Convert 7F hex to binary. f) Convert the EUI-48 address A1-B2-C3-44-5D-3C to binary. Leave a space between each octet. As a check, there must be 48 bits. g) What are the two components of the Ethernet data field? h) What is the purpose of the LLC subheader? i) If the length field is 1020, what is the length of the packet? (Hint: The answer is not 1020.) j) What is the purpose of the Frame Check Sequence Field? k) What happens if the receiver detects an error in a frame? l) If a company wishes to use priority in Ethernet, what fields must it add? m) Where are tag fields located if they are present?

---

[12] Although there is no minimum length, if the data field is less than 46 octets long, additional PAD bits are added so that the total of the data field and the PAD are 46 bits long. As noted in an earlier footnote, this is a holdover from early Ethernet technologies and is irrelevant today. However, it is still used in the standard for backward compatibility.

[13] Why does the data field have two parts? The answer is that the data field of the MAC layer frame actually is encapsulated in an LLC layer frame, which has a header (the LLC subheader) and a data field consisting of the packet being carried in the LLC frame. However, to avoid damaging neurons, it is best simply to think of the MAC layer data field as having two parts.

Basic Ethernet Data Link Layer Switch Operation

In this section, we will discuss the basic data link layer operation of Ethernet switches. This is also governed by the 802.3 MAC Layer Standard. In the section after this one, we will discuss other aspects of Ethernet switching that a firm may or may not use.

Frame Forwarding   Figure 5-21 shows an Ethernet LAN with three switches. Larger Ethernet LANs have dozens or hundreds of switches, but the operation of individual switches is the same whether there are a few switches or many. Each individual switch makes a decision about which port to use to send the frame back out to the next switch or to the destination host.

In the figure, Host A1 (we abbreviate the address) wishes to send a frame to Host E5. This frame must go to Switch 1, then Switch 2, and then Switch 3. Switch 3 will send the frame to Host E5.

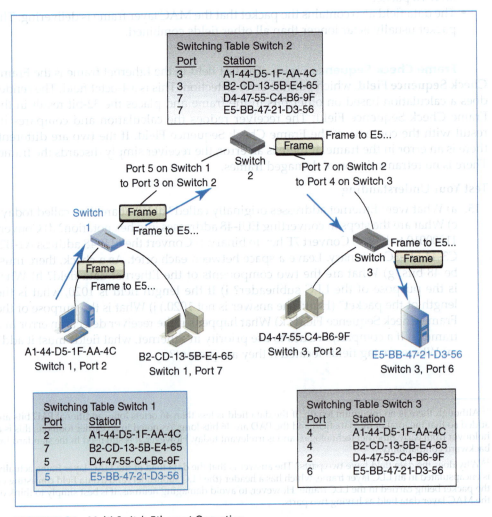

FIGURE 5-21   Multi-Switch Ethernet Operation

To begin this process, Host A1 puts E5-BB-47-21-D3-56 in the destination address field of the frame. It sends the frame to Switch 1, through Port 2.

- Switch 1 looks up the address E5 in its switching table. It sees that E5 is associated with Port 5, so it sends the frame out Port 5. This is a very simple process, so it requires little processing power. This means that Ethernet switches are inexpensive for the volume of traffic they carry.
- The frame going out Port 5 on Switch 1 goes into Port 3 on Switch 2. Switch 2 now looks up the address E5 in its switching table. This address is associated with Port 7, so Switch 2 sends the frame out Port 7.
- The frame arrives at Switch 3 through Port 4. Switch 3 now looks up the address E5 in the switching table. This time, the address is associated with Port 6. Switch 3 sends the frame out Port 6. This takes it to the destination Host E5.

Note that each switch only knows the information in its switching table. More specifically, it only knows what port to use to send the frame back out. Switches do not know the entire data link between the source host and the destination host.

Hierarchical Switch Organization   Note that the switches in Figure 5-21 form a **hierarchy**, in which each switch has only one parent switch above it. In fact, the Ethernet standard *requires* a **hierarchical topology** (physical organization of switches and transmission links). Otherwise, loops would exist, causing frames to circulate endlessly from one switch to another around the loop or causing other problems. Figure 5-1 shows another switched Ethernet LAN organized in a hierarchy.

Ethernet requires a hierarchical switch topology.

In a hierarchy, there is only a single possible path between any two hosts. (To see this, select any two hosts at the bottom of the hierarchy and trace a path between them. You will see that only one path is possible.) If there is only a single possible path between any two hosts, it follows that, in every switch along the path, the destination address in a frame will appear only once in the switching table—for the specific outgoing port needed to send the frame on its way.

In a hierarchy, there is only a single possible path between any two hosts.

This allows a simple table lookup operation that is very fast and therefore costs little per frame handled. This is what makes Ethernet switches inexpensive. As noted in the introduction, simple switching operation and therefore low cost has led to Ethernet's dominance in LAN technology.

The fact that there is only a single possible path between any two end hosts in an Ethernet hierarchy makes Ethernet switch forwarding simple and therefore inexpensive. This low cost has led to Ethernet's dominance in LAN technology.

In Chapter 8, we will see that routers have to do much more work when a packet arrives. Routers are connected in a mesh, so there are multiple alternative routes between any two hosts. Each of these alternative routes appears as a row in the routing table. Therefore, when a packet arrives, a router must first identify all possible routes (rows) and then select the best one—instead of simply finding a single match. This additional work per forwarding decision makes routers very expensive for the traffic load they handle.

Test Your Understanding

16. a) Do switches know the entire data link between the source and destination host? b) What does a switch know? c) In Figure 5-21, trace everything that will happen when Host E5 sends a frame to D4. d) Trace everything that will happen when Host E5 sends a frame to B2.

17. a) How are switches in an Ethernet LAN organized? b) Because of this organization, how many possible paths can there be between any two hosts? c) In Figure 5-1, what is the single possible path between Client PC 1 and Server X? d) Between Client PC 1 and Server Y?

18. a) What is the benefit of having a single possible path? Explain in detail. b) Why has Ethernet become the dominant LAN technology? c) Why are routers expensive for the traffic volume they handle?

ADVANCED ETHERNET SWITCH OPERATION

Having discussed basic Ethernet switch operation, we will begin looking at additional aspects of Ethernet switch operation that are important in larger Ethernet networks.

The Rapid Spanning Tree Protocol (RSTP)

Single Points of Failure   Having only a single possible path between any two hosts allows rapid frame forwarding and, therefore, low switch cost. However, having only a single possible path between any two computers also makes Ethernet vulnerable to **single points of failure**, in which the failure of a single component (a switch or a trunk link between switches) can cause widespread disruption.

> *Having only a single possible path between end hosts in a switched Ethernet network reduces cost, but it creates single points of failure, meaning that a single failure can cause widespread disruption.*

To understand this, suppose that Switch 2 in Figure 5-22 fails. Then the hosts connected to Switch 1 will not be able to communicate with hosts connected to Switch 2 or Switch 3. For a second example, suppose that the trunk link between Switch 1 and Switch 2 fails. In this case, too, the network also will be broken into two parts.

Although the two parts of the network might continue to function independently after a failure, many firms put most or all of their servers in a centralized server room.

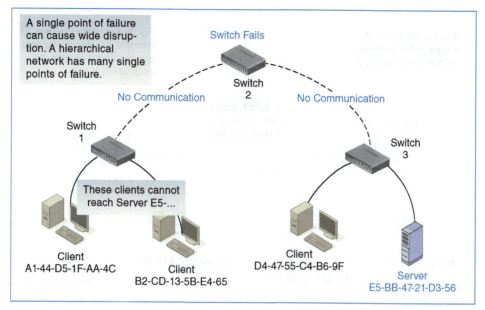

FIGURE 5-22 Single Point of Failure

In such firms, clients on the other side of the broken network would not be able to reach the servers they need. For example, Client A1-44-D5-1F-AA-4C, which connects to Switch 1, cannot reach Server E5-BB-47-21-D3-56, which connects to Switch 3. External connections to the Internet also tend to be confined to a single network point for security reasons. Computers on the wrong side of the divide after a breakdown would lose external access.

The Rapid Spanning Tree Protocol (RSTP) The traditional way to deal with single points of failure is to install backup links. This adds redundancy, which we saw in Chapter 4. Redundancy increases **reliability**, which is the probability that hosts can connect.

In Figure 5-23, the company has installed a transmission link between Switch 1 and Switch 3. As the figure shows, this creates a loop among the three switches. Loops create serious problems in Ethernet. Fortunately, there is a standard that Ethernet switches use to detect and break loops automatically and restore a strict hierarchy. This is the **Rapid Spanning Tree Protocol (RSTP)**. In the figure, RSTP has deactivated the backup link.

What happens if there is a failure? Switches will exchange messages via the RSTP protocol. They will agree to disable the links between Switch 2 and the other two switches. They will also agree to reactivate the backup link. Now, the two clients on the left can reach Server E5-... on the right.

Although RSTP was created to detect and break loops, using it to reactivate backup links is rather tricky. When a loop occurs, the switches hold an election to pick a new root (top level) switch. They then create a hierarchy beneath the root. To ensure that the restored hierarchy is the one the company wants to have, the networking staff

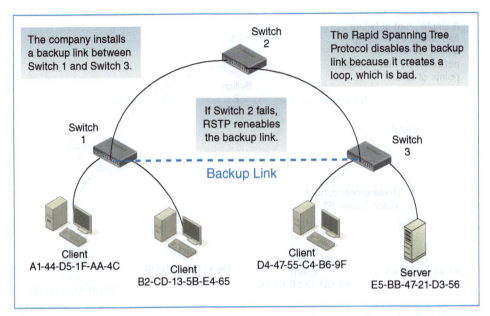

FIGURE 5-23 Backup Link and the Rapid Spanning Tree Protocol

must "rig the election." It does this by setting certain parameters on each switch. This is easy if there is a single backup link. If there are many backup links, this is very difficult.

Test Your Understanding

19. a) What is a single point of failure? b) Why is having a single possible path between any two hosts in an Ethernet network dangerous? c) What is the traditional way to address this problem? d) How does it bring redundancy? e) How does it improve reliability? f) What standard allows backup links for redundancy in Ethernet networks? g) Is it easy or difficult to create backup links effectively with RSTP? h) What do you think the outcome would be if a workgroup switch was elected as the root? Explain.

Priority

As we saw in Chapter 4, networks sometimes have momentary traffic peaks. When priority is used, the highest-priority frames go first. As we saw earlier, Ethernet switches can have up to eight priority levels, from 000 through 111.

Test Your Understanding

20. a) Can Ethernet switches implement priority? b) How many priority levels can they implement?

Manageability

If there is an Ethernet switch problem, discovering which switch is malfunctioning can be very difficult. Fixing the problem, furthermore, may require traveling to the switch to change its configuration. Switch troubleshooting can be very expensive,

Priority

Ethernet switches can provide up to eight priority levels

Manageability

Manageable switches can be managed by SNMP

Although manageable switches cost much more than non-manageable switches, this is more than made up for by lower management costs

Software-defined networking may bring a revolution in switch management

Power Over Ethernet (POE) Plus

USB ports provide both data transmission and power to hosts

Switches implementing POE Plus can provide up to 25 watts of power over UTP to hosts

This is sufficient for voice over IP phones, surveillance cameras, and most access points

This saves money because there is no need to install power lines to these devices

Not sufficient for desktop or laptop PCs

FIGURE 5-24 Advanced Ethernet Capabilities (Study Figure)

especially if the network staff must travel to distant switches to do diagnostics or configuration. As we saw in Chapter 4, the Simple Network Management Protocol allows the manager to contact the agents for individual managed devices. **Manageable switches** are likely to be the most numerous of these managed devices. For example, in a mid-size bank, there are likely to be around 500 switches to be managed. Manageable switches cost significantly more than "dumb" switches, but the reduction in management labor costs makes SNMP-compliant switches mandatory in large networks. As discussed in Chapter 4, strong security will allow a firm to use SNMP Set commands to remotely reconfigure switches.

Chapter 4 also noted that switches are beginning to implement software-defined networking (SDN). This may lead to radical increases in organizational control over its Ethernet switches. This would revolutionize the management of Ethernet and therefore of LANs in general.

Test Your Understanding

21. a) What communication protocol is used with manageable switches? b) Manageable switches cost more than dumb switches. Why is using them worthwhile anyway? c) What benefit does strong security bring for manageability?

Power over Ethernet (POE)

USB provides both data and electrical power to connected devices. With **Power over Ethernet (POE) Plus**, an Ethernet switch can do the same. It can provide up to 25 watts of power over the UTP access link. This is sufficient for voice over IP phones, surveillance cameras, and most access points. It is not enough for desktop or laptop computers.[14]

---

[14] However, some switch vendors offer higher wattages in their products, which are enough to support at least laptops. In the future, these may become standardized.

POE Plus might not seem like a major benefit, but companies installing access points, surveillance cameras, and other infrastructure devices may face significant cost to install the wiring needed to power these devices. With POE Plus, the company can simply plug the device into the Ethernet wall jack it uses for data transmission.

Test Your Understanding

22. a) What is POE Plus? (Do not just spell out the abbreviation.) b) Why is POE Plus attractive to corporations? c) What maximum standard power does the POE Plus standard specify? d) For what types of devices is POE Plus sufficient? e) Is POE Plus sufficient for desktop computers and most notebook computers?

ETHERNET SECURITY

Until recently, few organizations worried about the security of their wired Ethernet networks. Only someone within the site could get access to the LAN, and this seemed unlikely. Unfortunately, experience has shown that attackers can *usually* get into sites, especially if a site has public areas. Once into the site network, the attacker can plug into any wall jack. This bypasses the border firewall. While site networks are hard and crunchy to outside attackers, they tend to be soft and chewy to people on the inside.

Port-Based Access Control (802.1X)

To thwart the ability of attackers to simply plug into the internal network, companies can implement **802.1X**, which is a standard for **Port-Based Access Control** on the workgroup switches that give users access to the network. With 802.1X, whenever a host connects to the network, its user must prove his or her identity before the workgroup switch will pass further traffic.

Figure 5-25 illustrates 802.1X. The supplicant is called the **peer**. The workgroup switch is called the **authenticator**. It gets this name because the workgroup switch

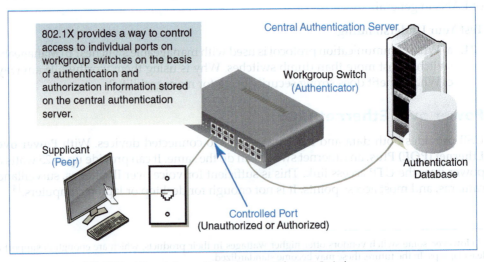

FIGURE 5-25   802.1X Port-Based Access Control on an Ethernet Switch

provides authentication service to the supplicant computer. The 802.1X standard also uses a central **authentication server** to do the actual supplicant credentials checking.

When the supplicant host (peer) transmits its authentication credentials (password, etc.), the authenticator passes these credentials on to the authentication server. The authentication server checks these credentials against its authentication database. If the authentication server authenticates the credentials, it sends back a confirmation to the workgroup switch. The workgroup switch then allows the supplicant PC to send frames to other devices in the network.

Using a central authentication server provides four benefits.

- *Switch Cost.* First, having the central authentication server check credentials instead of having the switch doing this minimizes the processing power needed in the workgroup switch. Given the large number of workgroup switches in firms, this reduces overall cost.
- *Consistency.* Second, having all credentials on the authentication server gives consistency in authentication. An attacker cannot try many different workgroup switches until he or she finds one that is misconfigured and gives the attacker access.
- *Reduced Management Cost.* Third, management cost is reduced because credentials only need to be changed on the central authentication server when a user joins the firm, leaves the firm, or needs other credential changes. Making all these changes on workgroup switches would be prohibitively expensive.
- *Rapid Changes.* Fourth, the credentials of individuals who are fired or suspended can be invalidated in seconds, removing access to all workgroup switches.

Note from its name that the 802.1X standard was created by the *802.1* Working Group, not by the *802.3* Working Group that creates Ethernet standards. The 802.1 Working Group produces standards that cut across all 802 network technologies. This includes security standards.

Test Your Understanding

23. a) What threat does 802.1X address? b) How does the standard address the threat? c) In 802.1X, what device is the authenticator? d) What are the four benefits of using a central authentication server instead of having the individual authenticators do all authentication work?

Man in the Middle Attack in an Ethernet LAN

If an attacker can compromise a host within an Ethernet LAN, he or she may be able to force all traffic to pass through the compromised host. This will allow the attacker to read all transmissions between hosts on the LAN. This is called a **man in the middle attack** because it places the attacker in the middle of compromised transmissions between two legitimate hosts, as shown in Figure 5-26.

Each host and router has an **Address Resolution Protocol (ARP) cache** (table) that lists IP addresses and their corresponding EUI-48 addresses. When a host wishes to transmit a packet to a certain IP address, it looks up the IP address in the ARP table and notes the EUI-48 address for that device. It uses this EUI-48 address as the destination

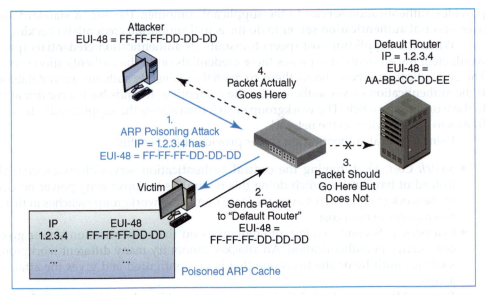

FIGURE 5-26 Man in the Middle Attack in an Ethernet LAN Using ARP Poisoning

address in the frame that delivers the packet. In the figure, the victim host wishes to transmit a packet to the default router, whose IP address is 1.2.3.4 and whose EUI-48 address is AA-BB-CC-DD-EE.

Unfortunately, the attacker has already transmitted an **ARP poisoning** attack packet to the victim host. This packet falsely tells the victim that the EUI-48 address for 1.2.3.4 is FF-FF-FF-DD-DD-DD. This is really the EUI-48 address of the attacker.

When the victim host transmits a packet to 1.2.3.4, it believes that this packet is going to the default router. In reality, the frame carries the packet to the attacker's address. The attacker reads the packet, stealing any important information. Not shown in the figure, the attacker then passes the frame on to the default router. Neither the victim host nor the router knows that the packet has been intercepted and read by the attacker.

Many Ethernet networks are wide open to ARP poisoning attacks. In the past, these attacks tended to be dismissed on the grounds that the attacker would have to be inside the network. Of course, if the attacker owns a compromised host, he or she is already there. Different switch vendors have different proprietary approaches to mitigating the danger of ARP cache poisoning man in the middle attacks. None are perfect, and all require attention from the user organization.

The 802.1 Working Group has developed a general solution, the **802.1AE** standard, which requires hosts and routers to authenticate the source of ARP messages and other messages before the receiver will accept them. A host will not accept an ARP message from another host. However, implementing authentication between each pair of devices on a network is time consuming, and the threat is viewed as rare; so the standard is not widely used, despite the fact that all modern switches implement it.

Test Your Understanding

24. a) How does a man in the middle attack benefit the attacker? b) How does a host use information in its ARP cache? c) How does the ARP cache poisoning packet change the ARP cache on a victim host or router? d) What are the consequences of this change? e) Are the victim and default router aware that the man in the middle attack is occurring? f) How can 802.1AE defeat man in the middle attacks? g) Is the standard widely used?

CONCLUSION

Synopsis

In this chapter, we looked at Ethernet switched wired LANs. In contrast to wide area networks (WANs), LANs are inexpensive per bit transmitted, so organizations can afford to provide extremely high-speed LAN service. There once were several switched wired LAN technologies, but Ethernet, which is standardized by the IEEE 802 Committee's 802.3 Working Group, is the only significant switched wired LAN technology.

All LANs are governed by physical and data link layer standards. We began by looking at physical layer standards—specifically at binary and digital signaling, which give resistance to transmission error. Ethernet uses two major transmission media. Four-pair unshielded twisted pair (4-pair UTP) copper wiring dominates in access links between hosts and the workgroup switches they connect to. Optical fiber, which can span longer distances, is used primarily in trunk links to connect switches to other switches. LANs use inexpensive 850 nm multimode fiber, which can span the distances needed in LANs. Normally, a single UTP or optical fiber link connects a pair of switches. However, with link aggregation (also called bonding), a pair of switches can be connected by two or more UTP or fiber links. Ethernet has many physical layer standards for both UTP and optical fiber. Standards set both transmission speed and maximum distance. They allow network designers to select media standards for specific media runs within the customer premises. For UTP, quality levels are indicated by category numbers. Today, Category 5e, 6, and 6A wiring are dominant. Optical fiber quality is standardized with OM numbers. Current fiber on sale fires the OM3 and OM4 standards.

Although Ethernet has many physical layer standards, it only has a single data link layer standard, the 802.3 MAC Layer Standard. We looked at some aspects of Ethernet's frame organization. The source and destination EUI-48 addresses are 48 bits long and are expressed for human consumption in hexadecimal notation. The length field gives the length of the data field. The final Frame Check Control Sequence field is for error checking. Ethernet does error detection but merely discards incorrect frames. There is no error correction, so Ethernet is an unreliable protocol. The data field has two subfields. The first is the 8-bit logical link control (LLC) subheader, which specifies the type of packet contained in the data field. The second is the packet itself—usually an IP packet, although other types of packets can be carried. If priority is used, two tag fields are inserted between the address fields and the length field.

We looked at how Ethernet switches forward frames. Ethernet networks must be organized as a hierarchy, in which there are no loops among the switches. Consequently, there is only a single path between any two hosts. This makes Ethernet switching tables very simple, so Ethernet switches are both fast and inexpensive.

Although basic Ethernet switch forwarding is simple, large Ethernet networks add complications to this basic operation. In a hierarchical LAN, a single point of failure, such as a transmission link or switch, can isolate client hosts from server hosts. Backup links would solve this problem but would create loops that would destroy the strict hierarchy. The Rapid Spanning Tree Protocol allows backup links to be installed but activated only if there is a break in the hierarchy.

An important switch capability is manageability. Manageable switches are controlled by an SNMP manager. Centralized management reduces labor cost substantially, more than making up for the higher costs of manageable switches.

The Ethernet POE Plus standard provides up to 25 watts of electrical power to each switch port. This allows simple devices such as access points to receive power from the switch instead of requiring a separate power connection, which might be expensive to install.

Ethernet security has not been seen as a major issue in most firms. However, we reviewed the 802.1X standard that requires a host to authenticate itself to a switch port before it is allowed to use the network. This prevents attackers from walking into a firm and simply plugging into any Ethernet wall jack. In 802.1X, the host is called a peer, the switch is the authenticator, and there is a back-end authentication server that actually checks authentication credentials. Having a central authentication server that keeps authentication data and makes authentication decisions reduces the work that must be done by the switch. This minimizes switch cost. Centralizing authentication data and decisions on the authentication server also brings consistency to authentication, reduces switch and management cost, and allows the status of individual users to be changed instantly. Note that this security standard comes from the 802.1 Working Group, not the 802.3 Working Group.

Another security threat in 802.3 networks is man in the middle attacks through ARP poisoning. This allows an adversary on a host inside an Ethernet LAN to force all traffic to pass through his or her host. This allows the adversary to eavesdrop on all traffic. The best defense against ARP poisoning is to force all hosts to authenticate themselves using the 802.1AE standard, but this standard is not widely used.

END-OF-CHAPTER QUESTIONS

Thought Questions

5-1. With power over Ethernet, what is the potential danger to users in having powered switch ports? How do you think this danger is avoided in the POE Plus standard?

5-2. a) List the security planning principles from Chapter 4. b)When implementing SNMP for managed switches, what security planning principle must be considered?

Design Questions

5-3. Design an Ethernet network to connect a single client PC to a single server. Both the client and the server will connect to their workgroup switches via UTP. The two devices are 900 meters apart. They need to communicate at 800 Mbps. Your design will specify the locations of any switches and the transmission link between the switches.

5-4. Add to your design in the previous question. Add another client next to the first client. This client will also communicate with the server and will also need 800 Mbps in transmission speed. Again, your design will specify the locations of switches and the transmission link between the switches.

Troubleshooting Question

5-5. You are connecting two switches in a large Ethernet switch with 32 switches. You are using 4-pair UTP. Suddenly, transmissions cannot travel over the network. What do you think might have happened? If you cannot come up with a good hypothesis, reread the synopsis and see which points might apply. Do not do other steps in the troubleshooting process.

Perspective Questions

5-6. What was the most surprising thing you learned in this chapter?

5-7. What was the most difficult part of this chapter for you?

Chapter 5a

Hands-On: Cutting and Connectorizing UTP[1]

LEARNING OBJECTIVES

By the end of this chapter, you should be able to:

- Cut, connectorize, and test 4-Pair UTP cabling.
- Explain the difference between solid wire and stranded-wire UTP.
- Know when to use patch cables.

INTRODUCTION

Chapter 5 discussed UTP wiring in general. This chapter discusses how to cut and connectorize (add connectors to) solid UTP wiring.

SOLID AND STRANDED WIRING

Solid-Wire UTP versus Stranded-Wire UTP

The TIA/EIA-568 standard requires that long runs to wall jacks use **solid-wire UTP**, in which each of the eight wires really is a single solid wire.

However, patch cords running from the wall outlet to a NIC usually are **stranded-wire UTP**, in which each of the eight "wires" really is a bundle of thinner wire strands. So stranded-wire UTP has eight bundles of wires, each bundle in its own insulation and acting like a single wire.

---

[1] This material is based on the author's lab projects and on the lab project of Professor Harry Reif of James Madison University.

Solid-Wire UTP

> Each of the eight wires is a solid wire

> Low attenuation over long distances

> Easy to connectorize

> Inflexible and stiff—not good for runs to the desktop

Stranded-Wire UTP

> Each of the eight "wires" is itself several thin strands of wire within an insulation tube

> Flexible and durable—good for runs to the desktop

> Impossible to connectorize in the field (bought as patch cords)

> Higher attenuation than solid-wire UTP—Used only in short runs

>> From wall jack to desktop

>> Within a telecommunications closet (see Chapter 3)

FIGURE 5A-1 Solid-Wire and Stranded-Wire UTP (Study Figure)

Relative Advantages

Solid wire is needed in long cords because it has lower attenuation than stranded wire. In contrast, stranded-wire UTP cords are more flexible than solid-wire cords, making them ideal for patch cords—especially the one running to the desktop—because they can be bent more and still function. They are more durable than solid-wire UTP cords.

Adding Connectors

It is relatively easy to add RJ-45 connectors to solid-wire UTP cords. However, it is very difficult to add RJ-45 connectors to stranded-wire cords. Stranded-wire patch cords should be purchased from the factory precut to desired lengths and preconnectorized.

In addition, when purchasing equipment to connectorize solid-wire UTP, it is important to purchase crimpers designed for solid wire.

CUTTING THE CORD

Solid-wire UTP normally comes in a box or spool containing 50 meters or more of wire. The first step is to cut a length of UTP cord that matches your need. It is good to be a little generous with the length. This way, bad connectorization can be fixed by cutting off the connector and adding a new connector to the shortened cord. Also, UTP cords should never be subjected to pulls (strain), and adding a little extra length creates some slack.

STRIPPING THE CORD

Now the cord must be stripped at each end using a **stripping tool** such as the one shown in Figure 5a-2. The installer rotates the stripper once around the cord, scoring (cutting into) the cord jacket (but not cutting through it). The installer then pulls off the scored end of the cord, exposing about 5 cm (about 2 inches) of the wire pairs.

It is critical not to score the cord too deeply, or the insulation around the individual wires may be cut. This creates short circuits. A really deep cut also will nick the wire, perhaps causing it to snap immediately or later.

WORKING WITH THE EXPOSED PAIRS

Pair Colors

The four pairs each have a color: orange, green, blue, or brown. One wire of the pair usually is a completely solid color. The other usually is white with stripes of the pair's color. For instance, the orange pair has an orange wire and a white wire with orange stripes.

Untwisting the Pairs

The wires of each pair are twisted around each other several times per inch. These must be untwisted after the end of the cord is stripped.

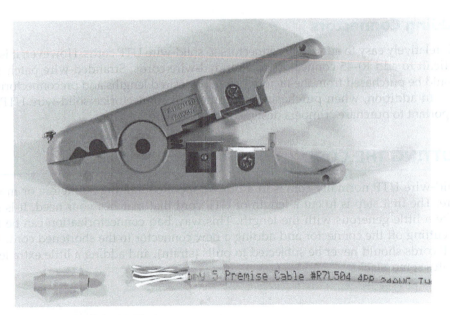

FIGURE 5A-2 Stripping Tool

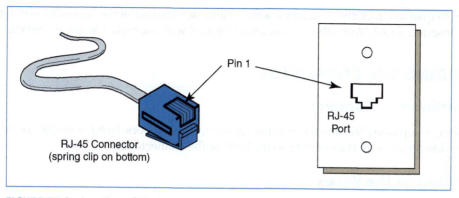

FIGURE 5A-3   Location of Pin 1 on an RJ-45 Connector and Wall Jack or NIC

Ordering the Pairs

The wires now must be placed in their correct order, left to right. Figure 5a-3 shows the location of Pin 1 on the RJ-45 connector and on a wall jack or NIC.

Which color wire goes into which connector slot? The two standardized patterns are shown in Figure 5a-4. The T568B pattern is much more common in the United States.

The connectors at both ends of the cord use the same pattern. If the white-orange wire goes into Pin 1 of the connector on one end of the cord, it also goes into Pin 1 of the connector at the other end.

Cutting the Wires

The length of the exposed wires must be limited to 1.25 cm (0.5 inch) or slightly less. After the wires have been arranged in the correct order, a cutter should cut across the wires to make them this length. The cut should be made straight across, so that all wires

Pin*	T568A	T568B
1	White-Green	White-Orange
2	Green	Orange
3	White-Orange	White-Green
4	Blue	Blue
5	White-Blue	White-Blue
6	Orange	Green
7	White-Brown	White-Brown
8	Brown	Brown

*Do not confuse T568A and T568B pin colors with the
TIA/EIA-568 Standard.

FIGURE 5A-4   T568A and T568B Pin Colors

are of equal length. Otherwise, they will not all reach the end of the connector when they are inserted into it. Wires that do not reach the end will not make electrical contact.

ADDING THE CONNECTOR

Holding the Connector

The next step is to place the wires in the RJ-45 connector. In one hand, hold the connector, clip side down, with the opening in the back of the connector facing you.

Sliding in the Wires

Now, slide the wires into the connector, making sure that they are in the correct order (white-orange on your left). There are grooves in the connector that will help. Be sure to push the wires all the way to the end or proper electrical contact will not be made with the pins at the end.

Before you crimp the connector, look down at the top of the connector, holding the tip away from you. The first wire on your left should be mostly white. So should every second wire. If they are not, you have inserted your wires incorrectly.[2]

Some Jacket Inside the Connector

If you have shortened your wires properly, there will be a little bit of jacket inside the RJ-45 connector.

CRIMPING

Pressing Down

Get a really good **crimping tool** (see Figure 5a-5). Place the connector with the wires in it into the crimp and push down firmly. Good crimping tools have ratchets to reduce the chance of your pushing down too tightly.

Making Electrical Contact

The front of the connector has eight pins running from the top almost to the bottom (spring clip side). When you **crimp** the connector, you force these eight pins through the insulation around each wire and into the wire itself. This seems like a crude electrical connection, and it is. However, it normally works very well. Your wires are now connected to the connector's pins. By the way, this is called an **insulation displacement connection (IDC)** because it cuts through the insulation.

---

[2] Thanks to Jason Okumura, who suggested this way of checking the wires.

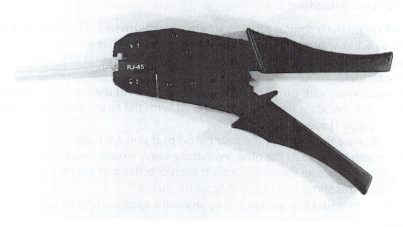

FIGURE 5A-5 Crimping Tool

Strain Relief

When you crimp, the crimper also forces a ridge in the back of the RJ-45 connector into the jacket of the cord. This provides **strain relief**, meaning that if someone pulls on the cord (a bad idea), they will be pulling only to the point where the jacket has the ridge forced into it. There will be no strain where the wires connect to the pins.

TESTING

Purchasing the best UTP cabling means nothing unless you install it properly. Wiring errors are common in the field, so you need to test every cord after you install it. Testing is inexpensive compared to troubleshooting subtle wiring problems later.

Testing with Continuity Testers

The simplest testers are **continuity testers**, which merely test whether the wires are arranged in correct order within the two RJ-45 connectors and are making good electrical contact with the connector. They cost only about $100.

Testing for Signal Quality

Better testers cost $500–$2,000 but are worth the extra money. In addition to testing for continuity problems, they send **test signals** through the cord to determine whether the cord meets TIA/EIA-568 signal-quality requirements. Many include **time domain reflectometry (TDR)**, which sends a signal and listens for echoes in order to measure the length of the UTP cord or to find if and where breaks exist in the cord.

Test Your Understanding

1. a) Explain the technical difference between solid-wire UTP and stranded-wire UTP. b) In what way is solid-wire UTP better? c) In what way is stranded-wire UTP better? d) Where would you use each? e) Which should only be connectorized at the factory?

2. If you have a wire run of 50 meters, should you cut the cord to 50 meters? Explain.

3. Why do you score the jacket of the cord with the stripping tool instead of cutting all the way through the jacket?

4. a) What are the colors of the four pairs? b) If you are following T568B, which wire goes into Pin 3? c) At the other end of the cord, would the same wire go into Pin 3?

5. After you arrange the wires in their correct order and cut them across, how much of the wires should be exposed from the jacket?

6. a) Describe RJ-45's insulation displacement approach. b) Describe its strain relief approach.

7. a) Should you test every cord in the field after installation? b) For what do inexpensive testers test? c) For what do expensive testers test?

Chapter 5b

Hands-On: Ethernet Switching

LEARNING OBJECTIVES

By the end of this chapter, you should be able to:

- Set up a small Ethernet switched network.
- Observe what happens if you create a loop among Ethernet switches.

THE EXERCISE

This is a class exercise rather than an individual exercise. It is rather quick (taking 15 to 20 minutes), but it takes an investment in resources.

What You Will Need

- A number of Ethernet switches. In general, it is good to have one switch for every two to four students, with the low ratio being much better. These can be very cheap switches.
- Enough UTP cords to connect the switches to each other and to the wall jack that bring the campus network into the classroom. Each will need to be 3–6 m in length, depending on the layout of the classroom. Each student group should have sufficient room to work.
- Each Ethernet switch is powered. You may need to have some power cables so that all of the teams have power for their switches.
- Two notebooks to plug into the network.

Creating the Network

The students should create a network like the one in Figure 5b-1. There should be a top-level switch at the front of the classroom. It should plug into the wall jack that connects the classroom to the campus network.

Below the top-level switch, other switches should be arranged in a hierarchy. I find it useful to have a simple hierarchy with two columns of switches as shown in the figure. It is important to keep a strict hierarchy among the switches.

After the switches are set up, attach PCs to switches at the end of each column. See if the PCs can connect to the Internet via the classroom wall jack. They should be able to do so.

At the end of this exercise, you can see how straightforward it is to set up a hierarchical Ethernet network. The switches are easy to power up, and RJ-45 connectors simply go "snap."

Creating a Loop

Now that the network is working, it is time to create a loop. Loops are not allowed in Ethernet, and you are about to see why. Connect two switches so that a loop is created, as Figure 5b-2 illustrates. Now see if the PCs can still access the Internet. They should not be able to do so.

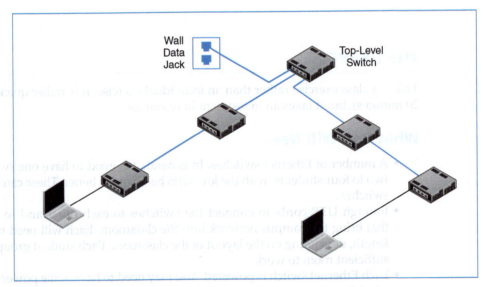

FIGURE 5B-1   The Network

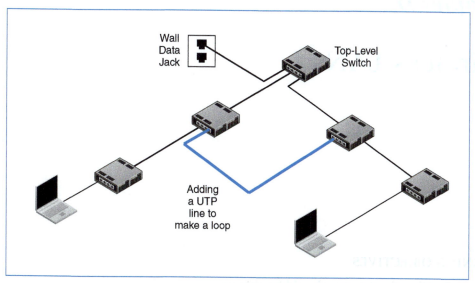

FIGURE 5B-2   Adding a Loop

Chapter 6

Wireless LANs I

LEARNING OBJECTIVES

By the end of this chapter, you should be able to:

- Explain basic radio signal propagation concepts, including frequencies, antennas, and wireless propagation problems.

- Explain the frequency spectrum, service bands, channels, bandwidth, licensed versus unlicensed service bands, and the type of spread spectrum transmission used in 802.11 Wi-Fi LANs.

- Describe 802.11 Wi-Fi WLAN operation with access points and a switched Ethernet distribution system to link the access points. Distinguish between BSSs, ESSs, and SSIDs. Discuss communication between access points.

- Compare the CSMA/CA+ACK and RTS/CTS media access control disciplines. (If you read the box on access control mechanisms).

- Compare and contrast the 802.11g, 802.11a, 802.11n, and 802.11ac transmission standards. Discuss emerging trends in 802.11 operation, including channels with much wider bandwidth, MIMO, beamforming, and multiuser MIMO.

- Briefly discuss the key points of wireless mesh networking.

INTRODUCTION

OSI Standards

In Chapter 5, we looked at wired switched Ethernet networks. Technologies for these networks require both physical and data link layer standards. Consequently, they use OSI standards. In this chapter and in Chapter 7, we will look at wireless LANs. Like wired LANs, wireless LANs are also single networks, which require physical and DLL standards. They too use OSI standards.

Test Your Understanding

1. a) At what layers do wireless LANs operate? b) Do wireless LAN standards come from OSI or TCP/IP? Explain.

802.11 versus Wi-Fi

Having discussed wireless transmission briefly, we will look at wireless networking's widest application, wireless local area networks. **Wireless LANs (WLANs)** use radio for physical layer transmission on the customer premises.

Ethernet 802.3 LANs

    Require standards at Layer 1 (physical) and Layer 2 (data link)

    Therefore, use OSI standards

    The 802.3 Working Group of the IEEE 802 Committee creates standards

Wireless LANs

    Operate at Layers 1 and 2

    Therefore, they are OSI standards

802.11 Wireless LAN Technology

    The dominant WLAN technology today

    Standardized by the 802.11 Working Group of the IEEE 802 Committee

Wi-Fi Alliance

    Industry association of 802.11 equipment manufacturers

    Purpose

        802.11 standards have many options

        Wi-Fi Alliance selects subsets of standards as profiles

        Does interoperability testing among vendors on these profiles

        Only products that pass can display the Wi-Fi logo on their products

    However, sometimes develops new standards

        Two have been security nightmares

FIGURE 6-1   802.11 / Wi-Fi Wireless LAN (WLAN) Technology (Study Figure)

Wireless LANs (WLANs) use radio for physical layer transmission on the customer premises.

In the last chapter, we saw that the 802.3 Working Group of the IEEE's 802 LAN/ MAN Standards Committee creates Ethernet standards. Other working groups create other standards. The dominant WLAN standards today are the **802.11** standards, which are created by the **IEEE 802.11 Working Group**.

It is common to call the 802.11 standards "Wi-Fi" standards. In fact, the terms have become almost interchangeable, and we will use them that way in this book. However, as an IT professional, you should understand the technical difference between 802.11 and Wi-Fi. The term **Wi-Fi** stems from the **Wi-Fi Alliance**, which is an industry consortium of 802.11 product vendors. When the 802.11 Working Group creates standards, it often creates many options. The Wi-Fi Alliance creates subsets of 802.11 standards with selected options. The Alliance conducts interoperability tests among products that claim to meet these "profiles." Only products that pass interoperability tests may display the Wi-Fi logo on their products. Products that do not pass are rarely sold, so when someone picks up a box containing an 802.11 product, they almost always see the Wi-Fi logo.

Test Your Understanding

2. a) Distinguish between 802.3 standards and 802.11 standards. b) Distinguish between 802.11 and Wi-Fi.

Wireless LAN Operation

It is possible to have a purely wireless LAN. In organizations today, however, the normal situation is to have a *hybrid switched/wireless single network*. Figure 6-2 shows that corporations already have comprehensive Ethernet switched LANs. These wired LANs reach almost everywhere on the corporate premises. Wireless clients (wireless devices

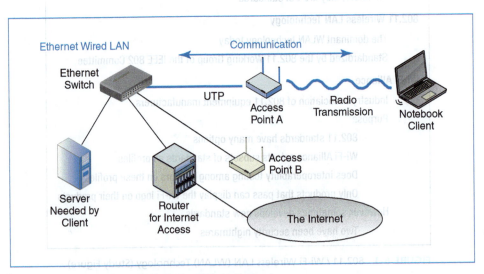

FIGURE 6-2 Hybrid Switched/Wireless 802.11 Network

are almost always clients) communicate wirelessly (by radio) to an 802.11 wireless access point, which is typically simply called an **access point**.

Wi-Fi clients rarely communicate with other 802.11 clients. Instead, they usually need to reach resources on the main Ethernet LAN. Obviously, clients need to reach servers, and corporate servers are on the firm's Ethernet network. In addition, of course, clients need to reach the Internet, and the firm's border router that connects it to the Internet is also on the firm's Ethernet network. In addition to orchestrating radio transmissions between itself and the wireless clients it serves, an access point connects the wireless devices to the firm's main Ethernet LAN.

> *In addition to orchestrating radio transmissions between itself and the wireless clients it serves, an access point connects the wireless devices to the firm's main Ethernet LAN.*

Only small firms can get by with a single access point. Larger firms disperse access points around their premises so that a wireless client can connect to another access point when it is moved to a different location.

Test Your Understanding

3. a) Why do wireless clients need access to the firm's main wired switched Ethernet network? b) How can firms provide WLAN coverage throughout a large building?

RADIO SIGNAL PROPAGATION

Chapter 5 discussed propagation effects in wired transmission media (UTP and optical fiber). Propagation effects in wired transmission can be well controlled by respecting cord distance limits and taking other installation precautions. This is possible because wired propagation is predictable. If you input a signal, you can estimate precisely what it will be at the other end of a cord. A wired network is like a faithful, obedient dog.

> *Propagation effects in wired transmission can be well controlled by respecting cord distance limits and taking other installation precautions.*

In contrast, radio propagation is very unreliable. Radio signals bounce off obstacles, fail to pass through walls and filing cabinets, and have other problems we will look at in this section. Consequently, Wi-Fi networks, which use radio to deliver signals, are more complex to implement than wired networks. They do not have a few simple installation guidelines that can reduce propagation effects to nonissues. Therefore, we will spend more time on wireless propagation effects than we did on wired propagation effects.

> *Propagation effects in wireless networks are complex and difficult to implement.*

Test Your Understanding

4. a) In 802.3 Ethernet networks, can simple installation rules usually reduce propagation effects to nonissues? b) In 802.11 Wi-Fi networks, can simple installation rules usually reduce propagation effects to nonissues?

Frequencies

Radios for data transmission are called **transceivers** because they both transmit and receive. When transceivers send, their wireless signals propagate as waves, as we saw in Chapter 5. Figure 6-3 again notes that waves have amplitude and wavelength. While optical fiber waves are described in terms of wavelength, radio waves are described in terms of another wave characteristic, **frequency**.

Frequency is used to describe the radio waves used in WLANs.

In waves, frequency is the number of complete cycles per second. One cycle per second is one **hertz** (Hz). Metric designations are used to describe frequencies. In the metric system, frequencies increase by a factor of 1,000 rather than 1,024. The most common radio frequencies for wireless transceivers range between about 500 **megahertz (MHz)** and 10 **gigahertz** (GHz).

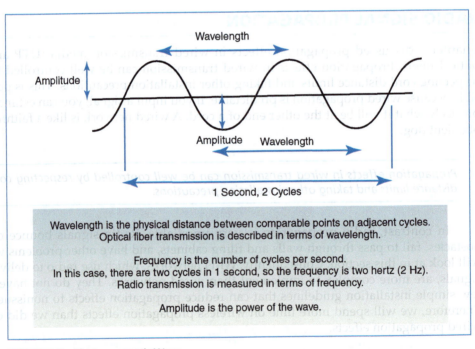

Wavelength is the physical distance between comparable points on adjacent cycles.
Optical fiber transmission is described in terms of wavelength.

Frequency is the number of cycles per second.
In this case, there are two cycles in 1 second, so the frequency is two hertz (2 Hz).
Radio transmission is measured in terms of frequency.

Amplitude is the power of the wave.

FIGURE 6-3   Electromagnetic Wave

Test Your Understanding

5. a) What is a transceiver? b) Is wireless radio transmission usually expressed in terms of wavelength or frequency? c) What is a hertz? d) Convert 3.4 MHz to a number without a metric prefix. (The use of metric prefixes was discussed in a box in Chapter 1.) e) At what range of frequencies do most wireless systems operate?

Antennas

A transceiver must have an **antenna** to transmit its signal. Figure 6-4 shows that there are two types of radio antennas: omnidirectional antennas and dish antennas.

- **Omnidirectional antennas** transmit signals equally strongly in all directions and receive incoming signals equally well from all directions. Consequently, the antenna does not need to point in the direction of the receiver. However, because the signal spreads in all three dimensions, only a small fraction of the energy transmitted by an omnidirectional antenna reaches the receiver. Omnidirectional antennas are best for short distances, such as those found in a wireless LAN or a cellular telephone network.

- **Dish antennas**, in contrast, point in a particular direction, which allows them to send stronger signals in that direction for the same power and to receive weaker incoming signals from that direction. (A dish antenna is like the reflector in a flashlight.) Dish antennas are good for longer distances because of their focusing ability, although users need to know the direction of the other radio. In addition, dish antennas are hard to use. (Imagine if you had to carry a dish with you whenever you carried your cellular phone. You would not even know where to point the dish!)

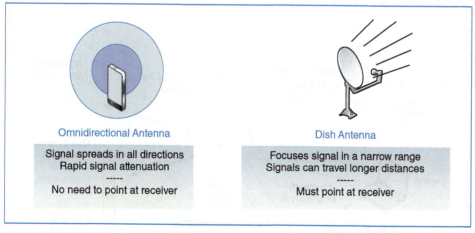

FIGURE 6-4 Omnidirectional and Dish Antennas

Test Your Understanding

6. a) Distinguish between omnidirectional and dish antennas in terms of operation. b) Under what circumstances would you use an omnidirectional antenna? c) Under what circumstances would you use a dish antenna? d) What type of antenna normally is used in WLANs? Why?

Wireless Propagation Problems

We have already noted that, although wireless communication gives mobility, wireless transmission is not very predictable, and there often are serious propagation problems. Figure 6-5 illustrates five common wireless propagation problems.

Inverse Square Law Attenuation Compared to signals sent through wires and optical fiber, radio signals attenuate very rapidly. When a signal spreads out from any kind of antenna, its strength is spread over the area of a sphere. (In omnidirectional antennas, power is spread equally over the sphere, while in dish antennas, power is concentrated primarily in one direction on the sphere.)

The area of a sphere is proportional to the square of its radius, so signal strength in any direction weakens by an **inverse square law** $(1/r^2)$, as Equation 6–1 illustrates. Here, S_1 is the signal strength at distance r_1, and S_2 is the signal strength at a farther distance r_2.

$$S_2 = S_1 * (r_1/r_2)^2 \qquad \textbf{(Equation 6–1)}$$

If you triple the distance $(r_1/r_2 = 1/3)$, the final signal strength (S_2) falls to only one-ninth $(1/3^2)$ of its original strength (S_1). With radio propagation, you have to be relatively close to your communication partner unless the signal strength is very high, a dish antenna is used, or both.

To give a specific example, at 10 meters, the signal strength is 30 milliwatts (mW). How strong will the signal be at 30 meters?

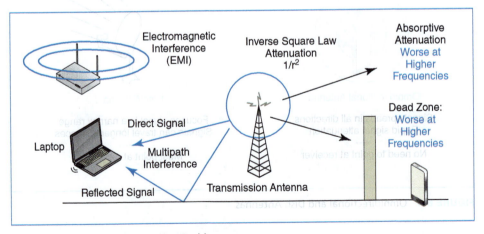

FIGURE 6-5 Wireless Propagation Problems

The Situation

Signals spread over the surface of a sphere

As the radius of the sphere increases with distance, the signal weakens

Weakens as the square of the distance

$$S_2 = S_1 * (r_1/r_2)^2 \qquad \text{(Equation 6–1)}$$

Example

At 10 meters (S_1), the signal strength is 30 mW

How strong will it be at 30 m?

The distance triples (so r_1/r_2 is 1/3).

So we multiply the signal strength at 10 meters by 1/9 (1/3 squared)

30 mW multiplied by 1/9 is 3.33 mW.

So the strength of the signal at 30 meters (S_2) will be 3.33 mW.

FIGURE 6-6   Inverse Square Law Attenuation (Study Figure)

- The distance triples (so r_1/r_2 is 1/3).
- So we multiply the signal strength at 10 meters by 1/9 (1/3 squared).
- 30 mW multiplied by 1/9 is 3.33 mW.
- So the strength of the signal at 30 meters will be 3.33 mW.

Absorptive Attenuation   As a radio signal travels, it is partially absorbed by the air molecules, plants, and other things it passes through. This **absorptive attenuation** is especially bad when the signal travels through rain or even office plants because water is an especially a good absorber of radio signals. Rain and moisture in plants can sharply reduce power.

Absorptive attenuation can be confusing because we have already seen inverse square law attenuation. Yes, wireless propagation suffers from *two* forms of attenuation. Inverse square law attenuation is due to the signal spreading out as a sphere and so becoming weaker at each point on the sphere. Absorptive attenuation is signal loss through energy absorption.

Wireless transmission suffers from two forms of attenuation—inverse square law attenuation and absorptive attenuation.

Dead Zones   To some extent, radio signals can go through and bend around objects. However, if there is a dense object (e.g., a thick wall) blocking the direct path between the sender and the receiver, the receiver may be in a **dead zone**, also called a shadow zone or dead spot. In these zones, the receiver cannot get the signal. If you have a mobile phone and often try to use it within buildings, you may be familiar with this problem.

Multipath Interference   In addition, radio waves tend to bounce off walls, floors, ceilings, and other objects. As Figure 6-7 shows, this may mean that a receiver will receive two or more signals—a direct signal and one or more reflected signals.

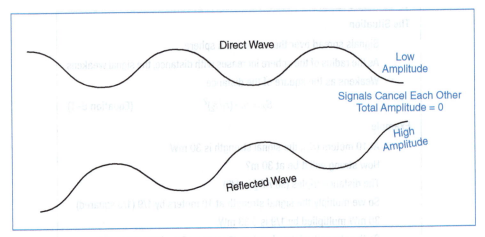

FIGURE 6-7 Multipath Interference

The direct and reflected signals will travel different distances and so may be out of phase when they reach the receiver. For example, one may be at its highest amplitude while the other is at its lowest, giving an average of zero. If their amplitudes are the same, they will completely cancel out. In real situation, multiple signals travelling different paths will interfere, so we call this type of interference multipath interference.

Multipath interference may cause the signal to range from strong to nonexistent within a few centimeters. If the difference in time between the direct and reflected signal is large, some reflected signals may even interfere with the next direct signal. Multipath interference is the most serious propagation problem at WLAN frequencies. We will see that it is controlled through spread spectrum transmission.

Multipath interference is the most serious propagation problem at WLAN frequencies.

Electromagnetic Interference (EMI)   A final common propagation problem in wireless communication is **electromagnetic interference (EMI)**. Many devices produce EMI at frequencies used in wireless data communications. Among these devices are cordless telephones, microwaves, and nearby access points. Consequently, placing access points so that they give good coverage without creating excessive mutual interference is difficult.

Frequency-Dependent Propagation Problems   To complicate matters, two wireless propagation problems get worse as frequency increases.

- First, higher-frequency waves suffer more rapidly from absorptive attenuation than lower-frequency waves because they are absorbed more rapidly by moisture in the air. Consequently, as we will see in this chapter, WLAN signals around 5 GHz attenuate more rapidly than signals around 2.4 GHz.
- Second, dead zone problems grow worse with frequency. As frequency increases, radio waves become less able to go through and bend around objects.

Test Your Understanding

7. a) If the signal strength from an omnidirectional radio source is 8 mW at 30 meters, how strong will it be at 120 meters, ignoring absorptive attenuation? Show your work. b) Contrast inverse square law attenuation and absorptive attenuation. c) How are dead zones created? d) Why is multipath interference very sensitive to location? e) What is the most serious propagation problem in WLANs? f) List some sources of EMI. g) What two propagation problems become worse as frequency increases?

RADIO BANDS, BANDWIDTH, AND SPREAD SPECTRUM TRANSMISSION

Service Bands

The Frequency Spectrum   The **frequency spectrum** is the range of all possible frequencies from zero hertz to infinity, as Figure 6-8 shows.

Service Bands   Regulators divide the frequency spectrum into contiguous spectrum ranges called **service bands** that are dedicated to specific services. For instance, in the United States, the AM radio service band lies between 535 kHz and 1,705 kHz. The FM radio service band, in turn, lies between 88 MHz and 108 MHz. The 2.4 GHz service band that we will see later in this chapter extends from 2.4 GHz to 2.4835 GHz. There are also service bands for police and fire departments, amateur radio operators, communication satellites, and many other purposes.

Channels   Service bands are subdivided further into smaller frequency ranges called **channels**. A different signal can be sent in each channel because signals in different channels do not interfere with one another. This is why you can receive different television channels successfully.

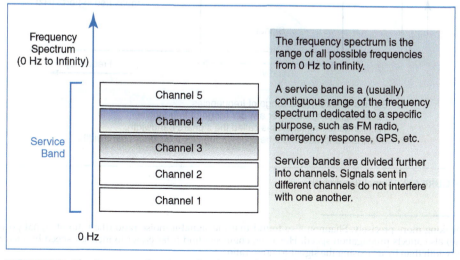

FIGURE 6-8   The Frequency Spectrum, Service Bands, and Channels

Test Your Understanding

8. a) Distinguish among the frequency spectrum, service bands, and channels. b) In radio, how can you send multiple signals without the signals interfering with one another?

Signal and Channel Bandwidth

Figure 6-3 showed a wave operating at a single frequency. In contrast, Figure 6-9 shows that real signals *do not* operate at a single frequency. Rather, real signals spread over a range of frequencies. This range is called the signal's **bandwidth**. Signal bandwidth is measured by subtracting the lowest frequency from the highest frequency.

A channel also has a bandwidth. For instance, if the lowest frequency of an FM channel is 89.0 MHz and the highest frequency is 89.2 MHz, then the **channel bandwidth** is 0.2 MHz (200 kHz). AM radio channels are 10 kHz wide, FM channels are 200 kHz wide, and television channels are 6 MHz wide. How wide must the channel bandwidth be? The channel bandwidth must be wide enough for a signal's bandwidth.

Claude Shannon discovered a remarkable thing about signal transmission. A signal carrying X bits per second only needs half the bandwidth of a signal carrying 2X bits per second.[1] Looked at the other way, if you want to transmit twice as many bits per second, you need to double your bandwidth. More generally, if you want to be able to transmit N times as fast, you need N times as much channel bandwidth. High bandwidth brings high radio transmission speed.

To transmit N times as fast, you need N times as much channel bandwidth.

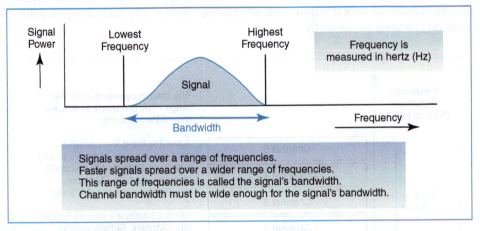

FIGURE 6-9 Signal Bandwidth

---

[1] Speaking more precisely, Shannon also found that the signal-to-noise ratio (the ratio of signal power to noise) also affects propagation speed. However, engineers find it far easier to increase speed by increasing bandwidth than by increasing the signal-to-noise ratio.

Required Transmission Speed and Required Channel Bandwidth

    There is a direct relationship between required transmission speed and required channel bandwidth

    Doubling bandwidth doubles the possible transmission speed

    Multiplying bandwidth by N makes possible N times the transmission speed

Broadband Channels

    Broadband means wide radio channel bandwidth and therefore high speed

    Popularly, fast systems are called "broadband" even if they are not radio systems

---

FIGURE 6-10   Channel Bandwidth and Transmission Speed (Study Figure)

Radio channels with large bandwidths are called **broadband** channels. They can carry data very quickly. Although the term *broadband* technically refers only to the width of a channel, broadband has come to mean "fast," whether or not radio is used.

Transmission systems that are very fast are usually called broadband *systems even when they do not use radio channels.*

Test Your Understanding

  9. a) Does a signal usually travel at a single frequency, or does it spread over a range of frequencies? b) If the lowest frequency in a channel is 1.22 MHz and the highest frequency is 1.25 MHz, what is the channel bandwidth? (Use proper metric notation.) c) If you want to transmit seven times as fast, how much wider must the channel be? d) Why is large channel bandwidth desirable? e) What do we call a system whose channels are wide? f) What other types of system do we call *broadband*?

The 2.4 GHz and 5 GHz Service Bands

802.11 Wi-Fi WLANs today use two service bands. One is the 2.4 GHz band. The other is the 5 GHz band.

    The 2.4 GHZ Service Band   The **2.4 GHz service band** is the same in most countries in the world, stretching from 2.4 GHz to 2.4835 GHz. Radio propagation is better in the 2.4 GHz service band than it is in the higher-frequency 5 GHz band, where absorptive attenuation is higher and dead zones are deader. Consequently, propagation differences are somewhat shorter.

    Unfortunately, the 2.4 GHz band only has 83.5 MHz of bandwidth. Traditionally, each 802.11 channel was 20 MHz wide, although 40 MHz bandwidth channels were introduced in 802.11n. Furthermore, due to the way channels are allocated, there are only three possible non-overlapping 20 MHz 802.11 channels, which are centered at

The 2.4 GHz Service Band

2.4 GHz to 2.485 GHz

Propagation characteristics are good

For 20 MHz 802.11 channels, only three nonoverlapping channels are possible

Channels 1, 6, and 11

This creates co-channel interference between nearby access points transmitting in the same channel

Except in very small networks, difficult or impossible to put nearby access points on different channels (Figure 6-12)

The 5 GHz Service Band

More bandwidth, so between 11 and 24 non-overlapping 20 MHz channels

Makes it easy to have nearby access points operate on non-overlapping channels

Increasing channel bandwidth in newer standards reduces the number of possible channels

FIGURE 6-11   The 2.4 GHz and 5 GHz Service Bands (Study Figure)

Channels 1, 6, and 11.[2] If nearby access points operate in the same channel, their signals will interfere with each other unless the access points are far apart. This is called **co-channel interference**. If an 802.11n station finds itself in a crowded area, it will drop back from 40 MHz channels to 20 MHz channels to reduce interference. Of course, speed roughly drops in half when this happens.

If you have only three access points that can all hear each other, there is no problem with having only three channels. You simply run each on a different channel, and there will be no co-channel interference. However, when you have multiple access points that can all hear each other, Figure 6-12 shows that there is no way to avoid having some

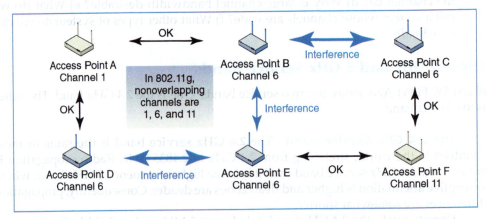

FIGURE 6-12   Co-Channel Interference in the 2.4 GHz Service Band

[2] Channel numbers were defined for the 2.4 GHz band when channels were narrower. A 20 MHz 802.11 channel overlaps several initially defined channels. Channels 1, 6, and 11 operate in the 2.402 GHz to 2.422 GHz, 2.427 GHz to 2. 447 GHz, and 2.452 GHz to 2.472 GHz frequency ranges, respectively. Note that there are unused 5 MHz "guard bands" between the channels to prevent inter-channel interference.

co-channel interference. You can minimize co-channel interference somewhat by giving the shared channel to the two access points that are farthest apart, but this will only reduce interference somewhat.

The 5 GHZ Service Band   Wi-Fi can also operate in the **5 GHz service band**. The big advantage of the 5 GHz band is that it is far wider than the 2.4 GHz band. In contrast to the 2.4 GHz band's mere three channels, the 5 GHz band provides between 11 and 24 non-overlapping 20 MHz channels today, depending on the frequencies allocated to this service band in a particular country. In addition, while the 2.4 GHz band is extremely crowded almost everywhere, it is only recently that companies have begun to use the 5 GHz band extensively.

The problem with the 5 GHz band has been simple economics. Radio transceivers in this band are inherently more expensive than they are in the 2.4 GHz band. However, technological advances have brought 5 GHz radio transceivers down to the price range that companies and households can now afford. Given the room in the 5 GHz band, this has led to a gold rush for vendors and users moving into this uncrowded service band.

Adding to the attractiveness of the 5 GHz band, regulators in several countries have been extending it to add more total bandwidth and therefore more channels. The United States added more bandwidth in 2003. In 2013, the Federal Communications Commission announced that it would add 35% more. In contrast, the 2.4 GHz band has no expansion potential because it is bordered by services that cannot be moved.

In addition, we will see that 802.11n and 802.11ac are using channels much wider than 20 MHz—up to 160 MHz. Wider channels mean fewer channels in the service band. Without growth in 5 GHz bandwidth, there would be too little bandwidth in the service band to permit enough very wide channels.

Test Your Understanding

10. a) In what two service bands does 802.11 operate? b) Which band dominated use initially? c) How many 20 MHz non-overlapping channels does the 2.4 GHz band support? d) Why is this a problem? e) Why are companies moving rapidly into the 5 GHz band? f) How many non-overlapping channels does the 5 GHz band support? g) Why is it important that governments add more bandwidth to the 5 GHz band? h) If you triple channel bandwidth, what happens to the number of channels in the service band?

NORMAL AND SPREAD SPECTRUM TRANSMISSION

Spread Spectrum Transmission

At the frequencies used by WLANs, there are numerous and severe propagation problems. In these service bands, regulators mandate the use of a form of transmission called spread spectrum transmission. **Spread spectrum transmission** is transmission that uses far wider channels than transmission speed requires.

Spread spectrum transmission is transmission that uses far wider channels than transmission speed requires.

Regulators mandate the use of spread spectrum transmission to minimize propagation problems—especially multipath interference. (If the direct and reflected signals cancel out at some frequencies within the band, they will be double at other frequencies and will average out over a wide enough frequency range.)

In commercial spread spectrum transmission, security is *not* a benefit. The military uses spread spectrum transmission for security, but it does so by keeping certain parameters of its spread spectrum transmission secret. Commercial spread spectrum transmission must make these parameters publicly known to allow parties to communicate easily.

In wireless LANs, spread spectrum transmission is used to reduce propagation problems, not to provide security.

Test Your Understanding

11. a) In Wi-Fi service bands, what type of transmission method is required by regulators? b) What is the benefit of spread spectrum transmission for business communication? c) Is spread spectrum transmission done for security reasons in commercial WLANs?

Licensed and Unlicensed Radio Bands

If two nearby transceivers send at the same frequency, their signals will interfere with each other. To prevent chaos, governments regulate how radio transmission is used. The International Telecommunications Union, which is a division of the United Nations, creates worldwide rules that define service bands and specify how individual radio service bands are to be used. Individual countries enforce these rules but are given discretion over how to implement controls.

Licensed Radio Bands   In **licensed radio bands**, transceivers must have a government license to operate. They also need a license change if they move. Commercial television bands are licensed bands, as are AM and FM radio bands. Government agencies control who may have licenses in these bands. By doing so, the government limits interference to an acceptable level. In some licensed bands, the rules allow mobile hosts to move about while only central transceivers are regulated. This is the case for mobile telephones.

Unlicensed Radio Bands   However, for companies that have wireless access points and mobile computers, even the requirement to license central antennas (in this situation, access points) is an impossible burden. Consequently, the International Telecommunications Union has created a few **unlicensed radio bands**. In these bands, a company can add or drop access points any time it chooses. It can also have as many wireless hosts as it wishes. All 802.11 Wi-Fi networks operate in these unlicensed radio bands.

Licensed Radio Bands

    If two nearby radio hosts transmit in the same channel, their signals will interfere

    Most radio bands are licensed bands, in which hosts need a license to transmit

    The government limits licenses to reduce interference

    Television bands, AM radio bands, etc. are licensed

    In cellular telephone bands, which are licensed, only the central antennas are licensed, not the mobile phones

Unlicensed Radio Bands

    Some bands are set aside as unlicensed bands

    Hosts do not need to be licensed to be turned on or moved

    802.11 Wi-Fi operates in unlicensed radio bands

    This allows access points and hosts to be moved freely

    However, there is no legal recourse against interference from other nearby users

    Your only recourse is to negotiate

    At the same time, you may not cause unreasonable interference by transmitting at illegally high power

---

FIGURE 6-13   Licensed and Unlicensed Radio Bands (Study Figure)

The downside of unlicensed radio bands is that companies must tolerate interference from others. If your neighbor sets up a wireless LAN next door to yours, you have no recourse but to negotiate with him or her over such matters as which channels each of you will use. At the same time, the law prohibits unreasonable interference by using illegally high transmission power.

Test Your Understanding

12. a) Do WLANs today use licensed or unlicensed bands? b) What is the advantage of using unlicensed bands? c) What is the downside?

Implementing Spread Spectrum Transmission

Normal versus Spread Spectrum Transmission   As noted earlier in our discussion of the bandwidth and speed, if you need to transmit at a given speed, you must have a channel whose bandwidth is sufficiently wide.

To allow as many channels as possible, channel bandwidths in *normal radio transmission* are limited to the speed requirements of the user's signal, as Figure 6-14 illustrates. For a service that operates at 10 kbps, regulators would allocate only enough channel bandwidth to handle this speed. Adding more channel bandwidth would not increase speed. It would be pure waste.

In contrast to normal radio transmission, which uses channels just wide enough for transmission speed requirements, spread spectrum transmission takes the original signal, called a **baseband signal**, and spreads the signal energy over a much broader channel than is required by the transmission speed.

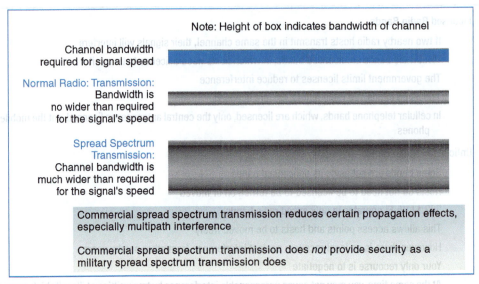

FIGURE 6-14 Normal Radio Transmission and Spread Spectrum Transmission

Orthogonal Frequency Division Multiplexing There are several spread spectrum transmission methods. The 802.11 Working Group's current standards all use **orthogonal frequency division multiplexing (OFDM)**, which Figure 6-15 illustrates.

In OFDM, each broadband channel is divided into many smaller subchannels called **subcarriers**. OFDM transmits part of a frame in each subcarrier. OFDM sends data redundantly across the subcarriers, so if there is impairment in one or even a few subcarriers, all of the frame will usually still get through.

Why use subcarriers instead of simply spreading the signal over the entire channel? The problem is that sending data over a very wide channel reliably is very difficult. It is much easier to send many slow signals in many small subcarriers.

Test Your Understanding

13. a) In normal radio operation, how does channel bandwidth relate to the bandwidth required to transmit a data stream of a given speed? b) How does this change in

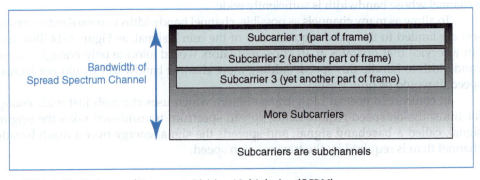

FIGURE 6-15 Orthogonal Frequency Division Multiplexing (OFDM)

spread spectrum transmission? c) What spread spectrum transmission method dominates today? d) Why does it use subcarriers instead of simply spreading the data over the entire channel?

802.11 WLAN OPERATION

As Figure 6-16 shows, an 802.11 Wi-Fi LAN typically connects a small number of mobile devices to a large wired Ethernet LAN because the servers and Internet access routers that mobile hosts need to use usually are on the wired LAN.[3] In 802.11 terminology, the wired Ethernet LAN to which access points connect is a **distribution system (DS)**.

The wired LAN to which access points connect is a distribution system (DS).

Test Your Understanding

14. In Figure 6-16, what is the distribution system?

Wireless Access Points

When a wireless host wishes to send a frame to a server, it transmits the frame to a wireless access point.

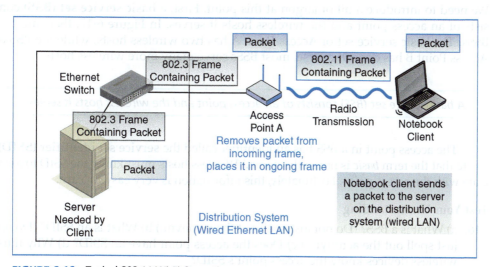

FIGURE 6-16 Typical 802.11 Wi-Fi Operation

---

[3] There is a rarely used 802.11 *ad hoc mode*, in which no wireless access point is used. In ad hoc mode, computers communicate directly with other computers without using an access point. (In contrast, when an access point is used, this is called 802.11 infrastructure mode.) In addition, 802.11 can create point-to-point transmission over longer distances than 802.11 normally supports. This approach, which normally is used to connect nearby buildings, uses dish antennas.

As Figure 6-16 shows, when a wireless host transmits to a server on the wired LAN, it puts the packet in an 802.11 frame.[4] An 802.11 frame cannot travel over the 802.3 LAN. Wi-Fi has an entirely different frame organization, and Ethernet switches have no idea how to handle 802.11 frames. To address this problem, the access point removes the packet from the 802.11 frame and places the packet in an 802.3 Ethernet frame. The access point sends this 802.3 frame to Ethernet network, which delivers the frame to the server. Later, when the server replies, the wireless access point receives the 802.3 frame, removes the packet from the Ethernet frame, and forwards the packet to the wireless host in a Wi-Fi frame.[5]

The packet goes all the way from the wireless host to a server. The 802.11 frame travels only between the wireless host and the wireless access point. The 802.3 frame travels only between the wireless access point and the server.

Test Your Understanding

15. a) Why must an access point remove an arriving packet from the frame in which the packet arrives and place the packet in a different frame when it sends the packet back out?

Basic Service Sets (BSSs)

We need to introduce a bit of jargon at this point. First, a **basic service set (BSS)** consists of an access point and the wireless hosts it serves. In Figure 6-17, there are two BSSs. The basic service set of Access Point A has two wireless hosts, while the BSS of Access Point B has one. Of course, most BSSs serve many more wireless hosts.

A basic service set (BSS) consists of an access point and the wireless hosts it serves

---

The access point in a BSS has an identifier called the **service set identifier (SSID)**. (Note that the term *basic* is not in the name.) Wireless hosts must know the SSID to associate with the access point. Fortunately, this information is very easy to learn.

Test Your Understanding

16. a) What is a BSS? (Do not just spell out the acronym.) b) What is an SSID? (Do not just spell out the acronym.) c) Does the access point have an SSID? d) Why must wireless devices know the access point's SSID?

---

[4] 802.11 frames are much more complex than 802.3 Ethernet frames. Much of this complexity is needed to counter wireless propagation problems.

[5] This sounds like what a router does. However, a router can connect any two single networks. Access points are limited to connecting 802.3 and 802.11 networks.

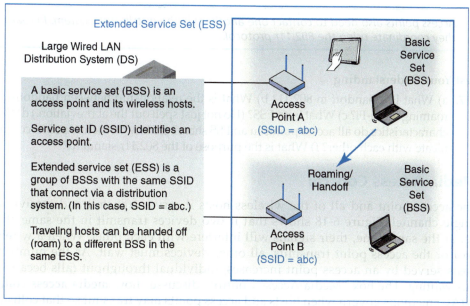

FIGURE 6-17   Basic Service Sets, Extended Service Set, Handoff, and Roaming

Extended Service Sets (ESSs), Handoffs, and Roaming

If a mobile host travels too far from a wireless access point, its signal will become too weak to reach the access point. However, if there is a closer access point, the host can be **handed off** to that access point for service. In WLANs, the ability to use handoffs is also called **roaming**.[6]

Roaming requires that both access points belong to the same extended service set. An **extended service set (ESS)** is a group of BSSs 1) that are connected to the same distribution system and 2) in which all access points have the same SSID.

An extended service set (ESS) is a group of BSSs 1) that are connected to the same distribution system and 2) in which all access points have the same SSID.

We said earlier in this section that one function of access points is to work together to coordinate service, and we gave roaming as an example of this. In roaming, the two access points involved have to coordinate the handoff. They do this by communicating over the distribution system. Specifically, they coordinate via **802.11r** messages, which are nicely named because they deal with roaming.

---

[6] In cellular telephony, which we will see in Chapter 10, the terms *handoff* and *roaming* mean different things.

> *Access points also need to contact one another via the distribution system. In roaming, they coordinate using the 802.11r protocol.*

Test Your Understanding

17. a) What is a handoff in 802.11? b) What is the relationship between handoffs and roaming in Wi-Fi? c) What is an ESS? (Do not just spell out the abbreviation.) d) What characteristics do all access points in an ESS share? e) How can access points communicate with each other? f) What is the purpose of the 802.11r standard?

Media Access Control

The access point and all of the wireless hosts it serves transmit and receive in a single channel. Figure 6-18 shows that if two devices transmit in the same channel at the same time, their signals will interfere with each other. When a wireless host or the access point transmits, all other devices must wait. As the number of hosts served by an access point increases, individual throughput falls because of this waiting. The box "Media Access Control" discusses how **media access control (MAC)** methods govern when hosts and access points may transmit so that collisions are avoided.[7]

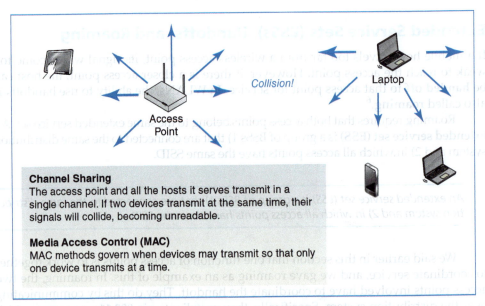

Channel Sharing
The access point and all the hosts it serves transmit in a single channel. If two devices transmit at the same time, their signals will collide, becoming unreadable.

Media Access Control (MAC)
MAC methods govern when devices may transmit so that only one device transmits at a time.

FIGURE 6-18   Hosts and Access Points Transmit on a Single Channel

---

[7] Yes, this is where the term MAC address comes from. Conceptually, Media Access Control is a sublayer of the data link layer. It applies to Ethernet, Wi-Fi, and other 802.11 standards. Addresses are defined at this layer so that all 802.11 standards use EUI-48 addresses.

Media access control (MAC) methods govern when hosts and access points may transmit so that collisions can be avoided.

The access point and all of the wireless hosts it serves transmit and receive in a single channel. When a wireless host or the access point transmits, all other devices must wait.

Test Your Understanding

18. All wireless hosts and the access point that serves them transmit on the same channel. a) What problem does this cause? b) How does media access control address this problem? c) Does media access control apply to wireless hosts, access points, or both?

BOX 1

Media Access Control (MAC)

The 802.11 standard has two mechanisms for media access control. The first, CSMA/CA+ACK, is mandatory. Access points and wireless hosts must support it. The second, RTS/CTS, is optional.[8]

CSMA/CA+ACK Media Access Control

The mandatory method is Carrier Sense Multiple Access with Collision Avoidance and Acknowledgement, which is mercifully shortened to CSMA/CA+ACK.

Carrier sense (CS) means to listen to (sense) traffic (the carrier, in radio parlance). **Multiple access (MA)** means that this method uses listening to control how multiple hosts can access the network to transmit. Quite simply, if another device is transmitting, the wireless host or access point does not transmit.

Collision avoidance (CA) means that the method attempts to avoid two devices transmitting at the same time. Most obviously, if one device has been sending for some time, two or more others may be waiting to send. If they both send as soon as the current sender stops, they will both transmit at the same time. This will cause a collision. Collision avoidance adds a random delay time to decide which device may transmit first. This works, but it is inefficient because it adds dead time when no one is transmitting.

ACK means that if the receiver receives a message correctly, it immediately sends an acknowledgment to the sender, not waiting at all. This is another reason to require stations to delay before sending when a sender stops transmitting.

If the sender does not receive an ACK, it retransmits the frame. Sending acknowledgments and retransmissions makes 802.11 Wi-Fi transmission *reliable* because it provides both error detection and error correction. CSMA/CA+ACK is the only reliable transmission method we will see in this book other than TCP. Most early DLL protocols were reliable because transmission then was unreliable, even in wired networks. Under these circumstances, error correction at the data link layer made sense. This is no longer true today generally. Wired transmission protocols such as Ethernet are unreliable. Doing error correction is simply not worth the effort when transmission errors are rare. We have seen that wireless transmission, however, is encumbered with propagation problems, and lost or damaged frames are far too common. It makes sense under these conditions to make 802.11 (and many other wireless protocols) reliable.

(continued)

---

[8] Actually, if you have even a single host with older 802.11b equipment connected to an access point, RTS/CTS becomes mandatory. However, 802.11b wireless hosts are almost never encountered anymore.

Carrier Sense Multiple Access with Collision Avoidance and Acknowledgement

> Mandatory for 802.11 Wi-Fi Operation

Carrier Sensing with Multiple Access

> Sender listens for traffic (senses the carrier)
>
> If another device is transmitting, it waits
>
> This controls access by multiple devices that must not transmit simultaneously

Collision Avoidance

> When the current sender stops, two or more waiting devices may immediately want to transmit
>
> This will cause a collision
>
> Instead, the devices must wait a randomized amount of time before sending
>
> This usually avoids collision, but it is inefficient

ACK (Acknowledgement) and Reliability

> Receiver *immediately* sends back an acknowledgement
>
> CA random delay for other devices guarantees there will be enough time for an immediate ACK
>
> If sender does not receive the acknowledgement, it retransmits using CSMA/CA+ACK
>
> CSMA/CA plus ACK is a reliable protocol
>
> Reliable transmission protocols are rare for wired networks
>
> However, radio transmission is unreliable enough to warrant it

Inefficiency

> There is a lot of waiting with CSMA/CA+ACK
>
> This makes it inefficient

FIGURE 6-19 CSMA/CA+ACK Media Access Control

Thanks to CSMA/CA+ACK, 802.11 is a reliable protocol.

CSMA/CA+ACK works well, but it is inefficient. Waiting before transmission wastes valuable time. Sending ACKs also is time consuming. Overall, an 802.11 LAN can only deliver throughput (actual speed) of about half the rated speed of its standard—that is, the speed published in the standard.

Test Your Understanding

19. a) What does CS mean? (Do not just spell out the abbreviation.) b) How is carrier sensing used in multiple access? c) Why is CA desirable? d) Does a frame's receiver transmit an ACK immediately or after a random delay? e) Is CSMA/CA+ACK reliable or unreliable? f) Why was 802.11 made reliable? g) Is CSMA/CA+ACK efficient?

Request to Send/Clear to Send (RTS /CTS)

Although CSMA/CA+ACK is mandatory, there is another control mechanism called **request to send/clear to send (RTS/CTS)**. Figure 6-20 illustrates RTS/CTS. As noted earlier, the RTS/CTS

(continued)

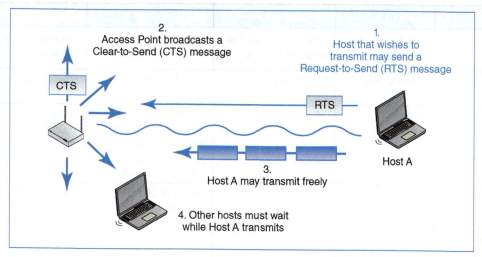

FIGURE 6-20   Request to Send/Clear to Send Media Access Control

protocol is optional. Avoiding RTS/CTS whenever possible is wise because RTS/CTS is much less efficient, and therefore slower, than CSMA/CA+ACK.

- When a host wishes to send, the host may send a **request-to-send (RTS)** message to the wireless access point. This message asks the access point for permission to send messages.
- If the access point responds by broadcasting a **clear-to-send (CTS)** message, then other hosts must wait. The host sending the RTS may then transmit, ignoring CSMA/CA.

Although RTS/CTS is widely used, keep in mind that it is only an option, while CSMA/CA is mandatory. Also, tests have shown that RTS/CTS reduces throughput when it is used even compared to CSMA/CA.

RTS/CTS makes sense primarily when two wireless clients can both hear the access point but cannot hear each other. With CSMA/CA+ACK, the two stations may transmit at the same time. RTS/CTS eliminates this.

Test Your Understanding

20. a) Describe RTS/CTS. b) Is CSMA/CA+ACK required or optional? c) Is RTS/CTS required or optional? d) Which is more efficient, RTS/CTS or CSMA/CA+ACK? e) When does it make sense to use RTS/CTS?

802.11 TRANSMISSION STANDARDS

The 802.11 Working Group has created several WLAN transmission standards since 1997. We will look at the most important of these standards today.

Characteristics of 802.11g, 802.11a, 802.11n, and 802.11ac

Figure 6-21 compares the 802.11g, 802.11a, 802.11n, and 802.11ac standards that companies must support today.

Characteristic	802.11g	802.11a	802.11n	802.11ac
Status	Obsolescent but still used	Obsolescent but still used in business	Dominant today in the installed base	Dominant today in sales
Unlicensed Band(s)	2.4 GHz only	5 GHz only	2.4 GHz and 5 GHz	5 GHz only
Channel bandwidth	20 MHz	20 MHz	40 MHz, but will drop back to 20 MHz if there is interference on the two selected channels	80 MHz or 160 MHz
Number of non-overlapping channels in the 5 GHz band in the USA (varies by country)	NA	20–25	20–25 at 20 MHz 8–12 at 40 MHz	4–6 at 80 MHz 1–2 at 160 MHz
MIMO?	No	No	Yes	Yes
Maximum number of spatial streams	NA	NA	4	8
Multi-User MIMO / Beamforming?	No	No	No	Yes
Rated Speed	54 Mbps	54 Mbps	100 Mbps to 600 Mbps; 150 to 300 Mbps common.	433 Mbps to 6.93 Gbps; 433 Mbps to 1.3 Gbps common.

FIGURE 6-21 Characteristics of Major 802.11 Wi-Fi Standards

- The 802.11g standard is obsolete, but access points must still deal with a considerable number of 802.11g devices. It achieved high penetration when it first brought 54 Mbps speed to the 2.4 GHz band, but 802.11n has largely replaced it.
- Not many people have even heard of 802.11a, but it saw some business use because of its operation in the uncrowded 5 GHz band. Today, it has a small installed base, but access points operating in the 5 GHz band still must support 802.11a clients.
- The 802.11n standard now dominates the installed base. Products that use this standard have higher speeds than 802.11g and 802.11a products and also have longer transmission ranges. As prices have fallen, 802.11n has become the low-price option in Wi-Fi.
- Products using the 802.11ac standard now dominate sales. Compared to 802.11n, 802.11ac offers very high speeds. 802.11ac will probably supplant 802.11n rapidly.

Test Your Understanding

21. a) Among the four standards listed, which are obsolete? **b)** Which dominates the installed base today? **c)** What is the market position of 802.11ac?

Bands and Channel Bandwidth

Earlier in this chapter, we saw that, other things being equal, doubling channel bandwidth doubles the possible transmission speed. However, service bands have limited total bandwidth, so doubling channel bandwidth means cutting the number of channels in half.

802.11g Channel Bandwidth   The 802.11g standard operates only in the crowded 2.4 GHz band. With channel bandwidth of 20 MHz, only three 802.11g channels are possible.

802.11a Channel Bandwidth   The 802.11a standard operates only in the less crowded 5 GHz band. It also uses 20 MHz channels. This permits many 802.11a channels. Unfortunately, radios in the 5 GHz band were expensive when 802.11a emerged, so 802.11a never achieved large market share.

802.11n Channel Bandwidth   The 802.11n standard can operate in both the 2.4 GHz band and the less-crowded and wider 5 GHz band. It also doubles 802.11g bandwidth, raising it to 40 MHz. This alone roughly doubles speed. However, to be a good neighbor, when there are stations operating on the three possible 20 MHz channels, 802.11n products will drop back to a 20 MHz channel bandwidth, losing their channel bandwidth advantage.

Dual-band 802.11n products also operate in the 5 GHz band. In this higher band, 40 MHz channels are widely available. In other words, 802.11n often reaches its full expression only in the 5 GHz band. Note, however, in Figure 6-21 that while 802.11n can use 20 to 25 channels in the 5 GHz band, it can only use 8 to 12 40 MHz channels. Why fewer than half the channels? The answer is that the 5 GHz band is not a solid band of frequencies. There are some gaps, and it is easier to fill available ranges with 20 MHz channels than with 40 MHz channels. We will see that the situation is even worse in 802.11ac.[9]

802.11ac Channel Bandwidth   The 802.11ac standard operates only in the 5 GHz band and has even wider channels than 802.11n. Support for 80 MHz channels is mandatory, and 160 MHz channels are optional. Doubling and quadrupling channel bandwidth compared to 802.11n means roughly a doubling and quadrupling of transmission speeds, other things being equal. Of course, having wider channels means having fewer channels, and the filling of available ranges with 80 MHz and

---

[9] Why are ranges of channels shown, rather than precise numbers? The answer is that regulatory limits apply in some situations. For instance, near an airport that uses weather radar, you may not use some parts of the "available" 5 GHz band.

160 MHz channels is even harder than with 40 MHz channels. There are only 4–6 channels at 80 MHz and 1–2 channels at 160 MHz.[10]

Test Your Understanding

22. a) Why is wider channel bandwidth good? b) What is the downside of wider channel bandwidth? c) What frequency band or bands do 802.11g, 802.11a, 802.11n, and 802.11ac use? d) For each, compare channel bandwidth and the number of possible channels.

MIMO

Increasing bandwidth is the easiest way to boost transmission speed, but there is also a more elegant way to increase speed without increasing bandwidth. Figure 6-22 notes that standards beyond 802.11g use a technique called **multiple input/multiple output (MIMO)** to double, triple, or quadruple transmission speed (or even increase it more) without increasing channel bandwidth.

The key to higher throughput in MIMO is that the host or access point sends two or more **spatial streams** (radio signals) in the *same channel* between two or more different antennas on access points and wireless hosts. Earlier, we said that that was impossible. That was a bit of a lie, actually. It used to be impossible, but newer technology has made this possible.

In the figure, there are two spatial streams. As we saw earlier in this chapter, two signals in the same channel should interfere with each other. However, the two spatial streams sent by different antennas will arrive at the two receiving antennas at slightly different times. Using detection and separation methods based on differences in arrival times for the two spatial streams, the receiver can separate the two spatial streams in the same channel and so can read them individually.

Even with only two spatial streams using two antennas each on the sender and receiver, MIMO can roughly double throughput. Using more antennas and therefore

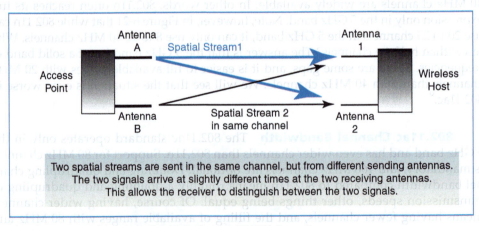

Two spatial streams are sent in the same channel, but from different sending antennas.
The two signals arrive at slightly different times at the two receiving antennas.
This allows the receiver to distinguish between the two signals.

FIGURE 6-22 Multiple Input/Multiple Output (MIMO) Operation

---

[10] The United States is currently in the process of adding about 35% more capacity to the 5 GHz band. Some of this will fill spaces between available ranges to give larger available ranges. This will add one or two 160 MHz channels, again depending on conditions.

more spatial streams can increase throughput even more. MIMO is not limited to two spatial streams.

The 802.11n standard introduced MIMO to Wi-Fi. With two spatial streams, the rated speed in 802.11n with 40 MHz channels is 300 Mbps. Three spatial streams raise the rated speed to 450 Mbps, and four raise it to 600 Mbps. The 802.11n standard requires access points to support four spatial streams, although wireless hosts are only required to support two spatial streams. Typical speeds in 802.11n products today have rated speeds of 150 Mbps to 300 Mbps.

The 802.11ac standard, in addition to doubling or quadrupling channel bandwidth compared to 802.11n, doubles the number of possible spatial streams to eight. The standard offers 16 possible combinations of bandwidth (80 MHz or 160 MHz) and number of spatial streams (1 to 8). This creates a large number of possible rated speeds: 433 MHz to 6.9 GHz. Products today typically provide rated speeds of 433 Mbps to 1.3 Gbps, but this is increasing rapidly.

Another benefit of MIMO, beyond greater transmission speed, is greater transmission range. Greater propagation distances may permit fewer access points to be installed, and this will lower equipment and installation cost.[11]

Test Your Understanding

23. a) How does MIMO use spatial streams to increase transmission speed? b) What is the main benefit of MIMO? c) What is its other benefit? d) Compare the range of rated speeds possible with 802.11n and 802.11ac.

Beamforming and Multiuser MIMO

Today, jet fighters use phased array radar systems that are flat dishes with many tiny antennas spread over the surface. Controlling the relative phases of the signals from these antennas can focus the radar beam in a particular direction very rapidly. Multiple antennas on MIMO systems can do the same, focusing the radio power instead of broadcasting it isotropically (in all directions equally). Figure 6-23 illustrates this **beamforming**.

Obviously, beamforming means that when the access point transmits to (or receives from) a wireless device the signal will be stronger. The radio can operate at lower power or send the signal farther.

Beamforming also allows **multiuser MIMO (MU-MIMO)**, in which the access point focuses on two wireless devices at the same time. With focused transmissions, it can communicate with two or more devices simultaneously. This eliminates the time a device may have to wait before transmitting in order to avoid collisions.

Theoretically, MU-MIMO was possible with 802.11n, but this aspect of the standard was never developed to a useable degree. With 802.11ac, however, beamforming and multiuser MIMO are intrinsic parts of the system's operation and well-defined.

Test Your Understanding

24. a) What is beamforming? b) What benefits can it bring? c) Distinguish between MIMO and multiuser MIMO.

---

[11] When a station transmits, it modulates the signal for physical layer transmission. (Modulation is covered in Module B). The 802.11n standard's best modulation method is 64 QAM. 802.11ac raises this to 256 QAM. This allows 802.11ac to send a third more bits per clock cycle as 802.11n (8 versus 6 bits per clock cycle).

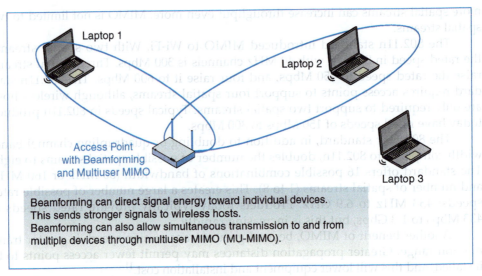

Laptop 1

Laptop 2

Laptop 3

Access Point
with Beamforming
and Multiuser MIMO

Beamforming can direct signal energy toward individual devices.
This sends stronger signals to wireless hosts.
Beamforming can also allow simultaneous transmission to and from
multiple devices through multiuser MIMO (MU-MIMO).

FIGURE 6-23   Beamforming and Multiuser MIMO

Speed, Throughput, and Distance

So far, we have been talking about rated speeds. However, what throughput—actual speed—can individuals expect to see? The general answer is complicated, but the single most important word is *less*. Individual users will always receive less than rated speeds, often much less.

Rated Speed versus Throughput   Rated speed is the number of bits that the host or access point will transmit per second according to the 802.11 standard it uses. The aggregate throughput is usually 25% to 50% lower.

Rated Speed versus Throughput

   Total throughput is substantially lower than rated speed—sometimes 50% lower

Aggregate versus Individual Throughput

   Access point throughput is aggregate throughput for all devices transmitting and receiving

   Its capacity is shared by all stations currently sending or receiving

   Individual throughput can be much lower than aggregate throughput

Throughput versus Distance

   As distance from the access point increases, signals get weaker

   Wireless hosts must use slower but more reliable bit encoding methods

   This reduces individual throughput for these devices

FIGURE 6-24   Speed, Distance, and Throughput (Study Figure)

Aggregate Throughput versus Individual Throughput   In addition, the access point's *aggregate* throughput is shared by all users of the access point. Suppose that the aggregate throughput is 100 Mbps per second and there are 10 users of an access point. If all 10 transmit or receive simultaneously, then *individual* throughput would be about 10 Mbps (actually somewhat less because of time lost in turn-taking). Of course, it would be rare for all stations to transmit simultaneously. But if even three are sending and receiving simultaneously, the individual throughput they experience would be about 33 Mbps.

What percentage of time do hosts transmit or receive? It depends entirely on what they are doing. Web downloads occur about every 30 seconds and take only a second or two. In contrast, streaming video creates an almost continuous data stream, consuming a good deal of the aggregate throughput.

Throughput versus Distance   As noted earlier, speed is highest when a user is near an access point. As the user moves away, speed falls. For each standard, such as 802.11g, 802.11n, and 802.11ac, there actually is a range of speeds. Each speed corresponds to a different way of modulating signals.[12] The fastest speeds use aggressive modulation methods that are fast but very sensitive to errors. As a station moves farther from an access point, the signal weakens and errors increase. The transceiver must switch to a less aggressive modulation method that is less sensitive to errors. Unfortunately, this modulation method also transmits more slowly. As a wireless hosts moves farther from an access point, its transmission speed will fall.

In General   Overall, it is impossible to say with any certainty what individual throughput a user will receive. A rule of thumb that frequently works is that individual throughput will be a quarter to a third of the rated speed if the access point is not heavily loaded.

Test Your Understanding

25. a) Distinguish between rated speed, aggregate throughput, and individual throughput. b) What factors influence individual throughput, given a certain level of aggregate throughput? c) Why does transmission speed drop as a computer moves farther from an access point?

Backward Compatibility

When new access points and wireless clients are sold, they must be able to work with older equipment. For instance, an 802.11ac client must be able to work with an older 802.11n access point. In the same way, an 802.11n access point must be able to work with an even older 802.11g client. Of course, when an 802.11ac device works with an 802.11n device, the 802.11ac device must drop back to 802.11n operation. Communication will take place at 802.11n speeds. This **backward compatibility** permits products meeting new standards to be installed gradually over time.

---

[12] Module A discusses common modulation techniques.

Devices Built for Newer Standards Still Implement Older Standards

This Allows Older and Newer Devices to Communicate

    Newer product: 802.11ac in the 5 GHz band

    Older product: 802.11n in the 2.4 GHz band

    The newer product will drop back to the standard the older product can use

    They will communicate using the 802.11n standard in the 2.4 GHz band

    They will only get 802.11n speeds

This is Backward Compatibility

FIGURE 6-25 Backward Compatibility (Study Figure)

Test Your Understanding

26. a) What is backward compatibility? b) Why is it important? c) When a device that implements 802.11ac communicates with an 802.11n access point, what standard do they use to communicate?

Standards and Options

We have looked at many standards in this section. However, just because two products are compliant with a particular standard, such as dual-band 802.11n, does not mean that they will have the same performance. This is true because most standards have options. One, for example, is the number of antennas on an 802.11n wireless access point. 802.11n calls for up to four antennas on a wireless client. However, most early 802.11n clients had only two antennas and therefore could only transmit two spatial streams. For a given piece of equipment, knowing what standards it complies with is not enough. The optional features of the standard implemented in the device must also be known.

Test Your Understanding

27. a) Why can two products that comply with the same standard perform differently? b) What implications does this have for making purchases? (The answer is not in the text.)

WIRELESS MESH NETWORKING

Do Wi-Fi devices in an organization usually connect to a wired switched Ethernet network? Yes, as we have seen throughout this chapter. Is it possible to avoid this by building an all-wireless network? The answer is that we are getting close. As Figure 6-26 shows, it is at least theoretically possible for wireless access points and wireless hosts to organize themselves into a mesh, forwarding frames from one to another until they reach the wireless destination host. With this arrangement, there is no wired network involved. The wireless devices provide their own wireless distribution system, with no need for Ethernet.

The **802.11s** standard for mesh networks exists. However, many related standards need to be developed before mesh networking's issues can be resolved sufficiently to be useful in corporations. New standards must address three main issues.

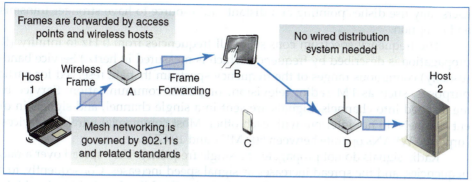

FIGURE 6-26 Wi-Fi Wireless Mesh Networking

- First, meshes must be self-organizing. Hosts and access points enter and leave the mesh frequently, and the network must respond immediately to changes.
- Second, it will be difficult to avoid overloading access points near the geographical center of the mesh. (Think of sitting in the middle seat at a table during a Christmas dinner and constantly having to pass food back and forth.) If mesh networking overloads wireless hosts and access points, it is useless.
- Third, an even bigger issue is security. With no central control, security will have to exist between *every pair* of devices, many of which will have just entered the mesh and are not well known. This is a recipe for security nightmares.

Test Your Understanding

28. a) What is wireless mesh networking? b) What is the current 802.11 standard for mesh networking? c) What devices forward frames in a mesh network? d) What three issues must be overcome to make mesh networking acceptable to corporations?

CONCLUSION

Synopsis

Chapter 5 looked at Ethernet switched local area networks. This chapter and Chapter 7 look at wireless LANs (WLANs). All single networks, whether point-to-point, switched, or wireless, operate at Layers 1 and 2. OSI standards dominate at those layers, so we can expect wireless network standards to be OSI standards.

This chapter focuses extensively on physical layer propagation. This detail is needed because wireless propagation effects are complex. We can predict what will happen as a signal travels down a copper wire or an optical fiber, but predicting how strong a radio signal will be at a user's location is far more difficult. We looked at five wireless propagation problems: absorptive attenuation, inverse square law attenuation (yes, there are two types of attenuation), interference, dead zones, and multipath interference. Multipath interference is the biggest propagation problem in wireless LANs. Absorptive attenuation and dead zones become worse at higher frequencies.

Wireless LANs use omnidirectional antennas because users would not know where to point a dish antenna and certainly do not want to carry a dish around. Fixed users may use dishes pointing at a distant radio source to have stronger transmission and reception.

The frequency spectrum consists of all frequencies from 0 Hz to infinity. (Radio propagation is described by frequency, which is measured in hertz.) Service bands are (usually) contiguous ranges of the frequency spectrum that are reserved for particular purposes, such as FM radio, television, or police communication. Service bands are divided into channels. Signals are sent in a single channel, and signals in different channels do not interfere with each other. Most commercial wireless services and corporate WLANs operate between 500 MHz and 10 GHz.

Radio signals do not propagate at a single frequency. They spread over a range of frequencies, and the spread increases as signal speed increases. Consequently, to carry fast signals, channels must have wide bandwidths. Doubling bandwidth should double possible signal speed.

Wireless LANs operate in unlicensed bands, in which you can set up your network the way you wish. However, you must tolerate interference from nearby WLANs built by others.

Initially, almost all WLAN technology operated in the 2.4 GHz band, in which radio prices were low. However, there are only three non-overlapping 20 MHz channels in this band, so nearby access points often interfere with one another. Increasingly, new WLAN equipment operates in the 5 GHz unlicensed band, in which there are more channels for a given channel bandwidth. The gap between 2.4 GHz prices and 5 GHz prices is narrowing. Consequently, the use of the 5 GHz band is growing rapidly.

In the 2.4 GHz and 5 GHz bands, the government requires the use of spread spectrum transmission, in which the signal is spread far more than it needs to be for its speed. Current 802.11 Wi-Fi standards use orthogonal frequency division multiplexing (OFDM), in which the channel is broken into much smaller subchannels called subcarriers. The frame is transmitted redundantly within the subcarriers. WLAN spread spectrum techniques, unlike military spread spectrum techniques, provide no security.

In 802.11 WLAN operation, access points normally attach to the firm's main wired Ethernet LAN so that wireless clients can access servers and Internet access routers on the wired LAN. When a wireless host transmits, it sends its packet in an 802.11 frame. The access point removes the packet from the 802.11 frame, puts it in an 802.3 frame, and sends the frame to the server or Internet access router. The packet travels all the way; the 802.11 frame does not. A basic service set (BSS) consists of an access point and the wireless hosts it serves. The SSID is the name of a radio on an access point. In an extended service set (ESS), all access points have the same SSID. Among other things, this permits roaming, which is also called being handed off.

The access point and the stations it serves all transmit in a single channel. Media access control (MAC) ensures that they take turns transmitting so that their signals do not interfere. In a box, we looked at 802.11 Wi-Fi's two MAC protocols. CSMA/CA+ACK is mandatory. Request to send/clear to send is optional but sometimes useful. Both create inefficiency by creating dead time in which there is no transmission.

WLAN products on the market follow different 802.11 standards. Figure 6-21 compares four 802.11 transmission standards. One consistent theme for newer versions is the use of wider channel bandwidths, which bring higher rated speeds. The 802.11g and 802.11a standards use 20 MHz channels. The 802.11n standard doubles this, except when there is interference from 802.11g devices in the 2.4 GHz band. The 802.11ac standard specifies 80 MHz and 160 MHz channels. While 802.11g uses the crowded and limited 2.4 GHz band, 802.11a, 802.11n, and 802.11ac can take advantage of the wider 5 GHz band's far greater total bandwidth.

Another way to boost speed is MIMO, which uses multiple antennas on the sender and receiver. The signals sent by different antennas are called spatial streams. The sender can transmit multiple spatial streams in the same channel, and the receiver will be able to read them. Roughly speaking, transmission speed increases in proportion to the number of spatial streams. The 802.11g and 802.11a standards do not use MIMO. The 802.11n standard uses MIMO and can support up to four spatial streams. The 802.11ac standard can support up to eight.

The 802.11ac standard can also use beamforming, which directs signals to individual devices instead of broadcasting signals omnidirectionally. Beamforming increases distance by focusing more of the sender's power on the receiver without using a dish antenna. A particularly sophisticated type of beamforming is multiuser MIMO, which allows multiple stations to communicate simultaneously with a single access point in a single channel. The access point can use their different spatial streams to separate their signals. If one station is sending, other stations do not have to wait to send.

It is easy to talk about rated speeds, but throughput is more difficult to discuss. Throughput is always slower than rated speed, and this is aggregate throughput, which is shared by all devices actively using an access point. Individual throughput is always lower than aggregate throughput. In addition, as a station moves farther from the access point, it must use slower bit encoding processes, further reducing individual throughput.

We looked briefly at two 802.11 mesh networks, which use access points and client hosts to forward 802.11 frames wirelessly between two wireless hosts. This forwarding process may require several hops among wireless devices. No Ethernet distribution system is involved. In Chapter 7, we will continue to look at 802.11 wireless LANs, focusing on security and management. We will then look at other local wireless technologies, including Bluetooth.

END-OF-CHAPTER QUESTIONS

Thought Questions

6-1. A building is cube-shaped. It uses 16 access points, which are, on average, 10 meters apart from one another. The company wishes to reduced this to 8 meters. About how many 5 GHz access points would the company need for the building?

6-2. The following matters were not addressed specifically in the text. However, if you understand the concepts of Layer 1 and Layer 2 standards, in each case, give your answer and explain your reasoning. a) Is multipath interference a Layer 1 or Layer 2 concern? b) Is media access control a Layer 1 or Layer 2 concern? c) Is MIMO a Layer 1 or Layer 2 concern? d) Are wireless propagation problems Layer 1 or Layer 2 concerns? e) Is 802.11ac a Layer 1 or Layer 2 standard? f) Is 802.11r a Layer 1 or Layer 2 standard?

Perspective Questions

6-3. What was the most surprising thing you learned in this chapter?

6-4. What was the most difficult part of this chapter for you?

Chapter 6a

Using Xirrus Wi-Fi Inspector

LEARNING OBJECTIVES

By the end of this chapter, you should be able to:

- Use Xirrus Wi-Fi Inspector with some facility.
- Interpret output from Wi-Fi Inspector in specific situations.
- Do a site survey.

INTRODUCTION

Wi-Fi analysis programs listen to nearby access points (and sometimes wireless hosts) to determine such things as how strong their signals are, what types of security they use, what their SSIDs and BSSIDs are, and sometimes the directions of the individual access points.

There are many Wi-Fi analysis programs for mobile devices. Many have "stumbler" in their names in homage to one of the first examples, NetStumbler. This chapter looks at *Wi-Fi Inspector* from Xirrus, which runs on Microsoft Windows and which is available as a free download from Xirrus. A comparable Windows Widget that always remains on the desktop is also available from Xirrus.

THE FOUR WINDOWS

Figure 6a-1 shows the ribbon menu and four tiled windows that appear when you bring up Wi-Fi Inspector. This view shows all information in a single window. This is the default. It is also what you see if you click on Show All in the Layout ribbon.

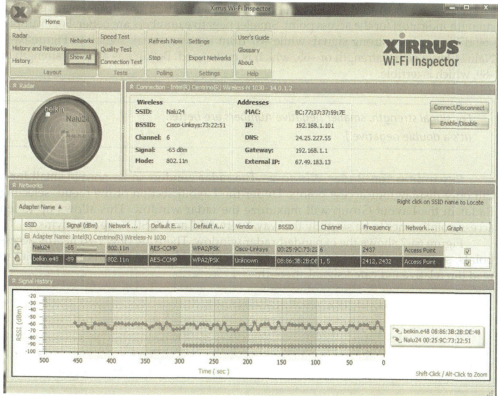

FIGURE 6A-1   Four Windows in Wi-Fi Inspector

The Radar Window (Read the Fine Print)

The most obvious window is the radar window, which shows all access points in the vicinity. The access points are spread out across the two-dimensional picture.

Relative Direction (Meaningless)   It appears that the radar window shows the relative directions of the access points, much as an air traffic radar display shows the directions of nearby aircraft. Actually, it does not. The access points are merely spread out for readability. Direction is meaningless. In this sense, the radar window is misleading. However, it looks cool.

Distance from the Center (Signal Strength)   What does distance from the center mean? It looks like it means physical distance, as it would on a physical radar screen. Rather, it means *signal strength*. Access points that are shown closest to the center are the *strongest*, and access points that are the farthest from the center are the *weakest*.

Measuring Signal Strength Signal strength gives the RSSI (relative signal strength indicator) for the access point. Smaller negative numbers are better. For example, –60 dBm is a very strong signal, while –87 dBm is a very weak signal. In Figure 6a-1, Nalu24 has a signal strength of –65, which is quite good. Belkin has a signal strength of –89, which is terrible.

For signal strength, smaller negative numbers are better.

(It's a double negative.)

Expanding the Radar Window The radar window in its normal small form can only display four access points. Under the Layout section of the menu, selecting Radar in the Layout Group will maximize the radar window. This allows up to ten access point names to be seen. By the way, "network" and "SSID" are synonyms.

Figure 6a-2 shows the expanded radar window. There are only two nearby access points, so there is no need for a large radar window. However, it certainly is easier to read the relative indicated signal strength.

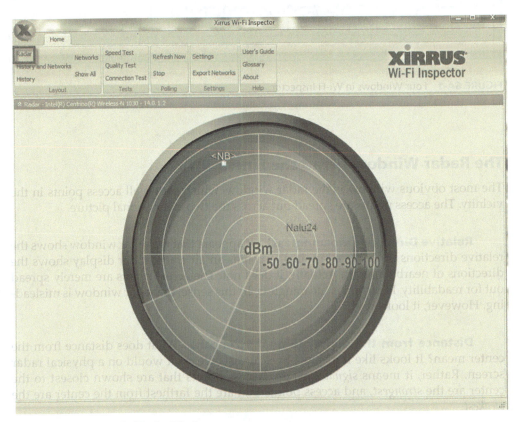

FIGURE 6A-2 Expanded Radar Window

Connection Window

The connection window (in the upper right in Figure 6a-1) shows information about the access point to which the computer running Wi-Fi Inspector is currently connected (Nalu24). It shows the SSID (the network name, in this case, Nalu24), the BSSID (the access point's MAC address, in this case, Cisco-Linksys:73:22:51[1]), the channel (6), the signal strength (–65 dBm), and the network mode (802.11n).

In the middle is information about the user's PC. It shows the user's MAC address and configuration information, including the user's IP address, the IP address of the destination server, the IP address of the default gateway (router), and the network's external IP address given to it by the ISP. (This is a home network.) This information does not tell the user about nearby access points, but it can be very useful in assessing connection problems.

On the right is a Connect/Disconnect button. Clicking this button shows a list of potential networks and allows the user's computer to disconnect from the current access point and pick another to connect to. The user can also turn off the computer's wireless adapter.

The Networks Window

The networks window shows detailed information about each of the nearby access points. This is what the user goes to when he or she wants detailed information. The row for the access point to which the user is currently connected is shown in orange highlighted. Wi-Fi Inspector updates the information in the networks window frequently. As Figure 6a-3 shows, the information in this window is detailed.

- SSID. The network name.
- Signal Level in either dBm or percentage. Remember that smaller negative dBm numbers indicate higher strength. Next to the number is a colored bar.
  - Green is for signals of –70 dBm and above (–60 dBm, etc.).

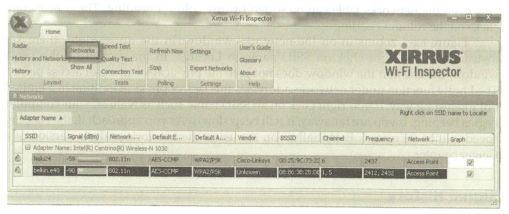

FIGURE 6A-3 Networks Window

---

[1] The first two octets in a MAC address identify the company making the network adapter in the access point. Wi-Fi Inspector converts this information into a humanly readable name.

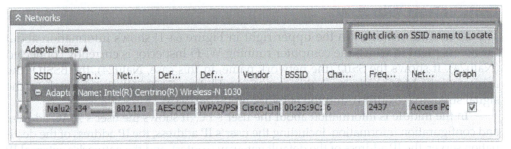

FIGURE 6A-4 Locating an Access Point

- Yellow is for signals between –71 dBm and –80 dBm.
- Orange is for signals between –81 dBm and –90 dBm.
- Red is for –91 dBm and below.
- Network Mode. 802.11g, 802.11n, etc.
- Default Encryption. None, WEP, TKIP (in WPA), or AES (802.11i).
- Default Authentication. Open (none), WPA/PSK, WPA2/PSK, WPA/802.1X, or WPA2/802.1X.
- Vendor. The name of the device manufacturer.
- BSSID. The access point's MAC address.
- Channel. The channel number.
- Frequency. The center frequency of the channel.
- Network Type. Access point or ad hoc (no access point).
- Graph. This is a checkbox that tells Wi-Fi Inspector to graph the signal level over time (checked) or not to do so (unchecked). In the figure, both are checked, so both will be graphed.

In the figure, the access points are listed in terms of declining signal strength. However, the networks table can be sorted by any column heading. The user merely clicks on the column heading.

Figure 6a-4 zooms in on the networks window. In the upper right, there are instructions to "Right click on SSID name to Locate." In the section on the radar window, we saw that the window does not give the physical locations of access points. The Locate function under networks addresses this lack of physical location in a limited but interesting way. If you right click on an SSID name such as Nalu24, your computer begins beeping. If you are far away, it will beep slowly. As you approach it, the beeping speed will be increased. Essentially, you are using the network analysis version of a Geiger counter.

Signal History

In the networks window, we saw that the user can check or uncheck whether graphing should be done. The Signal History window shows these graphs. The graphs in Figure 6a-5 show that the signal strength for Nalu24 is uniformly excellent, while the signal strength for Belkin is uniformly poor. Major fluctuations would indicate serious problems.

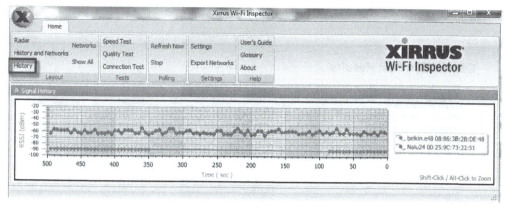

FIGURE 6A-5 Signal History

Other Groups on the Ribbon

The Layout group on the ribbon is the most-used feature of the Xirrus Wi-Fi Inspector.

Help Group The Help group provides a user's guide to explain the program's detailed functionality. There is also a helpful glossary of terms.

Settings Group The Settings group allows the user to adjust many settings, for example, expressing RSSI in percentage terms instead of in terms of dBm.

Tests Group The windows in Wi-Fi Inspector provide information visually. The Tests group allows the user to conduct more detailed tests. These tests are good for troubleshooting.

TESTS

As just noted, the Tests group actively tests the quality of your service. The Tests group performs three important tests.

Connection Test

The connection test shows how well you are connected to the outside world and to critical internal devices. Figure 6a-6 shows the results of a connection test. It shows that Wi-Fi Inspector uses ping to test latency to your DNS server, default gateway (router), and a host on the Internet (Internet Reachable). It also does a DNS lookup, in this case for www.google.com.

The test shows that the user has low latency for the default router and an Internet host. It also shows that the DNS lookup was successful. In color, these are shown in green, with the word *Pass*. However, there is relatively high latency to the user's DNS server (152 ms). This is indicated by a yellow bar with the text *Warning: high latency*. However, the latency is not very high. This connection looks good.

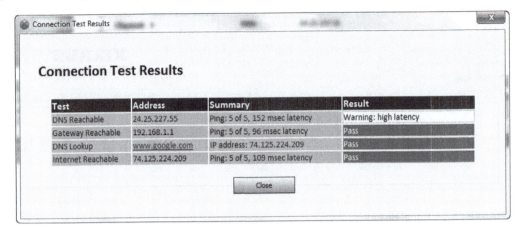

FIGURE 6A-6 Connection Test

Speed Test

The speed test takes the user to speedtest.net. Figure 6a-7 shows a test in which there was a download speed of 14 Mbps and an upload speed of just under 1 Mbps. These are reasonable numbers.

FIGURE 6A-7 Speed Test in Wi-Fi Inspector

Quality Test

Figure 6a-8 shows results from the quality test, which takes you to pingtest.net. The results give the user's quality level a B. However, the box on the left notes that the connection should be fine for anything but gaming.

- The ping (latency) averaged 84 ms, which is a little high for games. The server is less than 50 miles away. Connecting to a more distant server would increase latency.
- Jitter, which is variation in latency from packet to packet is 24 ms. This can affect voice and video, for which jitter can result in jittery voice or video. Again, the number is fairly good.
- There was zero packet loss. The connection appears to be reliable.
- There is a MOS score of 4.33. This is a traditional subjective indicator of voice call quality. A MOS score of 5 indicates toll-call quality on the telephone system. A MOS of 4.33 is quite good.

One caveat is that pingtest.net is a bit "grabby." It tries to sell you its tools and is slightly aggressive. In addition, the site uses Java, which you may have to download. You may also have to give a firewall exception to this Java program.

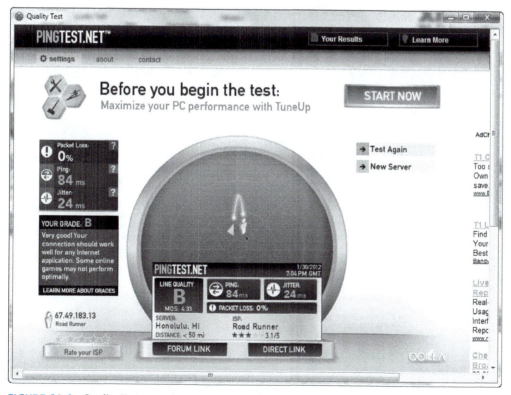

FIGURE 6A-8   Quality Test

ACTIVITIES

Questions

1. Why is the radar window's image of a radar scope misleading?
2. How would you locate an access point despite the limitations of the radar window? This will take one to four paragraphs.
3. There is a value of −44 dBm for signal strength. How good is this?
4. How can you sort the networks window?
5. What information does the Connection Test give you?
6. What information does the Speed Test give you?
7. What information does the Quality Test give you?

Activity

Select a building. Go to at least ten locations. At each location, record the information in the networks window. Also, do a connection and speed test. Write a brief report what you learned about Wi-Fi service in the building, referring to the data you collected.

Chapter 7

Wireless LANs II

LEARNING OBJECTIVES

By the end of this chapter, you should be able to:

- Explain 802.11i Wi-Fi security.
- Explain why 802.11i security is not enough for WLANs.
- Explain 802.11 WLAN management.
- If you read the box on decibels, work with decibel representations of power ratios.
- Describe other local wireless technologies, including Bluetooth, near field communication (NFC), and Wi-Fi Direct. Discuss security in the context of emerging local wireless network standards.

THE TJX BREACH

TJX Companies, Inc. (TJX) has over 2,500 retail stores in the United States, Canada, England, Ireland, and several other countries. These companies do business under such names as TJ Maxx and Marshalls. In its literature, TJX describes itself as "the leading off-price retailer of apparel and home fashions in the U.S. and worldwide." With this mission statement, there is strong pressure to minimize costs.

On December 18, 2006, TJX detected "suspicious software" on its computer systems. On December 22, the company informed law enforcement authorities in the United States and Canada. Five days later, security consultants determined that customer data had been stolen.

The consultants initially determined that the intrusion software had been working for seven months before TJX discovered it. A few weeks later, the consultants discovered that the attackers had also breached the company several times in 2005. All told, the consultants estimated that attackers stole 45.7 million customer records. At the time, this was by far the largest number of personal customer records ever stolen from any company.

The thieves did not steal these records for the thrill of breaking in or to enhance their "cred." They did it to make fraudulent credit card purchases in the names of the customers whose information they had stolen.

TJX did not tell customers that their data had been stolen for nearly a month. The company said that it had needed time to beef up its security. It also said that law enforcement officials had asked TJX to withhold information to avoid tipping off the data thieves about the investigation. Of course, the delay left the customers ignorant of the danger they faced.

How did the breaches occur? First, the data thieves broke into poorly protected wireless networks in some Florida stores.[1] The breached stores had protected their wireless networks, but they used the obsolete wired equivalent privacy (WEP) security standard instead of the newer and better 802.11i standard.

In the central TJX credit and debit card processing system in Massachusetts, poor firewall protection[2] allowed the data thieves to enter several systems and to install a sniffer that listened to the company's poorly encrypted traffic passing into and out of the processing center. Another problem was that TJX retained some sensitive credit card information that should not have been retained; it is this improperly retained information that the data thieves found most valuable.[3]

Previous data breaches had prompted the major credit card companies to create the **Payment Card Industry–Data Security Standard (PCI–DSS)** to specify how companies should protect credit card information. Failure to implement PCI–DSS control objectives can result in fines and even the revocation of a company's ability to accept credit card payments.

When TJX discovered the data breach, it was far behind in its PCI–DSS compliance program. The company complied with only three of the twelve required control objectives. Internal memos revealed that the company knew that it was in violation of the PCI–DSS requirements, particularly with respect to its weak encryption in retail store wireless networks.[4] However, the company deliberately decided not to move rapidly to fix this problem. In November 2005, a staff member noted that "saving money and being PCI compliant is important to us, but equally important is protecting ourselves against intruders. Even though we have some breathing room with PCI, we are still vulnerable with WEP as our security key. It must be a risk we are willing to take for the sake of saving money and hoping we do not get compromised."

When the staff member noted that "we have some breathing room with PCI," he was referring to the fact that TJX had been given an extension allowing it to be noncompliant beyond the standard's specified compliance date.[5] This additional time, ironically,

---

[1] Mark Jewel, "Encryption Faulted in TJX Hacking," *MSNBC.com*, September 25, 2007. www.msnbc.msn.com/id/20979359/.

[2] Ross Kerber, "Details Emerge on TJX Breach," *The Boston Globe*, October 25, 2007. http://www.boston.com/business/articles/2007/10/25/details_emerge_on_tjx_breach/.

[3] Jewel, op. cit.

[4] Jewel, op cit.

[5] Evan Schuman, "In 2005, Visa Agreed to Give TJX Until 2009 to Get PCI Compliant," *Storefront Backtalk*, November 9, 2007. www.storefrontbacktalk.com/story/110907visaletter.

was given after the data breaches had already begun. This extension was dependent upon evaluation of a self-written TJX report on its compliance project, due by June 2006. The letter that authorized the extension was sent by a fraud control vice president for Visa. It ended with, "I appreciate your continued support and commitment to safeguarding the payment industry."

When TJX finally announced the breach, it quickly faced commercial lawsuits and government investigations. TJX was first sued by seven individual banks and bank associations. In December 2007, TJX settled with all but one of these banks, agreeing to pay up to $40.9 million. This would reimburse the banks for the cost of reissuing credit cards and other expenses.

The company also received a large fine from Visa. Actually, Visa could not fine TJX directly but instead fined TJX's merchant bank. (Merchant banks are financial institutions that serve—and should control—retail organizations that accept credit card payments.) The merchant bank passed the fine on to TJX. During the summer of 2007, Visa fined TJX's merchant bank $880,000 and announced that it would continue to impose fines at $100,000/month until TJX had fixed its security problem. However, after the TJX settlement with the seven banks and banking associations, this fine was to be reduced by an undisclosed amount.

In this battle of corporate giants, consumers came last. In 2007, the Federal Trade Commission approved a settlement between TJX and the consumers who had their private information stolen. The FTC required TJX to do security audits every two years for the next 20 years and to report the results of those audits to the FTC.[6]

TJX reached a settlement that would only involve very limited measures such as help with ID theft through insurance and other measures for the roughly 455,000 victims who had given personally identifiable information when they returned goods without a receipt. Other victims received a small voucher or the opportunity to buy TJX merchandise at sale prices.[7] This settlement was approved.

In 2008, the Department of Justice charged 11 individuals with conducting the TJX break-in and with the subsequent use of the stolen information.[8] Three were Americans, and they were jailed rapidly. Two more were in China. The other six lived in Eastern Europe. Although the three Americans conducted the actual data theft, they fenced the stolen information overseas. Two of the American defendants entered plea deals to testify against the alleged ringleader, Albert Gonzalez of Miami, Florida. Gonzalez was sentenced in 2010 to 20 years in prison.

One surprising thing about this indictment was the revelation that these hackers had not only plundered TJX. Investigation found that the attackers had repeated the crime with at least a half dozen other major companies, including OfficeMax,

---

[6] Federal Trade Commission, "Agency Announces Settlement of Separate Actions Against Retailer TJX and Data Broker Reed Elsevier and Seisint for Failing to Provide Adequate Security for Customers' Data," March 27, 2008. www.ftc.gov/opa/2008/03/datasec.shtm.

[7] John Leyden, "TJX Consumer Settlement Sale Offer Draws Scorn," *TheRegister.com*, November 20, 2007. http://www.theregister.co.uk/2007/11/20/tjx_settlement_offer_kerfuffle/.

[8] U.S. Department of Justice, "Retail Hacking Ring Charged for Stealing and Distributing Credit and Debit Card Numbers from Major U.S. Retailers," August 5, 2008. www.usdoj.gov/criminal/cybercrime/gonzalezIndict.pdf.

7-Eleven, Dave & Busters, and Heartland Payment Systems.[9] The Heartland break-in was especially severe because Heartland does credit card payment processing for other firms. Most of these break-ins also began with the exploitation of WEP security.

Test Your Understanding

1. a) What was the attackers' first step in breaking into TJX and other companies? b) Why do you think TJX failed to upgrade to stronger security than WEP? (There may be more than one consideration.) c) How was the TJX break-in an international crime?

INTRODUCTION

In Chapter 6, we focused on how 802.11 wireless LANs operate. In this chapter, we will look at Wi-Fi security and management. We will then turn to other local wireless technologies.

802.11i WLAN SECURITY

WLAN Security Threats

Wireless transmission is inherently dangerous. Adversaries can potentially read transmissions and send packets into the network wirelessly, bypassing a site's border firewall. Companies face two classes of external attackers.

- Less importantly, war drivers are people who drive around a city looking for working access points that are unprotected. They record SSIDs (access point IDs), signal strength, and most of all security condition. They may even publish their results. War driving per se is not illegal. The information they collect is not protected private information once it leaves the building's walls.

War Drivers	Drive-By Hackers
Lurk outside a building	Lurk outside a building
Collect access point data: SSID Strength of Signal Security	Collect access point data: SSID Strength of Signal Security
May publicize findings Do not read wireless messages Do not send attacks	Read wireless messages Send attacks bypassing the firewall
Legal	Illegal

FIGURE 7-1 Wireless LAN Security Threats (Study Figure)

---

[9] Kim Zettrer, "TJX Hacker Charged with Heartland, Hannaford Breaches," *Wired Magazine*, August 17, 2009. http://wired.com/threatlevel/2009/tjx-hacker-charged-with-heartland/.

- More seriously, drive-by hackers do what war drivers do but go far beyond them. They try to intercept and read the firm's data transmissions. They can also hack servers, send malware into the network, and do other mischief. Drive-by hacking software is readily downloadable from the Internet. While war driving is legal, intercepting electronic conversations and attacking are definitely illegal.

Test Your Understanding

2. a) Distinguish between war drivers and drive-by hackers in terms of what they do. b) Are war drivers illegal? Why or why not? c) Are drive-by hackers illegal? Why or why not?

The 802.11i WLAN Security Standard

Realizing the danger of drive-by hackers, the 802.11 Working Group created the far better **802.11i** standard for Wi-Fi networks. Figure 7-2 shows that 802.11i provides cryptographic protection between the wireless access point and the wireless host. This protection includes initial authentication plus message-by-message confidentiality, integrity, and authentication (CIA). A drive-by hacker cannot intercept traffic or send his or her own messages to the access point.[10]

Note in the figure that 802.11i protection only extends between the wireless client and the wireless access point. It does not provide protection end-to-end between the

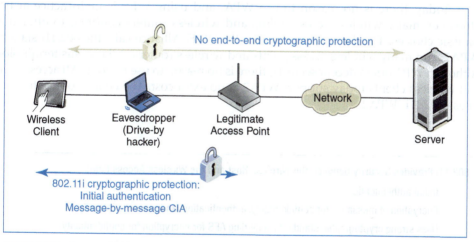

FIGURE 7-2 Scope of 802.11i Security Protection

---

[10] Some people recommend further security protections, such as turning off the periodic broadcasting of the access point's SSID. Users need to know this SSID to use an access point. However, the SSID is transmitted in the clear (without encryption) in every frame header. Another common recommendation is to accept only computers whose wireless network interface cards have pre-approved EUI-48 addresses. Again, however, the EUI-48 address is transmitted in the clear in any packet. Overall, these measures take a great deal of work, and they are easily cracked by readily available hacking software. They might make sense if you are only concerned about a home network and unsophisticated but nosy neighbors. Turning on 802.11i protection is easier, and it provides excellent security if you use it correctly.

wireless client and the server on the wired LAN (or a server on the Internet). The 802.11i standard has a very limited objective—to protect wireless transmission.

The protection provided by 802.11i only extends between the wireless access point and the wireless host.

Although its physical scope is limited, 802.11i protects transmissions within its scope very well. For example, the standard uses the Advanced Encryption Standard (AES) for confidentiality. It also uses strong standards for all other aspects of cryptology.

The 802.11i standard is actually the third standard created to protect communication between wireless clients and access points in 802.11 WLANs. The original standard was **wired equivalent privacy (WEP)**. The 802.11 Working Group created WEP as part of the original 802.11 standard in 1997. Unfortunately, it was not created by experts in security, and it was deeply flawed. The 802.11i standard was created to replace it. Many companies decided not to upgrade to 802.11i, and the results were predictably disastrous. TJX made this mistake, and it allowed the hackers into its network.

802.11i's development effort took several years. As a stop-gap measure, the Wi-Fi Alliance created an interim security standard based on an early draft of 802.11i but using much weaker standards for cryptographic protections than 802.11i called for. The Wi-Fi Alliance called their interim standard **Wireless Protected Access (WPA)**.

Today, there is no reason to use WPA, and using WEP is malpractice at best. However, many wireless access points and wireless routers continue to offer these Jurassic choices. To add to the confusion, the Wi-Fi Alliance calls the 802.11i standard **WPA2**, and many wireless access points and wireless routers still use this terminology. Although WPA offers decent security, there is no reason to use it today. All access points and wireless clients today support WPA2 at no extra cost. The choice today should be to use 802.11i/WPA2.

802.11i Provides Security between the Wireless Host and the Wireless Access Point

    Initial authentication

    Encryption of messages for confidentiality, authentication, and message integrity

    Uses strong cryptographic standards, including AES for encryption for confidentiality

Configuring an Access Point

    Select 802.11i (sometimes called WPA2)

    Do not select Wireless Protected Access (WPA), an earlier, weaker security standard created by the Wi-Fi Alliance

    Never ever select Wired Equivalent Privacy (WEP), an earlier security standard created by the 802.11 Working Group

    Earlier standards do not provide acceptable security

FIGURE 7-3 802.11i Security (Study Figure)

Mode of 802.11i Operation	Pre-Shared Key Mode	802.1X Mode
Environment	Home, business with single access point	Companies with multiple access points
Uses a central authentication server	No	Yes
Authentication	Knowledge of pre-shared key	Credentials on central authentication server
Security	Technologically strong, but weak human security can compromise the technological security	Extremely strong

FIGURE 7-4   802.11i Modes of Operation (Study Figure)

The choice today should be to use 802.11i/WPA2.

Test Your Understanding

3. a) What cryptographic protections does 802.11i provide? b) How is this protection limited? c) What Working Group created 802.11i? d) What were the two earlier 802.11 security standards? e) What does the Wi-Fi Alliance call 802.11i? f) When offered the choice while configuring a wireless access point, which WLAN security standard should you choose?

Pre-Shared Key (PSK) Mode in 802.11i

The 802.11i standard offers two modes of operation designed to be used in very different circumstances. We will begin with the simple **pre-shared key (PSK) mode**, which was created for home use, although it can be used in a business with a single access point. The Wi-Fi Alliance calls this **personal mode**. This is a good name in light of its intended use.

PSK mode in 802.11i is for homes and small businesses with a single access point.

Figure 7-5 shows that the access points and wireless hosts need to know the same **pre-shared key (PSK)** for authentication. Host X, Host Y, and Host Z all authenticate themselves to the access point using this pre-shared key. After they are authenticated, however, they will not use the PSK.

After authentication using the pre-shared key, the wireless access point gives each authenticated device a new **unshared session key** to use while communicating with the access point. In Figure 7-6, Host X has authenticated itself to Access Point A. The access point returns the unshared session key AX. Host X and Access Point A will encrypt all future communication between them using session key AX. Other hosts will get

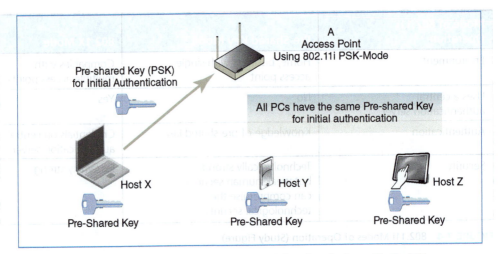

FIGURE 7-5 802.11i Pre-Shared Key (PSK) Mode: Initial Authentication with the PSK

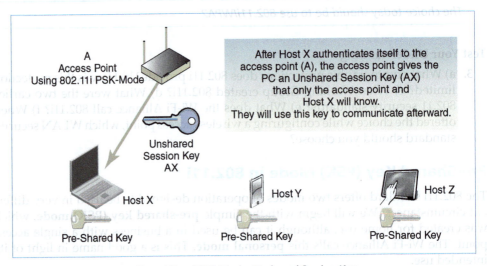

FIGURE 7-6 802.11i Pre-Shared Key (PSK) Mode: Unshared Session Key

different unshared session keys after they communicate. Hosts cannot decrypt and read transmissions between other hosts and the access point.

A **session key** is a key used only for a limited time. When the host stops using the access point, the session key is terminated. If the same wireless client connects to the same access point later, it will receive a different session key. Using session keys limits the amount of information encrypted with the key. If a sender encrypts too much information with a key, a cryptanalyst can crack the key. Session keys only encrypt a limited amount of data, making cryptanalysis impossible.

A session key is a key used only for a limited time, such as during a single session of a client using an access point.

Someone may give the pre-shared key to unauthorized people

It does not seem secret, so employees may give it out not realizing that it is secret

PSKs are generated from passphrases

Passphrases must be at least 20 characters long

Wireless Protected Setup (WPS)

Created to make PSK setup easier

User enters an 8-digit PIN for a particular WPS-capable access point instead of a long password

Unfortunately, easily cracked and should be turned off on the access point if possible

---

FIGURE 7-7 Security Threats in Pre-Shared Key Mode (Study Figure)

In a home or very small business, having a handful of people know the pre-shared key is not too dangerous. However, there is still the danger that someone in a small business, rationalizing that everyone knows the pre-session key, will give it to an unauthorized person.

Another danger is that the household or small business will select a weak passphrase. To create the pre-shared key, the household or company creates a long **passphrase**, which is much longer than a password. The client or access point uses this passphrase to generate the 64-bit PSK. The passphrase must be at least 20 characters long to generate a strong pre-shared key. If short passphrases are used, 802.11i in PSK mode is almost as easy to crack as WEP.

In 802.11i pre-shared key mode, the passphrase must be at least 20 characters long to generate a strong pre-shared key.

In addition, most PSK wireless access points have a serious security vulnerability. To simplify the configuration of wireless clients so that users can connect to access points more easily, the Wi-Fi Alliance created **Wireless Protected Setup (WPS)**. The user only has to know an 8-digit PIN associated with the access point. There is no need to remember and type a long passphrase.

The way the Alliance designed WPS, the PIN can be cracked easily.[11] Yet WPS is usually turned on by default on access points. Access points using Wireless Protected Setup should have this feature turned off. On many wireless access points and wireless access routers, unfortunately, there is no way to turn off WPS.

---

[11] WPS requires the user to know a secret PIN that has eight digits (the characters from 0 to 9). Exhaustive search on such a PIN should take about half of 108 or 50,000,000 attempts. This is not practical. However, the Wi-Fi Alliance made a poor decision in its design. It divided the PIN into two 4-digit halves. Then, it inexplicably gave an attacker feedback if the first half was entered correctly. Therefore, the attacker only has to try an average of 104 or 5,000 attempts to find the first four digits. Once these are known, cracking the second part only takes about half of 103 or 500 attempts. Why not half of 104 instead of 103? The answer is that one of the last four final numerals is a check digit that can be computed from the other seven. The take away is that by cutting the number of attempts required to learn the secret, guessing the PIN is reduced on average from 50,000,000 attempts to 5,500 attempts. The latter allows Wi-Fi Protected Setup to be broken in a few hours.

Test Your Understanding

4. a) For what use scenario was 802.11i PSK mode created? b) How does a user authenticate his or her device to the access point? c) What kind of key does a host use after initial authentication? d) What device or devices know this key? e) After authentication, can hosts using an access point understand the messages that other hosts using the access point are sending? f) Why is the key called a session key? g) Why are session keys good? h) What three threats should PSK consider? i) Why is this risk probably acceptable? j) How long must passphrases be in order to generate strong pre-shared keys?

5. a) Why is WPS desirable? b) Why should you not use it? c) What should users do about this problem?

802.1X Mode Operation

As we have seen, PSK mode is for homes and for small businesses with a single access point. Large firms with many access points must use a different 802.11i mode, **802.1X mode**. (The Wi-Fi Alliance calls this **enterprise mode**.) In Chapter 5, we saw that 802.1X was created for Ethernet switched networks. Its goal was to prevent attackers from simply walking into a building and plugging a computer into any wall jack or directly into a switch.

Figure 7-8 shows that the Ethernet workgroup switch acts as the authenticator with traditional 802.1X. A computer wishing to access the Ethernet network connects to the authenticator via a UTP connection. A central authentication server checks the supplicant's credentials and sends an accept/reject decision to the authenticator.

For Ethernet access, there is no need to have security between the computer seeking access and the workgroup switch that controls access. It is difficult for another person to tap the wired access line between the computer and the switch, and there

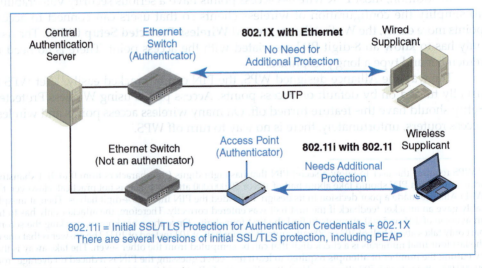

FIGURE 7-8   802.11i in 802.1X Mode

are easier ways to break into a network. Consequently, as Figure 7-8 shows, there is no protection in 802.1X during the transmission of authentication credentials.

In Wi-Fi, in contrast, the Ethernet switch is not the authenticator. Rather, the wireless access point is the authenticator. All transmission between the client and the authenticator is wireless and therefore easy to intercept. This is unacceptable for the transmission of authentication credentials.

To address this problem, the 802.11 Working Group extended the 802.1X standard to become 802.11i. The extension's job is to protect initial authentication exchanges in 802.1X.

802.11i does this by first creating an SSL/TLS connection between the wireless client and the wireless access point. This is the standard used to protect you when you visit secure websites. SSL/TLS was selected because it does not require the supplicant or verifier to exchange any secret information during the setup.[12]

Once SSL/TLS protection is in place, 802.1X authentication, which does require the exchange of secret information, takes place. This exchange is encrypted for confidentiality by SSL/TLS, so there is no danger of an eavesdropper being able to read credentials during authentication.

The 802.11i standard gives product designers flexibility over how to implement initial SSL/TLS protection. The most popular version is Microsoft's Protected Extensible Authentication Protocol (PEAP).

Test Your Understanding

6. a) If a firm has many access points, which 802.11i mode must it use? b) What mode or modes of 802.11i operation use a central authentication server? c) What does the Wi-Fi Alliance call 802.1X mode? d) In 802.1X operation, what device acts as the authenticator in Ethernet? e) What device acts as the 802.1X authenticator in Wi-Fi?
7. a) In Ethernet, why does 802.1X not need security between the authenticator and the host before 802.1X authentication is done? b) Why does 802.1X mode in 802.11i need security between the authenticator and the host *before* 802.1X authentication? c) What is the most common protocol for providing this initial security?

BEYOND 802.11i SECURITY

The 802.11i standard protects communication between the wireless access point and wireless clients. This greatly reduces risks. However, two types of attack can succeed even if a company implements 802.11i security well.

Rogue Access Points

The first is the creation of rogue access points. A **rogue access point** is an unauthorized access point set up within a firm by an employee or department. Rogue access points are dangerous because they are usually configured with no security or poor security. Figure 7-9 shows that even if a firm carefully applies 802.11i to all of its authorized

---

[12] The authenticator sends the supplicant a public key. The supplicant uses the public key to encrypt its credentials. Only the authenticator has the private key, so only it can decrypt and read the credentials.

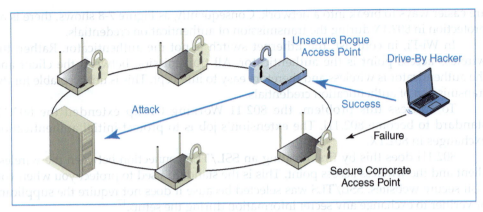

FIGURE 7-9 Rogue Access Point

access points, the presence of even a single unsecure rogue access point will give a drive-by hacker access to the firm's internal network. In other words, a single rogue access point destroys the security that the firm has so laboriously created with 802.11i. In the terminology of Chapter 4, this is a weakest link problem. The least secure access point determines the strength of the entire network.

A rogue access point is an unauthorized access point set up within a firm by an employee or department.

Test Your Understanding

8. a) What is a rogue access point? b) Who creates a rogue access point? c) Why is it dangerous?

Evil Twin Access Points and Virtual Private Networks (VPNs)

The second type of attack that 802.11i will not stop is the ominous-sounding evil twin access point.

Evil Twin Access Points   Figure 7-10 illustrates an evil twin access point attack. Normally, the wireless client shown in the figure will associate with its legitimate access point. The two will establish an 802.11i connection between them.

An **evil twin access point** (which usually is a notebook computer) has software to impersonate a real access point. The evil twin operates at very high power. If the wireless host is configured to choose the highest-power access point, it will associate with the evil twin access point instead of the legitimate access point. The evil twin will establish a secure 802.11i connection with the wireless victim client. This is Security Connection 1. It uses Key 1 for encryption.

An evil twin access point is a notebook computer configured to act like a real access point.

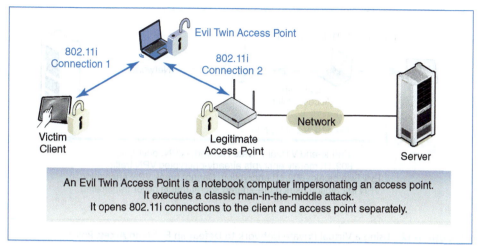

An Evil Twin Access Point is a notebook computer impersonating an access point.
It executes a classic man-in-the-middle attack.
It opens 802.11i connections to the client and access point separately.

FIGURE 7-10   Evil Twin Access Point Operation

Next, the evil twin associates with the legitimate access point using 802.11i, creating Security Connection 2. This connection uses Key 2 for encryption. The evil twin now has two symmetric session keys—one that it shares with the victim client and one that it shares with the legitimate access point. Figure 7-11 illustrates this process.

The evil twin can now read all traffic flowing between the wireless client and the legitimate wireless access point.

* When the wireless client sends a frame encrypted with Key 1, the evil twin decrypts the frame and reads it.
* It then re-encrypts the frame with Key 2 before sending it on to the wireless access point.

It does the same with traffic going in the other direction. Neither the wireless client nor the wireless access point knows that this is happening. Both seem to experience a normal, secure connection. The wireless client has no problem getting to servers on the main wired LAN or getting to Internet servers.

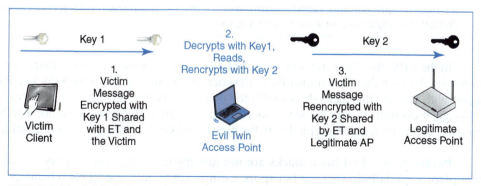

FIGURE 7-11   Evil Twin Decryption, Reading, and Reencryption

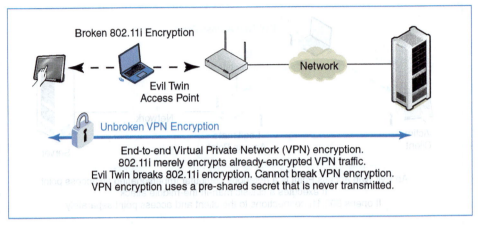

FIGURE 7-12 Using a Virtual Private Network to Defeat an Evil Twin Access Point

What damage can an evil twin access point do? Most obviously, it can eavesdrop on the communication between the wireless client and the servers it uses. This allows the evil twin to steal corporate trade secrets, personal information, and other sensitive information. In addition, the evil twin can also use Connection 2 to launch attacks against any server on the network, bypassing the company's firewall.

Virtual Private Network (VPN)   The evil twin attack is an example of a general class of attacks called **man-in-the-middle** attacks, in which an attacker intercepts messages and then passes them on. Man-in-the-middle attacks typically are very difficult to prevent. The main way to prevent them is to establish a virtual private network (VPN) connection between the wireless client and the server host it will use, as Figure 7-12 illustrates.

A **virtual private network (VPN)** is nothing more than a cryptographically secure connection all the way between a client and a server. A VPN gets its name from the fact that, as far as security is concerned, the client and server seem to have their own private network.

A virtual private network (VPN) is nothing more than a cryptographically secure connection all the way between a client and a server.

In the VPN, the client and server encrypt all communication with a key that is never transmitted. When the client transmits, it first encrypts its message with the VPN key, then again with the key the client shares with the evil twin. When the evil twin receives the message, it decrypts it with the key it shares with the client. However, it cannot read the message because it is still encrypted with the pre-shared key. Confidentiality is maintained.

Perspective   Evil twin attacks are not just theoretical concerns. They are commonplace, especially in wireless hot spots. Companies should use VPNs whenever clients and servers exchange sensitive communication wirelessly.

Without a VPN

    Client encrypts with the key it shares with the evil twin

    The evil twin decrypts the message and reads it

With a VPN

    Client encrypts first with the VPN key

    Client encrypts again with the key it shares with the evil twin

    Evil twin decrypts with the key it shares with the client

    This only gives the evil twin the message encrypted with the VPN key

    The evil twin cannot decrypt and read the original message

---

FIGURE 7-13   Using a VPN to Defeat Evil Twin Decryption (Study Figure)

Test Your Understanding

9. a) What kind of device is an evil twin access point? b) A company uses 802.11i. How many 802.11i connections will the evil twin access point set up when a victim client wishes to connect to a legitimate access point? c) What does the evil twin do when the client transmits subsequently to the legitimate access point? d) Distinguish between evil twin access points and rogue access points. (The answer is not explicitly in the text.)

10. a) Why are VPNs called "private networks?" b) How are VPNs able to defeat evil twin attacks? c) Why must the VPN key be pre-shared to thwart a VPN attack?

802.11 WI-FI WIRELESS LAN MANAGEMENT

Until recently, the term *WLAN management* was almost an oxymoron. Large WLANs were like major airports without control towers. Companies quickly realized that they needed tools to centralize WLAN management. Vendors began to provide these tools.

Access Point Placement

The first management issue is where to place access points throughout a building or site. If access points are placed poorly, there will be overloaded access points, dead spots, and crippling interference between access points.

Initial Planning   The first step in placing access points is to determine how far signals should travel. In many firms, a good radius is about 10 meters. If the radius is too great, many hosts will be far from their access points. Hosts far from the access point must drop down to lower transmission speeds, and their frames will take longer to send and receive. This will reduce the access point's effective capacity. If the radius is too small, however, the firm will need many more access points to cover the area to be served. Having access points too close together may also cause interference.

Once an appropriate radius is selected (say 10 meters), the company gets out its architecture drawings and begins to lay out 10-meter circles with as little overlap as

Must be done carefully for good coverage and to minimize interference between access points

Lay out roughly 10-meter overlapping circles on blueprints

Adjust for obvious potential problems such as thick walls and filing cabinets

In multistory buildings, must consider placement in three dimensions

Install access points and do site surveys to determine signal quality

Adjust placement and signal strength as needed

FIGURE 7-14 Access Point Placement in a Building (Study Figure)

possible but with all points being within a circle. Where there are thick walls, filing cabinets, or other obstructions, shorter propagation distances must be used.

Of course, in a multistory building, this planning must be done in three dimensions. The "circles" are now bubbles with radiuses of 10 meters. Again, the goal is to provide coverage to all points within the building while reducing overlap as much as possible.

Finally, planners assign channels to access point positions. They attempt to minimize interference while doing so.

Installation and Initial Site Surveys Next, the access points are installed provisionally in the planned locations. However, the implementation work has just begun. When each access point is installed, an initial **site survey** must be done of the area around the access point to discover whether there are any dead spots or other problems. This requires **signal analysis software**, which can run on a notebook computer or even a smartphone.

When areas with poor signal strength are found, surrounding access points must be moved appropriately, or their signal strengths must be adjusted until all areas have good signal strength. Users should now have good service.

Ongoing Site Surveys Although the initial site survey should result in good service, conditions will change with time. More people may be given desks in a given access point's range, signal obstructions may be put up for business purposes, and other changes may occur. Site surveys must be done frequently and routinely; they may also be done in response to specific reports of problems.

Test Your Understanding

11. a) Describe the process by which access point locations are determined. b) When must firms do site surveys to give users good service?

Remote Management

Large organizations have hundreds or even thousands of access points. Traveling to each one for manual configuration and troubleshooting would be extremely expensive. To keep management labor costs under control, organizations need to be able to manage access points remotely, from a central management console. Figure 7-16 shows that the management console constantly collects data from the individual access points. This includes signal strengths, indications of interference, configuration settings, and other diagnostic information.

The Manual Labor to Manage Many Access Points:

    Can be very high

    Automation is critical

Access Points are Managed Devices (Figure 7-16)

    Send data to the administrator at the management console

    Administrator can send commands to the access points

Desired Network Management Functionality

    Notify the WLAN administrators of failures immediately

    Should provide continuous transmission quality monitoring

    Support remote access point power adjustment

    Allow software updates to be pushed out to all smart access points or WLAN switches

    Work automatically whenever possible

Desired Security Management Functionality

    Notify administrator of rogue access points

    Notify administrator of evil twin access points

    Notify the administration of access points that have improperly configured security

    Do all this as automatically as possible

FIGURE 7-15   Remote Access Point Management (Study Figure)

     If the administrator reading the data detects a problem in the network, he or she can send commands to access points to increase power, decrease power, change channels, change configuration settings, and make other changes.

     Wireless LAN Management Functionality   Although technological approaches to centralized WLAN management vary, vendors generally agree on the types of functionality these systems should provide:

- These systems should have alarms that notify the WLAN administrators of failures immediately so that malfunctioning access points can be fixed or replaced.

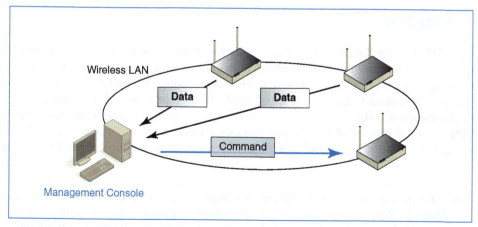

FIGURE 7-16   Remote Access Point Management

- They should provide continuous transmission quality monitoring at all access points. In effect, they should provide continuous site surveys.
- They should allow remote access point adjustment—for instance, telling nearby access points to increase their power to compensate for changes in the user environment. They may even need to make temporary adjustments if many users crowd into an area.
- They should allow software updates to be pushed out to all smart access points or WLAN switches, bypassing the need to install updates manually.
- They should help provide security by detecting rogue access points, evil twin access points, or legitimate access points that have improperly configured security. (Managed access points report on their neighbors as well as themselves; this permits unauthorized rogue and evil twin access points to be identified.) In other words, central management systems should include wireless intrusion detection system functionality.
- All of these functions should work as automatically as possible to minimize management labor.

Cost and Security   Centralized network management software and hardware on the management console and switches or access points is expensive. However, it should greatly reduce management labor, so there should be considerable net savings from its use.

In addition, centralized WLAN management's wireless intrusion detection functionality is the only real way to manage WLAN security. Manual detection of threats would be far too slow and require prohibitive amounts of labor.

Test Your Understanding

12. a) Why is centralized access point management desirable? b) What functions should remote access point management systems provide? c) Why should they provide these functions as automatically as possible? d) What are the security benefits from centralized access point management?

BLUETOOTH

Wi-Fi/802.11 is not the only standards family for wireless local networking. If you have a wireless headset for your mobile phone or pocket music player, or if you have a hands-free cellular system in your car, you may already be using Bluetooth. These are precisely the kinds of short-distance modest-speed applications that Bluetooth was created to handle. **Bluetooth** is a short-range radio technology designed for **personal area networks (PANs)**—small groups of networked devices around a person's body or in the area around a single desk. It is useful to think of Bluetooth as a cable replacement technology.

Bluetooth is a short-range radio technology designed for personal area networks (PANs)—small groups of networked devices around a person's body or in the area around a single desk. It is useful to think of Bluetooth as a cable replacement technology.

BOX 1

Expressing Power Ratios in Decibels

Signal power is usually measured in **milliwatts (mW)**. Networking professionals often have to compare two signal strengths. For instance, if signal power is 20 mW (milliwatts) at 10 meters and 2 mW at 20 meters, then the ratio of the second power to the first is 2:20 (1:10). To give another example, if a larger antenna doubles a transceiver's transmission power, then the ratio of the final power to the initial power is 2:1. Power ratios are expressed in several ways—as decimal numbers, percentages, or ratios (such as 2:1).

Calculating Decibel Values for Power Ratios

Networking professionals typically express the ratio of two powers in **decibels (dB)**, using Equation 7-1. L_{dB} is the decibel value of two power levels, P_1 and P_2. P_1 is the initial power level. P_2 is the final power level. The equation shows that the decibel expressions use a logarithmic scale.

$$L_{dB} = 10 * Log_{10}\left(\frac{P_2}{P_1}\right)$$ **(Equation 7-1)**

This looks complicated, but it really is not. Figure 7-17 shows how to do decibel calculations in Excel or some other spreadsheet program. In the first example, the initial power is 40 mW and the final power is 10 mW. This gives a power ratio of 0.25. Excel has a LOG10 function, and this is applied to the power ratio. The result is −0.60. This logarithm is multiplied by a factor of ten. This gives a value of −6.02 decibels. Whenever the second value is smaller than the initial value, the decibel value is negative.

Whenever the second value is smaller than the initial value, the decibel value is negative.

In the second example, the final power is *larger* than the initial power. For example, the signal may be amplified by a larger antenna. The initial power is 10 mW and the final signal power

$$L_{dB} = 10 * LOG10\left(\frac{P_2}{P_1}\right)$$

Data or Formula	Example 1: Attenuation	Example 2: Amplification
P_1 (mw)	40	10
P_2 (mw)	10	30
P_2/P_1	0.25	3
LOG10(P_2/P_1)	−0.60206	0.477121255
10*LOG10(P_2/P_1)	−6.0205999	4.771212547

FIGURE 7-17   Decibel Calculation for Power Levels

(continued)

is 30 mW. This gives a power ratio of 3:1. This time, the decibel value is 4.77 dB, a positive value. Whenever the second value is larger than the initial value, the decibel value is positive.

Whenever the second value is larger than the initial value, the decibel value is positive.

Test Your Understanding

13. a) The power level at 10 meters is 100 mW. At 20 meters, it is 5 mW. How many dB has it lost? b) Compared to an omnidirectional antenna, a dish antenna quadruples radiated power. How much is this change in decibels? c) Compute the decibel value for a power ratio of 17:1. d) Of 1:33.

Approximating Decibel Values

You do not always have a spreadsheet program with you. Nobody can calculate logarithms in their head. However, there are two useful approximations you can use to roughly estimate decibel values if you know the power ratio.

First, Figure 7-18 shows that if you double signal power, this is a gain of approximately 3 dB. If you quadruple the signal power, this is a gain of approximately 6 dB. For each additional doubling, the gain is another approximately 3 dB. This calculation is approximate, but it is close. The exact value is 3.0103.

Each doubling of power gives a gain of approximately 3 dB.

Each multiplying by ten in power gives a gain of approximately 10 dB.

What if the power ratio is less than one? If it is 0.5, then the decibel value is approximately –3 dB. Cutting this in half gives –6 dB. Every additional halving is another –3 dB. Again, if the power ratio is greater than one, the decibel value will be positive, and if the power ratio is less than one, the decibel value will be negative.

Powers of 2		Powers of 10	
Power Ratio	Approximate dB	Power Ratio	Exact dB
2	3 dB	10	10 dB
4	6 dB	100	20 dB
8	9 dB	1,000	
16		10,000	
32		100,000	
1/2	–3 dB	1/10	–10 dB
1/4		1/100	
1/8		1/1,000	

FIGURE 7-18 Decibel Approximations

(continued)

For positive or negative powers of ten, the situation is even simpler. A power ratio of 10:1 is exactly 10 dB. There is no approximation. A power ratio of 100 is 20 dB. Each further increase by a factor of ten is another 10 dB. Likewise, a power ratio of 0.1 is –10 dB, and a power ratio of 0.01 is –20 dB.

What if a ratio is *not* a power of two or ten? What if it is, for example, 3:1? Well, 2:1 is 3 dB; and 4:1 is 6 dB. So the answer is somewhere between 3 dB and 6 dB. That is not very precise, but it can be useful in practical situations. The 2:1 and 10:1 approximation will not always be useful, but they are good tools for networking professionals to have.

Test Your Understanding

14. a) Fill in the missing values in Figure 7-18. Approximate, without using Excel, the decibels for a ratio for b) 8:1. c) 9:1. d) 110:1. e) 1:7. f) 1:90.

dBm Values

Sometimes, you will see a transceiver's power expressed as dBm. The m is new. Also, we are seeing decibels expressed for a single device's power, not for a power ratio.

Actually, dBm *is* a power ratio. However, with dBm, P_1 is always one milliwatt (mW). This means that a transceiver power of two mW will be 2:1 or 3 dBm. A transceiver power of 100 mW would have a power of 20 dBm.

With dBm, P_1 is always one milliwatt (1 mW).

Test Your Understanding

15. a) What is the dBm value for a radio operating at 78 mW? b) At 7 W? c) Estimate, without using Excel, the dBm value for a radio operating at 2 mW. d) For a radio operating at 16 mW. e) For a radio operating at 1 W. f) For a radio operating at 0.1 W.

Transceiver Power	dBm
4 mW	6 dBm
10 mW	10 dBm
10 W	40 dBm
0.5 mW	–3 dBm

Note: In dBm calculations, P_1 is always 1 mW.

FIGURE 7-19   dBm Calculations (Study Figure)

Two Modes of Operation

How fast is Bluetooth? The answer is that the latest version of the Bluetooth standard, Bluetooth 4.0, has two popular modes of operation with different transmission speeds, distances, and power requirements. Figure 7-20 compares these two modes of operation.

Operating Mode	Classic Bluetooth	High-Speed Bluetooth
Principal Benefit	Good performance at low power	High-speed transfers available when needed; longer operating distances
Speed	Up to 3 Mbps	Up to about 24 Mbps
Expected Duty Cycle	Low to High	Low
Power Required	Low	High
Maximum Distance	~10 m	~30 m

FIGURE 7-20 Bluetooth Modes of Operation

Classic Bluetooth The 802.11 standards are created by the IEEE Standards Association's 802.11 Working Group. In contrast, Bluetooth is created by the **Bluetooth Special Interest Group**, an association of hardware manufacturers and other organizations. Bluetooth 2.0 introduced what most people think of as the **Classic Bluetooth** speed of 2 to 3 Mbps. This is slow compared to current versions of 802.11, but it is fast enough for wireless mice, voice communication, and many other things. Its published distance limit is about 10 meters, although useful range is shorter. We normally think of high power and long range as good things, but low power and short range mean that power consumption is low, so batteries last a long time. For keyboards, mice, wireless headsets, and other small wireless devices, this is important.

High-Speed Bluetooth In 2009, the Bluetooth SIG introduced Bluetooth 3.0. This introduced a new mode of Bluetooth transmission, **high-speed Bluetooth**. This new mode retains ordinary Bluetooth speeds for most operations. However, for operations that require higher speeds, such as webpage downloads, a Bluetooth device capable of high-speed Bluetooth can turn on a second radio that uses 802.11. This gives 802.11 speeds (up to about 24 Mbps).

In other words, the Bluetooth SIG "borrowed" radio transmission technology from its rival, 802.11. However, this is not full 802.11. High-speed Bluetooth operates in a one-to-one mode. It cannot use access points. In addition, only some 802.11 transmission modes and speeds are supported. If the last point sounds a bit vague, it is. Bluetooth support for 802.11 transmission modes is evolving rapidly.

Speed and distance are good, but high-speed Bluetooth consumes a good deal of electrical power, like regular 802.11. Bluetooth conserves battery power by using high-speed Bluetooth only when necessary.[13]

---

[13] In 2010, the Bluetooth SIG introduced Bluetooth 4.0. In addition to other improvements, this standard introduced a third mode of operation, low-energy Bluetooth. Low-energy Bluetooth is for device pairs that have low duty cycles, that is, that only communicate with each other a very small percentage of the time. These devices must also have low speed requirements because low-energy Bluetooth is limited to only about 200 kbps. Devices must also be within about 15 meters of each other. Using low-energy Bluetooth, devices like light switches that only rarely send brief messages can operate with "coin" batteries that last for several years between replacements.

Test Your Understanding

16. a) What is a PAN? (Do not just spell out the abbreviation.) b) What organization creates Bluetooth standards? c) Compare the relative benefits of classic Bluetooth and high-speed Bluetooth. d) Would two devices typically use high-speed Bluetooth during their total communication time? Explain.

One-to-One, Master–Slave Operation

Figure 7-21 shows several devices communicating with Bluetooth. The device in the top center is a mobile phone. To its right is a printer. The mobile phone user wishes to print a webpage showing on the mobile's screen. The user selects print, chooses the target printer, and prints. In seconds, the user walks up to the printer and picks up the output.

Bluetooth always uses a **one-to-one connection** between each pair of devices. Bluetooth cannot do many-to-many networking, which is possible with 802.11 and Ethernet. Reducing operation to one-to-one service simplifies Bluetooth protocols.

Bluetooth always uses point-to-point communication between a pair of devices.

Bluetooth also uses **master–slave control**. One device is the master, and the other device is the slave. The master controls the slave. In the printing scenario, the mobile device is the master and the printer is the slave. The mobile phone drives the printing process.

In Bluetooth, one device is the master and the other device is the slave. The master controls the slave.

Although communication is always one-to-one, a master may have multiple slaves. In addition to controlling the printer, the mobile phone in Figure 7-21 also controls the user's hands-free headset. In this case, a single master controls two slaves. However, the operation is still one-to-one in each case. The mobile phone's connections to the two devices are separate Bluetooth connections.

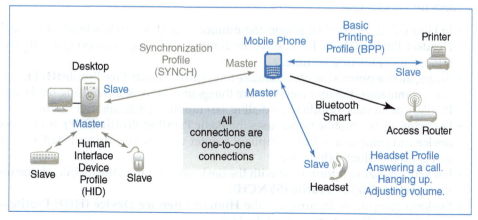

FIGURE 7-21 Bluetooth Operation

It is possible for a Bluetooth device to be a master and slave simultaneously. Consider the relationship between the mobile phone and the desktop computer. The two are synchronizing information. The mobile phone is the master, and the desktop is the slave. However, we have just seen that the desktop is master to the keyboard and mouse.

A Bluetooth device may be a master of one device and a slave to another device simultaneously.

Although one device is always the master and the other the slave, they sometimes switch roles during an interaction. For example, when the wearer of a hands-free headpiece initiates a call, the headset is the master and the mobile phone is the slave. However, they switch roles afterward, allowing the more powerful mobile phone to control the call interactions.

Test Your Understanding

17. a) What does it mean that Bluetooth uses one-to-one operation? b) Is this still true if a master communicates with four slaves? c) What does master–slave operation mean? d) Can a Bluetooth master have multiple slaves? e) Can a Bluetooth slave have two masters? f) Can a Bluetooth device be both a master and a slave? g) At the beginning of a telephone call placed through a Bluetooth headset, which device is initially the master? h) Which usually becomes the master later?

Bluetooth Profiles

Like 802.11, Bluetooth specifies transmission at the physical and data link layers. The 802.11 Working Group did not have to worry about applications because the desktop and laptop PCs on 802.11 WLANs already had many applications.

However, the Bluetooth SIG faced a different situation. Not only were there no transmission standards for short-range one-to-one communication; there also were no application protocols in existence for PAN applications such as wirelessly controlling keyboards, telephone headsets, and other devices. Consequently, in addition to defining transmission standards, the SIG also defined application profiles, which are called **Bluetooth profiles**. Profiles govern how devices share information and specify control messages for various uses.

- In Figure 7-21, the mobile phone communicates with a wireless headset using the **Headset Profile (HSP)**. Its features are limited, including answering a call, hanging up, and adjusting volume.
- In cars, mobile phones can communicate through the **Hands-Free Profile (HFP)**. Using voice commands, the user can do more things than he or she can using the Headset Profile. Commands include voice dialing, last number redial, and call waiting.
- For printing, the mobile phone uses the **Basic Printing Profile (BPP)**. A Bluetooth device can print to any BPP compliant printer without having to install a printer driver on the Bluetooth device.
- For synchronizing information with the desktop computer, the mobile phone uses the **Synchronization Profile (SYNCH)**.
- Desktop computers, in turn, use the **Human Interface Device (HID) Profile** for mice, keyboards, and other input devices.

Bluetooth Profiles

> Specify how devices will work together for different applications
>
> Nothing like this in 802.11

Headset Profile

> For using a mobile phone through a headset
>
> Features usually accessed through manual controls
>
> Rings, answers a call, hangs up, adjusts volume

Hands-Free Profile

> For using a mobile phone in an automobile
>
> Features accessed through voice commands
>
> Headset profile plus last number redial, call waiting, and voice dialing

Basic Printing Profile

> Print to any BPP printer without having to load a printer driver

Synchronization Profile

> For synchronizing information with a desktop computer

Human Interface Device Profile

> Bluetooth mice, keyboards, etc.

Bluetooth Smart

> Permits devices without full operating systems to interact
>
> Created for the Internet of Things
>
> The phone in Figure 7-21 can upload photos to a cloud service via a nearby access router

---

FIGURE 7-22 Bluetooth Profiles (Study Figure)

- Bluetooth Smart is actually more than a Bluetooth Profile. It is a general facility for allowing devices without full operating systems to work together. This will be important in tomorrow's Internet of Things. In Figure 7-21, the mobile phone is uploading photographs to a cloud service via an Internet access router.

Test Your Understanding

18. a) Why did the Bluetooth SIG have to develop Bluetooth profiles? b) What profile would a Bluetooth-enabled notebook use to print to a nearby printer? c) What profile would a tablet use with a Bluetooth keyboard? d) What profile can a mobile phone use to communicate with a headset? e) Why will Bluetooth Smart extend the types of devices that can communicate wirelessly?

OTHER LOCAL WIRELESS TECHNOLOGIES

There is no competitor for 802.11 Wi-Fi standards, but Bluetooth has two competitors for very-short-distance communications. These are Near Field Communication and Wi-Fi Direct.

Near Field Communication (NFC)

Reducing Distance and Power Requirements to the Extreme   Reducing the distance between devices reduces transmission power. Taken to the logical extreme, the greatest reduction in transmission power would occur if two devices were physically "bumped" together. In fact, there is a technology that does precisely that. It is called **near field communication (NFC)**. It is governed by the **NFC Forum.**

In NFC, the two devices do not actually have to touch physically. However, they must be within about 4 cm (roughly 2 in.). It is difficult to judge such small distances, so the normal practice is to bump the two devices to ensure communication.

NFC transmission speed is limited to 424 kbps. Slow transmission further minimizes transmission power. In addition, NFC operates at the 13.56 kHz service band. Low-frequency operation further reduces the need for transmission power. Overall, NFC devices are very energy efficient. They often use inexpensive "coin" batteries, and these batteries may last for months or even years.

NFC Applications   NFC has many possible uses. For example, consider Vishal, who is going to work. As Vishal leaves his house, he taps his mobile phone against the front door, deactivating the home intruder alarm. He walks to his car and taps the handle with his mobile. This unlocks the car. It also moves the driver's seat to his preferred position. Bumping the ignition with the mobile starts the car.

For Very Small Distances and Low Speed

    Up to 4 cm (about 2 inches)

    Limited to 424 kbps

    So uses very little battery power

Operation in the 13.56 kHz Band

    Dedicated for this use

    Also gives low power consumption

Sample Applications

    Payment of bus fares (already popular in some countries)

    Unlocking car doors and turning on the ignition

    Building door entry control

    Sharing electronic business cards and other files between mobile devices

    Retail payments, including loyalty points and coupons (beginning to be popular)

Passive Radio Frequency ID (RFID) Tags

    Goal: to replace bar codes

    Tags are electronic but have no power source

    When scanned by a reader, use power of the scan to generate a reply

    Inexpensive compared to powered devices

    Can only send a small amount of information

    Cannot do encryption

FIGURE 7-23   Near Field Communication (NFC) (Study Figure)

At work, Vishal taps his mobile against the building door to unlock it and walks in. To share business cards, he and a visitor tap their phones together. To share a file, they do the same.

At the building's convenience store, Vishal bumps his mobile against the reader to pay for a purchase. This also records his loyalty points for the purchase and makes use of any coupons Vishal had loaded onto his mobile last night.

Passive RFID Tags With NFC, one of the devices can even operate if it has no power at all. Some items on a store shelf can have small wire arrangements embedded in paper or plastic. These are **passive radio frequency ID (RFID) tags**.[14] When Vishal bumps his mobile against one of these tags, his phone receives the price and some other information about the product. RFID also speeds scanning at checkout. There is no need to line up the item's UPC bar code tag with a laser reader. Eventually, customers will be able to skip the checkout line entirely and just leave the store. A scanner at the door will record their purchases, charge their account, and print a receipt.

Passive RFID tags do not have power sources. Instead, when the reader sends a command pulse to the tag, the RFID tag absorbs some of the signal's energy. The absorbed power is tiny, but it is enough for the tag to transmit its information. With no need for a battery, passive RFID tags are inexpensive and never have to worry about batteries losing power.

Test Your Understanding

19. a) What is the distance limit for NFC? b) Why is bumping done? c) What factors account for NFC's low transmission power requirements? d) In what service band does NFC operate? e) List two NFC applications you would like to use. f) Passive RFID chips have no batteries. How can they transmit when queried?

Wi-Fi Direct

Bluetooth and NFC provide direct transmission between a pair of devices. Wi-Fi typically uses access points to transfer frames between 802.11 devices. However, 802.11 has always been capable of direct device–device transmission. As Figure 7-24 shows, this capability has recently been expanded and formalized as **Wi-Fi Direct**. Wi-Fi Direct is built into many mobile phones today. Wi-Fi Direct is likely to be popular because we almost always carry a Wi-Fi device with us.

Test Your Understanding

20. a) Compare normal Wi-Fi with Wi-Fi Direct. b) With what two transmission standards does Wi-Fi Direct compete?

Security in Emerging Local Wireless Technologies

Security is a complex situation for emerging local wireless transmission technologies. Like all wireless technologies, they are vulnerable to eavesdropping, data modification, and impersonation.

---

[14] Active RFID tags contain batteries and can be read from longer distances. They are much more expensive than passive RFID tags and become unreadable if their batteries die. They are sometimes used on cars that have to pass over toll bridges frequently.

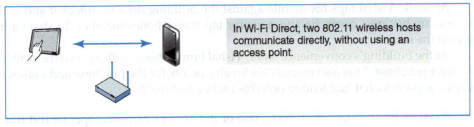

In Wi-Fi Direct, two 802.11 wireless hosts communicate directly, without using an access point.

FIGURE 7-24 Wi-Fi Direct

Some of these technologies have no cryptographic security at all. The classic example is using NFC to read passive RFID tags. These technologies assume that eavesdroppers cannot get close enough to read the information because maximum transmission distances are very small. However, distances in the standards are for normal devices. Eavesdroppers with highly directional antennas and amplifiers can intercept signals over much longer distances. Bluetooth probably has the best security among emerging wireless technologies, but its security is still weaker than 802.11i's security.

Threats

> Eavesdropping
>
> Data modification
>
> Impersonation

Cryptological Security

> Some have no cryptological security
>
> Example: Near field communication for reading passive RFID tags
>
> They rely on short transmission distances to foil eavesdroppers
>
> However, directional antennas and amplifiers can read signals that are far longer than distances in standards

Strength of Security

> Some have reasonably good security
>
> Example: Bluetooth
>
> However, still not as strong as 802.11i security

Device Loss or Theft

> In this age of bring your own device (BYOD) to work, this is a serious problem
>
> Most devices are only protected by short PINs

Maturity

> In general, new security technologies take some time to mature
>
> During this period, they often have vulnerabilities that must be fixed quickly
>
> User companies must master security for each new technology they use

FIGURE 7-25 Security in Emerging Local Wireless Technologies (Study Figure)

In today's world of bring your own device (BYOD) to work, emerging local wireless technologies make a worrisome corporate security situation even more problematic. For example, if devices such as mobile phones are lost or stolen, they are often protected only by brief PINs, if they are protected at all. Many of these devices contain sensitive corporate information, and even if they do not, they may allow attackers to log into sensitive servers on the corporate network.

As a general rule, new security technologies tend to have vulnerabilities that take time to discover and protect against. One must hope that technology vendors will be quicker to act than attackers. In any case, companies need to fully understand security for each technology.

Test Your Understanding

21. a) Why is short transmission range protection against eavesdroppers? b) Describe the state of cryptographic security for new transmission standards. c) Why is device theft or loss a serious risk?

CONCLUSION

Synopsis

This chapter continues our discussion of local wireless communication. We began with a discussion of 802.11 wireless LAN security threats, including drive-by hackers and war drivers.

The 802.11i cryptographic standard can protect transmissions between a wireless client and a wireless access point. (It does not provide end-to-end protection between the wireless client and the server it uses.)

The 802.11i standard has two operation modes. Pre-shared key (PSK) mode is for use in homes and small businesses with a single access point. The Wi-Fi Alliance calls this personal mode. All users must know a pre-shared key to be authenticated. After authentication, this pre-shared key is replaced by a one-time unshared session key to encrypt further communication between the access point and a particular wireless client. PSK mode provides strong security but only if it is carefully implemented with a strong passphrase.

Corporations with multiple access points must use 802.11i in 802.1X mode, which the Wi-Fi Alliance calls enterprise mode. In Chapter 5, we saw that the 802.1X security standard requires an authenticator and a central authentication server. In Ethernet, the authenticator is a switch. In 802.1X mode in 802.11i, the authenticator is the access point. The 802.11i standard adds extra SSL/TLS security to transmissions between the access point and the client *before* the 802.1X authentication phase. When you configure an access point's security, it is important to specify 802.11i security, which is sometimes listed as WPA2 security. It is important not to select WEP or WPA security.

The 802.11i standard offers very good security between the wireless client and the access point. However, it does not stop all security threats. Sometimes, individuals or departments install their own rogue access points. Even if all other access points are properly secured, a single rogue access point without security gives a drive-by hacker an easy way to get into the firm. A more complex problem is the evil twin access point, which is an attacker computer outside the walls of the company. The evil twin implements a man-in-the-middle attack, intercepting and reading all communication between the victim wireless client and the access point. A virtual private network (VPN) connection between the wireless client and the server it uses is needed to defeat evil twin access points.

We discussed wireless LAN management, including strategies for placing access points to give good coverage with a minimum of overlap and a minimum of interference from nearby access points. Good access point placement requires initial and ongoing site surveys of signal strength and interference. We also looked at the remote management of access points using smart access points or dumb access points controlled by wireless LAN switches. A central manager can detect rogue access points and evil twins, allow the remote adjustment of access point power, push software updates out to the access points, and do all this and more automatically, with a minimum of intervention.

An optional box showed how to express power relationships as ratios and as decibel values. Power ratios in radio transmission are often expressed in decibels, so it is useful to be able to work with decibels.

We looked at other local wireless technologies, including Bluetooth, which is for personal area networks (PANs) in which all devices are located nearby, often on the same desk or around the body of a person. We discussed Bluetooth in some detail because Bluetooth is growing rapidly in importance. We also looked at near field communication (NFC) and Wi-Fi Direct, which are competitors of Bluetooth for mobile device interactions. We finished by discussing the general level of security in emerging local wireless standards.

END-OF-CHAPTER QUESTIONS

Thought Questions

7-1. (If you read the box on expressing power ratios in decibels) If a power ratio is 20:1, this can be expressed as 10:1 times 2:1. You know that 10:1 is 10 dB and that 2:1 is 3 dB. Although power ratios multiply, decibels add. So a power ratio of 20 (10 times 2) is 10 + 3 dB or 13 dB. Learning from this example, what will a power ratio of 1:800 be in decibels?

7-2. a) List the security principles in Chapter 4. b) What principle do rogue access points compromise? c) What principle does the danger of giving out PSK keys to people who are not authorized to have them represent? d) What principle does having both 802.11i and centralized security management represent?

7-3. Create a policy for 802.11 Wi-Fi security in your wireless network at home. This is not a trivial task. Do not just jot down a few notes. Make it a document for people in your firm to read.

7-4. Create a policy for 802.11 Wi-Fi security in a wireless network in a five-person company with a one-access point WLAN. This is not a trivial task. Do not just jot down a few notes. Make it a document for people in your firm to read.

7-5. Create a policy for 802.11 Wi-Fi security in a wireless network in a 500-employee company with a 47-access point WLAN. This is not a trivial task. Do not just jot down a few notes. Make it a document for people in your firm to read.

Perspective Questions

7-6. What was the most surprising thing you learned in this chapter?

7-7. What was the most difficult part of this chapter for you?

Chapter 8

TCP/IP Internetworking I

LEARNING OBJECTIVES

By the end of this chapter, you should be able to:

- Define hierarchical IP addresses, networks and subnets, border and internal routers, and masks.
- Predict what the router will do with a packet given a routing table and an arriving packet's destination IP address.
- (In a box) Explain the purpose and operation of the Address Resolution Protocol on an Ethernet network.
- Explain the IPv4 packet header fields we did not see in earlier chapters.
- Explain the IPv6 packet header fields and IPv6's use of extension headers.
- Convert a 128-bit IP address into compressed hexadecimal notation.
- Explain TCP fields and session closings.
- Explain why application message fragmentation is not possible with UDP.

INTRODUCTION

Switched networks and wireless networks are governed by Layer 1 and Layer 2 standards. We looked at single network standards in Chapters 5, 6, and 7. In this chapter and the next, we will look at internetworking, which is governed by Layer 3 and Layer 4 standards.

We will only look at TCP/IP internetworking because TCP/IP dominates the work of network professionals at the internet and transport layers. However, real-world routers cannot limit themselves to TCP/IP internetworking. Commercial routers are multiprotocol routers, which can route not only IP packets but also IPX packets, SNA packets, AppleTalk packets, and other types of packets.

5 Application	User Applications			Supervisory Applications		
	HTTP	SMTP	Many Others	DNS	Dynamic Routing Protocols	Many Others
4 Transport	TCP			UDP		
3 Internet	IP			ICMP		ARP
2 Data Link	None: Use OSI Standards					
1 Physical	None: Use OSI Standards					

Note: Shaded protocols are discussed in this chapter.

FIGURE 8-1 Major TCP/IP Standards

We looked at the TCP/IP architecture in Chapters 1 and 2. We focused on IP, TCP, and UDP, although we looked at a few other TCP/IP standards. Figure 8-1 shows a few of the many standards the IETF has created within the TCP/IP architecture. Some of the standards are shaded in this figure. We will look at them in this chapter.

IP ROUTING

In this section, we will look at how routers make decisions about forwarding packets—in other words, how a router decides which interface to use to send an arriving packet back out to get it closer to its destination. (In routers, ports are called **interfaces**.)

Router ports are called interfaces.

This forwarding process is called **routing**. Router forwarding decisions are much more complex than the Ethernet switching decisions we saw in Chapter 5. Because of this complexity, routers do more work per arriving packet than switches do per arriving frame. Consequently, routers are more expensive than switches for a given level of traffic. A widely quoted network adage reflects this cost difference: "Switch where you can; route where you must."

When routers forward incoming packets closer to their destination hosts, this is routing.

Test Your Understanding

1. a) What are interfaces? b) What is routing?

Hierarchical IP Addressing

To understand the routing of IP packets, it is necessary to understand IP addresses. In Chapter 1, we saw that IP Version 4 (IPv4) addresses are 32 bits long. However, IP addresses are not simple 32-bit strings. They have internal structure, and this internal structure is important in routing.

Hierarchical Addressing As Figure 8-2 shows, IP addresses are **hierarchical**. They usually consist of three parts that locate a host in progressively smaller parts of the Internet. These are the network, subnet, and host parts. We will see later in this chapter how hierarchical IP addressing simplifies routing tables.

Network Part First, every IP address has a **network part**, which identifies the host's network on the Internet. In this case, *network* is an organizational concept. It is a user organization, such as a manufacturing corporation, or it is an ISP. Whichever organization receives the network part effectively controls part of the Internet.

In IP addressing, network is an organizational concept. A network is an organization that controls part of the Internet. It may be a user organization such as a manufacturing corporation or an ISP.

In Figure 8-2, the network part is 128.171. This is two IP address segments. Each segment is 8 bits long, so the network part for the University of Hawai`i is 16 bits long. All host IP addresses in the university begin with this network part.

Do not get hung up on the network part being 16 bits. This is only an example. Different organizations have different network parts that range from 8 bits to 24 bits in length.

Subnet Part Most large organizations further divide their networks into smaller units called **subnets**. After the network part in an IP address come the bits of the **subnet part**. The subnet part bits specify a particular subnet within the network.

For instance, Figure 8-2 shows that in the IP address 128.171.17.13, the first 16 bits (128.171) correspond to the network part, and the next 8 bits (17) correspond to a subnet on this network. (Subnet 17 is the Shidler College of Business subnet within the University of Hawai`i Network.) All host IP addresses within this subnet begin with 128.171.17.

Again, do not get hung up on the subnet part being 8 bits long. In different organizations, subnet lengths vary widely. Keep clear in your head that the UH Network is only being used as an example.

Host Part The remaining bits in the 32-bit IP address constitute the **host part**, which specifies a particular host on the subnet. In Figure 8-2, the host part is 8 bits long with a segment value of 13. This corresponds to a particular host, 128.171.17.13, on the Shidler College of Business subnet of the University of Hawai`i Network. Again, host parts in different organizations differ in length.

Variable Part Lengths Can you tell just by looking at an IP address which bits correspond to the network, subnet, and host parts? The answer is no. For instance, if you see the IP address 60.47.7.23, you may have an 8-bit network part of 60, an 8-bit subnet part of 47, and a 16-bit host part of 7.23. In fact, parts may not even break conveniently at 8-bit boundaries. The only thing you can tell when looking at an IP address is that it is 32 bits long.

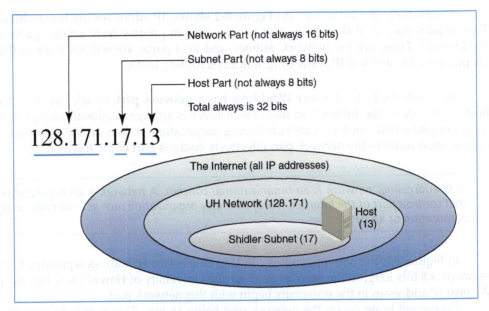

FIGURE 8-2 Hierarchical IPv4 Addresses

Test Your Understanding

2. a) What are the three parts of an IP address? b) How long is each part? c) What is the total length of an IP address? d) In the IP address 10.11.13.13, what is the network part?

Routers, Networks, and Subnets

Border Routers Connect Different Networks   As Figure 8-3 illustrates, networks and subnets are very important in router operation. Here we see a simple site internet. The figure shows that a **border router**'s main job is to connect different networks. This border router connects the 192.168.x.x network within the firm to the 60.x.x.x network of the firm's Internet service provider. Here, the *xs* are the remaining bits of the IP address, so 192.168 and 60 are the network parts of the two networks.

A border router's main job is to connect different networks

Internal Routers Connect Different Subnets   The site network also has an internal router. An **internal router**, Figure 8-3 demonstrates, only connects different subnets within a network—in this case, the 192.168.1.x, 192.168.2.x, and 192.168.3.x subnets. Many sites have multiple internal routers to link the site's subnets.

An internal router only connects different subnets within a network.

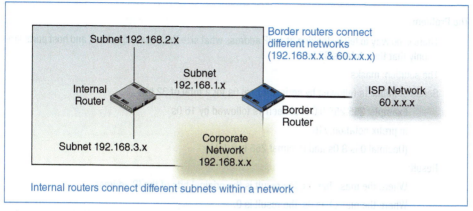

FIGURE 8-3 Border Routers, Networks, and Subnets

Test Your Understanding

3. a) Connecting different networks is the main job of what type of router? b) What type of router only connects different subnets?

Network and Subnet Masks

We have seen that in the University of Hawai`i network, the first 16 bits in IP addresses are the network part, the next 8 are the subnet part, and the final 8 are the host part. However, because the sizes of the network, subnet, and host parts differ, routers need a way to tell the sizes of key parts. The tool that allows them to do this is masks.

32-Bit Strings Figure 8-4 illustrates how masks work. A mask is a string of 32 bits, like an IP address. However, a mask always begins with a series of 1s; this is followed by a series of 0s. The total length of an IP address is always 32 bits, so if a mask begins with twelve 1s, it will end with twenty 0s.

In a network mask, the bits in the network part of the mask are 1s, while the remaining bits are 0s. In subnet masks, the bits of both the network and subnet parts are 1s, and the remaining bits are 0s. We have seen that the University of Hawai`i network part is 16 bits and the subnet part is 8 bits. So the network mask will have sixteen 1s followed by sixteen 0s. The subnet mask will have twenty-four 1s followed by eight 0s.

A mask is a 32-bit string of 1s and 0s.

The mask always has a certain number of initial 1s. The remaining bits are always 0s.

In network masks, the initial 1s correspond to the network part.

In subnet masks, the initial 1s correspond to the network and subnet parts.

For example, suppose that the mask is 255.255.0.0. This means that the four 8-bit segments of the mask have the values 255, 255, 0, and 0. In dotted decimal notation

The Problem

There is no way to tell by looking at an IP address what size the network, subnet, and host parts are—only that their total is 32 bits

The solution: masks

Series of initial 1s followed by series of final 0s for a total of 32 bits

Example: 255.255.0.0 is sixteen 1s followed by 16 0s

In prefix notation, /16

(Decimal 0 is 8 0s and Decimal 255 is 8 1s)

Result:

Where the mask has 1s, the result is the original bits of the IP address

Where the mask has 0s, the result is 0.

Mask Operation

Network Mask	Dotted Decimal Notation
Destination IP Address	128.171.17.13
Network Mask	255.255. 0. 0
Bits in network part, followed by 0s	128.171. 0 .0

Subnet Mask	Dotted Decimal Notation
Destination IP Address	128.171. 17.13
Subnet Mask	255.255.255. 0
Bits in network part and subnet parts, followed by 0s	128.171. 17. 0

FIGURE 8-4 IP Networks and Subnet Masks

eight 1s is 255 and eight 0s is 0. Therefore, the four segments have, in order, eight 1s, eight 1s, eight 0s, and eight 0s. Putting this together, the mask has sixteen 1s followed by sixteen 0s.

Prefix Notation for Masks Writing 255.255.255.0 is not very difficult, but networking professionals often use a shortcut called prefix notation. The mask 255.255.255.0 is twenty-four 1s followed by eight 0s. In prefix notation, this mask is represented as /24. Do you see the pattern? In **prefix notation**, a mask is represented by a slash followed by the number of initial 1s in the mask. What about 255.0.0.0? Yes, it is /8. Prefix notation is simpler to write than dotted decimal notation. By the way, we call this prefix notation because it focuses on the first part of the mask—the part that is all 1s.

In prefix notation, a mask is represented by a slash followed by the number of initial 1s in the mask.

Another advantage of prefix notation for a mask is that it is simple even if the number of leading 1s is not a multiple of eight. For example, suppose that the mask is eighteen 1s followed by fourteen 0s. The mask in prefix notation is obviously /18. What if you saw this mask in dotted decimal notation, in which would be 255.255.48.0? The first two octets are obviously all 1s. However, you would need your decimal-to-binary calculator to figure out that 48 is 00110000.

Masking IP Addresses   Figure 8-4 shows what happens when a mask is applied to an IP address, 128.171.17.13. The mask is 255.255.0.0. Where the mask has 1s, the result is the original bits of the IP address. There are sixteen 1s. This is two octets. So the first two octets of the result would be 128.171. For the remaining sixteen bits, which are 0s, the result of the masking is 0. So the masking result is 128.171.0.0.

Network Masks   Network masks, as noted earlier, have 1s in the network part and 0s for remaining bits. If the network mask is 255.255.0.0 and the IP address is 128.171.17.13, then the result of masking is 128.171.0.0. This tells us that 128.171 is the network part.

Subnet Masks   For subnet masks, in turn, the initial 1s indicate the number of bits in *both* the network and subnet parts. Therefore, if 128.171 is the network part and 17 is the subnet part, then the subnet mask will be 255.255.255.0 (/24). If you mask 128.171.17.13 with /24, you get 128.171.17.0.[1]

Test Your Understanding

4. a) How many bits are there in a mask? b) What do the 1s in a network mask correspond to in IP addresses? c) What do the 1s in a subnet mask correspond to in IP addresses? d) When a network mask is applied to any IP address on the network, what is the result?

5. a) A mask has eight 1s, followed by 0s. Express this mask in dotted decimal notation. b) Express this mask in prefix notation. c) In prefix notation, a mask is /16. Express this mask in dotted decimal notation. d) Express the mask /18 in dotted decimal notation. (You will need a calculator for this.)

HOW ROUTERS PROCESS PACKETS

Switching versus Routing

In Chapter 5, we saw that Ethernet switching is very simple. Ethernet switches must be organized in a hierarchy. Therefore, there is only a single possible path between any two hosts across the network. When a frame arrives, there is only one possible port to

---

[1] Why not make the network part 0s and the subnet part 1s instead of making both 1s? Think of a network as a state and a subnet as a city. In the United States, there are two major cities named Portland—one in Maine and the other in Oregon. You cannot just say "Portland" to designate a city. You must give both the state and city. Analogously, there may be many subnet parts with a value of 17, so you must give both the network and subnet parts to designate a specific subnet. Another way to look at it is that if you only had 1s in the subnet part of a subnet mask, you would break the rule that masks must have a number of leading 1s followed by a number of trailing 0s.

use to send the frame back out. Figure 8-5 shows an Ethernet switching table. Because an Ethernet frame can only be sent out one port, each Ethernet address only appears in one row. This row tells the switch which port to use to send the frame back out. This single row can be found quickly, so an Ethernet switch does little work per frame. This makes Ethernet switching fast and therefore inexpensive per frame handled.

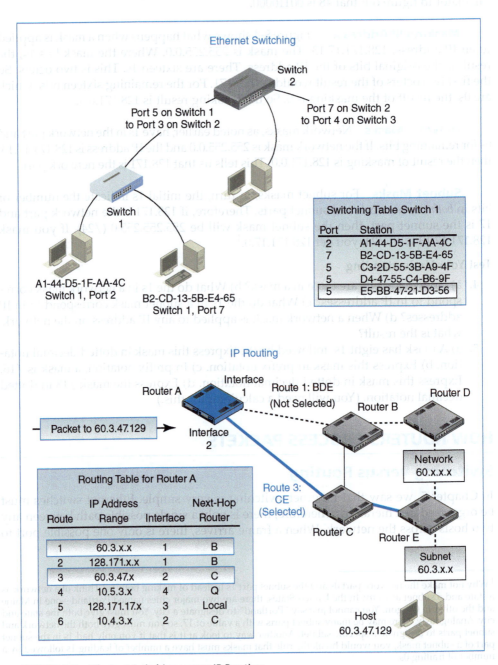

FIGURE 8-5 Ethernet Switching versus IP Routing

Routing

> Processing an individual packet and passing it closer to its destination host is called routing

The Routing Table

> Each router has a routing table that it uses to make routing decisions
>
> Routing tables have rows
>
> Each row represents a route for a range of IP addresses—often packets going to the same network or subnet

The Routing Decision

> Find all row matches
>
> Find the best-match row
>
> Send the frame out, based on information in the row

FIGURE 8-6 The Routing Process (Study Figure)

In contrast, routers are organized in meshes. This gives more reliability because it allows many possible alternative routes between endpoints. Figure 8-5 shows that in a routing table, each row represents an alternative route for a range of IP addresses. Consequently, to **route** (forward) a packet, a router must first find *all* rows representing alternative routes that a particular incoming packet can take. It must then pick the best alternative route from this list. This requires quite a bit of work per packet, making routing more expensive than switching.

Test Your Understanding

6. Why are routing tables more complex than Ethernet switching tables? Give a detailed answer.

Routing Table

Figure 8-7 shows a routing table. It has a number of rows and columns. We will see how a router uses these rows and columns to make the routing decision—what to do with an arriving packet.

Rows Are Routes for All IP Addresses in a Range

In the routing table, each row represents a route for all IP addresses within a range of IP addresses—typically addresses within a particular network or subnet. It does not specify the full route, however; it only specifies the next step in the route (either the next-hop router to handle the packet next or the destination host).

In the routing table, each row represents a route for all IP addresses within a range of IP addresses.

Row	Destination Network or Subnet	Mask (/Prefix)	Metric (Cost)	Interface	Next-Hop Router
1	128.171.0.0	255.255.0.0 (/16)	47	2	G
2	172.30.33.0	255.255.255.0 (/24)	0	1	Local
3	60.168.6.0	255.255.255.0 (/24)	12	2	G
4	123.0.0.0	255.0.0.0 (/8)	33	2	G
5	172.29.8.0	255.255.255.0 (/24)	34	1	F
6	172.40.6.0	255.255.255.0 (/24)	47	3	H
7	128.171.17.0	255.255.255.0 (/24)	55	3	H
8	172.29.8.0	255.255.255.0 (/24)	20	3	H
9	172.12.6.0	255.255.255.0 (/24)	23	1	F
10	172.30.12.0	255.255.255.0 (/24)	9	2	G
11	172.30.12.0	255.255.255.0 (/24)	3	3	H
12	60.168.0.0	255.255.0.0 (/16)	16	2	G
13	0.0.0.0	0.0.0.0 (/0)	5	3	H

FIGURE 8-7 Routing Table

This is important because the routing table does not need a row for each IP address as an Ethernet switching table does. It only needs a row for each group of IP addresses. This means that a router needs many fewer rows than an Ethernet switch would need for the same number of addresses.

However, there are many more IP addresses on the Internet than there are Ethernet addresses in an Ethernet network. Even with rows representing groups of IP addresses, core routers in the Internet backbone still have several hundred thousand rows. In addition, while an Ethernet switch only needs to find a single row for each arriving frame, we will see that routers need to look carefully at *all* rows.

Test Your Understanding

7. a) In a routing table, what does a row represent? b) Do Ethernet switches have a row for each individual Ethernet address? c) Do routers have a row for each individual IP address? d) What is the advantage of the answer to the previous subparts of this question?

Step 1: Finding All Row Matches

We will now see how the router uses its routing table to make routing decisions. The first step is to find which of the rows in the routing table match the destination IP address in an arriving packet. Due to the existence of alternative routes in a router mesh, most packets will match more than one row.

Step 1: Find All Row Matches

The router looks at the destination IP address in an arriving packet

For each row:

Apply the row's mask to the destination IP address in the packet

Compare the result with the row's destination value

If the two match, the row is a match

The router must do this to ALL rows because there may be multiple matches

This step ends with a set of matching rows

Example 1: A Destination IP Address that is NOT in the Range

Destination IP Address of Arriving Packet	60.43.7.8
Apply the (Network) Mask	255.255.0.0
Result of Masking	60.43.0.0
Destination Column Value	128.171.0.0
Does Destination Match the Masking Result?	No
Conclusion	Not a match.

Example 2: A Destination IP Address that IS in the Range

Destination IP Address of Arriving Packet	128.171.17.13
Apply the (Network) Mask	255.255.0.0
Result of Masking	128.171.0.0
Destination Column Value	128.171.0.0
Does Destination Match the Masking Result?	Yes
Conclusion	Row is a match.

Step 2: Find the Best-Match Row

The router examines the matching rows it found in Step 1 to find the best-match row

Basic rule: It selects the row with the longest match (Initial 1s in the row mask)

Tie breaker: If there is a tie on longest match, select among the tie rows based on a metric

For cost metric, choose the row with the lowest metric value

For speed metric, choose the row with the highest metric value

Step 3: Send the Packet Back Out

Send the packet out the interface (router port) designated in the best-match row

Address the packet to the IP address in the next-hop router column

If the address says Local, the destination host is out that interface

Sends the packet to the destination IP address in a frame

FIGURE 8-8 Steps in a Routing Decision (Study Figure)

Row Number Column   The first column in Figure 8-7 contains route (row) numbers. Routing tables actually do not have this column. We include it to allow us to refer to specific rows in our discussion. Again, each row specifies a route to a destination.

Row Matches   How does the router know which IP addresses match a row? The answer is that it uses the *Destination Network or Subnet* column and the *Mask* column.

Suppose that all IP addresses in the University of Hawai`i Network should match a row. The mask would be the network mask 255.255.0.0, because the UH Network has a 16-bit network part. If this mask is applied to any UH address, the result will be 128.171.0.0. This is the value that will be in the destination column. In fact, this matches Row 1 in Figure 8-7.

Let's see how routers use these two columns in Figure 8-7. Suppose that a packet arrives with the IP address 60.43.7.8. The router will look first at Row 1.

- In this row, the router applies the mask 255.255.0.0 to the arriving packet's destination IP address, 60.43.7.8. The result is 60.43.0.0.
- Next, the router compares the masking result, 60.43.0.0, to the destination value in the row, 128.171.0.0. The two are different, so the row is not a match.

However, suppose that a packet arrives with the IP address 128.171.17.13. Now, the situation is different.

- Again, the router applies the mask 255.255.0.0 in Row 1 to the destination IP address, 128.171.17.13. The result is 128.171.0.0.
- Next, the router compares 128.171.0.0 to the destination value in the row, 128.171.0.0. The two are identical. Therefore, the row is a match.

Mask and Compare   This may seem like an odd way to see if a row matches. A human can simply look at 60.43.7.8 and see that it does not match 128.171.0.0. However, routers do not possess human pattern-matching abilities.

While routers cannot do sophisticated pattern recognition, routers (and all computers) have specialized circuitry for doing masking and comparing—the two operations that row matching requires. Thanks to this specialized circuitry, routers can blaze through hundreds of thousands of rows in a tiny fraction of a second.

The Default Row   The last row in Figure 8-7 has the destination 0.0.0.0 and the mask 0.0.0.0. This row will match *every* IP address because masking any IP address with 0.0.0.0 will give 0.0.0.0, which is the value in the destination field of Row 13. This row ensures that at least one row will match the destination IP address of every arriving packet. It is called the **default row**. In general, a "default" is something you use if you do not have a more specific choice.

The Need to Look at All Rows   Thanks to their mesh topology, internets have many alternative routes. Consequently, a router cannot stop the first time it finds a row match for each arriving packet because there may be a better match further on. A router has to look at each and every row in the routing table to see which match. So far, we have seen what the router does in Row 1 of Figure 8-7. The router then goes on to Row 2 to see if it is a match by masking and comparing. After this, it goes on to Row 3, Row 4, Row 5, and so on, all the way to the final row (Row 13 in Figure 8-7).

Test Your Understanding

8. a) In Row 3 of Figure 8-7, how will a router test if the row matches the IP address 60.168.6.7? Show the calculations in the format given in the text. b) Is the row a

match? c) Why is the last row called the default row? d) Why must a router look at all rows in a routing table? e) Which rows in Figure 8-7 match 172.30.17.6? (Don't forget the default row.) Show your calculations for rows that match. f) Which rows match 60.168.7.32? Show your calculations for rows that match. g) Which rows in Figure 8-7 match 128.171.17.13? (Show your calculations for rows that match.)

Step 2: Selecting the Best-Match Row

List of Matching Rows At the end of Step 1, the mask and compare process, the router has a list of matching rows. For a packet with the destination IP address 128.171.17.13, three rows in Figure 8-7 match. The first is Row 1, as we have already seen. The second is Row 7, with a destination of 128.171.17.0 and a mask of 255.255.255.0. Finally, the default row (Row 13 in this figure) will always be a match. From these, the router must select the best-match row, the row that represents the best route for an IP address.

Basic Rule: Longest Match How does the router decide whether to follow Row 1, Row 7, or Row 13? The answer is that it follows the rule of selecting the **longest match** (the longest number of initial 1s in the mask). Row 1 has a mask of 255.255.0.0, which means that it has a 16-bit match. Row 7, in turn, has the prefix /24, meaning that it has a 24-bit match. Row 13 has a prefix of 0/. Row 7 has the longest match, so the router selects Row 7 as the best match.[2]

By the way, note that the default row always has a prefix of 0/. Consequently, if the default row and other rows are matches, the default row will never be chosen as the best-match row because it will always have the shortest length of match.

Tie-Breaker Rule: Best Metric Value What if two rows tie for the longest length of match? For instance, the destination IP address 172.29.8.112 matches both Row 5 and Row 8 in Figure 8-7. Both have a match length of 24 bits—a tie.

In case of a tie for longest match, the tie-breaker rule is to use the **metric** column, which describes the desirability of a route. For instance, in Figure 8-7, the metric is cost. Row 5 has a cost of 34, while Row 8 has a cost of 20. *Lower cost is better than higher cost,* so the router selects Row 8.

In this case, the row with the *lowest* metric won. However, what would have happened if the metric had been *speed* instead of cost? *More speed is better,* so the router would choose Row 5, with the *higher* speed (34).

Test Your Understanding

9. a) Distinguish between Step 1 and Step 2 in the routing process. b) If any row other than the default row matches an IP address, why will the router never choose the default row? c) Which rows in Figure 8-7 match 128.171.17.13? (Don't forget the default row.) Show your calculations for rows that match. d) Which of these is the best-match row? Justify your answer. e) What rows match 172.40.17.6? Show

---

[2] Why the longest match rule? The answer is that the closer a route gets a packet to the destination IP address, the better. Row 1 only gets the packet to the UH network, 128.171.x.x, while Row 7 gets the packet all the way to the Shidler College of Business subnet of the University of Hawai`i, 128.171.17.x—the subnet that contains host 128.171.17.13.

your calculations for rows that match. f) Which of these is the best-match row? Justify your answer. g) Which rows match 172.30.12.47? Show your calculations for rows that match. h) Which of these is the best-match row? Justify your answer. i) How would your previous answer change if the metric had been reliability?

Step 3: Sending the Packet Back Out

In Step 1, the router found all rows that matched the destination IP address of the arriving packet. In Step 2, it found the best-match row. Finally, in Step 3, the router sends the packet back out.

Interface   Recall that router ports are called interfaces. The fifth column in Figure 8-7 is interface number. If a router selects a row as the best match, the router sends the packet out the interface designated in that row. If Row 1 is selected, the router will send the packet out Interface 2.

Next-Hop Router   In a switch, a port connects directly to another switch or to a computer. However, a router interface connects to an entire subnet or network. Therefore, it is not enough to select an interface to send the packet out. It is also necessary to specify *a particular device* on the subnet.

In most cases, the router will send the packet on to another router, called the **next-hop router**. The next-hop router column specifies the router that should receive the packet. It will then be up to that next-hop router to decide what to do next. In Figure 8-7, the next-hop router value is G if Row 1 is selected.[3]

In some cases, however, the destination host will be on the subnet out a particular interface. In that case, the router will send the packet to the destination host instead of to another router. If the next hop is the destination host itself, the next-hop router field will say *local*.

Test Your Understanding

10. a) Distinguish between Step 2 and Step 3 in routing. b) What are router ports called? c) If the router selects Row 13 as the best-match row, what interface will the router send the packet out? d) To what device? e) Why is this router called the default router? (The answer is not in the text.) f) If the router selects Row 2 as the best-match row for packet 172.30.33.6, what interface will the router send the packet out? g) To what device? (Don't say, "the local device.")

Cheating (Decision Caching)

We have discussed what happens when a packet arrives at a router. However, what will the router do if another packet for the same destination IP address arrives immediately afterward? The answer is that the router *should* go through the entire process again. Even if a thousand packets arrive that are going to the same destination IP address, the router should go through the entire three-step process for each of them.

---

[3] Actually, this column should have the IP address of Router G, rather than its name. However, we include the letter designation rather than the IP address for simplicity of understanding.

As you might expect, a router might cheat, or as it is euphemistically named, cache (remember) the decision it made for a destination IP address. It will then use this decision for successive IP packets going to the same destination. Using a **decision cache** greatly reduces the work that a router will do for each successive packet.

Caching is not prescribed in the Internet Protocol. This is because it is dangerous. The Internet changes constantly as routers come and go and as links between routers

---

BOX 1

Masking When Masks Do Not Break at 8-Bit Boundaries

All of the masks we have seen up to this point have had their parts broken at 8-bit segment boundaries. For example, at the University of Hawai`i, the network part is 16 bits long, which corresponds to two segments (128.171), the subnet part is 8 bits long (17), and the host part is 8 bits long (13). All of the masks in Figure 8-7 break also at 8-bit segment boundaries.

Masks that break at 8-bit boundaries are easy for humans to read. In general, you can look at a mask in the table and decide if it matches a particular IP address. For instance, if the mask is 255.255.0.0 (/16) and if the destination column value is 128.171.0.0, this definitely matches the IP address 128.171.45.230.

However, masks do not always break at 8-bit boundaries. For example, suppose that a row in the routing table has the destination 3.136.0.0 and the mask 255.248.0.0. Does a packet with the destination IP address 3.143.12.12 match this row? At first glance, this certainly does not seem to be a match. However, it is.

To see why, look at Figure 8-9. This figure shows the matching analysis when the binary representations are given for each segment. If you follow the masking, you see that the result is a match. When a mask does not break at an 8-bit boundary, you must go back to the raw 32-bit IP address, mask, and destination field values.

Test Your Understanding

11. An arriving packet has the destination IP address 128.171.180.13. Row 86 has the destination value 128.171.160.0. The mask is 255.255.224.0. Does this row match the destination IP address? Show your work. You can use the Windows Calculator if you have a Windows PC. In Windows Vista and earlier versions of Windows, choose scientific when you open the calculator. In the Windows 7 calculator, choose programmer mode.

	Dotted Decimal Notation	Segment 1	Segment 2	Segment 3	Segment 4
IP address	3.143.12.12	00000011	10001111	00001100	00001100
Mask	255.248.0.0	11111111	11111000	00000000	00000000
Result	3.136.0.0	00000011	10001000	00000000	00000000
Destination	3.136.0.0	00000011	10001000	00000000	00000000
Match?	Yes	Yes	Yes	Yes	Yes

FIGURE 8-9   Using a Mask Whose 1s Do Not Break Down at an 8-Bit Boundary

change. Consequently, a cached decision that is used for too long will result in non optimal routing or even routes that will not work and that will effectively send packets into a black hole.

Test Your Understanding

12. a) What should a router do if it receives several packets going to the same destination IP address? **b)** How would decision caching speed the routing decision for packets after the first one? **c)** Why is decision caching dangerous?

BOX 2

The Address Resolution Protocol

The final step in the routing process for each arriving packet is to send the packet back out another interface, to a next-hop router or the destination host.

Address Resolution

To send the packet to a next-hop router or a destination host, the router's interface must place the packet into a frame and send this frame to the next-hop router or destination host. To do this, the interface must know the data link layer address of the destination host. The internet layer process must discover the DLL address of the destination host. This is called **address resolution**.

Address Resolution on an Ethernet LAN with ARP

Figure 8-10 shows the **Address Resolution Protocol (ARP)**, which provides address resolution on Ethernet LANs. There are other address resolution protocols for other subnet technologies.

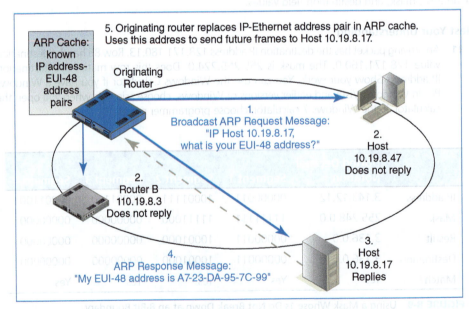

FIGURE 8-10 Address Resolution Protocol (ARP)

(continued)

ARP Request Message

Suppose that the router receives an IP packet with destination address 10.19.8.17. Suppose also that the router determines from its routing table that it can deliver the packet to a host on one of its Ethernet subnets.

- First, the router's internet layer process creates an ARP request message that essentially says, "Hey, device with IP address 10.19.8.17, what is your 48-bit EUI-48 address?" The router then broadcasts this ARP packet to all hosts on the subnet.[4]
- Second, the internet layer process on every host examines the ARP request message. If the target IP address is not that of the host, the host's internet layer process ignores the ARP request message. However, the host with IP address 10.19.8.17 composes an ARP response message that includes its EUI-48 address (A7-23-DA-95-7C-99). The target host sends this ARP response message back to the router.
- Third, the router's internet layer process now knows the EUI-48 address associated with IP address 10.19.8.17. It will deliver the packet to that host in a frame addressed to A7-23-DA-95-7C-99.

The ARP Cache

ARP is a time-consuming process, and the router does not want to do it for each arriving packet. Consequently, the internet layer process on the router saves the IP address–data link layer address information in its **ARP cache** (section of memory). Afterward, whenever an arriving packet has the IP address 10.19.8.17, the router looks up the DLL address in the ARP cache.

Using ARP for Next-Hop Routers

We have just looked at how routers use ARP when they deliver packets to destination hosts. A router also needs to know the data link layer destination addresses of next-hop routers so that it can send them packets encapsulated in frames. Routers use ARP to find the DLL destination addresses of both destination hosts and other routers.

ARP Encapsulation: Finally, Another Internet Layer Protocol!

In this book so far, we have only seen a single protocol at the internet layer—the Internet Protocol (IP). However, ARP is also a protocol at the internet layer, and ARP messages are called packets. ARP packets are encapsulated directly in frames, just like IP packets.

Test Your Understanding

13. A router wishes to send an IP packet to a host on its subnet. It knows the host's IP address. a) What else must it know? b) Why must it know it? c) What message will it broadcast? d) Which device will respond to this broadcast message? e) Does a router have to go through the ARP process each time it needs to send a packet to a destination host or to a next-hop router? Explain. f) Is ARP used to find the DLL destination addresses of destination hosts, routers, or both? g) At what layer does the ARP protocol operate? h) Why must client PCs use ARP to transmit packets? The answer is not in the text.

---

[4] Actually, the router passes the packet down to the data link layer process on the subnet's interface. It tells the data link layer process to broadcast its ARP packet. If the subnet standard is Ethernet, the DLL process places the packet into a frame with the destination Ethernet address FF-FF-FF-FF-FF-FF (forty-eight 1s). This is the Ethernet broadcast address. Switches will send frames with this broadcast address to all stations, and all stations will accept it as they would a frame addressed to their specific Ethernet address.

THE INTERNET PROTOCOL VERSION 4 (IPV4) FIELDS

We have focused on IP routing. However, the Internet Protocol has other properties that networking professionals need to understand.

As noted in Chapter 1, most routers today on the Internet and private internets are governed by the **IP Version 4 (IPv4)** standard. (There were no versions 0 through 3.) We looked at the header checksum, the source IP address, and the destination IP address in the first two chapters. Now we will look at the other fields in the IPv4 header.

The First Row

Figure 8-11 shows the IPv4 packet. Its first 4 bits constitute the **version** field. This field has the value 0100 (binary for 4). This indicates that this is an IPv4 packet. The next field gives the header length, and the last field on the first row gives the total length of the packet.[5]

Between the header and total length fields, two fields govern transmission quality. The **Differentiated Services Control Point** field can be used for priority or other

Bit 0   Bit 31

Version (4 bits) Value is 4 (0100)	Internet Header Length (4 bits)	DSCP (6 bits)	ECN (2 bits)	Total Length (16 bits) Length in octets
Identification (16 bits) Unique value in each original IP packet			Flags (3 bits)	Fragment Offset (13 bits) Octets from start of original IP fragment's data field
Time to Live (8 bits)		Protocol (8 bits) 1 = ICMP, 6 = TCP, 17 = UDP		Header Checksum (16 bits)
Source IP Address (32 bits)				
Destination IP Address (32 bits)				
Options (if any)				Padding
Data Field				

DSCP = Differentiated Services Control Point
ECN = Explicit Congestion Notification

FIGURE 8-11 IP Version 4 (IPv4) Packet Syntax

---

[5] The header length field gives the length of the header in 32-bit units. The length field gives the total length of the IP packet in octets.

quality of service purposes. The **Explicit Congestion Notification** field can be used to reduce the transmission frequency between a pair of hosts to cope with congestion in the transmission system between them.

Test Your Understanding

14. a) What is the main version of the Internet Protocol in use today? b) Which field can be used to specify quality of service? c) How can the ECN field be used?

The Second Row

TCP fragments application messages and sends them in individual packets. This has benefits that we saw in Chapter 1. When IPv4 was created, it was decided to allow routers to fragment packets as well. Although this seemed like a good idea at the time, it led to many problems. Today, operating systems by default tell routers not to fragment IPv4 packets. When IPv6 was developed, packet fragmentation was not allowed. The second row has information that the destination host uses to reassemble fragmented packets. Given the unimportance of IPv4 packet fragmentation, we will ignore the fields in this row.

Test Your Understanding

15. a) Distinguish between application message fragmentation and packet fragmentation. b) Under what circumstances would the identification, flags, and fragment offset fields be used in IP? c) Why did we not study them in detail? d) Does IPv6 allow packet fragmentation?

The Third Row

IP Time to Live (TTL) Field   In the early days of the ARPANET, which was the precursor to the Internet, packets that were misaddressed would circulate endlessly among packet switches in search of their nonexistent destinations. To prevent this, IP added a **time to live (TTL)** field that is assigned a value by the source host. Different operating systems have different TTL defaults. Most insert the TTL value 128. Each router along the way decrements (decreases) the TTL field by 1. A router decrementing the TTL to 0 will discard the packet.

IP Protocol Field   The **protocol field** tells the contents of the data field. TCP and UDP have protocol values 6 and 17, respectively. If the protocol field value is 1, the IP packet carries an ICMP message in its data field. As we will see later in the chapter, the IP header is a lean mean routing machine with no time for supervisory messages. ICMP is TCP/IP's tool for carrying internet layer supervisory messages. We will look at ICMP at the end of this chapter. After decapsulation, the internet layer process must pass the packet's data field to another process. The protocol field value determines which process should receive the data field.

Test Your Understanding

16. a) What does a router do if it receives a packet with a TTL value of 2? b) What does the next router do? c) What does the protocol field value tell the destination host?

IP Options

The IPv4 header allows options. There are several possible options, and they may come in any order. Some are only read by the destination host. However, a lack of required order means that each router must look at every option to see if it applies. This is time consuming.

Test Your Understanding

17. What problem is caused by the way that IPv4 handles options?

IP VERSION 6 (IPV6)

Outgrowing IPv4

Although IPv4 continues to dominate the Internet's traffic, the Internet Assigned Numbers Authority (IANA) did a poor job distributing IPv4 addresses, and there are no more to distribute. This is forcing more organizations to use IPv6 addresses. Firms that need new IP addresses are forced to apply for blocks of IPv6 addresses. To work with firms that only have IPv6 addresses, other firms must learn to support IPv6.

The most fundamental change in IPv6 is the move from 32-bit addresses to 128-bit addresses. This does not produce merely four times as many addresses. Each additional bit *doubles* the number of addresses. So while there are just under 4.3 billion (4.3×10^9) IPv4 addresses, there are 3.4×10^{38} IPv6 addresses—34 undecillion. To put this in perspective, there are about seven billion people in the world today. For each person, there are 5×10^{28} IPv6 addresses. Even with the Internet of Things, IPv6 will "solve" the address availability problem for many years to come.

Test Your Understanding

18. a) What is the main problem with IPv4 that IPv6 was created to solve? b) How does IPv6 solve this problem?

IPv6

In its 1994 meeting, the IETF decided to create a new version of the Internet Protocol. The IETF called this new version **IP Version 6 (IPv6)**. Over the next few years, the IPv6 standards family grew and matured. It was soon ready to be used, and many networking and computer vendors began to build IPv6 into their products.

Organizations soon found that using these new equipment capabilities, however, was a great deal more work than simply turning them on. For many years, few organizations saw the need to make the expensive upgrade to IPv6 because they had enough addresses. In addition, Network Address Translation (NAT) greatly extended the use of existing IP addresses in firms, at the cost of some complexity but at the gain of some security. IPv6 would have the mandatory inclusion of IPsec security functionality, but IPsec was quickly modified to work with IPv4 as well. Seeing no hard business case for upgrading, few companies did. Now that IPv4 addresses are no longer available, however, nearly all companies are beginning to at least plan for the implementation of IPv6, and many have already done so. As we will see in Chapter 9, companies have found that IPv6 implementation is a long and complex process. They need employees who understand this new protocol and other "v6" protocols such as ICMPv6 and DHCPv6.

Test Your Understanding

19. a) What has been holding back the adoption of IPv6? b) What is pushing IPv6 adoption now?

Writing 128-Bit IPv6 Addresses

We write IPv4 addresses in dotted decimal notation—four decimal numbers between 0 and 255 separated by dots. This gives addresses like 128.171.17.13. People can actually remember these addresses.

For the 128-bit addresses of IPv6, we would also like simpler ways to write them, but anything we do will still overload human memory. Consequently, when we write IPv6 addresses for human consumption, we do so to make the writing easier.

A 128-bit IPv6 address is shown in the following example. This is obviously difficult to write and read.

00100000000000010000000000100111111111110010101100000000000000000000000000000000
00000000000000000000000001100110100111111000011111100101 0

Figure 8-12 shows how to simplify this address for human reading and writing. First, IPv6 does not use dotted decimal notation as IPv4 does. Rather, IPv6 uses hexadecimal notation, which we saw in Chapter 5, in the context of Ethernet EUI-48 addresses. Each "nibble" of 4 bits is converted into a hex symbol from 0 through F. A 128-bit IPv6 address, then, would be translated into 32 hex symbols.

In Ethernet, we write hex symbols in pairs, separating each pair with a dash. This gives addresses like A1-B2-C3-D4-E5-F6. In IPv6, in contrast, we group hex symbols in tetrads (groups of four). Each tetrad is called a **field**. An example of a field is *fe56*. Note that we write the hex symbols in *lowercase* when writing IPv6 addresses. Each symbol is still 4 bits, so fe56 represents 16 bits. A full IPv6 address will have eight of these fields, which are separated by *colons* instead of dashes. The following is an IPv6 address written in hexadecimal notation.

128-bit IPv6 Address	0010000000000001000000000010011111111110001001100000000000000000000000000000000000000000000000001100110100111111100001111110010 10
Convert to hexadecimal notation; divide four-symbol fields by colons.	2001:0027:fe56:0000:0000:0000:cd3f:0fca
Remove leading 0s from each field.	2001:27:fe56::::cd3f:fca
If multiple 0000 fields are shortened, a series of colons can be reduced to a single pair of colons.	2001:27:fe56::cd3f:fca
Only shorten one run of colons. If there are multiple runs of multiple colons, shorten the longest. If two tie for the longest run, shorten only the first.	

FIGURE 8-12 Simplifying 128-bit IPv6 Addresses

2001:0027:fe56:0000:0000:0000:cd3f:0fca

This is still long. Fortunately, there are rules to help us shorten the writing of IPv6 addresses a little. The first is that in each field, *any leading 0s are dropped*. This is easy to understand. If the reader sees *:27:*, this must be *:0027:*. Note that only *leading* 0s are dropped. If trailing 0s or 0s anywhere were dropped, the reader could not know if *:27:* was *:0027:*, *:2700:*, or *0270:*. Dropping leading 0s is also natural because we do that when writing decimal numbers. Here is what the IPv6 address looks like after leading 0s are dropped. This is much shorter.

2001:27:fe56::::cd3f:fca

Note that if a field has four 0s, it will become :: by the first rule. In other words, all four "leading" 0s are dropped, and only the colons remain. A second rule is that if several consecutive fields of zero occur, *one* sequence of *all-zero fields* can be reduced to a simple ::. So if an IPv6 address has a sequence *:0000:0000:0000:*, this can be replaced by ::. This further simplifies our IPv6 address to the following:

2001:27:fe56::cd3f:fca

These two rules reduce length, but applying them has some subrules that appliers must follow.

- First, address simplification should be done whenever possible to the greatest extent possible.
- Second, only a single group of consecutive 0s may be shortened this way in an IP address.
- Third, if there are multiple sequences of all-0 fields, the *longest* group of all-0 fields should be shortened. This just makes sense. One might as well shorten things as much as possible.
- Fourth, if two groups of consecutive 0s tie for the longest number of all-zero groups, the *first* of these groups must be shortened.

These rules can be a little daunting, but it is important to know how to write IPv6 addresses properly. Following these rules means that everyone will write IP addresses the same way. If some people drop some initial 0s while others do not, and if some writers violate other rules, the same IP address will be written in different ways by different people. This will make it more difficult to determine if two written addresses are the same or different. It will also make string searching in databases and configuration fields far more difficult and error prone.

Test Your Understanding

20. a) Are IPv6 addresses written in uppercase or lowercase letters? b) Are IPv6 addresses written with decimal or hexadecimal symbols? c) How many symbols are there in a field? d) How are fields separated? e) How many fields are there in an IPv6 address?

21. a) List the rules for simplifying IPv6 addresses. b) Simplify the following IP address: 2001:0ed2:056b:00d3:000c:abcd:0bcd:0fe0. c) Simplify the following IP address: 2001:0002:0000:0000:0000:abcd:0bcd:0fe0. d) Simplify the following IP address: 2001:0000:0000:00fe:0000:0000:0000:cdef. e) What is the advantage of simplifying IPv6 addresses according to strict rules?

The IPv6 Header

Figure 8-13 shows the IPv6 header. The most obvious difference between the IPv6 and IPv4 headers is that IPv4 headers are usually 20 octets long, while IPv6 headers are 40 octets long. Actually, we will call this the **main IPv6 header** because, as we will see, an IPv6 packet can have multiple headers.

The second difference is that the IPv6 main header, although longer, is simpler than the IPv4 header, with fewer fields for routers and hosts to consider. This relative simplicity means that routers process longer IPv6 headers faster than they can process IPv4 headers.

Version Number Field   Both headers begin with a 4-bit **version number** field. For IPv4, the field value is 0100 (four). For IPv6, it is 0110 (six).

Traffic Class and Flow Label Fields   The first row of the IPv6 header also contains an 8-bit traffic class field and a 20-bit flow label field.[6] The two fields specify how routing will be handled in terms of priority and other quality of service matters.

The **traffic class field** has two subfields. The six-bit **diffserv (differentiated services)** subfield specifies whether *this particular packet* should be given routine best-effort service, high-priority low-latency service, or some other type of service. The last two bits are for congestion notification.

Bit 0   Bit 31

Version (4 bits) Value is 6 (0110)	Traffic Class (8 bits) Diffserv (6 bits) Congestion Notification (2)	Flow Label (20 bits) Marks a packet as part of a specific flow	
Payload Length (16 bits)		Next Header (8 bits) Name of next header	Hop Limit (8 bits)
Source IP Address (128 bits)			
Destination IP Address (128 bits)			
Next Header or Payload (Data Field)			

FIGURE 8-13   IP Version 6 (IPv6) Packet Syntax

---

[6] In the original definition of IPv6, these fields were 4 bits and 24 bits, respectively.

The **flow label field** value indicates that the packet is a member of a particular flow. The router has rules that apply to *every packet* in the flow.

Payload Length In IPv6, the **payload length field** gives the length of the packet payload, which is everything beyond the 40-octet main packet header. The payload length field is 16 bits long, so payloads can be up to 65,536 (2^{16}) octets long.

The payload length field gives the length of the packet payload, which is everything beyond the 40-octet main packet header.

Hop Limit Field IPv6 has a **hop limit field** that does the same thing the IPv4 time to live field does. Each router along the way decrements this field's value by 1, and if a router decrements it to 0, the router discards the packet.[7]

No Checksum Field? IPv4 has a header checksum field to check for packet header errors. When IPv4 was created, there was a concern that if packet headers contained errors, they could cause serious problems for the Internet. Experience showed that this concern was groundless. Consequently, IPv6 has no checksum field. The computations needed to check for errors in IPv4 were taxing, even for a 20-octet header. Dropping the checksum field significantly reduces packet handling time on routers.

Test Your Understanding

22. a) How do the version number fields in IPv4 and IPv6 differ? b) What is the general purpose of the diffserv subfield? c) Of the flow label field? d) In IPv6, how can the receiver tell the length of packet? e) Does the payload length field include the lengths of any extension headers in the packet? f) How is the hop limit field used? g) Does IPv6 have a header checksum field? h) What are the implications of this?

Extension Headers

The IPv4 packet has an options field that allows the sender to add options. Few IPv4 packets have options, but each router must check each packet for options, and it must examine each option. This adds to processing time and therefore cost per packet.

Main Header and Extension Header IPv6 took another approach. As Figure 8-14 shows, the main header can be followed by multiple extension headers. Each extension header has a well-defined purpose, such as providing information for security or mobile operation. Each extension header serves the role that an option does in IPv4.

Next Header Field The headers are daisy chained together based on the **next header** field. The main header's next header field gives the value of the first extension header. That extension header's next header field has the value of the next extension

---

[7] Internet old-timers know that when IPv4 was created, the time to live value was supposed to be measured in seconds. However, this proved to be unworkable. The value was then interpreted as the maximum number of hops permitted by the packet. The hop limit field name in IPv6 recognizes this.

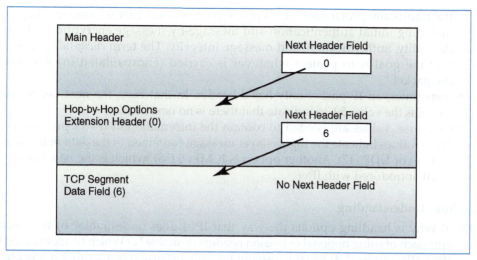

FIGURE 8-14 Main Header and Extension Headers in IPv6

headers. This continues until the last extension header. In the final extension header, the next header field value specifies the data field (TCP, UDP, etc.)

Next Header Values Each extension header has its own next-header field value. This value is placed in the next-header field of the main header or previous extension header. Figure 8-15 shows a few of the extension headers that have been defined for the next-header field, as well as their code values (in parentheses) in next header fields. The full list is much longer. We will discuss only a few of the headers mentioned in the table.

- The **hop-by-hop options** header carries options that must be considered by every router along the packet's route to its destination host. Its importance is indicated by its special extension code, 0. Successive headers usually only have to be dealt with by the destination host. This minimizes the work the router must do on each IPv6 packet.
- The encapsulating security payload (ESP) header (50) is used in IPv6's built-in cryptographic security protocol called IPsec (IP security). We will look at IPsec in the next chapter. Using information in the ESP header, IPsec gives all of

Extension Header Code (Value)	
Extension Header	Upper Layer Messages
Hop-by-Hop Options (0)	TCP (6)
Encapsulating Security Payload Header (50)	UDP (17)
Destination Options (60)	ICMPv6 (58)
Mobility Header (135)	
No Next Header (59)	

FIGURE 8-15 IPv6 Next Header Values

the traditional protections of cryptographic systems that we saw in Chapter 3, including initial authentication and message-by-message encryption for confidentiality, authentication, and message integrity. The term *encapsulating* means that the goal is to protect whatever is carried (encapsulated in) the rest of the packet.[8]

- Sometimes, an IP packet only has a header. In that case, the next header field contains the value 59, to indicate that there is no next header.
- Of course, values are needed to contain the information in IPv6's protocol field. These values indicate the higher-layer message contained in the data field, such as TCP (6) or UDP (17). Another option is ICMPv6 (58), which is the new version of ICMP introduced with IPv6.

Test Your Understanding

23. a) Why is handling options the way that IPv4 does undesirable? b) Why is the approach of using optional extension headers desirable? c) Which header is used by IPsec (IP security)? d) What is usually the only extension header that routers have to consider? e) How does the last extension header before a UDP datagram indicate that the UDP datagram comes next? (You must infer the answer from the text.) f) If you see 59 in the next header field of a header, what will follow this header?

THE TRANSMISSION CONTROL PROTOCOL (TCP)

Fields in TCP/IP Segments

In Chapter 2, we looked briefly at the syntax of TCP messages (segments). In this section, we will look at the syntax of this complex protocol in more depth. When IP was designed, it was made to be a very simple "best effort" protocol (although its routing tables are complex). The IETF left more complex internetwork transmission control tasks to TCP. Consequently, network professionals need to understand TCP very well. Figure 8-16 shows the organization of TCP segments.

Sequence Numbers TCP can handle messages of almost any length. In Chapter 2, we saw that it handles long application messages by fragmenting them into many TCP segments and sending each segment in its own packet. So that the receiver can put the segments back in order, each segment has a **sequence number** that gives its position in the stream of segments. The receiving TCP process puts the segments in order of increasing sequence number, reassembling the full application message. The TCP process then passes the application message up to the correct application process indicated in the port number.[9]

---

[8] Initially, security was supposed to be a competitive advantage for IPv6 compared to IPv4. However, the IETF quickly made the encapsulating security payload available in IPv4 by allowing its value (50) to appear in the IPv4 protocol field. In addition, while it is often said that the use of security is mandatory in IPv6, the truth is that providing the *capability* for ESP and authentication header security is mandatory. Their *use* is not mandatory. In general, making security an option in IPv4 stole the thunder from IPv6's touted security advantage.

[9] Module A has a detailed discussion of TCP sequence and acknowledgment numbers.

TCP Segment

Bit 0   Bit 31

Source Port Number (16 bits)	Destination Port Number (16 bits)
Sequence Number (32 bits)	
Acknowledgment Number (32 bits)	

Header Length (4 bits)	Reserved (3 bits)	Flag Fields (9 bits)	Window Size (16 bits)

TCP Checksum (16 bits)	Urgent Pointer (16 bits)

Options (if any)	Padding

Data Field

Flag fields are 1-bit fields. They include SYN, ACK, FIN, and RST.

UDP Datagram

Bit 0   Bit 31

Source Port Number (16 bits)	Destination Port Number (16 bits)
UDP Length (16 bits)	UDP Checksum (16 bits)

Data Field

FIGURE 8-16 TCP Segment and UDP Datagram

Acknowledgment Numbers In Chapter 2, we saw that TCP uses **acknowledgments (ACKs)** to achieve reliability. If a transport process receives a TCP segment correctly, it sends back a TCP segment acknowledging the reception. If the sending transport process does not receive an acknowledgment, it transmits the TCP segment again.

The **acknowledgment number field** indicates which segment is being acknowledged. One might expect that if a segment has sequence number X, then the acknowledgment number in the segment that acknowledges it would also be X. As Module A notes, the situation is more complex, but the acknowledgment number is at least related to the sequence number of the segment being acknowledged.

Flag Fields   As discussed in Chapter 2, TCP has nine single-bit fields. Single-bit fields are called flag fields, and if they have the value 1, they are said to be *set*. These fields allow the receiving transport process to know the kind of segment it is receiving. We saw several uses of these flag bits in Chapter 2.

- If the ACK bit is set, then the segment acknowledges another segment. If the ACK bit is set, the acknowledgment field must be filled in to indicate which message is being acknowledged.
- If the SYN (synchronization) bit is set, then the segment requests a connection opening.
- If the FIN (finish) bit is set, then the segment requests a normal connection closing.

Openings and Abrupt TCP Closes

In Chapter 2, we saw that TCP is a connection-oriented protocol. Connection-oriented protocols have formal openings and closings. Figure 8-17 recaps these openings and closings.

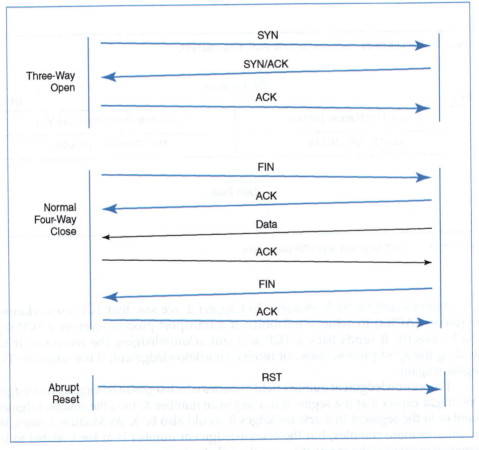

FIGURE 8-17 TCP Session Openings and Closings

In Chapter 2, we looked at *normal* closings. Just as you do not simply hang up on a telephone call when you want to finish talking if you are polite, a normal TCP close consists of two FIN segments, one in each direction, plus their acknowledgments.

However, Figure 8-17 shows that TCP also permits another type of close. This is an abrupt close. Whenever either side wishes to end a conversation, it can simply send a **TCP reset segment**. This is a segment with the **RST** (reset) flag bit set. This may occur if a problem is encountered during a connection, for security reasons, or for any other reason.

Note in Figure 8-17 that an RST segment is not acknowledged. The side that sent the RST segment is not listening any longer, so acknowledging a reset would be as pointless as saying goodbye after someone has hung up on you. The RST segment is one of two segment types that are not acknowledged. As noted in Chapter 2, a segment that is nothing more than acknowledgment (a pure acknowledgment) is not acknowledged because doing so would create an endless loop of acknowledgments.

Test Your Understanding

24. a) For what reason is TCP complex? b) Why is it important for networking professionals to understand TCP? c) What are TCP messages called?
25. a) Why are sequence numbers good? b) What are 1-bit fields called? c) If someone says that a flag field is set, what does this mean? d) If the ACK bit is set, what other field must have a value? e) What is a FIN segment? f) Distinguish between four-way closes and abrupt resets. g) Why is a reset segment not acknowledged?

THE USER DATAGRAM PROTOCOL (UDP)

We saw UDP in Chapter 2. This is a very simple protocol, so the discussion in that chapter is sufficient except for one point. This is the fact that UDP, unlike TCP, cannot do segmentation. This means that an application message must fit into a single UDP datagram. Figure 8-16 shows that the length field in the UDP header is 16 bits long, so the maximum length of the UDP data field, and therefore the maximum length of an application message, is 65,536 octets. UDP messages are called UDP datagrams.

UDP cannot do segmentation, so an application message must fit into a single UDP datagram.

Test Your Understanding

26. a) Why can TCP handle long application messages? b) Why can UDP not handle long application messages? c) What is the maximum application message size when UDP is used at the transport layer? d) What are UDP messages called?

	TCP	UDP
Can segment application messages?	Yes	No
Maximum application message size	Unlimited	65,536 octets

FIGURE 8-18 TCP, UDP, and Application Message Length (Study Figure)

CONCLUSION

Synopsis

IPv4 addresses are hierarchical. Their 32 bits usually are divided into a network part, a subnet part, and a host part. All three parts vary in length. A network mask tells what bits are in the network part, while a subnet mask tells what bits are in the total of the network and subnet parts. Masks always begin with a certain number of 1s followed by enough 0s to fill the mask out to 32 bits. For human reading, masks are expressed in dotted decimal notation or prefix notation.

Routers forward packets through an internet. Border routers move packets between the outside world and an internal site network. Internal routers work within sites, moving packets between subnets. Ports in routers are called interfaces. Different interfaces may connect to different types of networks. Most routers are multiprotocol routers, which can handle not only TCP/IP internetworking protocols, but also internetworking protocols from IPX/SPX, SNA, and other architectures. Routers are designed to work in a mesh topology. This creates alternative routes through an internet. Alternative routes are good for reliability. However, the router has to consider the best route for each arriving packet, and this is time consuming and therefore expensive.

To make a routing decision (deciding which interface to use to send an incoming packet back out), a router uses a routing table. Each row in the routing table represents a route to a particular network or subnet. All packets to that network or subnet are governed by the one row. Each row (route) has destination, mask, metric, interface, and next-hop router fields.

If the destination IP address in an arriving packet is in a row's range, that row is a match. After finding all matches in the routing table, the router finds the best-match row on the basis of match length and, in the case of tied match lengths, on metric values. Once a best-match route (row) is selected, the router sends the packet out a particular interface to the next-hop router specified in that row or to the destination host if the destination host is out the interface.

In the examples in the main text, masks broke at 8-bit boundaries, making it easy to specify them with dotted decimal notation. If you read the box "Masking When Masks Do Not Break at 8-Bit Boundaries," you can deal more realistically with the world of masking because masks often do not break at 8-bit boundaries.

If you read the box, "The Address Resolution Protocol (ARP)," you saw that the router must encapsulate the packet in a frame in order to send it out. The frame must be addressed to the DLL address of the host or router to which the packet will be sent. ARP identifies this DLL address.

IP Version 4 has a number of important fields besides the source and destination address fields. The time to live (TTL) field ensures that packets that are misaddressed do not circulate endlessly around the Internet. The protocol field value gives the contents of the data field—ICMP message, TCP segment, UDP datagram, and so forth.

IP Version 6 requires networking and security professionals to understand a new approach to expressing addresses. IPv6 addresses are 128 bits long. For human comprehension, they are expressed in hexadecimal notation. In addition, there are certain rules that compress the hex version of the address to reduce its length.

The IPv6 main header is simpler than the IPv4 header. The IPv6 header saves time on each router by not checking for errors and not allowing packet fragmentation. The IPv6 header has a mechanism for specifying quality-of-service parameters for the packet and for marking a packet as a member of a flow of packets with predefined quality-of-service parameters.

IPv4 has an inelegant method for handling options. A router must read through all options to see which ones are important to it, as opposed to the destination host. IPv6 expresses options as extension headers. The first extension header is the hop-by-hop extension header, which every router should read along the way. The router can probably ignore subsequent extension headers. Reading few if any additional extension headers reduces routing decision time.

The Transmission Control Protocol (TCP) has sequence numbers that allow the receiving transport process to place arriving TCP segments in order. The TCP header has several flag fields that indicate whether the segment is a SYN, FIN, ACK, or RST segment. Connection openings use a three-step handshake that uses SYN segments. Normal closes involve a four-step message exchange that uses FIN segments. Resets close a connection with a single segment (RST) instead of the normal four.

UDP has a very simple header, with two port number fields, a UDP length field, and a UDP checksum field that is often not used. It is lightweight but unreliable. In this chapter, we learned that UDP has another limitation. It cannot fragment application messages, so application messages must be of limited size.

END-OF-CHAPTER QUESTIONS

Thought Questions

8-1. a) How does the postal service use hierarchical sorting? b) How does this simplify delivery decisions?

8-2. Give a non-network example of hierarchical addressing, and discuss how it reduces the amount of work needed in physical delivery. Do not use any example in the book, the postal service, or the telephone network.

8-3. A client PC has two simultaneous connections to the same webserver application program on a webserver. (Yes, this is possible, and in fact, it is rather common.) What will be different between the TCP segments that the client sends on the two connections? (Hint: Consider all the fields in a TCP segment.)

8-4. A router that has the routing table in Figure 8-7 receives an incoming IPv4 packet. The source IP address in the arriving packet is 10.55.72.234. The destination IP address is 10.4.6.7. The TTL value is 1. The protocol field value is 6. What will the router do with this packet? (Hint: Consider all the fields in the IP and TCP headers.)

Perspective Questions

8-5. What was the most surprising thing you learned in this chapter?

8-6. What was the most difficult material for you in this chapter?

Chapter 9

TCP/IP Internetworking II

LEARNING OBJECTIVES

By the end of this chapter, you should be able to:

- Explain IPv4 subnet planning and do calculations needed for working with subnet and host parts and decide on part lengths.

- Explain the purposes of Network Address Translation (NAT), how NAT operates, and problems related to NAT.

- Explain how the Domain Name System (DNS) operates.

- Describe the object model in the Simple Network Management Protocol (SNMP) and describe the enabling value of good security in the use of Set commands.

- Describe IPv6 subnetting and IP protocol stacks.

- Describe how the DNS was modified to deal with IPv6 addresses for host names.

INTRODUCTION

In Chapter 8, we looked at core TCP concepts. In this chapter, we will focus on the security and management of TCP/IP networks.

CORE TCP/IP MANAGEMENT TASKS

If a firm uses TCP/IP as its internetworking protocol, it must do a considerable amount of work to build and maintain the necessary infrastructure of TCP/IP. While switched networks are (generally) capable of operating for long periods without intervention by network managers, TCP/IP internets require constant tuning and support. This results in a need for considerable TCP/IP expertise and management effort.

IP Subnet Planning

As Chapter 8 discussed, IP addresses are 32 bits long. Each organization is assigned a network part. We saw that the University of Hawai`i's network part (128.171) is 16 bits long. A firm has no control over its network part. However, it was up to the university to decide what to do with the remaining 16 bits.

Subnetting at the University of Hawai`i   The university, like most organizations, chose to subnet its IP address space. It divided the 16 bits over which it has discretion into an 8-bit subnet part and an 8-bit host part.

The $N = 2^b - 2$ Rule   With b bits, you can represent 2^b possibilities. Therefore, with 8 bits, one can represent 2^8 (256) possibilities. This would suggest that the university can have 256 subnets, each with 256 hosts. However, a network, subnet, or host part cannot be all 0s or all 1s.[1] Therefore, the university can have only 254 ($256 - 2$) subnets, each with only 254 hosts. Figure 9-1 illustrates these calculations.

If a part is b bits long, it can represent $2^b - 2$ networks, subnets, or hosts. For example, if a subnet part is 9 bits long, there can be $2^9 - 2$, or 510, subnets. Alternatively, if a host part is 5 bits long, there can be $2^5 - 2$, or 30, hosts.

If a part is b bits long, it can represent $2^b - 2$ networks, subnets, or hosts.

Step	Description				
1	Total size of IP address (bits)	32			
2	Size of network part assigned to firm (bits)	16		8	
3	Remaining bits for firm to assign	16		24	
4	Selected subnet/host part sizes (bits)	8/8	6/10	12/12	8/16
5	Possible number of subnets ($2^b - 2$)	254 ($2^8 - 2$)	62 ($2^6 - 2$)	4,094 ($2^{12} - 2$)	254 ($2^8 - 2$)
6	Possible number of hosts per subnet ($2^b - 2$)	254 ($2^8 - 2$)	1,022 ($2^{10} - 2$)	4,094 ($2^{12} - 2$)	65,534 ($2^{16} - 2$)

FIGURE 9-1   IP Subnetting

---

[1] If you have all 1s in an address part, this indicates that broadcasting should be used. All 0s parts are used by computers when they do not know their own addresses. As we will see later in this chapter, most client PCs get their IP addresses from DHCP servers. All-zero addresses can only be used in the source addresses of DHCP messages sent from a host to a DHCP server.

Balancing Subnet and Host Part Sizes The larger the subnet part, the more subnets there will be. However, the larger the subnet part is made, the smaller the host part will be. This will mean fewer hosts per subnet. There is always a trade-off. More subnets mean fewer hosts, and more hosts mean fewer subnets.

The University of Hawai`i's choice of 8-bit subnet and host parts was acceptable for many years because no college needed more than 254 hosts. Its advantage is that its subnet mask (255.255.255.0) was very simple, breaking at 8-bit boundaries. This made it easy to see which hosts were on which subnets. The host at 128.171.17.5, for instance, was the fifth host on the *17th* subnet. If the subnet mask did not break at an 8-bit boundary, you would not be able to see which subnet a host is on by looking at the address in dotted decimal notation.

However, many colleges in the university now have more than 254 computers, and the limit of 254 hosts required by its subnetting decision has become a serious problem. Several colleges have now been given two subnet numbers. These colleges must connect their two subnets with routers so that hosts on the two subnets can communicate. This is expensive and awkward.

The university would have been better served had it selected a smaller subnet part, say 6 bits. As Figure 9-1 shows, this would have allowed 62 college subnets, which probably would have been sufficient. A 6-bit subnet part would give a 10-bit host part, allowing 1,022 hosts per subnet. This would be ample for several years to come.

A Critical Choice In general, it is critical for corporations to plan their IP subnetting carefully, in order to get the right balance between the sizes of their network and subnet parts.

Test Your Understanding

1. a) Why is IP subnet planning important? b) If a subnet part is X bits long, how many subnets can you have? c) If you have a subnet part of 9 bits, how many subnets can you have? (Check figure: 510 subnets) d) If you have a subnet part of 6 bits, how many subnets can you have? e) Your firm has an 8-bit network part. If you need at least 250 subnets, what must your subnet part size be? (Check figure: 8 bits) f) Continuing the last question part, how many hosts can you have per subnet? (Check figure: 65,534 hosts per subnet) g) Your firm has an 18-bit network part. If you need at least 16 subnets, what must your subnet part size be? h) Continuing the last question part, how many hosts can you have per subnet? i) Your firm has a 22-bit network part. What subnet part would you select to give at least 10 subnets? j) Continuing the last question part, how many hosts can you have per subnet?

Network Address Translation (NAT)

One issue that firms face is whether to allow people outside the corporation to learn their internal addresses. This is a security risk. If attackers know internal IP addresses, this allows them to send attack packets from the outside world. To prevent this, companies can use **network address translation (NAT)**, which presents external IP addresses that are different from internal IP addresses used within the firm.

NAT

> Sends false external IP addresses that are different from internal IP addresses
>
> To expand the number of IP addresses inside the firm
>
> For security reasons

NAT Operation (Figure 9-3)

NAT is Transparent to Internal and External Hosts

Security Reason for Using NAT

> External attackers can put sniffers outside the corporation
>
> Sniffers can learn IP addresses
>
> Attackers can send attacks to these addresses
>
> With NAT, attackers only learn false external IP addresses

Expanding the Number of Available IP Addresses

> Companies may receive a limited number of IP addresses from their ISPs
>
> There are roughly 4,000 possible ephemeral port numbers for each IP address
>
> So for each IP address, there can be 4,000 external connections
>
> If a firm is given 254 IP addresses, there can be roughly one million external connections for clients (254 x 4000)
>
> Even if each internal client averages several simultaneous external connections, there should not be a problem providing as many external IP connections as a firm desires

Private IP Addresses

> Can only be used inside firms
>
> 10.x.x.x
>
> 192.168.x.x (most popular)
>
> 172.16.x.x through 172.31.x.x

Protocol Problems with NAT

> IPsec, VoIP, etc.
>
> These applications must know the receiving host's true IP address
>
> Firewall traversal techniques for such applications must be considered carefully.

FIGURE 9-2   Network Address Translation (NAT) (Study Figure)

NAT Operation   Figure 9-3 shows how NAT works. An internal client host, 192.168.5.7, sends a packet to an external server host. The source address in this packet is 192.168.5.7, of course. The source port number is 3333. As we saw in Chapter 2, this is an ephemeral port number that the source client host made up for this connection.

When the NAT firewall at the border receives the packet, it makes up a new row in its translation table. It places the internal IP address and port number in the table. It then generates a new external source IP address and external source port number. These are 60.5.9.8 and 4444, respectively.

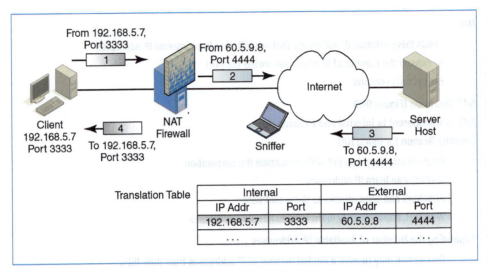

FIGURE 9-3 Network Address Translation (NAT) Operation

When packets arrive from the external host, they have 60.5.9.8 in their destination IP address fields and 4444 in their destination port number fields. The NAT firewall looks these values up in its translation table, replaces the external values with the internal values, and sends them on to the client PC.

Transparency NAT is transparent to both internal and external hosts. Hosts do not even know that NAT is happening. Consequently, there is no need to change the ways in which they operate.

NAT and Security Figure 9-3 shows how NAT brings security. An attacker may be able to install a **sniffer program** beyond the corporation's NAT firewall. This sniffer will be able to read all packets coming out of the firm. With NAT, an eavesdropper only learns false (external) IP addresses and port numbers. In theory, if an attacker can attack immediately, it can send packets to the external IP addresses and port numbers, and the NAT firewall will pass them on to the internal host. However, it is rarely possible for an attacker to act immediately, and NAT rows are only kept active for a few minutes at most. NAT provides a surprising amount of security despite its simple operation.

Expanding the Effective Number of IP Addresses An equally important potential reason for using NAT is to permit a firm to have many more internal IP addresses than its ISP gives it. Suppose that an ISP only gives a firm 254 IP addresses because it has a network part of 24 bits. In this case, the firm would not do subnetting. It would use all of the remaining 8 bits for the host part. Without NAT, the firm can only have 254 internal clients simultaneously using the Internet.

However, there are approximately 4,000 ephemeral port numbers, and therefore 4,000 possible external connections for each of the 254 public IP addresses. This gives a million external connections (4,000 times 254). NAT can map these millions of connections into any combination of hosts and connections per host that it wishes. For example, it could have connections for 100,000 internal clients, each with 10 external connections. This shows how NAT can give a company far more internal clients than the number of external IP addresses it has.

Using Private IP Addresses   To support NAT, the Internet Assigned Numbers Authority (IANA) has created three sets of **private IP address ranges** that can only be used *within* firms. These are the three ranges:

- 10.x.x.x
- 192.168.x.x
- 172.16.x.x through 172.31.x.x

The 192.168.x.x private IP address range is the most popular because it allows companies to use 255.255.0.0 and 255.255.255.0 network and subnet masks, respectively. These break at convenient 8-bit boundaries. However, the other two private IP address ranges are also widely used.

Protocol Problems with NAT   In terms of security and expanding IP effective address ranges, NAT is a simple and effective tool. However, some protocols cannot work across a NAT firewall or can work only with considerable difficulty. These include the popular IPsec cryptographic system in transport mode and several voice over IP (VoIP) protocols. The problem is that these applications must know the true IP address of the other party. A number of firewall traversal techniques occur for such applications, but each application requires considerable attention.

Test Your Understanding

2. a) What is NAT? (Do not just spell it out.) b) Describe NAT operation. c) What are the two benefits of NAT? d) How does NAT enhance security? e) How does NAT allow a firm to deal with a shortage of IP addresses given to it by its ISP? f) How are private IP address ranges used? g) What are the three ranges of private IP addresses? h) What problems may firms encounter when using NAT?

The Domain Name System (DNS)

As we saw in Chapter 1, if a user types in a target host's host name, the user's PC will contact its local Domain Name System (DNS) server. The DNS server will return the IP address for the target host or will contact other DNS servers to get this information. The user's PC can then send IP packets to the target host. In this chapter, we will look at DNS and its management in more detail.

Figure 9-4 looks at how a DNS provides an IP address when a host sends a DNS request message specifying a host name. In many cases, as we saw in Chapter 1, the local DNS server will know the IP address and send it back. In other cases, the local DNS host will not know the host's IP address. It must then find the **authoritative DNS server** for the domain in the host name. In the figure, dakine.pukanui.com's authoritative DNS server is authoritative for the pukanui.com domain. This DNS server will send the IP address to the local DNS server, which will pass the address on to the host that sent the DNS request.

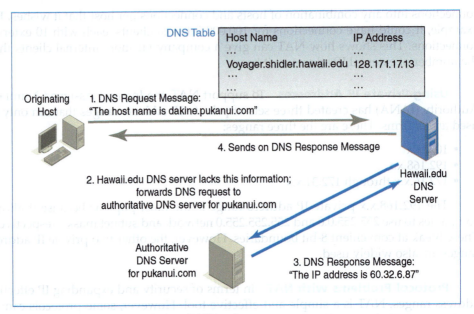

FIGURE 9-4 Domain Name System (DNS) Lookup

What is a Domain? Figure 9-5 shows that the **Domain Name System (DNS)** and its servers are not limited to providing IP addresses for host names. More generally, DNS is a general system for naming domains. A **domain** is any group of resources (routers, single networks, and hosts) under the control of an organization. The figure shows that domains are hierarchical, with host names being at the bottom of the hierarchy.

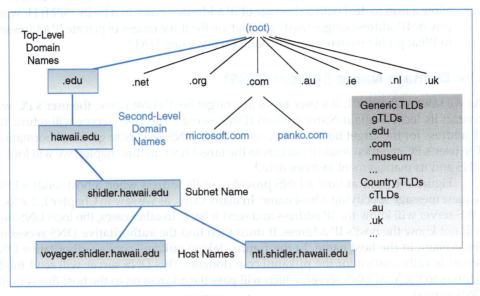

FIGURE 9-5 Domain Name System (DNS) Hierarchy

A domain is any group of resources (routers, single networks, and hosts) under the control of an organization.

Root   The domain name system is a hierarchy. At the top of the DNS hierarchy is the root, which consists of all domain names. The overall control of the root, and therefore of the entire directory tree, is managed by the Internet Corporation for Assigned Names and Numbers (ICANN). Thirteen **root DNS servers** keep overview information for the system.

Top-Level Domains   Under the root are **top-level domains** that categorize the domain in one of two ways.

- **Country top-level domains (cTLDs)** specify the country of the domain owner. Examples are .uk, .ca, .ie, .au, .jp, .nl, .tv, .md, and .ch.
- **Generic top-level domains (gTLDs)** specify that the organization owning the name is a particular type of organization. The first gTLDs included .com, .edu, .net, .info, .gov, and .org. Later, the IANA added several more gTLDs, such as .name and .museum. In 2012, ICANN opened the naming system widely, permitting any organization to propose new generic top-level domains.

Note the distinction between the root and top-level domains. The root consists of all domains. It is not named as a level, however. If you are familiar with the UNIX operating system, the root directory concept is similar.

Also, note that it is possible for a domain to have two top-level designations, for instance, AAAA.com.ie. Most organizations, however, tend to use either a country TLD or a generic TLD.

Second-Level Domains   Under top-level domains are **second-level domains**, which usually specify a particular organization (microsoft.com, hawaii.edu, cnn.com, etc.). Sometimes, however, specific products, such as movies, get their own second-level domain names. Competition for good second-level domain names is fierce. Organizations and individuals compete fiercely to get second-level domains because this is how the public will reach them.

Organizations and individuals compete fiercely to get second-level domains because this is how the public will reach them.

Companies get second-level domain names from domain registrars for nominal fees. However, getting a second-level domain name is only the beginning. Each organization that receives a second-level domain name must have a DNS server to host its domain name information. Large organizations have their own internal DNS servers that contain information on all subnet and host names. Individuals and small businesses that use webhosting services depend on the webhosting company to provide this DNS service.

In addition, a second-level domain name does nothing for the firm until the firm buys or rents a webserver, builds a website, and pays an ISP to connect the website to the Internet.

Lower-Level Domains Domains can be further qualified. For instance, within hawaii.edu, which is the University of Hawai`i's second-level domain, there is a *shidler. hawaii.edu domain*. This is the Shidler College of Business. Within shidler.hawaii.edu is *voyager.shidler.hawaii.edu*, which is a specific host within the college.

Test Your Understanding

3. a) Is the Domain Name System only used to send back IP addresses for given host names? Explain. b) What is a domain? c) Distinguish between the DNS root and top-level domains. d) What are the two types of top-level domains? e) Which level of domain name do corporations most wish to have? f) What are DNS root servers? g) How does a company or individual obtain a second-level domain name? h) After you get a second-level domain name, what more must you do to have a working website for your company?

Simple Network Management Protocol (SNMP)

We saw the Simple Network Management Protocol (SNMP) in Chapter 4. We will now look at SNMP in more detail, focusing on the management information base (MIB) and the security implications of the Set command.

The Management Information Base (MIB) When the manager retrieves information from agents on managed devices, it stores this information in a database called the **management information base (MIB)**. As in databases in general, "MIB" refers both to the physical database and to the schema (organization) of the information in the database. We will focus on the latter.

The MIB schema is not relational. Instead, the SNMP MIB schema is organized as a hierarchy of objects. This term is a little confusing at first. An **object** is a piece of information about a managed device. The managed device itself is not an object. Figure 9-7 shows the basic schema for organizing SNMP objects.

SNMP Objects (see Figure 9-7)

Not the managed devices themselves

Objects are specific pieces of information about a managed device

Information is kept in the management information base (MIB)

Set Commands

Dangerous if used by attackers

Many firms disable set to thwart such attacks

However, they give up the ability to manage remote resources without travel

Password used to encrypt manager–agent communication

SNMPv1: password was a "community name" used by the manager with all devices (poor)

SNMPv3: each manager–agent pair has a different password (good)

FIGURE 9-6 Simple Network Management Protocol (SNMP) (Study Figure)

System Objects

    System name

    System description

    System contact person

    System uptime (since last reboot)

IP Objects

    Forwarding (for routers). Yes if forwarding (routing), No if not

    Subnet mask

    Default time to live

    Traffic statistics

    Number of discards because of resource limitations

    Number of discards because could not find route

    Number of rows in routing table

    Rows discarded because of lack of memory

    Individual row data

TCP Objects

    Maximum/minimum retransmission time

    Maximum number of TCP connections allowed

    Opens/failed connections/resets

    Segments sent

    Segments retransmitted

    Errors in incoming segments

    No open port errors

    Data on individual connections (sockets, states)

UDP Objects

    Error: no application on requested port

    Traffic statistics

ICMP Objects

    Number of errors of various types

Interface Objects (One per Interface)

    Type (e.g., 69 is 100Base-FX; 71 is 802.11)

    Status: up/down/testing

    Speed

    MTU (maximum transmission unit—the maximum packet size)

    Traffic statistics: octets, unicast/broadcast/multicast packets

    Errors: discards, unknown protocols, etc.

FIGURE 9-7 SNMP MIB Hierarchical Object Model

- There is one set of objects for the system (switch, router, host, etc.) as a whole. For example, the manager may ask a router its system uptime—how long it has operated since its last reboot. If this is only a few minutes, the router may be suffering intermittent failures that cause it to crash and reboot frequently.
- There is also one set each of IP objects, TCP or UDP objects, and ICMP objects. For example, the manager can ask the agent for a router' routing object's value. If the value is "no," the router does not route packets. Rows discarded because of lack of memory is another useful object value to know. If a router is discarding more than a tiny number of packets because its memory is full, it is time to add more memory.
- A router may have multiple interfaces, and so will a switch (although switch *interfaces* are called ports). Each interface will have its own set of objects, including its interface speed and numbers of errors it has experienced. If an interface has too many errors, it may have problems that need attention.

Each SNMP Get command asks a managed device for the value of an object. By polling managed devices with Get commands wisely, the manager can maintain a database of important information about each managed device. The network visualization program can use this information to provide useful pictures of how well individual devices and sections of the network are functioning.

SNMP Set Security   Get is very useful, but the SNMP *Set* command is even more powerful. The manager can use a Set command to tell an agent to change the configuration of a managed device. If a router interface seems to be malfunctioning, for example, the manager can tell the agent to set the value of an interface to "testing." The agent will then put the interface into testing mode. Set commands can also turn off interfaces to avoid using expensive transmission lines when demand is low.

By allowing administrators to manage devices remotely, the Set command can save companies a great deal of money by avoiding travel to fix problems. Unfortunately, many firms are reluctant to use Set commands because of security dangers. If Set is permitted and attackers learn how to send Set commands to managed devices, the results could be catastrophic. Fortunately, SNMP security has improved over time.

- The original version of SNMP, SNMPv1, had very weak authentication security, making this danger a distinct possibility. The manager and all managed devices merely had to be configured with the same secret **community name**. With hundreds or thousands of devices sharing the same community name, it becomes easy for attackers to learn the community name and thus be able to implement massive attacks. Of course, "everybody" knows the community name, so there is usually little effort to keep it secret.
- SNMPv3[2] supports passwords for each manager–agent pair, and these pairwise passwords are used to authenticate and encrypt transmissions. This requires a great deal of work to set up, but it is the only way to secure SNMP. An attacker learning one of the pairwise passwords will not be able to take over the network.

---

[2] SNMPv2 was largely ignored in the marketplace.

Of course, poor implementation can defeat SNMPv3 security. If a lazy administrator uses the same password for all manager–agent pairs, then this is no better security than community names. On the other hand, if a company has strong security, this will allow it to use Set and save a great deal of network management labor. This is an example of good security being an enabler, not merely a nuisance.

Test Your Understanding

4. a) Explain the difference between managed devices and objects. b) What type of SNMP object is the number of rows in the routing table? c) The number of segments sent? d) Speed? e) Why are firms often reluctant to use *Set* commands? f) Describe SNMPv1's poor authentication method. g) Describe SNMPv3's good authentication method. h) How can good security be an enabler with SNMP?

SECURING INTERNET TRANSMISSION

When the Internet was created, little thought was given to security. As Jon Postel, who edited the main Internet RFCs, explained to the first author, "It just wasn't a problem then, and we were stretched thin." Today, however, Internet security is very much a pressing issue. Companies are beginning to address the security of transmissions across the Internet (and within site networks as well) by using virtual private networks.

Virtual Private Networks

Figure 9-8 shows that corporations can cryptographically protect traffic flowing between two sites or between a site and a remote user. In Chapters 3 and 7, we saw host-to-host virtual private networks. Figure 9-8 shows a **remote-site-access VPN** connecting a remote user to a site and a **site-to-site VPN** that connects two corporate sites.

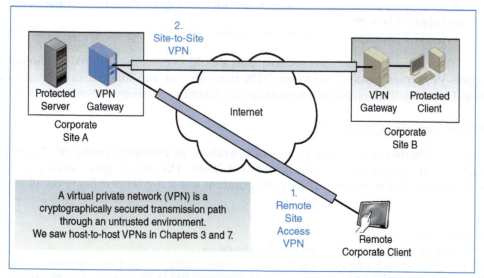

FIGURE 9-8   Remote Access and Site-to-Site Virtual Private Networks (VPNs)

> *A remote-site-access VPN connects a remote user to a site.*
>
> *A site-to-site VPN connects two corporate sites.*

- Remote-site-access VPNs are attractive because single hosts trying to connect to a corporate site via the Internet are extremely vulnerable. They are even more vulnerable if they connect to their network wirelessly.
- Site-to-site VPNs protect all traffic flowing between a pair of sites. Typically, traffic between sites is heavy, so site-to-site VPNs tend to carry much more traffic than remote-site-access VPNs.
- In Chapters 3 and 7, we also saw host-to-host VPNs, in which a client connects to a particular server using a VPN.

Both remote-site-access VPNs and site-to-site VPNs usually terminate in a **VPN gateway** at the border of each site. This VPN gateway handles cryptographic protections when dealing with remote users or a VPN gateway at another site.

IPsec VPNs

For security over the Internet, the Internet Engineering Task Force created a family of standards collectively called **IP security (IPsec)**.[3] As its name suggests, IPsec operates at the internet layer. It provides protection to at least part of the IP header. More importantly, it also provides protection to all content at the transport and application layers and to part of the IP packet header.[4] This protection is transparent, meaning that nothing has to be done to upper-layer content in order to be protected and that all upper-layer content is protected. By securing packets and their contents, the IETF provided a single mechanism to protect TCP/IP traffic.

> *IPsec operates at the internet layer. It provides security to all content at the transport and application layers.*

IPsec offers the strongest security and should eventually dominate remote-site-access VPN transmission, site-to-site VPN transmission, and internal site IP transmission. However, IPsec is complex to manage and therefore relatively expensive to manage.

IPsec Transport Mode

Figure 9-9 shows IPsec's two modes of operation. In **transport mode**, the two computers that are communicating implement IPsec. This mode gives strong end-to-end security, but it requires IPsec configuration *and* a digital certificate on all hosts.

---

[3] IPsec is pronounced "eye-pea-sek," with emphasis on the sek.

[4] Actually, the term *all* is a bit too strong. In transport mode, which is discussed later, attackers can read the IP addresses because the packet is addressed to the destination host instead of to the IPsec gateway server. However, on exams, call it all.

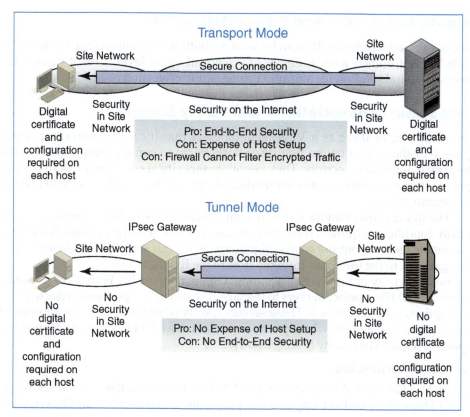

FIGURE 9-9   IPsec in Transport Mode and Tunnel Mode

Although the cost per host for configuration and for the digital certificate is small, the large number of computers in a company makes the aggregate cost of transport mode setup high.

Although IPsec transport mode offers end-to-end cryptographic security, there is also a security impairment to accept when IPsec transport mode is used. There is no way for firewalls between the source and destination host to decode, read, and filter the traffic. The firewall will simply pass the packet if it is part of an approved IPsec transport mode VPN.

IPsec Tunnel Mode

In contrast, in **tunnel mode**, the IPsec connection extends only between **IPsec gateways** at the two sites. This provides no protection within sites, but the use of tunnel mode IPsec gateways offers simple security. The two hosts do not have to implement IPsec security and, in fact, do not even have to know that IPsec is being used between the IPsec gateways. Most importantly, there is no need to install digital certificates on individual hosts. Only the two IPsec gateways need to have IPsec configuration and digital certificates. Tunnel mode minimizes costs but provides no protection for the traffic within the sites.

Remote-Site-Access and Site-to-Site VPNs

IPsec is a versatile protocol that can be used for both remote-site-access VPNs and site-to-site VPNs. Coupled with its ability to protect all upper-layer content transparently, IPsec is a general solution for a firm's cryptographic protection needs.

IPsec Security Associations and Policy Servers

One advantage of IPsec as a VPN technology is that it can be centrally managed. Figure 9-10 shows that before two IPsec hosts begin to communicate, they negotiate how they will perform security. They negotiate **security associations (SAs),** which are agreements about what security methods and options the two devices will use when they communicate.

The figure shows that the gateways implement an association in each direction. If security conditions require it, these SAs can use different security options. For example, for a remote user, remote site access might have a stronger security association from the IPsec gateway to the user than from the user to the IPsec gateway.

Some security options are very strong. Others may not be. With IPsec, companies can use central **IPsec policy servers** to manage IPsec security options in order to prevent weak options from being used. These servers specify what SA options are allowable for various gateway pairs and what options must not be used. Policy servers are especially important if a firm has many IPsec gateways.

Test Your Understanding

5. a) At what layer does IPsec operate? b) What layer content does IPsec protect? c) Does IPsec protect upper-layer protocols transparently? d) Describe IPsec

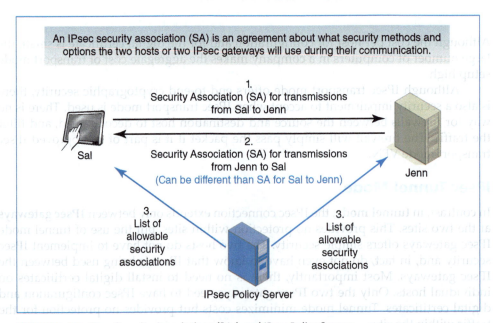

FIGURE 9-10 IPsec Security Associations (SAs) and IPsec Policy Servers

tunnel mode. e) What is the main advantage of tunnel mode? Explain. f) What is the main disadvantage of tunnel mode? Explain. g) Describe IPsec transport mode. h) What is the main advantage of transport mode? Explain. i) What is the main disadvantage of transport mode? Explain. j) Describe the problem that firewalls have with IPsec transport mode VPNs. k) In which IPsec mode are clients and servers required to have digital certificates? l) Which IPsec mode does not require clients and servers to have digital certificates? m) Is IPsec used for remote-site-access VPNs, site-to-site VPNs, or both?

6. a) In IPsec, what are security associations (SAs)? b) Must security associations be the same in the two directions? c) Describe how IPsec gateways can be managed centrally to ensure that weak SAs are not permitted.

SSL/TLS VPNs

Although IPsec is an enormously powerful tool for creating highly secure VPNs, it is expensive to implement. For many purposes, companies implement VPNs using the SSL/TLS. SSL/TLS, which we saw briefly in Chapter 3 for VPNs, is far less expensive to implement than IPsec, yet it offers reasonably strong security.

Figure 9-11 compares IPsec VPNs with SSL/TLS VPNs. It shows that the Internet Engineering Task Force is the standards agency for both. The IETF created IPsec directly. The Netscape Corporation created **Secure Sockets Layer (SSL)** standard but later passed it to the IETF. Not recognizing the concept of a "sockets layer," and noting that SSL operates at the transport layer, the IETF renamed the standard **Transport Layer Security (TLS)**. The SSL abbreviation is still widely used. Consequently, we will refer to these standards as SSL/TLS. Note that the IPsec standard operates at the internet layer.

Characteristic of VPN Technology	IPsec	SSL/TLS
Standards Organization	IETF	IETF (created by Netscape as SSL, renamed TLS by the IETF)
Layer	Layer 3	Layer 4
Built into Browsers, Webservers, and Mail Servers, So Protects These Applications at Little or No Cost	No	Yes
Can Protect any Application	Yes (also protects transport-layer header and some of the IP header)	No (only SSL/TLS-aware applications such as web and e-mail)
Type of VPNs Supported in the Standard	Host-to-Host Remote Site Access Site-to-Site	Host-to-Host
Strength of Security	Excellent	Good
Security Can Be Managed Centrally	Yes	No

FIGURE 9-11 SSL/TLS VPNs

The table emphasizes the relative strengths of IPsec and SSL/TLS by shading the box of the superior standard for selected characteristics. Note that SSL/TLS has only one "win." It is built into every browser, webserver, and e-mail program. This makes it free and simple to implement. Free and simple are powerful benefits. However, SSL/TLS can only protect a few "SSL/TLS–aware" applications and is designed only for host-to-host VPNs.

In contrast, IPsec protects everything in the transport header and application message and part of the IP header as well. It provides this protection transparently, meaning that nothing has to be changed at the transport or application layers for protection to work. In addition, IPsec supports all three types of VPNs. It is the gold standard for VPN security, and devices using IPsec can be managed centrally to ensure that they follow company policy for IPsec. Overall, SSL/TLS is a tactical VPN security tool that works for some needs, while IPsec is a strategic tool for protecting all IP and higher communication within a company.

Overall, SSL/TLS is a tactical VPN security tool that works for some needs, while IPsec is a strategic tool for protecting all IP and higher communication within a company.

You have personally used SSL/TLS. In fact, you probably used it today. If you have ever purchased something online, your URL at some point began with https://. The *s* signified that the transaction was secured with SSL/TLS. In addition, if you use a webmail e-mail service, it is likely that all communication between you and the webserver from which you get your mail is secured by SSL/TLS.

Test Your Understanding

7. a) Why are SSL/TLS VPNs attractive? b) Compare the relative advantage of SSL/TLS over IPsec. c) Compare the relative advantages of IPsec over SSL/TLS. d) How can you tell if your connection to a server uses SSL/TLS?

MANAGING IP VERSION 6 (IPV6)

In this chapter, we have looked at some aspects of managing IPv4. IPv6 generally has the same management needs. In this section, we will focus on important differences in managing IPv4 and IPv6.

Internet Layer Protocol Stacks

The internet layer sits between the transport layer and the data link layer. As Figure 9-12 illustrates, there has traditionally been a single internet layer process sitting between a host's transport layer process and its data link layer process. The internet layer process is called an **internet layer protocol stack** because it handles more than the Internet Protocol (IP). For example, it also handles the Internet Control Message Protocol (ICMP) and, in the case of IPv4, the Address Resolution Protocol (ARP). It is usually called, simply, the **IP stack**.

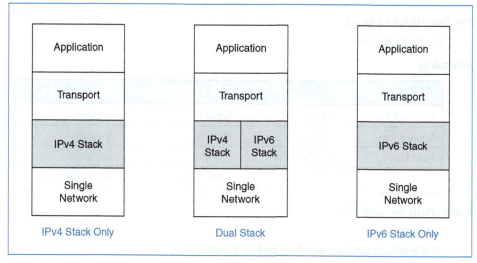

FIGURE 9-12 Internet Layer Protocol Stacks

Figure 9-12 shows that there was only a single IP stack on hosts originally—the **IPv4 stack**. The coming of IPv6 created two more alternatives.

- One is for hosts to have a single **IPv6 stack** *instead of* a single IPv4 stack.
- The other is to have a **dual-stack** host with both IPv4 and IPv6 stacks. This allows the host to transmit either IPv4 or IPv6 packets and to execute IPv4 or IPv6 internet layer protocols as needed.

The Internet Engineering Task Force expected that dual-stack implementation would become the norm. After a while, all hosts and other network devices would have both stacks. Support for IPv4 would be gradually turned off.

However, the exhaustion of IPv4 addresses has created a growing number of hosts that only have an IPv6 stack and no IPv4 stack. In addition, although IPv6 was defined in the 1990s, many vendors still sell operating systems that have the IPv6 stack turned off, weak IPv6 stacks that cause problems if turned on, and sometimes no IPv6 stack at all. If an IPv6-only client wishes to communicate with an IPv4-only server, this will be impossible. Network elements that cannot handle IPv6 may also impede communication from an IPv6-only device to another device even if it is an IPv6-only device or a dual-stack device.

Test Your Understanding

8. a) What is the advantage of having a dual stack for IP? b) Why is having only an IPv6 stack problematic?

IPv6 Subnetting

Earlier in this chapter, we looked at IPv4 subnetting. Subnetting in IPv6 is similar, but 128-bit addresses change the situation considerably. Figure 9-13 summarizes some of the key changes.

IPv6 Global Unicast Address

    Like IPv4 addresses

Terminology

IPv4	IPv6	IPv4 Part Length	IPv6 Part Length
Network Part	Routing Prefix	Variable	Variable
Subnet Part	Subnet ID	Variable	Variable
Host Part	Interface IDs	Variable	64 bits
		Total: 32 bits	Total: 128 bits

Routing Prefix and Subnet ID

    Subnet ID is 64 bits

    Total length of routing prefix and subnet ID is therefore 64 bits

    If the routing prefix is 20 bits, the subnet ID must be 44 bits long

    A longer routing prefix means a smaller subnet ID and therefore fewer subnets

    A shorter routing prefix means a larger subnet ID and therefore more subnets

FIGURE 9-13 IPv6 Subnetting

IPv6 Global Unicast Addresses Earlier in this chapter, we saw that IPv4 addresses have three parts—a host part, a subnet part, and a network part. Although the total length is always 32 bits, the lengths of the three parts are all variable. We also saw that these IPv4 addresses are normally public, meaning that they can be used on the Internet. In contrast, private IPv4 addresses can be used only within a corporate site or home network.

Global We will now see that **IPv6 global unicast addresses** are organized in the same way. *Global* means that packets with such addresses can be transmitted over the Internet. This is like public IP addresses in IPv4. *Unicast* means that these are addresses to use for one host to transmit to another host. The term *global unicast IPv6 address* is long, so we will call them, simply, *IPv6 addresses*.

The Three Parts Figure 9-13 also illustrates how IPv6 addresses are organized. The figure shows that IPv6 addresses, like IPv4 addresses, are divided into three parts. IPv6 does not use the terms *host part*, *subnet part*, and *network part*, but it does use similar concepts.

- The equivalent of the IPv4 network part is the *routing prefix*. The **routing prefix** lets routers on the Internet route packets to an organization.
- The equivalent of the IPv4 subnet part is the *subnet ID*. The **subnet ID** lets routers within a firm route packets to individual subnets within the firm.
- The equivalent of the IPv4 host part is the *Interface ID*. The **interface ID** identifies an individual host in the firm.

In IPv4, the size of the host part varies. In contrast, the size of the Interface ID in global unicast IPv6 addresses is fixed at 64 bits. It may seem wasteful to "use up" half of all bits in the IPv6 addresses to designate a host. However, with 64 bits left for the routing prefix and the subnet ID, there are still 1.8×10^{19} possibilities for the routing prefix and subnet ID.

The size of the Interface ID in global unicast IPv6 addresses is fixed at 64 bits.

Routing Prefix and Subnet ID   Figure 9-13 indicates that the routing prefix and subnet ID are variable in length, although their total must be 64 bits because the interface ID has already consumed 64 of the 128 bits. To give an example, if the routing prefix is 20 bits, the subnet ID must be 44 bits. If an address registrar gives a firm a short routing prefix, then the company can have a large subnet ID and can therefore have many subnets. Smaller firms, needing fewer subnets, are given longer routing prefixes.

Creating the 64-bit Interface ID   Returning to the 64-bit Interface ID, it would be nice to be able to use a host's data link layer address as the interface ID. However, the most common type of data link layer address is the EUI-48 address, which is only 48 bits long. Fortunately, the IEEE 802 Committee has defined a way to create a **64-bit modified extended unique identifier (EUI-64)** from a 48-bit EUI-48 address. This modified EUI-64 address can go into the interface ID field.

Creating a modified EUI-64 address from a EUI-48 address requires a series of steps, which Figure 9-14 illustrates. These steps are straightforward, and there are good technical reasons for each step. However, without a lot of in-depth knowledge, which

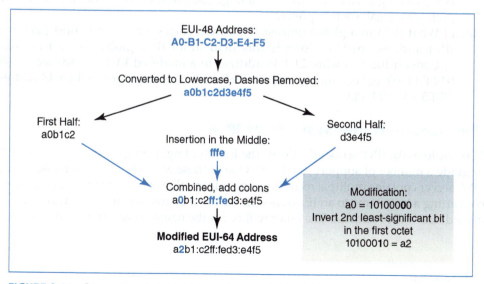

FIGURE 9-14   Converting an EUI-48 Address into an EUI-64 Address

frankly is not worth learning for information systems professionals, these five steps can appear to be illogical and weird. Just think of them as a mystical protocol for joining an obscure secret society.

- First, if the EUI-48 address is displayed in hexadecimal notation, the dashes are removed from the EUI-48 address, and the letters are changed to lowercase. So *A0-B1-C2-D3-E4-F5* becomes *a0b1c2d3e4f5*.
- Second, the 48 bits are divided into two half. Each half has 24 bits. In this case, the first half is *a0b1c2* and the second half is *d3e4f5*.
- Third, the hex symbol *fffe* is inserted between the two halves.[5] This gives a0b1c2fffed3e4f5.
- Fourth, the first half, the new group, and the second half are written together and regrouped into four fields with four hex symbols apiece. Colons separate these fields. This gives the result: *a0b1:c2ff:fed3:e4f5*. Notice that a colon separates the *ff* and the *fe*. Use this as a cross-check to make sure you have done things right.
- Fifth, now we come to the *modified* part of the name. In this final step, the *second least-significant bit* (the second bit from the right end) in the first octet is inverted. For instance, the EUI-48 address in our example begins with a0. These two hex symbols constitute the first octet. In binary, they are *1010 0000*.[6] This must be changed to *1010 0010* by inverting the *second* least-significant bit—the bit that is the second from the right. Inverting a bit means changing it to 1 if it is 0 and changing it to 0 if it is 1. The inversion gives *a2* instead of *a0*. So the final modified EUI-64 is *a2b1:c2ff:fed3:e4f5*.

Test Your Understanding

9. a) What field in an IPv6 global unicast address corresponds to the network part of an IPv4 address? b) What field in an IPv6 global unicast address corresponds to the subnet part of an IPv4 address? c) If the subnet ID is 16 bits long, how long is the routing prefix? d) If you are a large company, do you want a large routing prefix or a small routing prefix?

10. a) What field in a global unicast IP address corresponds to the host part of an IPv4 address? b) How long is this field in an IPv6 global unicast address? c) Convert the following EUI-48 address to a modified EUI-64 address: AA-00-00-FF-FF-00. (Check figure: ae00:00ff:feff:ff00) d) Repeat for this EUI-48 address: 9B-E5-33-21-FF-0D.

The Domain Name System for IPv6

In order to make IPv6 work effectively, the Internet Engineering Task Force also had to upgrade a number of support standards. One of these was DNS. For each host name, a DNS server contains multiple records giving information about that particular host. For converting a host name to an IP address, there must be two records. One will be for the named host's IPv4 address. The other will be for the named host's IPv6 address.

---

[5] Don't ask why.
[6] See previous footnote.

- **DNS A Record.**   The A record contains the IPv4 address for a target host. When your computer sends a DNS message to request the IPv4 address for a particular host name, the DNS server replies with information in the target host's A record.
- **DNS AAAA Record.**   For IPv6 addresses, a new address field had to be added. IPv6 addresses are four times as long as IPv4 addresses, so the added record is called the AAAA record.

Test Your Understanding

11. In the Domain Name System, distinguish between the information contained in the A and AAAA records for a host name.

OTHER TCP/IP STANDARDS

In this section, we will look briefly at several other important TCP/IP standards that network administrators need to master.

Dynamic Routing Protocols

How does a router get the information in its routing table? One possibility is to enter routes manually. However, that approach does not scale to large internets. Instead, as Figure 9-15 shows, routers constantly exchange routing table information with one another using **dynamic routing protocols.**[7]

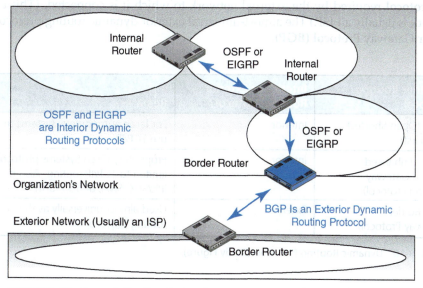

FIGURE 9-15   Dynamic Routing Protocols

---

[7] Note that TCP/IP uses the term *routing* in two different but related ways. First, we saw that the process of forwarding arriving packets is called routing. Second, the process of exchanging information for building routing tables is also called routing.

Interior Dynamic Protocols: OSPF and EIGRP   Recall from Chapter 1 that the Internet consists of many networks owned by different organizations. Within an individual organization's network or internet, the organization decides which **interior dynamic routing protocol** to use for its internal routers, as shown in Figure 9-15. There are two[8] popular interior dynamic routing protocols.[9] Each has relative strengths and weaknesses.

- **Open Shortest Path First (OSPF).**   For interior routing, the IETF created the **Open Shortest Path First (OSPF)** dynamic routing protocol. OSPF is very efficient, having a complex metric based on a mixture of cost, throughput, and traffic delays. It also offers strong security. However, it only does TCP/IP routing. Although TCP/IP is dominant today, many corporations still have legacy protocols from other standards architectures, such as IBM's SNA architecture and Novel's SPX/IPX. Corporations cannot use OSPF for routing in these other architectures.

- **EIGRP.**   Cisco Systems is the dominant manufacturer of routers. Cisco has its own proprietary interior dynamic routing protocol for large internets—**Enhanced Interior Gateway Routing Protocol (EIGRP)**. The term **gateway** is another term for *router*. EIGRP's metric is very efficient because it is based on a mixture of interface bandwidth, load on the interface (0% to 100% of capacity), delay, and reliability (percentage of packets lost). EIGRP is comparable to OSPF, but unlike OSPF, it can route SNA and IPX/SPX traffic as well as TCP/IP traffic.

Exterior Dynamic Protocol: BGP   For communication outside the organization's network, the organization is no longer in control. It must use the **exterior dynamic routing protocol** required by the external network to which it is connected. (This exterior network is usually an ISP.) The almost-universal exterior dynamic routing protocol is the **Border Gateway Protocol (BGP)**.

Dynamic Routing Protocol	Interior or Exterior Routing Protocol?	Remarks
OSPF (Open Shortest Path First)	Interior	For large autonomous systems that only use TCP/IP
EIGRP (Enhanced Interior Gateway Routing Protocol)	Interior	Proprietary Cisco Systems protocol. Not limited to TCP/IP routing. Also handles IPX/SPX, SNA, and so forth
BGP (Border Gateway Protocol)	Exterior	Used almost universally as the exterior routing protocol

FIGURE 9-16   Dynamic Routing Protocols (Study Figure)

---

[8] A third interior dynamic routing protocol of historical note is the Routing Information Protocol (RIP). RIP is very simple, making it attractive economically. However, its poor security excludes it from organizations today.

[9] A third interior dynamic routing protocol is RIP, the Routing Information Protocol. RIP is simpler than OSPF or EIGRP and was once popular. However, its almost complete lack of security features make it an unacceptable choice today.

Test Your Understanding

12. a) What is the purpose of dynamic routing protocols? **b)** For its own network, can an organization choose its interior dynamic routing protocol? **c)** What is the IETF interior dynamic routing protocol? **d)** When might you use EIGRP as your interior dynamic routing protocol? **e)** May a company select the routing protocol its border router uses to communicate with the outside world? **f)** What is the almost-universal exterior dynamic routing protocol?

Internet Control Message Protocol (ICMP) for Supervisory Messages at the Internet Layer

Supervisory Messages at the Internet Layer   IP is only concerned with packet delivery. For supervisory messages at the internet layer, the IETF created the **Internet Control Message Protocol (ICMP)**. IP and ICMP work closely together. As Figure 9-17 shows, IP encapsulates ICMP messages in the IP data field, delivering them to their target host or router. There are no higher-layer headers or messages.

Error Advisement   IP is an unreliable protocol. It offers no error correction. If the router or the destination host finds an error, it discards the packet. Although there is no retransmission, the router or host that finds the error may send an ICMP error message to the source device to inform it that an error has occurred, as in Figure 9-17. The ICMP error message contains type and code values indicating what the problem is. For example, a host unreachable message is Type 3/Code 1.

Note that this is error advisement (notification) rather than error correction. There is no mechanism within IP or ICMP for the retransmission of lost or damaged packets. ICMP error messages are only sent to help the sending process or its human user diagnose problems. They do not make IP reliable.

One important subtlety is that sending error advisement messages is not mandatory. For security reasons, many firms do not allow error advisement messages to leave their

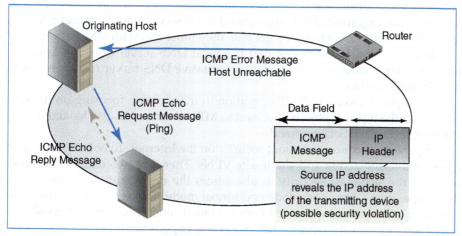

FIGURE 9-17   Internet Control Message Protocol (ICMP) for Supervisory Messages at the Internet Layer

internal internets because hackers can exploit the information contained in them. Most obviously, the ICMP message will be carried in a packet that contains the IP address of the sending router or other device. If adversaries have an exploit to use against routers, they have a target IP address for their attacks.

Echo (Ping)   Perhaps the most useful ICMP messages are the echo request and response messages. As we saw in Chapters 1 and 4, one host can use these message to "ping" another host. As in the case of error response messages, the IP header for the echo response message reveals the presence of a potential target at the source IP address.

Test Your Understanding

13. a) For what general class of messages and at what layer is ICMP used? b) Explain error advisement in ICMP. c) What two ICMP message types are used in *ping*? d) What security concern do ICMP error advisement messages and echo response messages create?

CONCLUSION

Synopsis

Chapter 8 dealt with TCP/IP concepts. This chapter focuses on TCP/IP management. The TCP/IP standards that dominate internetworking require a great deal of management attention, both initially and on an ongoing basis. The first step is to develop an IP subnet schema for the firm. This creates a basic trade-off between the number of subnets and the number of hosts per subnet. The firm also has to decide whether or not to use network address translation (NAT). NAT has several benefits, including adding security and increasing the effective number of public IP addresses a firm has; but NAT causes problems for certain protocols.

In this chapter, we looked more closely at the Domain Name System (DNS). We saw that DNS is a hierarchical system of named domains (collections of resources under the control of an organization). Corporations want second-level domain names, such as pearsonhighered.com. After they get one, they must maintain DNS servers for their second-level domain. We also saw that if a local DNS server does not know the IP address for a host name, it contacts the authoritative DNS server for the second-level domain in the IP address.

This chapter looked at SNMP operation in more detail, focusing on the concept of objects and the types of objects specified in MIB schemas. We also looked at security concerns regarding the Set command.

Companies are concerned about security on the Internet. To obtain better security, they use remote-site-access and site-to-site VPNs. There are two main VPN protocols. IPsec offers the strongest security. It also offers the important choice between two modes of operation—transport mode and tunnel mode. Transport mode offers host-to-host security but is more expensive to implement. Tunnel mode only offers site-to-site security (with no security within sites) but is less expensive. When transport mode is used, firewalls cannot read the content of packets. Most importantly, IPsec offers central manageability.

SSL/TLS can be used for remote-site-access VPNs. SSL/TLS is attractive because all browsers know how to create a secure SSL/TLS connection with host computers. This means that there is no need to add anything to the client computer. However, there are limitations on the services that SSL/TLS can provide easily.

We ended the chapter with a long discussion on the management of IPv6. Managing IPv6 is similar to managing IPv4, but it is not the same. We began with a discussion of single-stack IPv4-only hosts, single-stack IPv6-only hosts, and dual-stack IPv4/IPv6 hosts. Originally, the IETF believed that dual-stack hosts would make the introduction of IPv6 painless. However, there is a growing number of IPv6-only devices, which may have trouble communicating with the large number of existing IPv4-only hosts.

In IPv4, addresses have three parts: network, subnet, and host. In IPv6 global unicast addresses, the comparable parts are called the routing prefix, the subnet ID, and the interface ID. The interface ID is always 64 bits long. It is created from the host's EUI-48 address by a somewhat complex process that we reviewed. This process results in a 64-bit modified extended unique identifier (EUI-64) that is used as the interface ID. The company is assigned a routing prefix. This sets the size of its subnet ID and determines how many subnets it can have.

IPv6 required the extension of a number of existing TCP/IP standards. The major change to DNS is the introduction of an AAAA record for host names. This record contains the IPv6 address of the named host. (IPv4 addresses are contained in traditional A records.)

Routers build their routing tables by communicating with other routers. Routers frequently exchange messages, giving information stored in their routing tables. These messages are governed by dynamic routing protocols.

IP itself does not have supervisory messages. For internet layer supervisory messages, hosts and routers use the Internet Control Message Protocol (ICMP). We looked at two types of ICMP messages—error advisement messages and echo messages (ping). ICMP messages are carried in the data fields of IP packets.

END-OF-CHAPTER QUESTIONS

Thought Questions

9-1. Both DNS servers and DHCP servers send your client PC an IP address. Distinguish between these two addresses.

9-2. Assume that an average SNMP response message is 100 bytes long. Assume that a manager sends 400 SNMP *Get* commands each second. a) What percentage of a 100 Mbps LAN link's capacity would the resulting response traffic represent? b) What percentage of a 1 Mbps WAN link would the response messages represent? c) What are the management implications of your answers?

9-3. A firm is assigned the network part 128.171. It selects an 8-bit subnet part. a) Write the bits for the four octets of the IP address of the first host on the first subnet. b) Convert this answer into dotted decimal notation. (If you have forgotten how to do this, it was covered in Chapter 1.) c) Write the bits for the second host on the third subnet. (In binary, 2 is 10, while 3 is 11.) d) Convert this into dotted decimal notation. e) Write the bits for the last host on the third subnet. f) Convert this answer into dotted decimal notation.

9-4. A firm is assigned the network part 128.171. It selects a 10-bit subnet part. a) Draw the bits for the four octets of the IP address of the first host on the first subnet. (Hint: Use Windows Calculator.) b) Convert this answer into dotted decimal notation. c) Draw the bits for the second host on the third subnet. (In binary, 2 is 10, while 3 is 11.) d) Convert this into dotted decimal notation. e) Draw the bits for the last host on the third subnet. f) Convert this answer into dotted decimal notation.

Troubleshooting Question

9-5. In your browser, you enter the URL of a website you use daily. After an unusually long delay, you receive a DNS error message that the host does not exist. a) List the five troubleshooting steps discussed in Chapter 1. b) Apply them to this situation.

Hands-On Project

9-6. After Sal Aurigemma received his PhD from the University of Hawaii, he became an assistant professor at the University of Tulsa. There, he introduced the school to Aloha Friday, when people come to work in their colorful Aloha shirts. He got the idea of creating Aloha shirts with Tulsa's school colors and an emblem of the university on the shirt pocket. Suppose that he wants to create a company to sell school-specific Aloha shirts. He will need a company name and a second-level domain name. Got to an Internet domain name registrar. Thoughtfully come up with three appropriate and available domain names. Explain why each is good. Select one and explain why it is best.

Perspective Questions

9-7. What was the most surprising thing to you about the material in this chapter?

9-8. What was the most difficult thing for you in the chapter?

Chapter 10

Carrier Wide Area Networks (WANs)

LEARNING OBJECTIVES

By the end of this chapter, you should be able to:

- Contrast LANs and WANs in terms of technology, diversity, economics, speed, and need for optimization.
- Describe the three carrier WAN components and the two typical business uses for carrier WANs.
- Describe how the telephone system is organized, including its hierarchy of switches. (Most carrier WAN networks use the public switched telephone network for some or all of their communication.)
- Explain and compare the ADSL and cable modem residential Internet access services.
- Discuss trends in cellular data transmission speeds.
- Distinguish between access lines and leased lines. Select a leased line for a given application speed requirement. Explain how companies use leased lines in Internet access.
- Explain how networks of leased lines, public switched data networks (PSDNs), and MPLS can be used for site-to-site communication in a firm. Discuss the relative advantages and disadvantages of each.
- Explain carrier Ethernet and MPLS in some detail.
- Explain the capabilities of WAN optimization devices.
- Explain key concepts in software-defined networking.

> *Albert Einstein was reportedly asked how the telegraph worked. He said it was like a very long cat with its head in one city and its tail in another. When you pull on the tail in one city, it howls in the other city. Wireless transmission is the exactly the same but without the cat.*

LANs AND WANs (AND MANs)

One of the most fundamental distinctions in networking is the one between local area networks (LANs) and wide area networks (WANs). Figure 10-1 shows how these two types of networks differ. We will also see how they compare to intermediate-distance networks called metropolitan area networks (MANs).

LANs versus MANs and WANs

On and Off the Customer Premises   Some authors base the difference between LANs and WANs on physical distance. For instance, some say that the dividing line between LANs and WANs is one mile or one kilometer. However, the real distinction appears to be that **local area networks (LANs)** exist within a company's site, while **wide area networks (WANs)** connect different sites within an organization or between organizations.

Category	Local Area Network	Metropolitan Area Network	Wide Area Network
Abbreviation	LAN	MAN	WAN
Service Area	*On customer premises* (home, apartment, office, building, campus, etc.)	*Between sites* in a metropolitan area. (city and its suburbs) A Type of WAN	*Between sites* in a region, a country, or around the world.
Implementation	Self	Carrier	Carrier
Ability to Choose Technology	High	Low	Low
Who Manages the Network?	Self	Carrier	Carrier
Price	Highly related to cost	Based on pricing strategy. Highly unpredictable	Based on pricing strategy. Highly unpredictable
Cost per Bit Transmitted	Low	Medium	High
Typical Transmission Speed	1 Gbps and more	10 Mbps to 1 Gbps	1 to 100 Mbps
Diversity of Technologies	Low: 802.3 and 802.11	Medium	High

FIGURE 10-1   LANs versus WANs (and MANs)

Local area networks (LANs) exist within a company's site, while wide area networks (WANs) connect different sites within an organization or between organizations.

For LANs, then, the company owns the property and can do anything it wants. It can choose any LAN technology it wishes, and it can implement it any way it wishes.

There is no such freedom for WANs. A company cannot legally lay wires between two of its sites. (Consider how your neighbors would feel if you started laying wires across their yards.) The government gives certain companies called **carriers**[1] permissions (**rights of way**) to lay wires in public areas and offer service to customers. In return, carriers are subject to government regulation.

When you deal with carriers, you can only get the services they offer, and you must pay their prices. Although there may be multiple carriers in an area, the total number of service choices is likely to be quite limited.

On the positive side, you do not need to hire and maintain a large staff to deal with WANs because carriers handle nearly all of the details. In contrast, if you install a LAN, you also have to maintain it. As the old saying goes, anything you own ends up owning you.

Economics   Another fundamental difference between LANs and WANs stems from economics. You know that if you place a long-distance call, this will cost more than a local call. An international call will cost even more. As distance increases, the price of transmission increases. The cost per bit transmitted therefore is higher in WANs than in LANs.

You know from basic economics that as unit price increases, fewer units are demanded. Or, in normal English, when the price for an item increases, you usually buy less of it. Consequently, companies tend to purchase lower-speed WAN links than LAN links. Typically, LANs bring 1 Gbps to each desktop. WAN speeds more typically vary from 1 Mbps to about 100 Mbps. MAN speeds fall between the two.

In addition, companies spend more time optimizing their expensive WAN traffic than their relatively inexpensive LAN traffic. For example, companies may be somewhat tolerant of looking at YouTube videos on LANs, but they usually clamp down on this type of information on their WAN links. They also tend to compress data before sending across a WAN so that it can be handled with a lower-capacity WAN link.

Another aspect of economics is pricing. For LANs, you have a good idea of what installing and using a wired or wireless LAN will cost you. In carrier WANs, however, the price of services is only somewhat related to costs. Carriers change their prices

---

[1] Carriers were originally called common carriers. The name reflected the fact that these carriers were required by law to provide service to anyone or any organization requesting services. Regulation was originally instituted in the railroad industry because many companies that owned railroads also owned other companies and refused to provide services to competitors of these other companies.

strategically, for example, to encourage users to switch from one service to another. Consequently, price changes for WANs are less predictable than they are for customer-owned LAN technology.

Technologies   Another difference between LANs and WANs is that LAN technology has largely settled on two related families of standards—Ethernet (802.3) for wired LANs and Wi-Fi (802.11) for wireless LANs. As we saw in Chapter 6, 802.11 WLANs are primarily used today to extend corporate Ethernet wired LANs to mobile devices.

The technological situation is more complex in wide area networking. Multiple technologies are used, including leased line data networks, public switched data networks, and wireless networks. Within these categories are multiple options. Furthermore, WAN technologies are at different stages in their life cycles, with some increasing rapidly in use and others declining.

Test Your Understanding

1. a) Distinguish between LANs and WANs. b) What are rights of way? c) What are carriers? d) Why do you have more flexibility with LAN service than with WAN service? Why?
2. a) Why are typical WAN speeds slower than typical LAN speeds? Give a clear and complete argument. b) Why are future WAN prices difficult to predict? c) Compare the diversity of technologies in LANs and WANs.

Other Aspects of WANs

Metropolitan Area Networks (MANs)   All WANs connect sites between customer premises and cost more per bit transmitted than LANs. However, WANs differ considerably in the distances they span. Some are international and others span single nations. At the small end, some WANs are **metropolitan area networks (MANs)**, which connect sites in a city and its suburbs.

Although MANs are WANs, their relatively short distance span means that the cost per bit transmitted is lower than it is in national and international WANs. Consequently, typical transmission speeds are faster. If you have a smartphone or tablet with 3G or 4G cellular access, then you already use a MAN. Cellular networks almost always span a single MAN or even a single city. However, we will see that wired MANs are important for corporations because site-to-site traffic is large and is more efficiently transmitted over wires.

Single Networks versus Internets   Some people think that LANs are single networks, while WANs are internets. However, as Figure 10-2 shows, that is not the case. Small LANs usually will be single networks, but a larger LAN, such as one on a university campus, is likely to be a local internet.

For WANs, there can also be single networks or internets. Of course, the global Internet is a WAN, and we will see that many companies use it extensively for data transmission among their premises. We will also see that companies also use wide area single switched networks. These are large networks, but they are still switched single networks.

Technology	LAN	WAN
Can be a single switched or wireless network?	Yes	Yes
Can be an internet?	Yes	Yes

FIGURE 10-2   Single Networks versus Internets

Test Your Understanding

3. a) Why do MANs have higher typical speeds than broader-scope WANs? b) Are LANs single networks or internets? c) Are WANs single networks or internets? d) Is the Internet a WAN?

Carrier WAN Components and Business Uses

Figure 10-3 shows that there are three basic components to carrier wide area networks:

- First comes the customer premises with the **customer premises equipment (CPE)** needed to connect to the WAN. With mobile devices, your customer premises is wherever you are, and your mobile device is your customer premises equipment. For connecting corporate sites to wired access lines, the customer premises equipment is likely to be a border router.

- **Access links** connect the customer premises to the network core of the WAN. We will focus on wired access links because they are so prevalent. Later in the chapter, we will look at wireless access links.

- The **network core** connects access links to other access links. Again, we show it as a cloud because customers do not have to understand how it works in detail. The carrier takes care of the network core. Of course, as an IT professional, you have to understand what happens inside the cloud, and we will spend time looking at network core technologies.

The Internet connects everyone to everyone else. In contrast, **carrier WANs** primarily see two business uses. As Figure 10-3 shows, companies use carrier WANs to

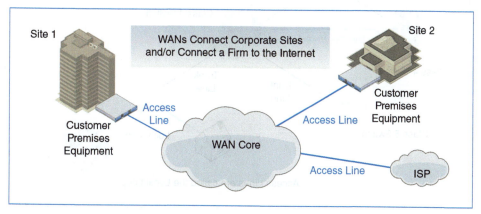

FIGURE 10-3   Basic WAN Components and Business Uses

link their sites to the Internet and to connect their own sites together. Carrier WANs are not frequently used to connect multiple companies together because all must be customers of the same carrier WAN. When multiple companies connect with a carrier WAN, it is generally because they need more security than the Internet provides.

Test Your Understanding

4. a) List the three basic components of wide area networks. b) Are access links wired or wireless? c) What is CPE? d) What are the two common business uses for carrier WANs? e) Distinguish between the Internet and carrier WANs. f) Why are carrier WANs not often used to link multiple firms together?

The Telephone System

The worldwide telephone system was created by voice. However, telephone carriers now provide data service to residential and business customers. In addition, other WAN carrier providers typically find it attractive to lease their transmission lines from telephone companies. This allows WAN providers to focus on data switching.

Figure 10-4 shows the **Public Switched Telephone Network (PSTN)**, which is the official name of the telephone system. Per our discussion earlier, there is a central core, and there are access lines. The access portion of the PSTN is the **local loop**. It extends from the final telephone company switch to the customer premises.

The **PSTN Core** is a modified hierarchy of switches. **End office switches** connect the PSTN to the customer. These are usually **Class 5 switches**—the lowest in the hierarchy. For perspective, there are about 100 Class 5 end office switches in the state of Hawaii. There are fewer switches at each subsequent level. For example, Hawaii has a single Class 3 switch.

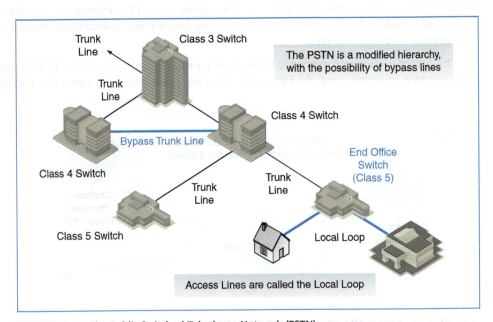

FIGURE 10-4 The Public Switched Telephone Network (PSTN)

The PSTN is a modified hierarchy in the sense that unlike Ethernet, the PSTN includes bypass trunk lines between switches that are at the same level if there is an unusually large volume of traffic between those switches. It is more efficient for such pairs of switches to communicate directly instead of having to involve a higher-level switch.

Test Your Understanding

5. a) Why is the PSTN important in WAN data transmission? b) What is the local loop? c) What class of switches are most end office switches? d) What is the structure of the PSTN core?

RESIDENTIAL WIRED INTERNET ACCESS

We will begin our discussion of WAN technology with residential Internet access. This will permit us to start with something familiar to most readers. This will give us a base of knowledge for looking at corporate WAN technologies.

Residential Asymmetric Digital Subscriber Line (ADSL) Service

Some readers are directly familiar with residential ADSL services. Figure 10-5 shows **asymmetric digital subscriber line (ADSL)** services provide simultaneous voice and data to residential customers. Data transmission speed is asymmetric, with faster download speed than upload speed. This is reasonable. Website downloading often requires a great deal of downstream speed. So does video streaming. In contrast, few residential applications require full two-way high-speed service.

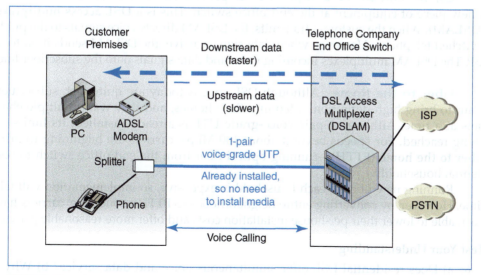

FIGURE 10-5 Asymmetric Digital Subscriber Line (ADSL) for Residential Access

Digital Subscriber Lines Telephone companies have traditionally served residential customers with **one-pair voice-grade (1PVG) UTP** in the local loop. This single unshielded pair was created for voice, not data. It is only twisted about once a foot. However, advances in signaling algorithms have allowed telephone companies to transmit data at high speeds over these lines—while continuing to deliver voice at the same time.

The line between the end office switch and the customer is called the subscriber line. When the telephone company transmits digital signals over it, it is called a **digital subscriber line (DSL)**. These are also called DSL lines, despite the fact that expanding the acronym gives digital subscriber line lines.

Sending data over 1-pair voice grade UTP is important because subscriber lines using this technology already run to every home and business. They have been used since the 1880s to deliver voice telephone service. There is no need to run new subscriber lines to homes in order to provide data transmission. In contrast, the business-focused leased lines that we will see later require carriers to run new transmission lines to each organization. This is extremely expensive.

Residential Customer Equipment and Service For ADSL service, a residential customer installs **ADSL modems**, although it is best to install splitters in each outlet. These **splitters** have two jacks—one for voice and one for data. Splitters separate voice and data signals, preventing possible transmission impairment.

How fast are transmission speeds in ADSL? The answer changes by the minute. In mid-2004, the first author was getting downstream speeds of just under 10 Mbps and upstream speeds a little over 2 Mbps. This is fast enough even for a high-definition movie download. ADSL vendors hope to raise downstream speeds to 100 Mbps or more in the near future. This will permit several high-definition telephone streams into the house. Faster upstream speeds will make online backup for hard disks reasonably painless.

Carrier End Office Equipment To provide ADSL, the carrier has to install a new piece of equipment at the end office switch. This is a **DSL access multiplexer (DSLAM)**. When the customer transmits, the DSLAM directs voice signals to the public switched telephone. However, when data signals arrive, the DSLAM sends it on to an ISP. The DSLAM multiplexes incoming voice and data signals onto the subscriber line.

Fiber to the Home Although DSL speeds today are quite fast, subscribers want to bring high-definition video into their homes, and they want multiple channels at a time. Although 1-pair voice-grade UTP is already installed, its limits are being reached. For speeds beyond about 100 Mbps, carriers are beginning to bring **fiber to the home (FTTH)**—running optical fiber from the end office switch to residential households.

Running new fiber to each household is expensive, so implementation will take time. However, by converting entire neighborhoods to FTTH at one time, carriers have been able to lower their per-house installation costs and offer more reasonable prices.

Test Your Understanding

6. a) Does residential DSL offer simultaneous voice and data service? b) Why is asymmetric speed acceptable in residential ADSL service? c) What is beneficial

about transmitting data over 1-pair voice-grade UTP? d) What equipment does the customer need in his or her home? e) What is the purpose of the DSLAM? f) Why is FTTH attractive? g) How are carriers attempting to reduce the cost of installing FTTH?

Cable Modem Service

Telephone Service and Cable TV In the 1950s, **cable television** companies sprang up in the United States and several other countries, bringing television into the home. Initially, cable only brought over-the-air TV to rural areas. Later, it began to penetrate urban areas by offering far more channels than urban subscribers could receive over the air. In the 1970s, many books and articles forecast a "wired nation" in which two-way cable and the advent of 40-channel cable systems would soon turn cable into an information superhighway. (After all, it would be impossible to fill 40 channels just with television, wouldn't it?) However, available services did not justify the heavy investment to make cable a two-way service until many years later.[2]

Figure 10-6 shows how cable television operates. The cable television operator has a central distribution point, called a **head end**. From the head end, signals travel out to neighborhoods via optical fiber.

From neighborhood splitters, signals travel through **coaxial cable**. The transmission of an electrical signal always requires *two* conductors. In UTP, the two conductors are the two wires in a pair. Figure 10-7 shows that in coaxial cable, the first conductor is a wire running through the center of a coaxial cable. The second

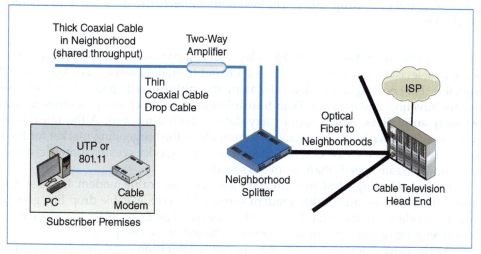

FIGURE 10-6 Cable Modem Service

---

[2] This was proven in the dissertation of a Stanford PhD student. The student received a contract from the White House to do the study. Unfortunately, when the study was finished, Richard Nixon was being impeached, and the Executive Office of the President of the United States refused to release the study—despite the fact that the results of the study were already widely known. The study was released a year later, and the student was able to get his doctorate.

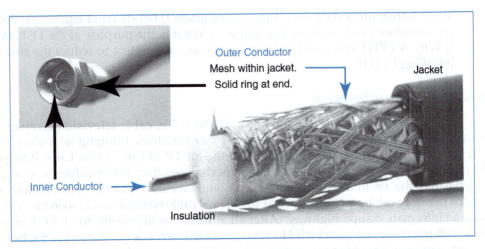

FIGURE 10-7 Coaxial Cable

conductor is a mesh wire tube running along the cable. The two conductors have the same axis, so the technology is called **coaxial cable**. Before the advent of high-definition HDMI cables, you typically connected your VCR to your television with coaxial cable.

The cable television company runs signals through the neighborhood using *thick coaxial cable* that looks like a garden hose. The access line to individual homes is a *thin coaxial cable* **drop cable**. The resident connects the drop cable to his or her television.

Cable Modem Service   Cable television companies eventually moved beyond one-way television service to two-way broadband (fast) data service. For television, the repeaters that boost signals periodically along the cable run only had to boost television signals traveling downstream. Data transmission required cable companies to install **two-way amplifiers**, which could carry data in both directions. Although this was expensive, it allowed cable companies to compete in the burgeoning market for broadband service. As in the case of ADSL, cable television service was asymmetric, offering faster downstream speeds than upstream speeds.

Instead of having a DSL modem, the subscriber has a **cable modem**. In general, this cable data service is called **cable modem service**. The coaxial cable drop line goes into the cable modem. The cable modem has a USB port and an Ethernet RJ-45 connector. The subscriber plugs a computer or access router into one of the two ports.

At the cable television head end, the cable television company connects to an Internet service provider. This allows subscribers to connect to hosts on the Internet.

Test Your Understanding

7. a) What transmission media do cable television companies use? b) Why is coaxial cable called "coaxial"? c) Distinguish between the coaxial trunk cable and drop cable. d) What types of amplifiers are needed for cable data service? e) What device do customers need for cable modem service?

ADSL versus Cable Modem Service

Telephone carriers and cable television companies constantly argue about the relative advantages of their two technologies. In reality, however, things boil down to speed and cost. The situation is changing rapidly. Both are increasing speeds frequently, and both are moving to FTTH. At most points in time, ADSL has been a little cheaper and a little slower. It will be interesting to see how competition drives them to improve in the future.

Test Your Understanding

8. a) What are the important things to consider when deciding between ADSL and cable modem service for your residence? b) In the past, how has ADSL compared to cable modem service? c) Which of these two services are moving toward FTTH?

CELLULAR DATA SERVICE

ADSL and cable modem service provide wired access to the Internet by linking users to their ISPs. Cellular telephony now connects users to their ISPs while they are away from home, in the office, or in hotspots. Businesses use cellular telephone service the same way.

Cellular Service

Nearly everybody today is familiar with cellular telephony. In most industrialized countries, well over half of all households now have a cellular telephone. Many now have *only* a cellular telephone and no traditional *wireline* public switched telephone network phone.

Cells and Cellsites   Figure 10-8 shows that cellular telephony divides a metropolitan service area into smaller geographical areas called **cells**. A city the size of Honolulu will have a few hundred cells.

The user has a cellular telephone (also called a mobile phone, **mobile**, or cellphone). Near the middle of each cell is a **cellsite**, which contains a transceiver (transmitter/receiver) to receive mobile phone signals and to send signals out to the mobiles. The cellsite also supervises each mobile phone's operation (setting its power level, initiating calls, terminating calls, and so forth).

Mobile Telephone Switching Office (MTSO)   All of the cellsites in a cellular system connect to a **mobile telephone switching office (MTSO)**, which connects cellular customers to one another and to wired telephone users.

The MTSO also controls what happens at each of the cellsites. It determines what to do when people move from one cell to another, including deciding which cellsite should handle the transmission when the caller wishes to place a call.[3]

---

[3] Several cellsites may hear the initial request at different loudness levels; if so, the MTSO selects a service cellsite based on signal strength, not physical distance.

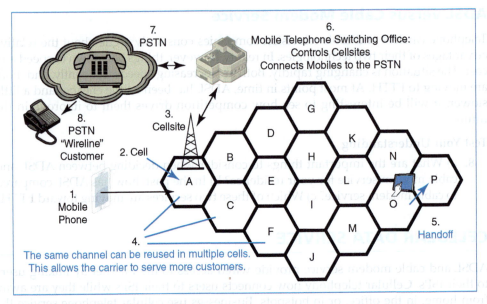

FIGURE 10-8 Cellular Telephone Service

Cellsite Figure 10-9 shows a typical small cellsite on top of a residential building. The three large "paddles" are cellular antennas.

Handoffs If a subscriber moves from one cell to another within a city, the MTSO will implement a **handoff** from one cellsite to another. For instance, Figure 10-8 shows a handoff from Cell O to Cell P. The mobile phone will change its

FIGURE 10-9 Cellsite with Paddle Antennas

sending and receiving channels during the handoff, but this occurs too rapidly for users to notice.[4]

Test Your Understanding

9. a) In cellular technology, what is a cell? b) What is a cellsite? c) What are the two functions of the MTSO? d) In cellular system, distinguish between handoffs and roaming.

Why Cells?

Why not use just one central transmitter/receiver in the middle of a metropolitan area? Early pre-cellular radio telephone systems did use a single antenna, and this was much cheaper than using multiple cellsites.

The answer is **channel reuse**. The number of channels permitted by regulators is limited, and subscriber demand is heavy. Cellular telephony uses each channel multiple times, in different cells in the network. This multiplies the effective channel capacity, allowing more subscribers to be served with the limited number of channels available.[5]

Test Your Understanding

10. a) Why does cellular telephony use cells? b) What is the benefit of channel reuse?

Cellular Data Speeds

Cellular data speeds have increased steadily since about 2000, when speeds jumped from about 20 kbps to a few hundred kilobits per second. Today, most carriers deliver peak downstream speeds of up to 5 to 10 Mbps, and the best carriers provide 15 to 20 Mbps. On the horizon is 100 Mbps. Nearly all carriers today follow the **LTE** (long-term evolution) standard. The **LTE Advanced** standard that most carriers are planning to implement next currently defines a peak downstream speed of 3 Gbps and a peak upstream speed of half that amount.[6]

Although speeds will continue to increase, making new applications attractive and older applications better, price is becoming a barrier to using high speeds. Many residential consumers have found to their shock that downloading a few high-definition movies can put them over the monthly maximums in their contracts. Companies too have to balance high speeds with high bills.

We did not talk about the difference between 3G and 4G because "G" has become meaningless. The International Telecommunications Union defined 4G service as

---

[4] In contrast, if a subscriber leaves a metropolitan cellular system and goes to another city or country, this is roaming. To confuse matters, many carriers only call going to another city roaming if the home carrier does not offer service there.

[5] In a sense, enterprise wireless LANs with many access points are like cellular technologies. They allow users to employ the limited number of frequencies available in WLANs many times within a building.

[6] The 3G Partnership Project (3GPP) defines the LTE and LTE Advanced standards. The Partnership frequently adds new "user equipment" categories that permit higher speeds. The "maximum" LTE or LTE Advanced is a constantly moving target.

Speeds

Early cellular systems were limited to about 20 kbps

Today, most carriers give peak download speeds of 5 to 10 Mbps with the best giving 15 to 20 Mbps

100 Mbps is on the horizon

Nearly all carriers now use LTE (long-term evolution) technology

LTE Advanced

The next generation of LTE

Currently, speeds are required to be 3 Gbps downstream, half of that upstream

3G, 4G, and 5G

The ITU creates definitions of generations

Marketers are using the terms in a meaningless manner

Throughput Differs Widely from Rated Speeds

There is extensive overhead in cellular transmission. The data transmission rate is always less than the bit transmission rate.

If the user is riding in a car, throughput will fall.

If more customers use a cellsite, the cellsite may have to decrease the transmission speed to each.

In particular, speed will depend on the time of day.

If the user travels into an area with an overloaded cellsite, speed will be lower.

At greater distances from a cellsite, speed falls, just as in Wi-Fi.

Weakened signal strength caused by transmission through buildings will also reduce speed.

FIGURE 10-10 Cellular Data Speeds (Study Figure)

having a downstream speed of at least one gigabit per second for stationary or walking customers and 100 Mbps for customers in cars or trains. No current offering meets the ITU's 4G standards, but carriers are marketing their systems as 4G and even 5G. It is actual speed that matters.

One problem in evaluating the speeds of different cellular carriers is that throughput is always considerably lower than advertised speed and varies widely within a system. There are several reasons for this.

- There is extensive overhead in cellular transmission. The data transmission rate is always less than the bit transmission rate.
- If the user is riding in a car, throughput will fall.
- If more customers use a cellsite, the cellsite may have to decrease the transmission speed to each. In particular, speed will depend on time of day.
- If the user travels into an area with an overloaded cellsite, speed will be lower.
- At greater distances from a cellsite, speed falls, just as in Wi-Fi.
- Weakened signal strength caused by transmission through buildings will also reduce speed.

Test Your Understanding

11. a) How fast can the best systems today download data? b) What speed is on the horizon? c) What is today's dominant cellular technology? d) What speed does the LTE Advanced standard currently require? e) Why does the book not distinguish between 3G and 4G service? f) What factors affect what throughput an individual user will receive?

WIRED BUSINESS WANs

To communicate with customers and for access to remote employees, companies use the Internet. However, they still need to use carrier WANs to reach the Internet and to connect their sites to one another. Figure 10-11 illustrates this situation.

Leased Lines

To connect to the Internet, Figure 10-11 shows that companies typically use leased lines from a carrier, most commonly the local telephone company. **Leased lines** are fast, point-to-point, always-on connections. As the name suggests, if a company wishes to use a leased line, it must sign a lease for a specified duration. Specifying the wrong speed when a leased line is ordered creates a persistent problem.

Figure 10-12 shows that a leased line is really a complex transmission path between the two points it connects. This path passes through customer access lines at the two ends and trunk lines between carrier switches along the path. To the user, however, the access line seems to be a simple data pipe all their own.

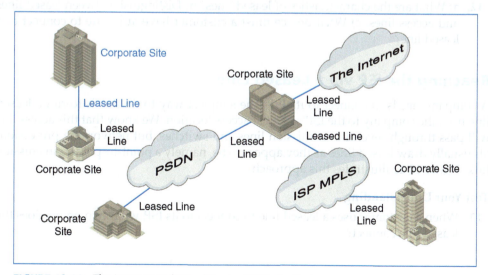

FIGURE 10-11   The Internet and Wired Carrier WANs for Business

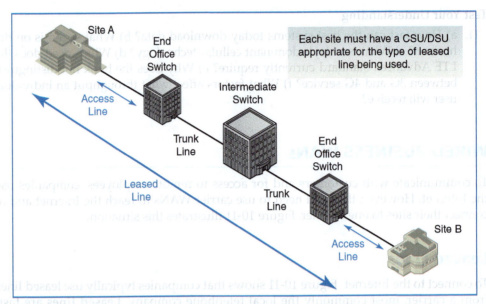

FIGURE 10-12   Leased Line, Trunk Lines, and Access Lines

To use a leased line, a company needs a piece of customer premises equipment called a **CSU/DSU**.[7] The purpose of this device is to translate the physical layer signals of network devices on the customer premises into physical layer signals in a format that leased lines require.

Test Your Understanding

12. a) What are the characteristics of leased lines? b) Distinguish between leased lines and access lines. c) What device must a customer have at its site to connect to a leased line?

Reaching the ISP via a Leased Line

A company needs to connect to its ISP. The simplest way to do this is to run a leased line from the company to the ISP's nearest access location. We know that this access line will pass through several transmission lines and switches, but networking professionals usually draw leased lines as they appear to be, namely a point-to-point transmission link. Figure 10-11 illustrates this approach.

Test Your Understanding

13. When a customer uses a leased line to connect to its ISP, what two points does the leased line connect?

---

[7] Channel Service Unit/Data Service Unit. Not very informative.

Leased Line Private Corporate WANs

Companies need to communicate with their ISPs. If they have multiple sites, they also need to connect these sites into a coherent network for internal communication. Figure 10-13 shows that they can do this by building a leased line network that will create a private internal WAN. Site routers route packets among the sites.

Figure 10-14 shows that leased line speeds vary widely. Under 50 Mbps, leased line speed standards were set regionally. The United States and Canada use the North American Digital Hierarchy Standard. Europe uses the CEPT Hierarchy. Other countries may use different standards. Fortunately, it is possible to translate between different leased line hierarchies, but the diversity of standards does cause minor problems.

Above 50 Mbps, carriers have standardized on a single standard that is called Synchronous Optical Network (SONET)[8] or Synchronous Digital Hierarchy (SDH). SONET and SDH use different naming conventions for their lines. For example, SONET labels its lines with OC (optical carrier) numbers, while SDH uses STM (synchronous transport module) designations. Other than naming differences, their services are identical and compatible.[9]

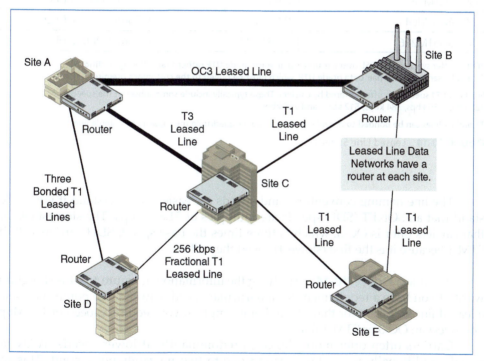

FIGURE 10-13   Leased Line Private Corporate WAN

---

[8] SONET is the terminology used in the United States and Canada. The rest of the world uses the SDH nomenclature.

[9] Apart from a few unimportant differences.

North American Digital Hierarchy		
Line	Speed	Typical Transmission Medium
T1*	1.544 Mbps	2-Pair Data-Grade UTP
T3	44.736 Mbps	Carrier Optical Fiber
CEPT Hierarchy		
Line	Speed	Typical Transmission Medium
E1*	2.048 Mbps	2-Pair Data-Grade UTP
E3	34.368 Mbps	Carrier Optical Fiber
SONET/SDH Speeds		
Line	Speed (Mbps)	Typical Transmission Medium
OC3/STM1	155.52	Carrier Optical Fiber
OC12/STM4	622.08	Carrier Optical Fiber
OC48/STM16	2,488.32	Carrier Optical Fiber
OC192/STM64	9,953.28	Carrier Optical Fiber
OC768/STM256	39,813.12	Carrier Optical Fiber

*Often offer synchronous DSL over existing 1-pair voice grade UTP rather than offering traditional T1 and E1 service over 2-pair data grade UTP, which must be pulled to the customer's premises.

Fractional T1 speeds are often offered by carriers. These typically include some subset of the speeds 128 kbps, 256 kbps, 384 kbps, 512 kbps, and 768 kbps.

T1 and E1 lines can be bonded to provide double, triple, or quadruple the capacity of a single line.

FIGURE 10-14 Leased Line Speeds

The line naming conventions and speeds are easier to understand if you understand that all SONET/SDH speeds are multiples of 51.84 Mbps. The slowest OC line that carriers offer is OC-3, which is three times the base speed. SDH carriers call this STM-1 because it is the first (slowest) speed they offer.

Applying Figure 10-14 Applying the information in Figure 10-14 is straightforward. If you have a requirement for a particular speed between two points, you select a leased line sufficient for that speed. For example, if you require a speed of 100 Mbps, you select an OC-3 or STM-1 line.

Carriers often offer more choices, predominantly at lower speeds. WAN line speeds traditionally were slow, around one to two megabits per second. This was roughly T1/E1 speed. Given frequent demand for a fraction of a T1 or E1 line, carriers typically offer fractional T1/E1 speeds for a fraction of the cost of a full T1/E1 line. If you need 200 kbps, you could get a fractional T1 line running at 256 kbps, which is 16.5% of a T1 line. As you might suspect, carriers will charge more than 16.5% of what they charge for a full T1 line.

Carriers also allow a customer to bond two or more T1/E1 lines together between a pair of sites. For example, if you need 2.8 Mbps between a pair of sites, you might bond two T1 or E1 lines.

Traditionally, T1/E1 leased lines required running a new 2-pair data grade UTP line to the customer's premises. This is expensive. In addition, the telephone system already runs 1-pair voice grade UTP to all premises, including business premises. We saw earlier in this chapter that carriers run digital subscriber line (ADSL) services over these lines. We also saw that ADSL today is much faster than T1/E1 speeds. Consequently, many carriers who offer "T1" and "E1" lines today are really offering DSL service over 1-pair VG UTP.

However, carriers do not offer asymmetric DSL service because businesses need symmetric speed—the same speed in both directions. Consequently, carriers offer **synchronous DSL** services to businesses. Businesses also require QoS guarantees, so these synchronous DSL lines come with service level agreements. SLAs mean that the DSL services offered to businesses are more expensive per bit transmitted than residential ADSL service.

Managing the WAN   Leased line corporate WANs do not design and operate themselves. A company that uses leased line networks to connect its sites faces substantial labor and customer premises equipment costs.

Test Your Understanding

14. a) If you need a speed of 1.2 Mbps between two points in the United States, what leased line would you specify in the United States and in Europe? b) Repeat for 160 Mbps. c) Repeat for 3 Mbps. d) Why do carriers offer low-speed "leased lines" that are really DSL lines? e) How do business DSL lines differ from residential DSL lines? f) Why is the need to manage the leased line network an issue?

Public Switched Data Network (PSDN) Carrier WANs

As packet switching matured in the 1970s, carriers began to create **public switched data networks (PSDNs)** that absorbed most of the corporate burden of managing WAN connections. As Figure 10-15 shows, the customer only needs to run a leased line from each of its corporate sites to the PSDN's nearest **point of presence (POP)**. The PSDN is shown as a cloud to signify that the PSDN handles all switching and forwarding tasks without concerning customers about the details.

The customer only needs to run a leased line from each of its corporate sites to the PSDN's nearest point of presence (POP).

Carriers have economies of scale in management costs because they manage the PSDN services of many customers. Consequently, PSDNs usually are cheaper than deploying a network of leased lines to link corporate sites together.

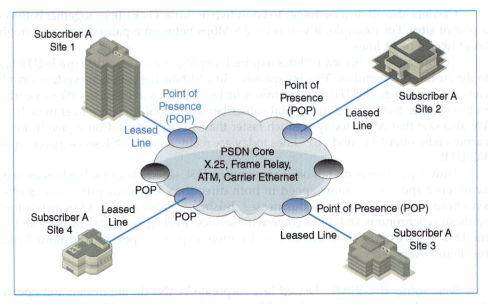

FIGURE 10-15 Public Switched Data Network (PSDN)

Due to economies of scale, PSDNs usually are cheaper than deploying a network of leased lines to link corporate sites together.

Historical PSDN Technologies PSDNs are switched, which means that they operate at Layer 2, the data link layer. (This is why one PSDN technology is called *Frame Relay*.) There have been several PSDN technologies to date.

- The first, **X.25**, emerged in the 1980s but never grew large. It was too expensive for what it provided.
- Things changed in the 1990s, when **Frame Relay** began to grow rapidly. Around the turn of the century, Frame Relay and leased line data networks each accounted for about 40% of WAN traffic. However, part of this growth was due to aggressive Frame Relay pricing, which resulted in poor profit margins. Around 2000, carriers began raising their Frame Relay prices, and market share dropped considerably.
- Another PSDN technology, **ATM**,[10] was created to replace the core of the public switched telephone network and has to a considerable extent done so. It offers very high speeds and many expected it to replace Frame Relay as WAN speeds increased. However, ATM was expensive and never grew as expected. As one pundit said, "ATM is the wave of the future and always will be."

---

[10] Asynchronous Transfer Mode. This is not very illuminating, so the acronym is rarely spelled out.

Carrier Ethernet (CE)   In the 1980s, there were several competing LAN technologies. However, Ethernet became the only survivor thanks to its low-cost switch operation and its ability to grow to ever faster speeds. One reason why carriers raised the price of Frame Relay dramatically in the early 2000s was that they wanted to move customers to either MPLS IP networks, which we will see a little later in this chapter, or to **carrier Ethernet (CE)**. As the name applies, this is Ethernet for WAN service offered by carriers. Carrier Ethernet was originally limited to metropolitan area network, so it was originally called *metro Ethernet*. However, when Ethernet began to span distances beyond metropolitan area networks, MEF (formerly called the Metropolitan Ethernet Forum) which standardizes Ethernet services in WANs, changed the name to carrier Ethernet.[11]

Although CE is relatively new, it is growing rapidly—the only PSDN technology to be doing so. Many carriers have told their customers that Frame Relay service will soon be discontinued, and this is accelerating carrier Ethernet's growth even faster.

MEF has standardized eight Carrier Ethernet services. Figure 10-16 shows the two that have dominated so far.

- **E-LINE** service is a site-to-site service. It competes directly with leased lines but offers other benefits.
- **E-LAN** service essentially extends the LAN to the wide area. Sites can use Ethernet to communicate back and forth as if the Carrier Ethernet PSDN was simply a set of trunk lines between switches.

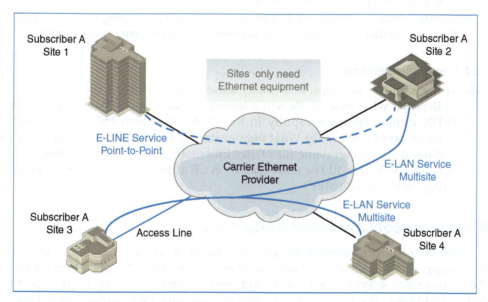

FIGURE 10-16   Carrier Ethernet Services

---

[11] MEF has long worked closely with the 802.3 Working Group. Knowing that carrier Ethernet would run over SONET/SDH lines, 802.3 developed two standards for its fastest speeds. For instance, short-reach versions of 10 Gbps were designed for LANs and operate at exactly 10 Gbps. In turn, long-reach versions of 10 Gbps Ethernet operate at 9,953 Gbps to run over OC192/STM64 lines. The 802.3 Working Group has defined a number of standards specifically designed for transmitting Ethernet over the local loop, including both carrier optical fiber and 1-pair voice-grade UTP.

> Low cost and familiarity of the technology to the firm's networking staff
>
> High speeds are available
>
> Speed agility: Increases in speed can be provisioned rapidly
>
> Quality of service
>
> Security

FIGURE 10-17   Carrier Ethernet Attractions (Study Figure)

Carrier Ethernet has a number of attractions.

- *Cost.* Using Ethernet's familiar low-cost MAC layer functionality, CE is inexpensive. In addition, sites only have to plug carrier termination equipment into an Ethernet switch port. There is no need to learn a new technology.
- *Speed.* Companies that need fast connections can get 100 Mbps, 1 Gbps, or 10 Gbps at attractive cost.
- *Speed Agility.* If companies need extra capacity for a limited period of time, such as a year-end crunch, CE carriers can usually reprovision their services quickly.
- *Quality of Service.* CE carriers can offer quality of service guarantees for speed, availability, frame delay, frame jitter, and frame loss.
- *Security.* Although Carrier Ethernet does not include cryptographic protections, the traffic of different customers is kept separate to prevent eavesdropping.

Test Your Understanding

15. a) If a firm has ten sites, how many leased lines will it need to use a PSDN? b) Between what two points will a leased line run for PSDN access? c) Which PSDN technology grew rapidly in the 1990s? d) Which PSDN technology is growing rapidly today? e) What organization is standardizing carrier Ethernet? f) What is the former name for carrier Ethernet? g) Distinguish between E-Line and E-LAN service. h) For what reasons is CE attractive? i) Is the 802.3 Working Group working with MEF?

Multiprotocol Label Switching (MPLS)

Making Routing More Efficient   In Chapter 8, we saw that routers look at an incoming packet's destination IP address. They compare that IP address to every row in the routing table, select the best match, and send the packet back out a certain port to a certain IP address. The next packet to arrive gets the same treatment—even if it goes to the same IP address.

Many routers can do decision caching, in which they remember their decisions for certain IP address ranges. We saw that this is dangerous. Fortunately, there is a more robust way to avoid having to look at all rows for all packets. This is **Multiprotocol Label Switching (MPLS)**, which Figure 10-18 illustrates.

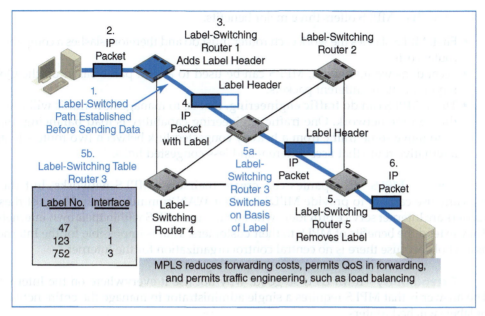

FIGURE 10-18 Multiprotocol Label Switching (MPLS)

Operation When two hosts start to converse, an MPLS network first determines the best path for the packets. This is the **label switched path**. Routers will send all packets along this path rather than making traditional routing decisions for each packet at each router.

As Figure 10-18 shows, after the label switched path is established, the source host transmits packets normally. The first router is a **label switching router**. It inserts a 32-bit **label header** in front of the IP header and after the frame header. The IP packet syntax and the frame syntax are unchanged.

The label header's **label number** identifies the label switched path selected for this conversation. The first label switched router and all others along the label switched path have MPLS look-up tables. These tables allow routers to look up the label number, read the corresponding interface, and send the packet out the indicated interface. For example, if the label number is 47, the router in Figure 10-18 will send it out Interface 1. Table lookups are fast because only one row will match the destination IP address. There is no need to look at all routing table rows to select the best interface to send a packet back out. The hard work was done when the label switched path was created. The last label switching router removes the label. Note that neither the source host nor the destination host knows that label switching was done. MPLS operation is transparent to hosts.

Often, all traffic between two sites is assigned a single label number. Or, traffic between two sites might receive one of a handful of label numbers. Different label numbers might correspond to label switched paths with different quality of service characteristics.

Benefits   MPLS offers three major benefits.

- First, MPLS slashes the work each router must do and therefore slashes a company's router costs.
- Second, as we just noted, MPLS can be used to assign paths based on the QoS requirements of different packets.
- Third, MPLS can do **traffic engineering**, that is, to manage how traffic will travel through the network. One traffic engineering capability is **load balancing**, that is, to move some traffic from a heavily congested link between two routers to an alternative route that uses different and less-congested links.

Carrier MPLS   Companies can create their own MPLS networks, but they typically use carriers to provide MPLS for their WAN communication. Many of these carriers are Internet service providers who already use MPLS within their own internets. They extend the benefits of MPLS to their customers. That is impossible for the Internet as a whole because there is no central control organization for the Internet.

Extendibility   If MPLS is so good, why not use it everywhere on the Internet? The answer is that MPLS requires a single administrator to manage the entire network of label switched routers.

Test Your Understanding

16. a) In MPLS, is selecting the best interface for each packet at each router done when the packet enters the network or before? b) Why is this beneficial? c) What is the name of the path selected for a particular conversation? d) When a source host first transmits to a destination host after a label switched path is established, what will happen? e) Do label switching routers along the MPLS path look at the packet's IP address? The answer is not explicitly in the text. Explain your reasoning. f) On what basis does each label switched router base routing decisions? g) Why is MPLS transparent to the source and destination hosts? h) What are MPLS's attractions? i) What is traffic engineering? j) Can MPLS provide traffic load balancing? k) Is it possible to implement MPLS across the entire Internet? Explain.

WAN Optimization

Given the high cost of long-distance transmissions, companies need to squeeze out every bit of performance improvement they can find for data over WANs. Figure 10-19 shows that one approach is to install **WAN optimization devices** at each end of important shared lines between sites.

Compression   The most important action that the WAN optimization devices take is to compress all data being transmitted into the line and decompress the data at the other end. **Compression** is possible because almost all data contains redundancy that can be reduced through encoding. For movies and voice, compression can be substantial. For word processing documents and spreadsheets, compression will be less effective. In the figure, the WAN optimization devices can provide an average of 10:1 compression. Source A is transmitting at 3 Gbps, and Source B is transmitting at

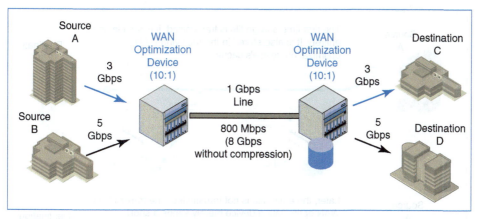

FIGURE 10-19 WAN Optimization: Compression

5 Gbps. This is a total of 8 Gbps arriving at the WAN optimization device. However, with 10:1 compression, the transmission line only has to carry 0.8 Gbps. This will fit in a 1 Gbps transmission line. Without compression, the company would need a much more expensive 10 Gbps transmission line.

Caching Another way to reduce the number of bits flowing through the transmission line is **caching**. (See Figure 10-20.) Suppose the company produces a large annual report. The server holding the report is in Source A. The annual report is likely to be transmitted multiple times from Source A to recipients in Source C and Source D. With a WAN optimization device that has caching, when the annual report is first delivered, it is copied onto the receiving WAN optimization device's disk **cache**. Later, when the annual report is to be transmitted again, the WAN optimization device near Source A and Source B will not transmit the entire file. Instead, it will send a brief message to the WAN optimization device near Source C and Source D. This message asks the WAN optimization device on the right to retrieve the annual report from the cache and send it to the receiver. Avoiding the retransmission of frequently transmitted files can reduce traffic considerably.

Traffic Shaping In many cases, unfavored applications take up too much capacity. Unfavored applications may include YouTube, Netflix, and BitTorrent for file sharing. Some WAN optimization devices do **traffic shaping**. (See Figure 10-21.) When undesired traffic reaches an optimization device, the device may simply prohibit it. The device can also take a less drastic action—limiting the application to a small percentage of the total traffic. Both can dramatically reduce overall traffic, allowing the firm to avoid upgrading its transmission lines.

Application and Network Protocol Acceleration (Tuning) Many applications and network protocols are somewhat inefficient when they transmit over long-distance lines. TCP, for example, tends to have conservative transmission

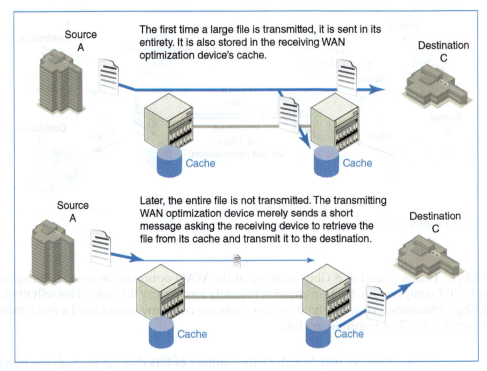

The first time a large file is transmitted, it is sent in its entirety. It is also stored in the receiving WAN optimization device's cache.

Later, the entire file is not transmitted. The transmitting WAN optimization device merely sends a short message asking the receiving device to retrieve the file from its cache and transmit it to the destination.

FIGURE 10-20   WAN Optimization: Caching

defaults that slow transmission. It may be possible to tune TCP by adjusting such things spent waiting for acknowledgments. To give another example, when a WAN optimization device receives a TCP SYN segment, it may send back an ACK even before it passes the segment on to its intended host. Application and network acceleration is a family of tactics the WAN optimization devices can use to reduce *latency*,

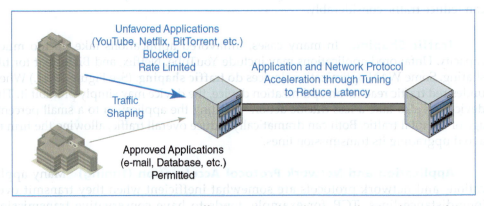

FIGURE 10-21   WAN Optimization: Traffic Shaping and Application and Network Protocol Acceleration

which tends to be a problem when signals must travel long distances. Although tuning can take place on hosts, WAN optimization devices provide a central point for tuning and tuning tools.

Application and network acceleration is a family of tactics the WAN optimization devices can use to reduce latency, which tends to be a problem when signals must travel long distances.

Test Your Understanding

17. a) Where are WAN optimization devices found? b) List the four mechanisms we discussed for optimizing transmission over a transmission link. c) How does compression reduce traffic? d) How does caching reduce traffic? e) Explain traffic shaping. f) How does traffic shaping reduce traffic? g) What is the main benefit of application and network protocol acceleration?

SOFTWARE DEFINED NETWORKING (SDN)

Having covered both LANs and WANs, we have finished looking at the transmission parts of networking. Although we still need to look at applications, this is a good time to cover an overall aspect of data transmission. This is **software defined networking (SDN)**, which may permit a vast expansion in our ability to manage entire corporate networks. The word "may" is key. The future of SDN is uncertain, but its potential importance makes it critical to cover.

Concepts and Benefits

Figure 10-22 shows SDN in more detail. It shows that software defined networking has three layers—individual switches and routers, the SDN controller, and SDN applications.

We saw in Chapter 4 that switches and routers traditionally both did forwarding and handled control—managing the rules for deciding how to forward specific frames or packets. **Control** involves routing protocols for exchanging routing table information in routers, Ethernet switch administrative frames for the Rapid Spanning Tree Protocol and other matters, and other administrative chores beyond the forwarding of each message as it arrives.

Placing the control function in individual routers allowed the Internet to scale because one can simply add more routers and be confident that they will participate fairly effectively. The same occurs in switched networks. However, each switch and router needs to be configured separately when it is installed. More importantly, it becomes almost impossible to make radical changes in the operation of an Ethernet network or a corporate internet. Administrators have to configure most or all individual devices to make such radical changes.

The limitations of traditional switching and routing first became serious when large data centers began to add virtual machines. VMs appear suddenly and many last only minutes or hours. A multitenant data center must do **traffic segregation** so that

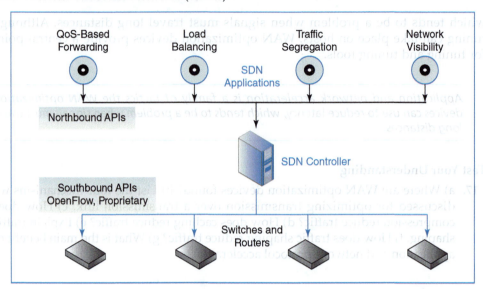

FIGURE 10-22 Software Defined Networking (SDN)

customers cannot reach the VMs of other customers. This and other changes required by growing data center size and an increasing pace of change led to constant router reconfiguration.

In SDN, switches and routers still do the forwarding function as usual. However, an SDN controller decides how switching and routing should be done, then pushes appropriate forwarding table changes out to individual switches and routers. This separation of traditional functionality brings several crucial benefits.

- *Agility*. Changes in forwarding patterns can be made rapidly. When a new VM appears, the information can be added immediately to its aggregation group for processing on all switches and routers. If a firm needs additional bandwidth between its servers and backup facilities overnight, to give another example, it can do so easily although many switches and routers may be involved.
- *Lower OpEx Cost through Automation*. **OpEx** is operating cost. It is primarily labor. By avoiding constant reconfiguration at many devices, SDN can dramatically trim labor costs. This is especially true because SDN controllers are programmable, meaning that many repetitive tasks can be automated.
- *Lower CapEx Cost*. **CapEx** is capital expense. Switches and routers are pricey because of their need to be able to perform control functions. Companies using SDN may be able to buy lower-cost "dumb" switches and routers, although switch and router vendors are trying to make this difficult.
- *Radical Changes*. If a company wishes to drastically change the way it does forwarding or routing or wishes to experiment with a new routing protocol or switch supervisory protocol, the firm can do this for a subset of its forwarding devices to experiment and then roll out innovations. Individual forwarding devices can even run traditional modes of operation for some traffic and new modes of operation for other traffic.

Test Your Understanding

18. a) What are the three layers in SDN? b) Distinguish between forwarding and control. c) Traditionally, where have these functions been located? d) How does this change in SDN? e) What pressing management issues does SDN address? f) Why did SDN begin in large data centers? g) What is the ability to change forwarding tables rapidly called? h) How can SDN reduce OpEx? i) How can it reduce CapEx? j) How can it facilitate radical changes in the network's operation?

Forwarding Tables

We saw Ethernet forwarding tables in Chapter 5 and router forwarding tables in Chapter 8. Actually, forwarding table rules can be considerably more intricate, as Figure 10-23 shows. Each row is a rule. **Forwarding rules** can use considerable information in a frame or packet.

Test Your Understanding

19. a) Was the information we presented about switching and routing tables in earlier chapters complete? b) From where does an SDN switch or SDN router get its forwarding table rules? c) Explain the rule in the first row. An Ethernet VLAN is used to segregate hosts. Hosts in a VLAN can only communicate with hosts on the same VLAN. d) Explain the rule in the second row. e) On what device is the forwarding table—a controller, switch, or router?

SDN Applications

SDN allows controllers to manage many aspects of forwarding on switches and routers. However, these abilities do not come pre-baked in controllers. Each requires the creation or purchase of an SDN application to do a particular thing. The real future of

Row	IP Src Addr	IP Dest Addr	TCP Dest Port	Ethernet Priority	IP Class Number	Action
1	External	128.3.2.8	443	7	Any	Pass with Priority
2	External	128.3.2.8	443	Any	17	Pass Apply Class Rule 17
3	External	128.3.2.8	443	Any	Any	Drop
4	Not Finance	Finance	Any	Any	Any	Drop Log
5	Internal	128.7.65.123	443	Any	Any	Authenticate
6	Internal	External	80	Any	Any	Drop
7	Internal	External	443	Any	Any	Pass
8	Any	Honeypot	Any	Any	Any	Pass Alarm

Note: All, Internal, External, Finance, and Honeypot are ranges of IP addresses.

FIGURE 10-23   Forwarding Table Rules

SDN rests on whether firms and vendors will build the applications that organizations need to administer their networks. Here are four important SDN applications (there are countless more):

- *Quality of Service Applications.* Most obviously, SDN can specify QoS-dependent message forwarding. SDN applications can add new QoS methods.
- *Load Balancing Applications.* When individual routers make routing decisions, they sometimes overload some paths while leaving others only slightly filled. **Load balancing** applications even out traffic on different paths.
- *Traffic Segregation Applications.* For security and other reasons, the traffic flows of different user groups or applications often need to be segregated from one another. Ethernet does this with virtual LANs (VLANs). SDN controllers can use VLAN IDs within Ethernet frames to do this, or they can use more sophisticated and robust methods.
- *Network Visibility.* Communication between the controller and the devices they control takes place in both directions. SDN applications can collect detailed data on forwarding device statistics. They can present this information in coherent form to network administrators.

Test Your Understanding

20. a) What good is a controller without SDN applications? b) List the four application categories listed in the text.

Application Program Interfaces (APIs)

Communication between SDN applications and SDN controllers must be standardized to allow competition among vendors. Communication between controllers and forwarding devices also needs standards. Standards are implemented through **application program interfaces (APIs)**. Each API exposes a function or set of functions to commands from the next higher layer. Figure 10-22 shows that it is common to call SDN APIs between applications and controllers **northbound APIs**. APIs between the controller and forwarding devices are **southbound APIs**.

Standards are implemented through **application program interfaces (APIs)**. *Each API exposes a function or set of functions to commands from the next higher layer.*

For southbound APIs, the **OpenFlow** standards are becoming popular. With OpenFlow, there is theoretically no need to purchase expensive switches and routers. For example, Google uses OpenFlow in its data centers. It built its own "dumb" routers with no internal control mechanisms. This permitted Google to reduce its CapEx considerably.

Naturally, switch and router vendors are disquieted by the prospect of their boxes being turned into low-cost commodities. To address this worry, they are adopting OpenFlow but are also offering their own southbound **proprietary APIs**. In many cases, these functions already existed in the forwarding device. Vendors hope that their proprietary APIs will be more fully featured and therefore more attractive to customers. Some, like Hewlett Packard, even have their own SDN app stores.

Test Your Understanding

21. a) What is an API? b) For SDN, distinguish between northbound and southbound APIs. c) What is OpenFlow, and why is it significant? d) Is OpenFlow a northbound or southbound API? e) What threat does OpenFlow create for switch and router vendors? f) How are vendors responding?

CONCLUSION

Synopsis

In Chapters 5, 6, and 7, we looked at local area networks. The technology picture was simple. Ethernet dominates wired LANs, and 802.11 dominates wireless LANs. In wide area networks, which take transmission beyond the customer premises, the situation is anything but simple. Most corporations have multiple WAN technologies that must work in an integrated way. In this chapter, we stepped through these technologies.

LANs and WANs also differ economically. LAN distances are short, so the cost per bit transmitted is low. In WAN transmission, however, the cost per bit transmitted is comparatively high, so companies need to be more frugal, living with lower transmission speeds and optimizing technology carefully. Metropolitan Area Networks (MANs) are intermediate in cost and speed. Overall, LAN and WAN managers must have different mind-sets. In this chapter, you learned to think like a WAN manager.

The Internet connects nearly everybody. However, it offers no performance guarantees or inherent security. Carrier WAN services, in turn, can offer QoS guarantees and enhanced security, but only companies who use the same carrier WAN service can communicate over carrier WAN technology. WANs are used primarily for connecting sites in the same corporation and connecting an organization to the Internet.

In this chapter, we looked at the main elements of wide area networks. These are the network core and the access link that connects the customer premises to the network core. In many cases, carriers use transmission lines from the public switched telephone network. Customers need customer premises equipment to connect to carrier WANs. For leased lines, the CPE is a CSU/DSU.

We looked first at wired residential Internet access, including ADSL from telephone companies and cable modem service from cable television companies. We also looked at cellular data transmission, which is increasing rapidly in speed.

Companies use the Internet to communicate with their customers. They also use a variety of wired networks to connect them to the Internet and to connect their sites together. These include Layer 1 networks of leased lines, Layer 2 public switched data networks, and Layer 3 MPLS services from ISPs. Companies still use leased lines to connect them to PSDNs and MPLS services from ISPs. Leased lines come in a wide range of speeds. To reduce costs, companies often apply WAN optimization devices at the two ends of a transmission link. These devices can reduce data transmission requirements and reduce latency.

Software defined network (SDN) may revolutionize the way in which we manage our networks. Controllers will allow us to centralize the control function that tells individual switches and routers how to forward arriving frames and packets. This will allow us to make changes rapidly in the way our networks operate, and it may lead to far cheaper switches and routers. The future of SDN depends heavily on how smart developers are at building SDN applications to implement control functions intelligently.

END-OF-CHAPTER QUESTIONS

Thought Questions

10-1. Distinguish between dial-up telephone service you use as a consumer and leased line services used in business. (You will have to extrapolate from your own experience with dial-up lines.)

10-2. If you have a network of leased lines, you have options for how many sites you connect. Sites can communicate directly or through intermediate sites. a) In a full mesh, every pair of sites will be directly linked by a leased line. If there are N sites, there will be $N*(N-1)/2$ connections. In Figure 10-13, how many leased lines would be used in a full mesh? b) In a hub-and-spoke network, there is a central site, and a leased line radiates from it to each other site. In Figure 10-13, how many leased lines would be used in a hub-and-spoke network with the hub located at Site A? c) What is the benefit of full mesh networks over hub-and-spoke networks?

d) What is the advantage of hub-and-spoke networks over full mesh networks? e) How would you use this information about advantages to advise a company about what to do when it installs a network of leased lines?

10-3. In ADSL service, there is a single UTP pair running from the end office switch to the individual household. In cable modem service, the thick coaxial cable in the neighborhood is shared by many subscribers. Yet typically, cable modem service provides faster service to individual customers than ADSL. How can this be? Hint: Draw a picture of the entire situation for both ADSL and cable modem service.

10-4. a) What wired WAN technologies are growing? b) Why will leased lines continue to be important even if networks of leased lines are no longer used?

Hands-On

10-5. If you have a smartphone, download an app to tell your data transmission throughput. What did you find?

Perspective Questions

10-6. What was the most surprising thing in this chapter for you?

10-7. What was the most difficult part of this chapter for you?

Chapter *11*

Networked Applications

LEARNING OBJECTIVES

By the end of this chapter, you should be able to:

- Describe the concept and importance of networked applications.
- Describe how taking over an application can give an attacker the ability to control the computer.
- Describe electronic mail standards and security.
- Describe voice over IP (VoIP) operation and standards.
- Describe the World Wide Web in terms of standards and explain how a webpage with text, graphics, and other elements is downloaded.
- Explain peer-to-peer (P2P) computing including BitTorrent, Skype, SETI@home, and the Tor network.

GhostNet

After the Dali Lama fled Tibet in 1959, he set up a government in exile. Today it is located in Dharamsala, India. It is called the Office of His Holiness the Dalai Lama (OHHDL). In 2008, the staff suspected it was under cyberattacks when it sent an invitation to a certain person. Immediately afterward, this person reported that he received a call from a Chinese government official who discouraged him from accepting the invitation. In addition, a woman working for a group making Internet contacts between Tibetan exiles and Chinese citizens was stopped by Chinese intelligence officers on her way back to Tibet. She was shown transcripts of her online conversations and warned to stop her political activities. These incidents led to an investigation that began to dissect a sophisticated cyberattack. This investigation was conducted by researchers at Cambridge University.[1]

The investigation found that the attack began with a spear phishing campaign that sent a legitimate-sounding message designed to entice staff members to open an attachment. Figure 11-1 shows one of these messages. It appears to be completely legitimate. However, when the monk opened the attachment, a Trojan horse was dropped on the monk's computer. This was a remote access Trojan (RAT) that allowed the attackers to remotely control the computer. (One monk reported seeing Outlook open by itself and send a message.) The Trojan could also do video and audio surveillance from the client computer, using the computer's camera and audio capability. Analysis showed that the malware searched computers for sensitive files and did keystroke logging. Using a modified version of HTTP, the attackers exfiltrated these files to Sichuan, China, which is where the Chinese intelligence group had been tasked with monitoring the OHHDL.

Using stolen credentials, the attackers then installed malware on the hosted OHHDL mail server in California. The malware frequently replaced attachments in legitimate e-mail with a malicious attachment. This allowed more and more client computers to be compromised with Trojan horses. Analysis of the mail server logs indicated successful logins from ISPs in China. No logins from China could have been legitimate.

```
Subject: Kalon Tripa Succession
From:    "Pema Rinzin" <prinzintibet@yahoo.com>
Date:    Thu, September 18, 2008 8:14 am
To:      choejor@dalailama.com
-----------------------------------------------------------------------

Dear Sir,

Attached please find the final Tibetan translation of my English
announcement for the Kalon Tripa succession initiative. Response to my
press release on September 2nd has been very positive and I have been
receiving lots of email and phone messages from Tibetans everywhere.

I am trying to get someone to translate the Kalon Tripa Hochoe into
English, but if you already have it translated, please send it to me.

Any advice from you in this initiative of mine would be greatly appreciated.

Yours sincerely,

Pema Rinzin
President
TAC



Official Photographer/webmaster
Office of His Holiness the Dalai Lama
Thekchen Choeling
P/O Mcleod ganj 176219
Dharamsala (H.P.)
India
```

FIGURE 11-1 Spear Phishing E-Mail with an Attachment

[1] Shishir Nagaraja and Ross Anderson, *The Snooping Dragon: Social-Malware Surveillance of the Tibetan Movement*, Technical Report Number 746, University of Cambridge Computer Laboratory, 15 JJ Thomson Avenue, Cambridge CB3 0FD, United Kingdom, March 2009.

While this investigation by Cambridge University researchers was underway, researchers from the University of Toronto[2] were finding that the attack on OHHDL was not an isolated incident. The techniques used against the Dali Lama, they discovered, were the tools of a large network of attack servers and other sites that the researchers named GhostNet. They were able to identify 1,295 infected computers in 103 countries, with a concentration in Southeast Asia. Almost a third of the victim organizations were high-value diplomatic, political, economic, or military targets.

Attackers are increasingly working through application programs and social engineering to implement their cyberattacks. Operating system exploits have been increasingly difficult to use with success, so attackers have largely turned to using application programs.

Test Your Understanding

1. a) How did the attackers gain their initial foothold on client PCs? b) What could the Trojan RAT do? c) Once they extended their control to the e-mail server, what did they do to get users to install additional RATs? d) What protocol did the attackers use to exfiltrate the files they discovered? e) What types of organizations were the most frequent victims of GhostNet?

INTRODUCTION

Networked Applications

Applications that require networks to operate are called **networked applications**. The World Wide Web and e-mail are networked applications. So is the Salesforce franchise management application used by Papa Murphy's.

Application Architectures   In this chapter, we will focus on **application architectures**—that is, how application layer functions are spread among computers to deliver service to users.

- Early PCs used stand-alone operation in which all processing was done on the PC.
- Today, we have seen that client/server processing is dominant.
- We are now seeing the emergence of peer-to-peer (P2P) processing, in which user devices communicate directly, with little or no use of servers.

An application architecture describes how functions are spread among computers to deliver service to users.

Important Networked Applications   In addition to looking broadly at application architectures, we will look at some of the most important of today's networked applications, including e-mail, voice over IP, the World Wide Web, cloud computing, peer-to-peer (P2P) computing, and mobile applications.

---

[2] Ronald J. Deibert and Rafal A. Rohozinski, "Tracking 'GhostNet': Investigating a Cyber Espionage Network," Report JR02-2009, Munk Center for International Studies, University of Toronto, Toronto, Canada, March 2009.

Networked Applications

   Applications that require networks to operate

   World Wide Web, e-mail, etc.

Application Architectures

   How application layer functions are spread among computers to deliver service to users

   Stand-alone operation

   Client/server operation

   Peer-to-peer (P2P) operation

Important Networked Applications

   E-mail, voice over IP, the World Wide Web, cloud computing, peer-to-peer (P2P) computing, and mobile applications

Importance of the application layer to users

   The only layer whose functionality users see directly

   What happens at lower layers should simply happen

FIGURE 11-2 Basic Networked Application Concepts (Study Figure)

Importance of the Application Layer to Users   In this chapter, we will focus on the application layer. This is the only layer whose functionality users see directly. When users want e-mail, it is irrelevant what is happening below the application layer, unless there is a failure or performance problem at lower layers.

Test Your Understanding

2. a) What is a networked application? b) What is an application architecture? c) Why do users focus on the application layer?

The Evolution of Client Devices and Networking

Some years ago, the president of the Stanley Works told his Board of Directors, "Last year, we sold 4 million drill bits that nobody wanted." After pausing to let that provocative statement sink in, he went on to explain by saying, "What they wanted was holes." Drill bits and drills are expensive. They are merely tolerated, despite their expense and difficulty of use, because the customer needs holes. The message he was trying to emphasize is that drills are not the only ways to make holes. The company needed to focus on customer needs, not technology. Of course, although he was fundamentally correct, quite a few customers do like drills a lot. So technology can, to some extent, drive demand.

With networked applications, the same dynamic occurs. Obviously, applications must serve customer needs. However, as client devices and networks have evolved, each step in their evolution has brought new "killer apps" that were impossible before new devices and new networks appeared. Figure 11-3 shows important steps in the evolution of client devices.

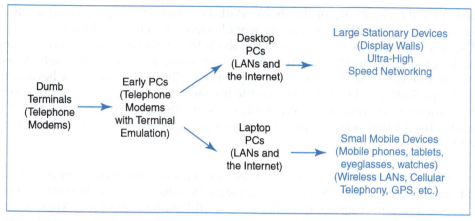

FIGURE 11-3 The Evolution of Client Devices and Networking

Dumb Terminals When computers were first built, the only way to interact with them was to throw binary switches, rewire boards, and place programs on punch cards into readers. Then, in the 1960s, remote terminals appeared. People could interact with computers via keyboards and printers (later keyboards and displays). This was before the days of microprocessors, so these devices were dumb terminals. They could merely send keystrokes to the large central computer and send characters from the central computer to the printer or display. Transmission used the telephone system. Dumb terminals were plugged into telephone modems, which sent their data over the telephone network. This limited speeds to around 10 kbps initially. At such low speed, the user interface on displays was very limited, consisted of monochrome text (plain text in a single color against a contrasting color background), which only required a few bytes to send per screen. In terms of application architecture, all processing had to be done on the large host computer.

Early PCs In the mid-1970s, the first personal computers appeared. Thanks to microprocessors, they were complete computers. These could be used by average employees in average companies and even homes. There was an explosion in new types of computer applications, including word processing, spreadsheet programs, graphics, and games. A few began to communicate to large computers by emulating (acting like) dumb terminals, but they were primarily stand-alone devices. They again used telephone modems, which again limited the user interface.

Desktop and Laptop PCs In the 1980s, a fundamental divide began between desktop PCs and laptop PCs. For desktop use, the key was processing power, massive amounts of storage, larger screens, and other performance-enhancing technologies. For laptop PCs, the keys were decreasing size and weight while gradually adding processing power. Both categories of PCs benefitted from the growth of local area networks in the 1990s.

In addition, while stand-alone applications were very popular, LANs created a new type of application architecture, client/server processing, which we have seen since the beginning of this book. With PCs growing in performance, client/server processing split the processing work between the client and the server. Before PCs, this was not possible. In the 1990s, the Internet caused client/server processing to grow explosively. All computers soon came with browsers, which were initially universal clients for webserver programs. Browsers soon grew beyond this single application to be clients for the file transfer protocol, e-mail, and many other applications. With tremendous economies of scale, the cost of using the Internet fell rapidly. In addition, telephone modem access quickly gave way to broadband access services.

Small Mobile Devices   The 21st century expanded the divide between desktop and smaller devices. New technology has allowed vendors to pack a substantial amount of processing power and battery life into small handheld products. These include tablets, smartphones, and new devices such as smart glasses and smart watches. Even laptops are becoming smaller, and they are getting touch screens as well.

Small device technology and wireless networking (including 802.11 WLANs, cellular telephony, and GPS) have combined to create a blizzard of new types of applications. Ever-growing transmission speeds have created rich applications impossible even on large desktop computers only a few years before.

Large Stationary Devices   Small mobile devices are dominating the news on client evolution. However, working on a small screen can be difficult. Many office workers already have desktop PCs with multiple displays, offering a great deal of "real estate" for laying out windows for multiple applications. In some cases, these are already touch screens.

In the future, tables, desks, and walls will themselves be displays and will all be linked together by ultra-high-speed networks. Presumably, these devices too will create a revolution in applications. If history has taught us anything, it is that when new computer and networking technologies are invented, we always see a flood of startling new applications.

Test Your Understanding

3. Create a table. The first column should list the client device (dumb terminal, PC, etc.). The second column should list the technical advance embodied in the client. The third should be networking advances associated with the client. The fourth and last should be new networked applications made possible by the client and networking.

4. What advance made the client/server application architecture possible?

Application Security

In the past, hackers focused primarily on vulnerabilities in the operating system in order to break into computers. Today, however, hackers primarily attack individual applications running on the computer.

The reason for this is shown in Figure 11-4. If a hacker can take over an application, then he or she receives all of the permissions that the operating system gave to the

If a hacker takes over a vulnerable application program, he or she receives the privileges of that program.

If the hacked program has root privileges, the attacker can do anything he or she wishes to do on the computer.

The hacker effectively "owns the box."

Hacked Vulnerable Application

Operating System

Hacker has the Hacked Program's Privileges on the Computer

Hardware

FIGURE 11-4 Application Hacking

application. Many applications run with **root privileges**, which means that they can do anything on the computer. Taking over such an application gives the hacker total control over the computer.

> *If a hacker can take over an application, then he or she receives all of the permissions that the operating system gave to the application.*

Finding a vulnerability in the operating system is increasingly difficult. However, with the many applications running on most computers, and with inconsistent security quality across applications, the probability of finding a vulnerable application on a computer is high. Security vulnerabilities in specific applications are listed in many hacker forums that are readily available to attackers.

We are now seeing an explosion in apps created for mobile devices. In addition, we are seeing diversity in mobile operating systems. The newness of mobile operating systems and mobile applications has led many inexperienced developers to create applications with severe vulnerabilities. Coupled with a lack of corporate control over mobile devices, this lack of experience has created a flood of application (and operating system) vulnerabilities.

Test Your Understanding

5. a) Why are hackers now focusing on taking over applications? b) What can hackers do if they take over an application with root privileges? c) Why is the explosion of applications and small mobile devices a particular concern?

Cross-Site Scripting (XSS)

There are many ways to hack application programs. One popular attack vector is the **cross-site scripting (XSS)** attack. In these attacks, the user is asked for an input variable such as their name. The user may enter the name "Pat." The website then creates a webpage that contains something like "Hello Pat." This is called **reflection**. It is dangerous because the webpage will contain whatever the user chooses to give.

An attacker may be able to misuse sites that reflect user input. Figure 11-5 shows that an attacker has begun by sending the CEO of a corporation an e-mail message that purports to be from a subordinate. The message contains an apparently safe link to devour.com. Presumably, the company uses devour.com extensively, so the CEO sees the site as "safe."

In HTTP, the text that appears for a link may not be the true link. In Figure 11-5, the actual link is *http://www.devour.com/Default.aspx?name=<script>alert('Hacked!')</script>*. The link does take the victim to default.com. However, the problem is that it does more than that.

Most importantly, it will pass information to a particular program on Devour.com, Default.aspx. Default.aspx expects an input string for its name variable. Not shown in the figure, Default.aspx will reflect this name on a webpage. Probably, it will include something like "Hello *name*" on the webpage.

Given the e-mail message's crafted URL, however, the webpage being visited will reflect the script *<script>alert(Hacked!')</script>* on the webpage. When scripts are placed on a webpage, the user does not see them. However, the script executes when the page is rendered. This particular script is not too damaging. The user will see a pop-up alert box that contains the message "Hacked!"

Most XSS attacks have far more damaging scripts. For example, the script may steal the user's login cookie and send it to the attacker. This may give the attacker the

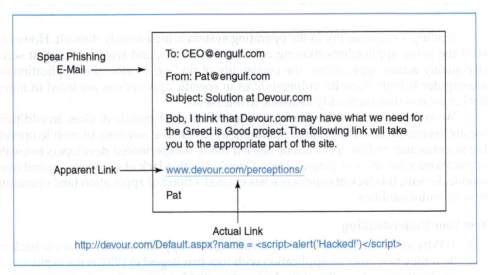

FIGURE 11-5 Cross-Site Scripting (XSS) E-Mail Message

victim's username and password. XSS attacks can also redirect the victim to another webpage, install malware, or even rewrite the contents of a webpage.

Cross-site scripting attacks do not always use e-mail or websites with deceptive links. For example, suppose a legitimate site allows user comments on webpages. Typically, the user enters text in a dialog box. The website then writes the comments onto the bottom of the webpage. If the comment contains a script, the script will execute every time someone visits the webpage afterward. This is a persistent XSS attack.

How can website designers thwart XSS attacks? At the broadest level, programmers should never trust user input. If information is to be reflected onto a webpage, the programmer must test the user input. It may seem simple to identify <script>and</script> tags, but scripts can be obfuscated (made less obvious). Also, there are many cross-site scripting attacks that do not use scripts. Thwarting cross-site scripting attacks is a difficult skill. This may explain why XSS vulnerabilities are pandemic on websites.

Programmers should never trust user input.

Test Your Understanding

6. a) Why is reflecting a user's input dangerous? b) What attitude should programmers have about user input?

SQL Injection Attacks

In many cases, user input becomes the basis for an SQL database query. If a malicious user knows this, he or she can enter specially crafted text to cause unanticipated damage. For example, suppose that a user enters a shipping destination in a dialog box. The website will compute the shipping cost. To do this, it will have to look up the shipping cost in a database using an SQL query.

To compute the shipping cost, the program may contain the following three lines of code. The first defines a new variable, destination. This is the destination city. The second gives the destination variable the destination name (inputdestination) the user has input into the form. The third creates an SQL query string. When this text string is entered into an SQL program, the program will find the destination city in the ShippingTable. It will return the value of the shippingcost column in that row. For instance, if the destination city is Tulsa, the program might tell the user that shipping the good will cost $20.

```
var destination;
destination = input.form ("inputdestination");
var sql = "select shippingcost from ShippingTable where destination = '" + inputdestina-
tion + "'";
```

However, if a user is malicious, he or she might enter the following information in the inputdestination field of the dialog box:

Tulsa'; drop table ShippingTable --

This string will be placed into the third line in the code. The "–" indicates that the rest of the line is a comment. This essentially "eats up" the rest of the line. The effect will be the following:

---

select shippingcost from ShippingTable where destination = 'Tulsa'; drop table ShippingTable

---

This will cause SQL to execute *two* statements instead of just one. First, it will tell the user the shipping cost to Tulsa. Second, it will delete the ShippingTable table. When the next person tries to look up the shipping cost for a particular city, they will only receive an error message.

Test Your Understanding

7. In an SQL injection attack, what does the user input instead of the expected input?

ELECTRONIC MAIL (E-MAIL)

Having discussed some factors that are driving new networked applications, we can now turn to specific applications. We will begin with electronic mail (e-mail) which was one of the earliest applications on wide area networks and that is still growing rapidly today.

E-Mail Standards

A major driving force behind the wide acceptance of Internet e-mail is standardization. Figure 11-6 shows that e-mail uses multiple standards for different aspects of its operation.

Message Body Standards

Obviously, message bodies have to be standardized, or we would not be able to read arriving messages. In physical mail, message body standards include the language the partners will use (English, etc.), the formality of language, and other matters.

RFC 2822 (Originally RFC 822) Bodies   The initial standard for e-mail bodies (and headers) was **RFC 822**, which has been updated as **RFC 2822**. This is a standard for plain text messages—multiple lines of typewriter-like characters with no boldface, graphics, or other amenities. The extreme simplicity of this approach made it easy to create early client e-mail programs.

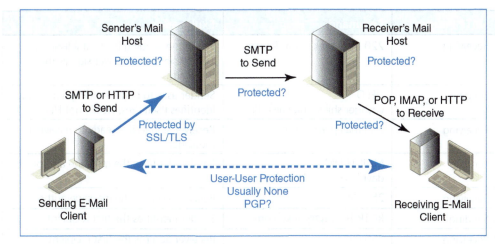

FIGURE 11-6   Classic E-Mail Standards

HTML Bodies   Later, as HTML became widespread on the World Wide Web, most mail vendors adopted **HTML bodies** with richly formatted text and even graphics.

UNICODE Bodies   RFC 822 specified the use of the ASCII code to represent printable characters. Unfortunately, ASCII was developed for English, and even European languages need extra characters. The **UNICODE** standard allows characters of all languages to be represented, although most mail readers cannot display all UNICODE characters well yet.

Simple Mail Transfer Protocol (SMTP)

We also need standards for delivering RFC 2822, HTML, and UNICODE messages. In the postal world, we must have envelopes that present certain information in certain ways, and there are specific ways to post mail for delivery, including putting letters in post office drop boxes and taking them to the post office.

Figure 11-6 shows how e-mail is posted (sent). The e-mail program on the user's PC sends the message to its outgoing mail host, using the **Simple Mail Transfer Protocol (SMTP)**. Figure 11-7 shows the complex series of interactions that SMTP requires between the sender and the receiver before and after mail delivery.

Receiving Mail (POP and IMAP)

Figure 11-6 also shows two standards that are used to *receive* e-mail. These are the **Post Office Protocol (POP)** and the **Internet Message Access Protocol (IMAP)**. These standards allow the e-mail user to download new messages whenever they find convenient.

SMTP Process	Command	Explanation
Receiving	220 mail.panko.com Ready	When the sending host establishes a TCP session, the receiver signals that it is ready.
Sending	HELO voyager.shilder.hawaii.edu	Sender asks to begin sending a message. Identifies itself (Yes, HELO, not HELLO).
Receiving	250 mail.panko.com	Receiver signals it is ready to receive a message.
Sending	MAIL FROM: david@voyager.hawaii.edu	Sender identifies the message author.
Receiving	250 OK	Receiver accepts the message author.
Sending	RCTP TO: ray@panko.com	Sender identifies the first recipient.
Receiving	250 OK	Receiver accepts the first recipient.
Sending	RCTP TO: lee@panko.com	Sender identifies the second recipient.
Receiving	550 No such user here	Receiver rejects the second recipient but will deliver the message to the first recipient.
Sending	DATA	Message will follow.
Receiving	354 Start mail input; end with <CRLF><CRLF>	Gives permission to begin sending the message.
Sending	*When in the course...*	Sender sends the message. Multiple lines of text. Ends with two carriage return/ line feeds, which gives a blank line.
Receiving	250 OK	Accepts the message.
Sending	QUIT	Sender requests termination of the SMTP session.
Receiving	221 Mail.Panko.COM Service closing transmission channel.	Receiver terminates session.

FIGURE 11-7 Simple Mail Transfer Protocol (SMTP)

Web-Enabled E-Mail

All client PCs have browsers. Many mail hosts are now Web-enabled, meaning that users only need browsers to interact with them in order to send, receive, and manage their e-mail. As Figure 11-8 shows, all interactions take place via HTTP. These systems use HTML to render pages on-screen.

SMTP for Transmission between Mail Hosts

So far, we have been looking at interactions between client hosts and their mail hosts. Figure 11-6 shows that mail hosts use SMTP when they transmit to each other. This is even true if client hosts communicate with their mail hosts using HTTP.

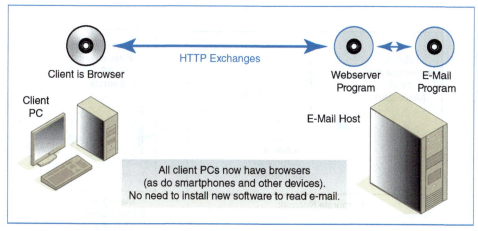

FIGURE 11-8 Web-Enabled E-Mail Operation

Test Your Understanding

8. a) Distinguish among the major standards for e-mail bodies. b) In traditional e-mail, when a station sends a message to its mail server, what standard does it use? c) When the sender's mail server sends the message to the receiver's mail server, what standard does it use? d) In traditional e-mail, when the receiver's e-mail client downloads new mail from its mail server, what standards is it likely to use? e) What is Web-enabled e-mail? f) What do you think are the advantages of a Web-enabled e-mail system? (The answer is not explicitly in the text.)

Malware Filtering in E-Mail

Although e-mail is tremendously important to corporations, it is a source of intense security headaches. As we learned in Chapter 3, the most widespread security compromises are attacks by malware. Malware enters an organization primarily, although by no means exclusively, through e-mail attachments and (sometimes) through scripts in e-mail bodies. E-mail attachments can also be used to install worms and Trojan horse programs on victim PCs.

The obvious countermeasure to e-mail-borne viruses is antivirus software, which scans incoming messages and attachments for viruses, worms, and Trojan horses. One problem is that most companies attempt to confront security threats by installing virus scanning on the user PCs. Unfortunately, too many users either turn off their antivirus programs if they seem to be interfering with other programs (or appear to slow things down too much) or keep their programs active but fail to update them regularly. In the latter case, newer viruses will not be recognized by the antivirus program.

Consequently, many companies are beginning to do central scanning for e-mail-borne viruses and Trojan horses. As Figure 11-9 shows, there are several places that this scanning can be done.

One popular place to do this is the corporate mail server. Users cannot turn off antivirus filtering on the mail server, and the e-mail staff (hopefully) updates virus definitions on these servers frequently.

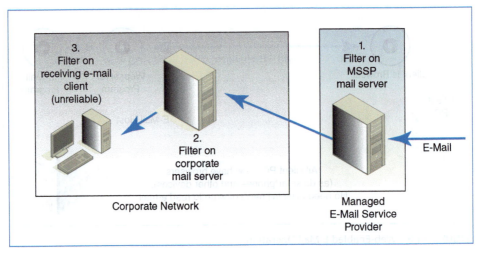

FIGURE 11-9 Possible Scanning Locations for E-Mail Malware

Some companies are even outsourcing antivirus/anti-Trojan horse scanning to outside security firms called managed e-mail service providers. To do this, they must redirect all incoming e-mail to a managed e-mail service provider. Fortunately, this is easy to do. Each second level domain's DNS server has an MX record that gives the IP address of the company's main mail server. The company simply changes the MX record to give the IP address of the managed e-mail service provider. The outsourcing firm has specialized expertise in searching for malware in e-mail. In addition, it handles the mail traffic of many firms. This gives it a large volume of e-mail, which allows it to analyze traffic for subtle malware trends.

Test Your Understanding

9. a) What is the main tool of firms in fighting viruses and Trojan horses in e-mail attachments? b) Why does filtering on the user's PC often not work? c) What options do firms have for where antivirus filtering may be done? d) According to the principle of defense in depth, how should firms do antivirus filtering?

Encryption for Confidentiality in E-Mail Transmission

Given the importance of e-mail and the sensitive information it often carries, you might expect that corporations would rigorously protect all e-mail through encryption for confidentiality. Actually, this is not often the case.

Link-by-Link Security   Figure 11-10 shows a typical situation in e-mail security. The sending client is transmitting a message to its mail host. This transmission is protected by SSL/TLS. The user knows that the message is encrypted for confidentiality. This may cause the user to believe that there is end-to-end encryption for confidentiality with the other user.

However, SSL/TLS only protects communication between the sending client and the sender's mail host. SSL/TLS gives **link protection**, not an end-to-end protection. The link in this case is the transmission between the sending client and the sender's mail host.

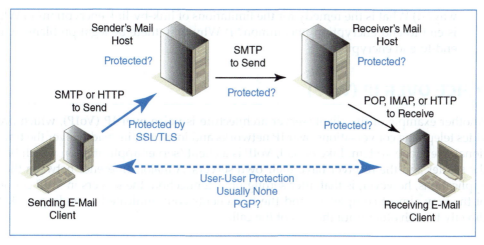

FIGURE 11-10 Encryption for Confidentiality in E-Mail

SSL/TLS provides link protection, not an end-to-end protection.

Is there any protection during the rest of the message's trip over the Internet? The answer is, "Perhaps." There may be encryption over the SMTP link between the sender's mail host and the receiver's mail host, but there is no guarantee. The receiving client may encrypt between itself and its mail host, but there is no guarantee of that either.

Even if encryption for confidentiality is implemented in all three links, the message is still not entirely safe. The sender's mail host must decrypt incoming messages, then re-encrypt the message to send it on to the receiver's mail host. For a brief period of time, the message will be in plaintext. A hacker who has planted spyware on the sender's or receiver's mail host will be able to capture the unencrypted message.

End-to-End Security The obvious remedy to the limits of link encryption is **end-to-end encryption** between the sending client and the receiving client. However, this is rarely done in practice. There is no widely accepted standard for end-to-end client encryption. The two clients must agree upon an encryption method if they wish to use one. Even if there is an end-to-end encryption method available, furthermore, users rarely use it.

There may even be legal issues with end-to-end encryption for confidentiality in a corporate environment. A number of laws require corporations to retain certain types of e-mail messages for later reading. For example, if an employee is fired, all electronic correspondence involved in the firing must be retained for a certain period of time. With end-to-end encryption, how would this be possible?

Test Your Understanding

10. a) If a message sender uses SSL/TLS when it sends a message, how is protection likely to be limited? b) Distinguish between link encryption and end-to-end encryption for confidentiality. c) Why is link-by-link encryption for confidentiality not fully secure even if there is encryption for confidentiality in all links along the way? d) What is the remedy for the limitations of link-by-link encryption? e) Why is end-to-end encryption uncommon? f) Why may there be legal problems with end-to-end encryption?

VOICE OVER IP (VoIP)

Another example of the client/server architecture is **voice over IP (VoIP)**, which provides telephone conversations over IP networks and internets, instead of over the traditional telephone system. Like e-mail, VoIP is a client/server application in which both the sender and the receiver have their own servers. A major difference between these applications, however, is that after setting up a connection, the servers in VoIP get out of the way almost completely, and the two clients communicate by sending packets directly to each other until the end of the call.

Voice over IP (VoIP) provides telephone conversations over IP networks and internets, instead of over the traditional telephone system.

Basics

VoIP offers the promise of reducing telephone costs by moving from traditional telephone transmission, which reserves capacity for a call even when neither side was transmitting, to more efficient packet switching, which only charges for information actually sent. This can substantially reduce cost.

Clients Figure 11-11 illustrates VoIP operation. The figure shows two clients. One is a client PC with multimedia hardware (a microphone and speakers) and VoIP software. The other is a **VoIP telephone**, which has a **codec** (the electronics to encode voice for digital transmission) and the ability to send and receive packets over a TCP/IP internet. With VoIP, these two client users can talk with each other.

Media Gateway The figure also shows a media gateway. The **media gateway** connects a VoIP system to the ordinary public switched telephone network. Without a media gateway, VoIP users can talk only to one another, but they could not call people on landlines. The media gateway translates both signaling and transport communication across IP networks and traditional telephone networks.

The media gateway translates both signaling and transport transmissions.

Test Your Understanding

11. a) What is VoIP? b) What is the promise of VoIP? c) What devices can be used by VoIP callers? d) What is a codec? e) What is the purpose of a media gateway? f) Why is having a media gateway in a VoIP system important? g) Does the media gateway translate signaling transmissions or transport transmissions?

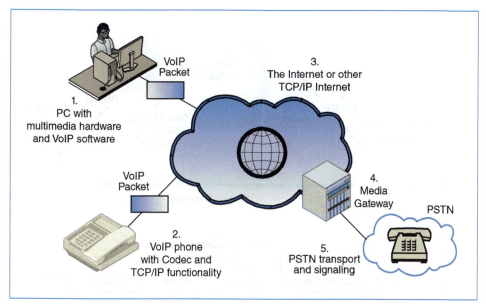

VoIP
Packet

3.
The Internet or other
TCP/IP Internet

1.
PC with
multimedia hardware
and VoIP software

VoIP
Packet

4.
Media
Gateway

PSTN

2.
VoIP phone
with Codec and
TCP/IP functionality

5.
PSTN transport
and signaling

FIGURE 11-11   Voice over IP (VoIP) Operation

VoIP Signaling

In telecommunications, there is a fundamental distinction between signaling and transport. Signaling consists of the communication needed to set up circuits, tear down circuits, handle billing information, and do other supervisory chores. Transport is the actual carriage of voice.

> *In telecommunications, there is a fundamental distinction between signaling and transport. Signaling consists of the communication needed to set up circuits, tear down circuits, handle billing information, and do other supervisory chores. Transport is the actual carriage of voice.*

There are two major VoIP signaling protocols. The first was the ISO **H.323** standard, which was effective but very complex. More recently, the IETF created the **Session Initiation Protocol (SIP)** standard. Most older VoIP systems use H.323 to control signaling. However, the use of SIP is growing rapidly, and most VoIP systems today use SIP for signaling.

Figure 11-12 illustrates the SIP protocol. Each subscriber has an SIP proxy server. The calling VoIP telephone sends a SIP INVITE message to its SIP proxy server. This message gives the IP address of the receiver. The caller's SIP proxy server then sends the SIP INVITE message to the called party's SIP proxy server. The called party's proxy server sends the SIP INVITE message to the called party's VoIP telephone or multimedia PC.

Test Your Understanding

12. a) What are the two major protocols for VoIP signaling? b) Which of these protocols is growing rapidly? c) Describe how SIP initiates a communication session.

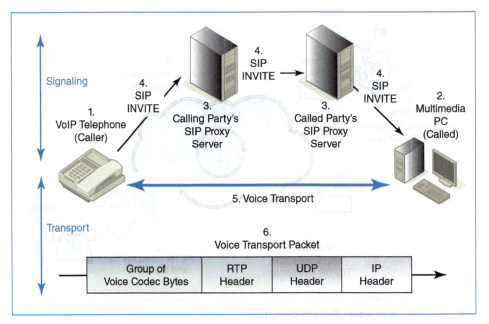

FIGURE 11-12   Voice over IP (VoIP) Signaling and Transmission Standards

VoIP Transport

After SIP or H.323 creates a connection, the two VoIP clients begin communicating directly. This is the beginning of transport, which is the transmission of voice between callers. VoIP, as its name suggests, operates over routed IP networks. Therefore, digitized voice has to be carried from the sender to the receiver in packets.

Codecs   VoIP telephones and multimedia PCs need codecs to convert analog voice signals into digital voice data streams. VoIP systems can use many different codecs. Figure 11-13 shows that some codecs convert voice streams into bit streams as small as 5.3 kbps. However, the codecs that do the most compression also lose the most voice quality. Selecting codec in a VoIP network means making a trade-off between voice quality and cost reduction.

VoIP Transport Packets   As noted in Chapter 1, long application messages have to be fragmented into smaller pieces that can be carried in individual packets. Each packet carries a small part of the application message.

Figure 11-12 shows a VoIP transport packet. The application message is a stream of voice codec bytes. Each packet carries a few bytes of the conversation.

TCP allows reliable application message delivery. However, the retransmission of lost or damaged TCP segments can take a second or two—far too long for voice conversations. Voice needs to be transmitted in real time. Consequently, VoIP transport uses UDP at the transport layer. UDP reduces the processing load on the VoIP telephones, and it also limits the high network traffic that VoIP generates. If packets are lost, the

Codec Standard	Bits Transmitted per Second
G.711	64 kbps
G.722	48, 56, or 64 kbps
G.721	32 kbps
G.722.1	24, 32 kbps
G.726	16, 24, 32, 40 kbps
G.728	16 kbps
G.729AB	8 kbps
G.723	5.33, 6.4 kbps
G.7231A	5.3, 6.3 kbps

FIGURE 11-13 Codec Standards

receiver creates fake noise for the lost codec bytes. It does this by extrapolating between the content of the preceding and following packets.

Between the UDP header and the application message, VoIP adds an additional header, a **Real Time Protocol (RTP)** header, to make up for two deficiencies of UDP:

- First, UDP does not guarantee that packets will be delivered in order. RTP adds a sequence number so that the application layer can put packets in the proper sequence.
- Second, VoIP is highly sensitive to jitter, which is variable latency in packet delivery. Jitter literally makes the voice sound jittery. RTP contains a time stamp for when its package of octets should be played relative to the octets in the previous packet. This allows the receiver to provide smooth playback.

Test Your Understanding

13. a) What is the purpose of a VoIP codec? b) Some codecs compress voice more. What do they give up in doing so? c) In a VoIP transport packet, what is the application message? d) Does a VoIP transport packet use UDP or TCP? Explain why. e) What two problems with UDP does RTP fix? f) List the headers and messages in a VoIP transport packet, beginning with the first packet header to arrive at the receiver. (Hint: See Figure 11-12.)

THE WORLD WIDE WEB

HTTP and HTML Standards

We have discussed the World Wide Web throughout this book. Figure 11-14 shows that the Web is based on two primary standards.

- First, webpages themselves are created using the Hypertext Markup Language (HTML).
- Second, the transfer of requests and responses uses the Hypertext Transfer Protocol (HTTP).

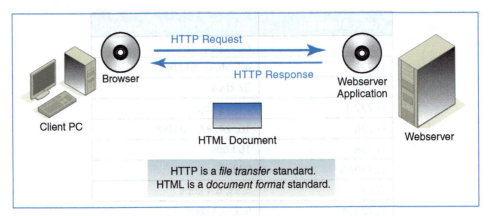

FIGURE 11-14 World Wide Web (WWW) Standards

To give an analogy, an e-mail message may be created using RFC 2822, but it will be delivered using SMTP. Many application standards consist of a document format standard and a file transfer standard.

Many application standards consist of a document format standard and a file transfer standard.

Complex Webpages

Actually, most "webpages" really consist of several files—a master text-only HTML file plus graphics files, audio files, and other types of files. Figure 11-15 illustrates the downloading of a webpage with two graphics files.

The HTML file consists merely of the page's text, plus **tags** to show where the browser should render graphics files, when it should play audio files, and so forth.[3] The HTML file is downloaded first because the browser needs the tags to know what other files should be downloaded.

Consequently, several HTTP request–response cycles may be needed to download a single webpage. Three request–response cycles are needed in the example shown in the figure.

Test Your Understanding

14. a) Distinguish between HTTP and HTML. b) You are downloading a webpage that has six graphics and two sound clips. How many request–response cycles will be needed?

---

[3] For graphics files, the IMG tag is used. The keyword *IMG* indicates that an image file is to be downloaded. The SRC parameter in this tag gives the target file's directory and file name on the webserver.

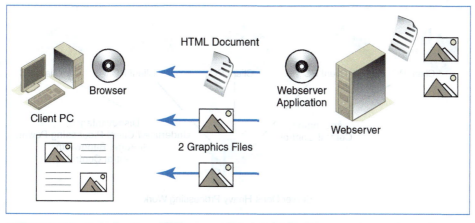

FIGURE 11-15 Downloading a Webpage with Two Graphics Files

PEER-TO-PEER (P2P) APPLICATION ARCHITECTURES

So far, we have examined two different application architectures: traditional terminal–host processing and client/server processing. Another application architecture is the **peer-to-peer (P2P) architecture**, in which most or all of the work is done by cooperating user computers, such as desktop PCs. If servers are present at all, they play only facilitating roles and do not control the processing.

> *In a peer-to-peer (P2P) architecture, most or all of the work is done by cooperating user computers, such as desktop PCs.*

Traditional Client/Server Applications

Figure 11-16 shows a traditional client/server application. In this application, all of the clients communicate with the central server for their work.

Advantage: Central Control One advantage of this *server-centric* approach is central control. All communication goes through the central server, so there can be good security and policy-based control over communication.

Disadvantages Although the use of central service is good in several ways, it does give rise to two problems.

- One disadvantage is that client/server computing often uses expensive server capacity while leaving clients underused. Clients normally are modern PCs with considerable processing power, not dumb terminals or early low-powered PCs. Thus, power, storage, and bandwidth are all wasted in this model.

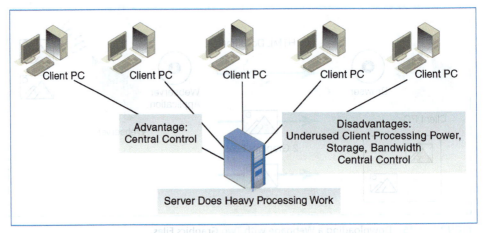

FIGURE 11-16 Traditional Client/Server Operation

- From the end users' point of view, central control can be a problem rather than an advantage. Central control limits what end users can do. Just as PCs freed end users from the red tape involved in using mainframe computers, peer-to-peer computing frees end users from the red tape involved in using a server. There is a fundamental clash of interests between central control and end user freedom.

P2P Applications

Figure 11-17 shows that, in a P2P application, user PCs work directly with one another, at least for part of their work. In this figure, all of the work involves P2P interactions. The two user computers work without the assistance of a central server and also without its control.

Advantages The benefits of P2P computing are the opposite of those of client/server computing. Client users are freed from central control, for better or worse, and less user computer capacity is wasted.

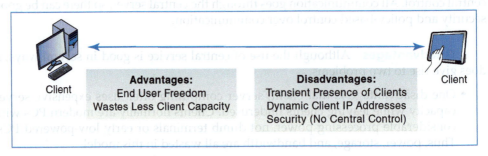

FIGURE 11-17 Simple Peer-to-Peer (P2P) Operations

Disadvantages P2P architectures have a number of unique disadvantages.

- *Transient Presence.* Most obviously, user PCs have transient presence on the Internet. They are frequently turned off, and even when they are on, users may be away from their machines. There is nothing in P2P like always-present servers.
- *Transient IP Addresses.* Another problem is that each time a user PC connects to the Internet, its DHCP server is likely to assign it a different IP address. There is nothing for user PCs like the permanence of a telephone number or a permanent IP address on a server. Dynamic IP addresses make finding PCs that provide service difficult.
- *Security.* Even if user freedom is a strong goal, there needs to be some kind of security. P2P computing is a great way to spread viruses and other illicit content. Without centralized filtering on servers, security will have to be implemented on all user PCs, or chaos will result.

Test Your Understanding

15. a) What are peer-to-peer (P2P) applications? b) What are the advantages of P2P applications compared to traditional server-centric client/server applications? c) What are the disadvantages?

P2P File-Sharing Applications: BitTorrent

One particularly popular type of P2P application is file sharing. In P2P file sharing, one client PC downloads a file that it needs from one or more other clients. Figure 11-18 shows **BitTorrent**, which is a popular peer-to-peer file sharing program.

Figure 11-18 shows the main steps in BitTorrent operation. First, your computer uses a **BitTorrent client program**. The BitTorrent client program searches for the file it wants, typically by going to an **index website**, which contains **.torrent** files giving information about specific files and where they are stored (Step 1). Next, the BitTorrent client program contacts a **tracker**, a server that coordinates the actual file transfer (Step 2). Trackers are usually run by independent clients, rather than being directly managed by BitTorrent.

To coordinate the file transfer, the tracker program examines all of the computers currently connected to its network to find out which have all or part of the file (Step 3). These computers are called the **swarm** for that particular file. The tracker passes this information to the BitTorrent client program, which begins to download different parts of the same file from multiple computers in the swarm (Step 4). These downloads occur simultaneously. The individual pieces are reassembled on the receiving computer to form the complete file (Step 5).

In order to encourage its users to share files, the BitTorrent system gives faster download speeds to users who opt to make their own files available for others to download. As more users share the same file, the download speeds for that file will become even higher, since a client program can take even smaller pieces of each file from each computer in the swarm.

Corporate Security Concerns Corporations that decide to use BitTorrent should consider several security concerns. First, BitTorrent uses specific port numbers, usually the TCP ports 6881 through 6889. Since firewalls commonly block these ports

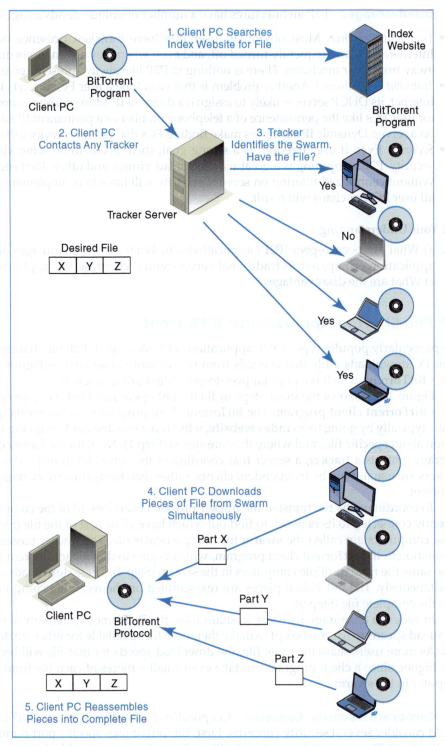

FIGURE 11-18 BitTorrent P2P File Retrieval

by default, using BitTorrent requires reconfiguring the firewall, possibly putting the firm at risk for attacks that exploit these ports.

Another security concern is that employees might use BitTorrent to download an infected file, which could then compromise the corporation's computers. Also, while using BitTorrent to share files is not itself illegal, one problem is that people have used the technology to share copyrighted material. A corporation must consider whether it will be held responsible if an employee uses BitTorrent to distribute illegal content.

Corporate Benefits   Despite these potential problems, BitTorrent has started to see corporate use. The main advantage of using BitTorrent is that it allows the corporation to use clients (whose capacity is often underused) rather than expensive server processing power. This results in cost savings.

BitTorrent's efficient method of sharing files has been used by broadcasters like Canada's CBC and Norway's NPK to distribute their television programs. Video game developer and publisher Blizzard Entertainment has used the BitTorrent protocol to deliver updates and patches for its World of Warcraft game. The BitTorrent company has also released BitTorrent DNA, a content delivery product designed to aid corporations that want to use BitTorrent to handle large downloads and streaming video.

Test Your Understanding

16. a) Distinguish between client/server file retrieval and P2P file sharing. b) In BitTorrent, what is an index website? c) What are .torrent files? d) In BitTorrent, what is a tracker? e) In BitTorrent, what is a swarm? f) What security concerns must firms address if they plan to use BitTorrent? g) What is the main advantage of BitTorrent file sharing?

P2P Communication Applications: Skype

Another popular P2P application is Skype. While BitTorrent is used for file sharing, Skype is used for communication between people. Early in this chapter, we saw how voice over IP (VoIP) worked in the traditional client/server architecture. With Skype, we will see how VoIP works as a P2P application.

Skype is a P2P VoIP service that currently offers free calling among Skype customers over the Internet and reduced-cost calling to and from Public Switched Telephone Network customers. Skype offers a range of features, from phone calls to instant messaging and video calling. At the time of this writing, Skype is the most popular P2P VoIP service. Skype's free calls from computer to computer have greatly contributed to this popularity. Figure 11-19 illustrates how Skype operates.

There are three main elements in the Skype network: the Skype login server, host nodes, and super nodes.

- The **Skype login server** is a central server managed directly by Skype. It is the only centralized component in the Skype network.
- A **host node** is a Skype application that runs on a user's computer.
- A **super node** is a host node that takes on the work of signaling. Any regular host node may be made a super node if it has enough memory, network bandwidth, and CPU.

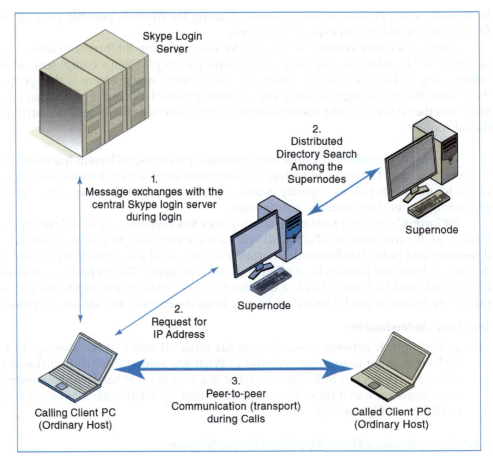

FIGURE 11-19   Skype P2P VoIP Operation

These elements are involved in the three steps that must occur for a user to place a call with Skype.

- *Step 1 Login.* First, a user must log in to the Skype login server. In this step, the username and password are authenticated. The Skype server also notes the user's IP address, which will be needed later, in the directory search process. Login is the only step that involves a central server; the rest of the call process is done peer-to-peer, using host nodes and super nodes. This step is similar to the login process in traditional voice over IP, where each client must log in to its own proxy server.

- *Step 2 Signaling/Directory Search.* After login, the user can place calls. His or her host will begin the signaling process. One of the main aspects of Skype signaling is the *directory search*, the process where a Skype application looks up the username and IP address of the party it wants to contact. A Skype directory search is a completely P2P process that is done using the super nodes. This is a major difference from traditional voice over IP, where signaling uses servers (proxy servers).

	Traditional VoIP	Skype	Comparison
Login	Server: user logs into his or her proxy server	Server: User logs into the Skype login server	Similar
Signaling	Server: proxy server manages signaling	Peer-to-Peer: Super nodes manage signaling, using P2P searching	Major difference
Transport	P2P between the two hosts	P2P between the two hosts	Similar

FIGURE 11-20 Traditional VoIP and Skype

- *Step 3 Transport.* Figure 11-20 compares Skype with traditional VoIP. While Skype's super nodes handle signaling, transport is done entirely by the two host nodes involved in the call. In transport, the voice packets are routed completely P2P, from caller to called party and vice versa. This is similar to traditional voice over IP transport, where the two clients also communicate directly.

Because the signaling and transport are done by peers rather than going through a central server, Skype only carries the burden of managing a login server. This greatly reduces Skype's operational costs, resulting in its low-cost calls.

Test Your Understanding

17. a) What is Skype? b) Do you have to pay a fee to make calls using Skype? Explain. c) What is the most popular P2P VoIP service?

18. a) List and define Skype's three main elements. b) Explain how login works in Skype. c) What is a directory search in Skype? d) Which element of the Skype network is in charge of signaling? e) Which element of the Skype network is in charge of transport? f) Which of Skype's three steps is done P2P? g) Compare Skype and traditional voice over IP in terms of whether login, signaling, and transport are P2P or whether they use servers.

P2P Processing Applications: SETI@home

As noted earlier, most PC processors sit idle most of the time. This is even true much of the time when a person is working at his or her keyboard. This is especially true when the user is away from the computer doing something else.

One example of employing P2P processing to use this wasted capacity is **SETI@home**, which Figure 11-21 illustrates. SETI is the Search for Extraterrestrial Intelligence project. Many volunteers download SETI@home screen savers that really are programs. When the computer is idle, the screen saver awakens, asks the SETI@home server for work to do, and then does the work of processing data. Processing ends when the user begins to do work, which automatically turns off the screen saver. This approach allows SETI to harness the processing power of millions of PCs to do its work. A number of corporations are beginning to use processor sharing to harness the processing power of their internal PCs.

Test Your Understanding

19. How does SETI@home make use of idle capacity on home PCs?

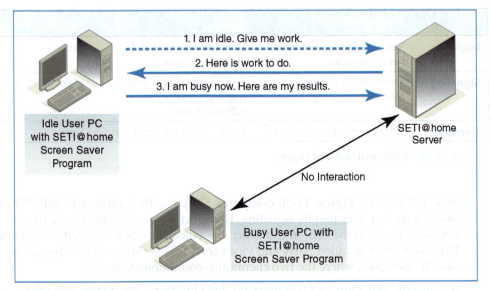

FIGURE 11-21 SETI@home P2P Application Processing

Privacy Protection: Tor

Even before we learned of the National Security Agency's eavesdropping on American Internet traffic, some people wished to use the Internet anonymously to preserve their privacy. This is difficult because IP packets have source IP addresses that identify the sender.

The **Tor** project was created to allow anonymous Internet use. In Figure 11-22, Client A wishes to connect anonymously with Server B. Client A knows that many P2P devices acting as Tor routers (relays) offer anonymous Internet transmission. These Tor routers are numbered in the figure. Collectively, they constitute the **Tor network**.

Client A negotiates a specific path through the Tor network using the **Tor protocol**. Client A then creates a message for Server B. The Tor path will go through three Tor routers. Client A will encrypt the message three times. Each Tor router decrypts the outermost layer of the cryptographic "onion" and passes the semi-decrypted message to the next Tor router on the path.

The final Tor router is an *exit node*. When it finishes its decryption, it has the original plaintext message from Client A to Server B. It passes this decrypted message to the server. The exit node is a concern because it can read the message. However, it does not know the IP address of Client A. It only knows the IP address of the previous Tor router. This provides a good degree of anonymity to Client A. However, if the exit node is malicious, it may be able to analyze the messages for an indication of Client A's identity.

Test Your Understanding

20. a) What is the goal of the Tor network? b) How does Tor use P2P devices? c) Does Tor provide confidentiality? (This is not a simple question.)

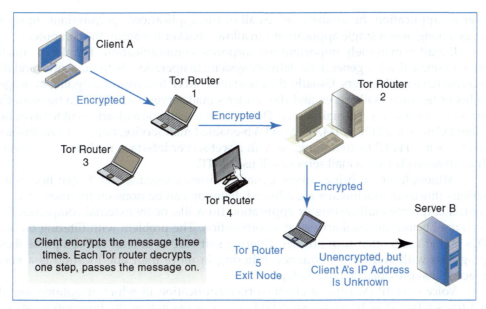

FIGURE 11-22   Tor Anonymity

Facilitating Servers and P2P Applications

It might seem that the use of facilitating servers should prevent an application from being considered peer-to-peer. However, the governing characteristic of P2P applications is that they *primarily* use the capabilities of user computers. Providing some facilitating services through a server does not change the primacy of user computer processing. For example, Skype is still considered a P2P application despite its use of a login server. Similarly, SETI is considered P2P even though it uses a server that downloads to and accepts data from the SETI@home users.

Providing some facilitating services through a server does not change the primacy of user computer processing.

Test Your Understanding

21. Explain how P2P applications may use facilitating servers yet still be called P2P applications.

CONCLUSION

Synopsis

Networked applications are applications that require a network to function. Although IT professionals must understand all layers in networking, users are only concerned with applications. Applications are also critical in terms of security. If an attacker takes over an application, he or she receives all of the application's permissions. In some cases, taking over a single application can allow a hacker to control the computer.

E-mail is extremely important for corporate communication. Thanks to attachments, e-mail also is a general file delivery system. In operation, both the sender and the receiver have mail servers. Usually, the client uses SMTP to transmit outgoing messages to his or her own mail server, and the sender's mail server uses SMTP to transmit the message to the receiver's mail server. The receiver usually downloads mail to his or her client PC by using POP or IMAP. With Web-enabled mail service, however, senders and receivers use HTTP to communicate with a webserver interface to their mail servers. Transmissions between mail servers still use SMTP.

Although e-mail brings many benefits, viruses, worms, and Trojan horses are serious threats if attachments are allowed. Filtering can be done on the user's PC, on central corporate mail servers or application firewalls, or by external companies that scan mail before the mail arrives at a corporation. The problem with filtering on user PCs is that users often turn off their filtering software or at least fail to update these programs with sufficient frequency. Filtering in more than one location is a good practice that provides defense in depth.

Voice over IP (VoIP) is a client/server application in which telephone signals are transmitted over IP packet-switched networks (including the Internet) instead of over circuit-switched networks. There are two major VoIP signaling protocols: the ISO H.323 standard and the Session Initiation Protocol (SIP), which is growing rapidly. While servers are involved in signaling, transport is done directly between the two VoIP clients. Transport packets have an IP header, a UDP header, an RTP header, and a segment of application data.

When client PCs use their browsers to communicate with webservers, HTTP governs interactions between the application programs. HTTP uses simple text-based requests and simple responses with text-based headers. HTTP can download many types of files. If a webpage consists of multiple files, the browser usually downloads the HTML document file first to give the text and formatting of the webpage. It then downloads graphics and other aspects of the webpage. MIME fields are used to describe the format of a downloaded file.

Most applications today are client/server applications. In peer-to-peer applications, in contrast, user PCs do most or all of the work. In a few P2P applications, no servers are used. However, it often makes sense to use servers to facilitate limited aspects of P2P applications. For instance, Skype is still considered a P2P application despite its use of a login server. Similarly, SETI@home is considered P2P even though it uses a server that downloads to and accepts data from the SETI@home user PCs. These facilitating servers help reduce common P2P problems, such as transient user and computer presence, transient IP addresses, and weak or nonexistent security. However, the application uses peer processing for *most* of its work—just not all of it.

There are several categories of P2P applications. So far, P2P has been dominated by file-sharing applications (such as BitTorrent), communication applications (such as Skype), and processor-sharing applications (such as SETI@home). New types and categories are appearing, including tools to anonymize Internet use (such as the Tor network).

END-OF-CHAPTER QUESTIONS

Thought Questions

11-1. Do you think that pure P2P architectures will be popular in the future? Why or why not?

11-2. Come up with a list of roles that facilitating servers can play in P2P applications. This will require you to read through the section on P2P applications carefully. You should also try to think of an example not in the text.

Troubleshooting Question

11-3. You perform a BitTorrent search and get no responses. Troubleshoot this problem.

Perspective Questions

11-4. What was the most surprising thing for you in the chapter?

11-5. What was the most difficult material for you in the chapter? Why was it difficult?

GLOSSARY

1000Base-SX: A fiber version of gigabit Ethernet for short wavelengths (transmitting at 850 nm).

1000Base-T: Ethernet physical layer signaling standard for transmission over 4-pair UTP at one gigabit per second.

100Base-TX: The dominant Ethernet physical layer 100 Mbps standard brought to desktop computers today. Uses UTP for transmission.

2.4 GHz Service Band: Unlicensed frequency band around 2.4 GHz. Used for Wi-Fi, Bluetooth, and other services.

25-Pair UTP Cord: The cabling used by telephony for vertical wiring that runs within a building.

2-Pair Data-Grade UTP: The traditional telephone access line for lower-speed leased lines. (Higher-speed leased lines use optical fiber.) Two pairs optimized for data transmission run out to each customer.

3G: Third-generation cellular technology. Although defined in a specific way, often used otherwise by cellular vendors. Considered to be obsolete today.

4G: Fourth-generation cellular technology. Although defined in a specific way, often used otherwise by cellular vendors. Considered to be the best cellular technology today.

4-Pair Unshielded Twisted Pair (UTP): The type of wiring typically used in Ethernet networks. 4-pair UTP contains eight copper wires organized as four pairs. Each wire is covered with dielectric insulation, and an outer jacket encloses and protects the four pairs.

5 GHz Service Band: Unlicensed radio band around 5 GHz. Used for Wi-Fi and other services.

50-micron Fiber: Optical fiber with a core diameter of 50 microns.

50-Pin Octopus Connector: The type of connector in which vertical cords typically terminate.

802 Committee: See 802 LAN/MAN Standards Committee.

802 LAN/MAN Standards Committee: IEEE standardization committee for local area network and metropolitan area network technology.

802.11 Wireless Network: Wireless network that uses 802.11 standards. Also called a Wi-Fi network.

802.11 Working Group: The IEEE working group that creates wireless LAN standards.

802.11a: Version of the 802.11 WLAN standard that has a rated speed of 54 Mbps and operates in the 5 GHz unlicensed radio band.

802.11g: Version of the 802.11 WLAN standard that has a rated speed of 54 Mbps and operates in the 2.4 GHz unlicensed radio band.

802.11i: An advanced form of 802.11 wireless LAN security.

802.11n: Version of the 802.11 WLAN standard that uses MIMO and sometimes doubled bandwidth to achieve a rated speed of 100 Mbps or more and longer range than earlier speed standards.

802.11r: Roaming standard for 802.11 wireless devices.

802.11s: Wi-Fi standard for mesh networking.

802.1X: Security standard for both wired and wireless LANs. Mode of operation in 802.11i security.

802.2: The single standard for the logical link control layer in 802 standards.

802.3 MAC Layer Frame: See Ethernet Frame.

802.3 MAC Layer Standard: The standard that defines Ethernet frame organization and NIC and switch operation.

802.3 Working Group: The 802 Committee's working group that creates Ethernet-specific standards.

900 Number: A number that allows customers to call into a company; callers pay a fee that is much higher than that of a regular toll call.

Absorptive Attenuation: In wireless transmission, the attenuation of a signal but water along the way absorbing its signal power. In optical fiber, attenuation due to the absorption of signal strength as a signal propagates.

Access Card: Small card with a magnetic stripe or microprocessor that gives you access to your computer or to a room.

Access Control: Limiting who may have access to each resource and limiting him or her permissions when using the resource.

Access Control List (ACL): An ordered list of pass/deny rules for a firewall or other device.

Access Line: 1) In networks, a physical transmission line that connects a station to a switch. 2) In telephony, the line used by the customer to reach the PSTN's central transport core.

Access Link: Same as Access Line although may be wireless.

Access Point: A bridge between a wireless station and a wired LAN.

Access Router: In home networking, a device that connects to the transmission vendor's modem and that provides a number of services including Ethernet connectivity, Wi-Fi connectivity, NAT, and DHCP.

Access System: In telephony, the system by which customers access the PSTN, including access lines and termination equipment in the end office at the edge of the transport core.

Account: An identifiable entity that may own resources on a computer.

ACK: See Acknowledgment.

ACK Bit: See Acknowledgement Bit.

Acknowledgment (ACK): 1) An acknowledgment message, sent by the receiver when a message is received correctly. 2) An acknowledgment frame, sent by the receiver whenever a frame is received; used in CSMA/CA+ACK in 802.11.

Acknowledgment Bit: In TCP, a bit that is set to indicate that a TCP segment contains an acknowledgement for a previous TCP segment the sending device received.

Acknowledgment Number Field: In TCP, a header field that tells what TCP segment is being acknowledged in a segment.

ACL: See Access Control List.

Active Directory: Microsoft's directory server product.

Active Directory Domain: A group of hosts served by one or more active directory domain controllers.

Active Directory Tree: An hierarchy of Active Directory domains.

Address Resolution: A process for determining a host's data link layer address if you know its IP address.

Address Resolution Protocol (ARP): Protocol for address resolution used in Ethernet networks. If a host or router knows a target host's or router's IP address, ARP finds the target's data link layer address.

ADSL: See Asymmetric Digital Subscriber Line.

Advanced Encryption Standard (AES): Currently dominant symmetric encryption standard that offers 128-bit, 192-bit, or 256-bit encryption efficiently.

Advanced Research Projects Agency (ARPA): An agency within the U.S. Department of Defense that funded the creation of the ARPANET and the Internet.

AES: See Advanced Encryption Standard.

Agent: See Network Management Agent.

Aggregate Throughput: Throughput shared by multiple users; individual users will get a fraction of this throughput.

Agility: The ability to change quickly. Typically offered by new technologies such as virtual machines and cloud computing that allow faster action than older technologies.

Alternative Route: In mesh topology, one of several possible routes from one end of the network to the other, made possible by the topology's many connections among switches or routers.

Amazon Web Services: Cloud service provided by Amazon.com.

Amplitude: The maximum (or minimum) intensity of a wave. In sound, this corresponds to volume (loudness).

Amplitude Modulation: A simple form of modulation in which a modem transmits one of two analog signals—a high-amplitude (loud) signal or a low-amplitude (soft) signal.

Analog Signal: A signal that rises and falls smoothly in intensity, analogously to the way the voice input signal rises and falls, and that does not have a limited number of states.

Antivirus Software: Software that scans computers to protect them against viruses, worms, and Trojan horses arriving in e-mail attachments and other propagation methods.

Application Architecture: The arrangement of how application layer functions are spread among computers to deliver service to users.

Application-Aware Firewall: A firewall that can tell what application is creating traffic and can understand actions taken by the application in messages, so that pass/deny decisions can be made about an application's traffic.

Application Layer: The standards layer that governs how two applications communicate with each other; Layer 7 in OSI, Layer 5 in the hybrid TCP/IP–OSI architecture.

Architecture: A broad plan that specifies what is needed in general and the components that will be used to provide that functionality. Applied to standards, networks, and applications.

ARP Cache: Section of memory that stores known pairs of IP addresses and single-network standards.

ARPA: See the Advanced Research Projects Agency.

ARPANET: A network created in the late 1960s by the Advanced Research Projects Agency. Became the first backbone for the Internet.

ASCII Code: A code for representing letters, numbers, and punctuation characters in 7-bit binary format.

Asymmetric Digital Subscriber Line (ADSL): The type of DSL designed to go into residential homes, offers high downstream speeds but limited upstream speeds.

Asynchronous Transfer Mode (ATM): The packet-switched network technology, specifically designed to carry voice, used for transmission in the PSTN transport core. ATM offers quality-of-service guarantees for throughput, latency, and jitter.

AT&T: U.S. telecommunications carrier.

ATM: See Asynchronous Transfer Mode.

Attenuate: For a signal's strength to weaken during propagation.

Auditing: Collecting data about events to examine actions after the fact.

Authentication: The requirement that someone who requests to use a resource must prove his or her identity.

Authentication Server: A server that stores data to help the verifier check the credentials of the applicant.

Authenticator: In 802.1X authentication, the device to which the supplicant connects—a workgroup switch or a wireless access point.

Authoritative DNS Server: DNS server that manages host names for a particular domain.

Availability: The ability of a network to serve its users.

Backward-Compatible: Able to work with all earlier versions of a standard or technology.

Bandwidth: The range of frequencies over which a signal is spread.

Baseband Signal: 1) The original signal in a radio transmission. 2) A signal that is injected directly into a wire for propagation.

Base Unit: In the metric system, the basic unit being measured: bits per second, hertz, meters, and so forth.

Basic Service Set (BSS): An access point and the set of hosts it serves.

Basic Service Set ID (BSSID): The MAC address of the specific access point.

Beamforming: In radio transmission, directing energy toward a wireless device without using a dish antenna.

BER: See bit error rate.

Best-Match Row: In routers, the row that provides the best forwarding option for a particular incoming packet.

BGP: See Border Gateway Protocol.

Binary Data: Data that has only two possible values (1s and 0s).

Binding: In Bluetooth, after peering is complete, two devices are bound and may communicate. If they are brought together later, they are still bound and can communicate without peering.

Biometrics: The use of bodily measurements to identify an applicant.

Bit: A single 1 or 0.

Bit Error Rate (BER): The percentage of bits that contain transmission errors.

Bits per Second (bps): The number of bits transmitted in a single second. Used as the basic measure of speed in networking, not bytes per second.

BitTorrent: A P2P file-sharing protocol where, instead of downloading a complete file from a single peer, you download different parts of the file you want from multiple peers.

BitTorrent Client Program: Program that runs on a user host. Allows the user host to participate in a BitTorrent network.

Bluetooth: A wireless networking standard created for personal area networks.

Bluetooth Profile: An application layer standard designed to allow devices to work together automatically, with little or no user intervention.

Bluetooth Special Interest Group: An association of hardware manufacturers and other organizations that sets Bluetooth standards.

Bonding: See Link Aggregation.

Border Gateway Protocol (BGP): The most common exterior routing protocol on the Internet. Recall that gateway is an old term for router.

Border Router: A router that sits at the edge of a site to connect the site to the outside world through leased lines, PSDNs, and VPNs.

Bot: A type of malware that can be upgraded remotely by an attacker to fix errors or to give the malware additional functionality.

Bps (bps): Bits per Second.

Breach: A successful attack.

Bring Your Own Device (BYOD): The practice of employees using personal devices such as laptops, cellular phones, and tablets for business purposes. BYOD reduces device cost to the firm, but it creates security issues.

Broadband: 1) Transmission where signals are sent in wide radio channels. 2) Any high-speed transmission system.

Broadcast: To send a message out to all other stations simultaneously.

Brute-Force Attack: A password-cracking attack in which an attacker tries to break a password by trying all possible combinations of characters.

BSS: See Basic Service Set.

BSSID: See Basic Service Set ID.

BYOD: See Bring Your Own Device.

CA: 1) See Certificate Authority. 2) See Collision Avoidance.

Cable Modem: 1) Broadband data transmission service using cable television. 2) The modem used in this service.

Cable Modem Service: Asymmetrical cable data service offered by a cable television company.

Cable Television: Form of television delivery that distributes signals to the home over coaxial cable.

Call Waiting: A service that allows the user to place an original caller on hold if someone else calls the user, shift briefly to the new caller, and then switch back to the original caller.

Caller ID: Service wherein the telephone number of the party calling you is displayed on your phone's small display screen before you pick up the handset; allows the user to screen calls.

Carder: Someone who steals credit card numbers.

Career Criminal: In security, an attacker who is primarily interested in making money from security breaches.

Carrier: A transmission service company that has government rights of way.

Carrier Sense Multiple Access with Collision Avoidance and Acknowledgments (CSMA/CA + ACK): A mandatory mechanism used to reduce problems with multiple simultaneous transmissions, which occur in wireless transmission. CSMA/CA+ACK is a media access control discipline, and it uses both collision avoidance and acknowledgment frames.

Cat: A short form for "category" in UTP.

Category: In unshielded twisted-pair wiring, a designation of quality for a UTP cord. Common Category numbers are Cat 5e, Cat 6, and Cat6A.

Category (Cat) 5e: Quality type of UTP wiring; required for 100Base-TX and gigabit Ethernet.

Category 6: The newest quality type of UTP wiring being sold; not required for even gigabit Ethernet. Can carry 10 Gbps Ethernet up to 55 feet.

Category 6A: Augmented Category 6 wiring that can carry 10 Gbps Ethernet up to 100 meters.

CDN: See Content Delivery Network.

Cell: In cellular telephony, a small geographical region served by a cellsite.

Cellphone: A cellular telephone, also called a mobile phone or mobile.

Cellsite: In cellular telephony, equipment at a site near the middle of each cell, containing a transceiver and supervising each cellphone's operation.

Cellular Telephone Service: Mobile telephone service in which there are multiple antenna sites to which a customer can connect. This permits channel reuse and therefore the ability to provide service to more customers simultaneously.

Certificate Authority (CA): Organization that provides public key–private key pairs and digital certificates.

Challenge Message: In authentication, a message that the verifier sends to the supplicant. The supplicant must process the challenge message and return the correct response message based on the challenge message in order to be authenticated.

Channel: A small frequency range that is a subdivision of a service band.

Channel Bandwidth: The range of frequencies in a channel; determined by subtracting the lowest frequency from the highest frequency.

Channel Reuse: The ability to use each channel multiple times, in different cells in the network.

Cipher: An encryption method.

Cladding: A thick glass cylinder that surrounds the core in optical fiber.

Classic Bluetooth: Early version of Bluetooth that operated at speeds of 2 to 3 Mbps.

Clear to Send (CTS): In 802.11, a message broadcast by an access point, which allows only a station that has sent a Request-to-Send message to transmit. All other stations must wait.

CLEC: See Competitive Local Exchange Carrier.

Client Host: In client/server processing, a server program on a server host provides services to a client program on a client host.

Client/Server Processing: The form of client/server computing in which the work is done by programs on two machines.

Clock Cycle: A period of time during which a transmission line's state is held constant.

Cloud: In the depiction of network and computer resources, indicates a part of the network the user does not have to understand in detail.

Cloud Computing: Service in which computer service in the form of hardware, applications, or other resources is provided to a customer for a fee. Frees the customer from having to provide the resources to its employees or customers.

Cloud Service Provider: A company that provides cloud computing services.

Coaxial Cable: Copper transmission medium in which there is a central wire and a coaxial metal tube as the second connector.

Co-Channel Interference: In wireless transmission, interference between two devices transmitting simultaneously in the same channel.

Codec: The device in the end office switch that converts between the analog local loop voice signals and the digital signals of the end office switch.

Collision: If two wireless devices transmit at the same time, their signals interfere with each other.

Collision Avoidance (CA): In 802.11, used with CSMA to listen for transmissions, so if a wireless NIC detects a transmission or a very recent transmission, it must not transmit. This avoids collision.

Communication Satellite: Satellite that provides radio communication service.

Community Name: In SNMP Version 1, only devices using the same community name will communicate with each other; very weak security.

Competitive Local Exchange Carrier (CLEC): A competitor to the ILEC.

Comprehensive Security: Security in which all avenues of attack are closed off.

Compression: Reducing the number of bits needed to be transmitted when the traffic has redundancy that can be removed.

Compromise: A successful attack.

Computer: Any computer attached to a network, including small devices.

Confidentiality: Assurance that interceptors cannot read transmissions.

Connectionless: Communication protocol in which the parties do not set up a formal association between themselves at the beginning of a conversation and do not end the association formally at the end of the conversation. One side simply sends a message to the other.

Connection-Oriented: Type of conversation in which there is a formal opening of the interactions, a formal closing, and maintenance of the conversation in between.

Connectorize: To add a connector to a wire or optical fiber cord.

Content Delivery Network: A network designed to provide content quickly to consumers; uses local content servers that cache frequently seen programs in order to deliver content with less latency (delay).

Continuity Testers: UTP tester that ensures that wires are inserted into RJ-45 connectors in the correct order and are making good contact.

Cord: A length of transmission medium—usually UTP or optical fiber but sometimes coaxial cable.

Core: 1) In optical fiber, the very thin tube into which a transmitter injects light. 2) In a switched network, the collection of all core switches.

Core Diameter: In optical fiber, the diameter of the core, through which the light signal propagates. 8.5, 50, or 62.5 microns.

Core Switch: A switch further up the hierarchy that carries traffic between pairs of switches. May also connect switches to routers.

Country Top-Level Domain: First-level domain name that specifies the owner's country (.UK, .AU, .CN, etc.)

Crack: To guess a password.

Credentials: Proof of identity that a supplicant can present during authentication.

Crimping Tool: Tool used to compress an RJ-45 connector onto the untwisted wires of a UTP cord.

Cross-Connect Device: The device within a wiring closet that vertical cords plug into. Cross-connect devices connect the wires from the riser space to 4-pair UTP cords that span out to the wall jacks on each floor.

Crosstalk Interference: Mutual EMI among wire pairs in a UTP cord.

Cryptographic System: A security system that automatically provides a mix of security protections, usually including confidentiality, authentication, message integrity, and replay protection.

Cryptography: Mathematical methods for protecting communication.

CSMA/CA + ACK: See Carrier Sense Multiple Access with Collision Avoidance and Acknowledgments. See definitions of the individual components.

CTS: See Clear to Send.

Customer Premises Equipment (CPE): Equipment owned by the customer, including PBXs, internal vertical and horizontal wiring, and telephone handsets.

Cyberterror: A computer attack made by terrorists.

Cyberwar: A computer attack made by a national government.

Data Field: A field containing the content delivered in a message.

Data Link: The path that a frame takes across a single network (LAN or WAN).

Data Link Layer: The layer that governs transmission within a single network all the way from the source station to the destination station across zero or more switches; Layer 2 in OSI. Governs switch or access point operation and the syntax of frames.

dB: See Decibels.

dBm: Decibels expressed relative to one milliwatt (mW), which is one thousandth of a watt, in the denominator.

DDoS: See Distributed Denial-of-Service.

Dead Spot: An area that cannot receive a radio signal due to the inability of the signal to pass through physical objects.

Decapsulation: When a device receives a frame, the procedure by which a layer process checks its layer message and passes the content up to the next higher level.

Decibels (dB): A way of expressing the ratio between two power levels, P_1 and P_2, on a logarithmic basis.

Decision Cache: In routing, a list a router keeps of recent routing decisions for specific IP addresses so that it does not have to go through an entire routing decision again if another packet to that IP address arrives. This is nonstandard and somewhat risky.

Decrypt: Conversion of encrypted ciphertext into the original plaintext so an authorized receiver can read an encrypted message.

Deep Inspection: Firewall filtering mechanism that looks at content in all layers of a packet. Typically also looks at streams of packets.

Default Router: 1) The next-hop router that a router will forward a packet to if the routing table does not have a row that governs the packet's IP address except for the default row. 2) The router to which a host will send packets unless it has specific instructions to send a packet to a different router.

Default Row: The row of a routing table that will be selected automatically if no other row matches; its value is 0.0.0.0.

Defense in Depth: The use of successive lines of defense.

Denial-of-Service (DoS): The type of attack whose goal is to make a computer or a network unavailable to its users.

Deregulation: Taking away monopoly protections from carriers to encourage competition.

Destination: In a routing table, a column that shows the destination network's network part or subnet's network part plus subnet part, followed by 0s. This row represents a route to this network or subnet.

DHCP: See Dynamic Host Configuration Protocol.

Dictionary Attack: A password-cracking attack in which an attacker tries to break a password by trying all words in a standard or customized dictionary.

Diff-Serv: The field in an IP packet that can be used to label IP packets for priority and other service parameters.

Digital Certificate: A document that gives the name of a true party, that true party's public key, and other information; used in authentication.

Digital Certificate Authentication: Authentication in which each user has a public key and a private key. Authentication depends on the applicant knowing the true party's private key; requires a digital certificate to give the true party's public key.

Digital Signaling: Signaling that uses a few states. Binary (two-state) transmission is a special case of digital transmission.

Digital Subscriber Line (DSL): A technology that provides digital data signaling over the residential customer's existing single-pair UTP voice-grade copper access line.

Direct Distance Dialing: Long-distance calls made at the standard long-distance rate.

Directory Server: Server that stores information about an organization's resources hierarchically.

Directly Propagating: A type of worm that tries to jump from the infected computer to many other computers without human intervention.

Disgruntled Employee or Ex-employee: Employee who is upset with the firm or an employee and who may take revenge through a computer attack.

Dish Antenna: An antenna that points in a particular direction, allowing it to send stronger outgoing signals in that direction for the same power and to receive weaker incoming signals from that direction.

Distributed Denial-of-Service (DDoS): DOS attack in which the victim is attacked by many computers.

DNS: See Domain Name System.

Domain: 1) In DNS, a group of resources (routers, single networks, and hosts) under the control of an organization. 2) In Microsoft Active Directory, a grouping of resources controlled by one or more Active Directory Servers.

Domain Controller: In Microsoft Active Directory, a computer that manages the computers in a domain.

Domain Name System (DNS): A server that provides IP addresses for users who know only a target host's host name. DNS servers also provide a hierarchical system for naming domains.

Domestic: Telephone service within a country.

DoS: See Denial-of-Service.

Dotted Decimal Notation: The notation used to ease human comprehension and memory in reading IP addresses.

Downlink: Downward transmission path for a communications satellite.

Downloader: Malware that downloads and installs another program on the computer.

Drive-By Hacker: Attacker outside a corporate building who hacks into the site through an access router, thus bypassing the site firewall.

Drop Cable: A thin coaxial cable access line that runs from the cable television company line in a neighborhood to individual homes.

DSL: See Digital Subscriber Line.

DSL Access Multiplexer (DSLAM): A device at the end office of the telephone company that sends voice signals over the ordinary PSTN and sends data over a data network such as an ATM network.

DSLAM: See DSL Access Multiplexer.

Dumb Access Point: A remotely managed access point that has insufficient resources to be managed directly and must be managed through a wireless switch.

Dumb Terminal: A desktop machine with a keyboard and display but little processing capability; processing is done on a host computer.

Dynamic Host Configuration Protocol (DHCP): The protocol used by DHCP servers, which provide each user PC with a temporary IP address to use each time he or she connects to the Internet.

Dynamic IP Address: A temporary IP address that a client PC receives from a DHCP server.

Dynamic Routing Protocol: A protocol that allows routers to exchange routing table information.

E1 Leased Line: The slowest leased line in the CEPT hierarchy used in Europe; has a speed of 2.048 Mbps.

Echo Message: An ICMP message that one host sends to another to tell if the receiver is active and reachable.

Egress Filtering: The filtering of traffic from inside a site going out.

EIGRP: See Enhanced Interior Gateway Routing Protocol.

Electromagnetic Interference (EMI): Unwanted electrical energy coming from external devices, such as electrical motors, fluorescent lights, and even nearby data transmission wires.

Electronic Signature: A bit string added to a message to provide message-by-message authentication and message integrity.

EMI: See Electromagnetic Interference.

Encapsulation: The placing of a message in the data field of another message.

Encapsulating Security Payload: For IPsec security, a block of bits that is added before the encrypted portion of the packet; added as an option in IPv4 packets or as an extension header in IPv6 packets.

Encoding: The conversation of messages into bits.

Encrypt: A mathematical process that substitutes a stream of bits for an original stream of bits; the substituted steam can be decrypted (returned to the original stream) by the receiver but not by an eavesdropper.

End Office Switch: The nearest switch of the telephone company to the customer premises.

End-to-End: 1) A layer where communication is governed directly between the transport process on the source host and the transport process on the destination host. 2) All the way from the source host to the destination host, as opposed to part of the path between the two hosts.

Enhanced Interior Gateway Routing Protocol (EIGRP): Interior routing protocol used by Cisco routers.

Enterprise Mode: In WPA and 802.11i, operating mode that uses 802.1X.

Ephemeral Port Number: The temporary number a client selects whenever it connects to an application program on a server. According to IETF rules, ephemeral port numbers should be between 49153 and 65535.

Error Advisement: In ICMP, a message that advises a host or router that there has been a transmission error.

Error Rate: In biometrics, the normal rate of misidentification when the subject is cooperating.

ESP: See Encapsulating Security Payload.

ESS: See Extended Service Set.

Ethernet: The dominant wired LAN standard. Now being used for metropolitan and wide area networking.

Ethernet Address: The 48-bit source and destination addresses in Ethernet 802.3 frames; these are EUI-48 addresses, previously called media access control (MAC) addresses.

Ethernet Frame: A message at the data link layer in an Ethernet network.

Ethernet Switch: Switch following the Ethernet standard. Notable for speed and low cost per Ethernet frame sent. Dominates LAN switching.

EUI-48 address: An extended unique identifier address that is 48 bits long. Formerly designated media access control (MAC) addresses. Still widely informally called MAC addresses.

Evil Twin Access Point: Attacker access point outside a building that attracts clients inside the building to associate with it.

Exhaustive Search: Cracking a key or password by trying all possible keys or passwords.

Exploit: A break-in program or attack method; a program that exploits known vulnerabilities.

Extended Service Set (ESS): A group of BSSs that are 1) connected to the same distribution system (network) and 2) have the same SSID.

Extended Unique Identifier: A type of address managed by the IEEE. The most common types are the EUI-48 addresses used in Ethernet and Wi-Fi networks and the EUI-64 addresses used in IPv6.

Extension Header: In IPv6, a header that follows the main header.

Exterior Dynamic Routing Protocol: Routing protocol used between autonomous systems.

Facilitating Server: A server that solves certain problems in P2P interactions but that allows clients to engage in P2P communication for most of the work.

False Alarm: In security, a system that provides an indication of an attack that proves not to be an attack upon further investigation.

Fiber to the Home (FTTH): Optical fiber brought by carriers to individual homes and businesses.

Field: 1) A subdivision of a message header or trailer. 2) A hexadecimal tetrad in an IPv6 address. Each field represents 16 bits. Fields are separated by colons.

File Sharing: The ability of computer users to share files that reside on their own disk drives or on a dedicated file server.

Filtering Method: A method used by firewalls and intrusion detection systems to make decisions about whether packet or stream of packets is malicious.

Fin Bit: One-bit field in a TCP header; indicates that the sender wishes to close a TCP connection.

Fingerprint Scanning: A form of biometric authentication that uses the applicant's fingerprints.

Firewall: A security system that examines each packet passing through it. If the firewall identifies the packet as an attack packet, the firewall discards it and copies information about the discarded packet into a log file.

Flag Field: A one-bit field.

Flat Rate: Local telephone service in which there is a fixed monthly service charge but no separate fee for individual local calls.

Flow Control: The ability of one side in a conversation to tell the other side to slow or stop its transmission rate.

Flow Label Field: In IPv6, all packets in a stream of packets are given the same flow label number.

Footprint: Area of coverage of a communication satellite's signal.

Forwarding Decision: In switches (and routers), the decision about which port (interface) the switch (router) will use to send an incoming frame (packet) back out.

Fractional T1: A type of private line that offers intermediate speeds at intermediate prices; usually operates at one of the following speeds: 128 kbps, 256 kbps, 384 kbps, 512 kbps, or 768 kbps.

Fragment (Fragmentation): To break a message into multiple smaller messages. TCP fragments application layer messages, while IP packets may be fragmented by routers along the packet's route.

Frame: 1) A message at the data link layer. 2) In time division multiplexing, a brief time period, which is further subdivided into slots.

Frame Check Sequence Field: A four-octet field used in error checking in Ethernet. If an error is found, the frame is discarded.

Frame Relay: A popular Public Switched Data Network that operates at speeds of about 256 kbps to 40 Mbps.

Fraud: Theft that involves lying in the form of incorrect information that by law must be correct or in the form of not providing information that must be provided by law.

Frequency: The number of complete cycles a radio wave goes through per second. In sound, frequency corresponds to pitch.

Frequency Modulation: Modulation in which one frequency is chosen to represent a 1 and another frequency is chosen to represent a 0.

Frequency Spectrum: The range of all possible frequencies from zero hertz to infinity.

FTTH: See Fiber to the Home.

Full-Duplex Communication: A type of communication that supports simultaneous two-way transmission. Almost all communication systems today are full-duplex systems.

Gateway: An obsolete term for "router"; still in use by Microsoft.

Gbps: See Gigabit per Second.

Generic Top-Level Domain: First-level domain name that specifies the type of organization that owns the domain (.com, .edu, etc.).

GEO: See Geosynchronous Earth Orbit Satellite.

Geosynchronous Earth Orbit Satellite (GEO): The type of satellite most commonly used in fixed wireless access today; orbits the earth at about 36,000 km (22,300 miles).

Get: An SNMP command sent by the manager that tells the agent to retrieve certain information and return this information to the manager.

GHz: See Gigahertz.

Gigabit Ethernet: 1 Gbps versions of Ethernet.

Gigabit per Second: A speed of 1,000,000,000 bps.

Gigahertz (GHz): One billion hertz.

Guideline: A directive that should be followed but that need not be followed, depending on the context.

H.323: In IP telephony, one of the protocols used by signaling gateways.

Hacker: Someone who intentionally uses a computer resource without authorization or in excess of authorization.

Hacking: The intentional use of a computer resource without authorization or in excess of authorization.

Handoff: a) In wireless LANs, a change in access points when a user moves to another location. b) In cellular telephony, transfer from one cellsite to another, which occurs when a subscriber moves from one cell to another within a system.

Hands-Free Profile (HFP): In Bluetooth, profile that governs device–device communication for voice dialing, adjusting volume, hanging up, number redial, call waiting, and other telephone use actions.

Head End: The cable television operator's central distribution point.

Header: The part of a message that comes before the data field.

Header Checksum: The UDP datagram field that allows the receiver to check for errors.

Hertz (Hz): One cycle per second, a measure of frequency.

Hex Notation: See Hexadecimal Notation.

Hexadecimal Notation: A way of writing addresses based on Base 16 (hexadecimal) symbols; used in Ethernet and IPv6.

Hierarchical Topology: A network topology in which all switches are arranged in a hierarchy, in which each switch has only one parent switch above it (the root switch, however, has no parent); used in Ethernet.

High-Speed Bluetooth: Bluetooth operating mode that retains ordinary Bluetooth speeds for most operations but that can turn on a second radio that uses a version of 802.11 limited to peer-to-peer transmission between two devices.

Hop Limit Field: In IPv6, the field that limits the number of hops an IPv6 packet may make among routers.

Host: Any computer attached to a network.

Host Computer: 1) In terminal–host computing, the host that provides the processing power. 2) On an internet, any host.

Host Name: An unofficial designation for a host computer.

Host Part: The part of an IP address that identifies a particular host on a subnet.

Hot Spot: An area served by Wi-Fi, typically offered by a coffee shop, airport lounge, or other public or semipublic area; may be free or may require a fee.

HTML: See Hypertext Markup Language.

HTML Body: Body part in a Hypertext Markup Language message.

HTTP: See Hypertext Transfer Protocol.

HTTP Request Message: In HTTP, a message in which a client requests a file or another service from a server.

HTTP Request–Response Cycle: An HTTP client request followed by an HTTP server response.

HTTP Response Message: In HTTP, a message in which a server responds to a client request;

contains either a requested file or an error message explaining why the requested file could not be supplied.

Human Interface Device (HID) Profile: In Bluetooth, this profile is used for mice, keyboards, and other input devices.

Hybrid Switched/Wireless Network: A network that uses Ethernet as the distribution system but that connects some hosts to Ethernet switches using Wi-Fi. Although not technically a single network because two standards are involved, the two work together so well that it is considered a single network if it is part of an internet.

Hypertext Markup Language (HTML): A document format standard used in webpages.

Hypertext Transfer Protocol (HTTP): The protocol that governs interactions between the browser and webserver application program.

Hz: See Hertz.

ICC: See International Common Carrier.

ICMP: See Internet Control Message Protocol.

ICMP Error Message: ICMP supervisory message sent by an internet layer process to another to indicate that an error has occurred; not mandatory and does not provide error correction and therefore reliability.

IDC: See Insulation Displacement Connection.

Identity Theft: Stealing enough information about a person to impersonate him or her in large financial transactions.

IEEE: See Institute for Electrical and Electronics Engineers.

IETF: See Internet Engineering Task Force.

ILEC: See Incumbent Local Exchange Carrier.

IMAP: See Internet Message Access Protocol.

Implementation Guidance: Instructions that are more specific than policies but less specific than implementation.

Incident: A successful attack.

Incumbent Local Exchange Carrier (ILEC): The traditional monopoly telephone company within each LATA.

Index Website: In BitTorrent, a website that contains .torrent files giving information about specific files and where they are stored.

Individual Throughput: The actual speed a single user receives (usually much lower than aggregate throughput in a system with shared transmission speed).

Infrastructure as a Service: A cloud service that provides processing power in the form of a virtual machine. The customer manages the machine and adds its own applications.

Ingress Filtering: The filtering of traffic coming into a site from the outside.

Initial Sequence Number (ISN): The sequence number placed in the first TCP segment aside transmits in a session; selected randomly.

Initial Site Survey: For 802.11 LANs, an electromagnetic field strength survey performed at the beginning of an installation instantiate. In virtualization, create a new virtual machine.

Institute for Electrical and Electronics Engineers (IEEE): Professional society whose Standards Agency creates networking standards.

Insulation Displacement Connection (IDC): A connection in which a metal prong is pushed through insulation into another wire.

Interexchange Carrier (IXC): A telephone carrier that transmits voice traffic between LATAs.

Interface: 1) The router's equivalent of a network interface card; a port on a router that must be designed for the network to which it connects. 2) In webservices, the outlet through which an object communicates with the outside world.

Interference: Occurs when external electromagnetic energy adds to a signal's electromagnetic energy; may make the original signal unreadable.

Interior Dynamic Routing Protocol: Routing protocol used within a firm's internet.

Internal Router: A router that connects different LANs within a site.

International Common Carrier (ICC): A telephone carrier that provides international service.

International Organization for Standardization (ISO): A strong standards agency for manufacturing, including computer manufacturing. One of the two standards agencies that creates OSI standards.

International Telecommunications Union–Telecommunications Standards Sector (ITU–T): Agency of the United Nations that creates telecommunications standards; one of the two standards agencies that creates OSI standards.

Internet: 1) A group of networks connected by routers so that any application on any host on any network can communicate with any application on any other host on any other network. 2) A general term for any internetwork (spelled with a lowercase i). 3) The worldwide Internet (spelled with a capital I).

Internet Backbone: The set of Internet service providers that carries traffic between ISPs that provide service to users; a single ISP can be both.

Internet Control Message Protocol (ICMP): The protocol created by the IETF to oversee supervisory messages at the internet layer.

Internet Engineering Task Force (IETF): TCP/IP's standards agency.

Internet Layer: The layer that governs the transmission of a packet across an entire internet.

Internet Message Access Protocol (IMAP): One of the two protocols used to download received e-mail from an e-mail server; offers more features but is less popular than POP.

Internet of Things: A term to denote direct host-to-host communication when no human is involved at either end.

Internet Protocol (IP): The TCP/IP protocol that governs operations at the internet layer. Governs packet delivery from host to host across a series of routers.

Internet Service Provider (ISP): Carrier that provides Internet access and transmission.

Interoperate: To work together effectively.

Inverse Square Law: Radio signal strength declines with the square of transmission distance.

IP: See Internet Protocol.

IP Address: An Internet Protocol address; the address that every computer needs when it connects to the Internet; IP addresses are 32 bits long.

IP Packets: In TCP/IP, messages at the internet layer.

IP Security (IPsec): A set of standards that operate at the internet layer and provide security to all upper layer protocols transparently.

IPsec Policy Server: In IP Security, a server that controls IPsec security parameters on a number of hosts.

IP Version 4 (IPv4): The standard that governs most routers on the Internet and private internets.

IP Version 6 (IPv6): A new version of the Internet Protocol.

IPsec: See IP Security.

IPsec Gateway: Border device at a site that converts internal data traffic into protected data traffic that travels over an untrusted system such as the Internet.

IPv4: See IP Version 4.

IPv6: See IP Version 6.

Iris: The colored part of the human eye; used in biometric authentication.

Iris Scanning: A form of biometric authentication that scans the pattern in the colored part of the applicant's eyes.

ISN: See Initial Sequence Number.

ISO: See International Organization for Standardization.

ISP: See Internet Service Provider.

ITU-T: See International Telecommunications Union–Telecommunications Standards Sector.

IXC: See Interexchange Carrier.

Jacket: The outer covering of a wire or optical fiber bundle.

Jitter: Variability in latency.

kbps: See Kilobits per Second.

Key: In encryption, a string of bits used by a cipher to encrypt or decrypt (or both) as string of bits; the cipher method cannot be kept secret, so the key is must to prevent unauthorized use.

Label Header: In MPLS, the header added to packets before the IP header; contains information that aids and speeds routers in choosing which interface to send the packet back out.

Label Number: In MPLS, number in the label header that aids label switching routers in packet sending.

Label Switched Path: A path that all packets to a particular address will take across an MPLS network.

Label Switching Router: Router that implements MPLS.

LAN: See Local Area Network.

LATA: See Local Access and Transport Area.

Latency: Delay, usually measured in milliseconds.

Latency-Intolerant: Applications that do not operate well if there is too much latency (delay) in the network.

Layer 1: The physical Layer.

Layer 2: The data link Layer.

Layer 3: See Internet Layer.

Layer 4: See Transport Layer.

Layer 5: See Application Layer.

Leased Line: A high-speed, point-to-point, always-on circuit.

Least Permissions: Giving each user the minimum permissions that he or she needs to do his or her specific job on a system.

Length Field: 1) The field in an Ethernet MAC frame that gives the length of the data field in octets. 2) The field in a UDP datagram that enables the receiving transport process to process the datagram properly.

LEO: See Low Earth Orbit Satellite.

Licensed Radio Band: Radio band in which stations must have a government license to operate.

Lightweight Directory Access Protocol: Simple protocol for accessing directory servers.

Link Aggregation: The use of two or more trunk links between a pair of switches; also known as trunking or bonding.

LLC: See Logical Link Control.

LLC Subheader: See Logical Link Control Layer Header.

Load Balancing: Dividing traffic across routers in order not to overload any single route.

Local Access and Transport Area (LATA): One of the roughly 200 site regions the United States has been divided into for telephone service.

Local Area Network (LAN): A network within a customer's premises.

Local Calling: Telephone calls placed to a nearby caller; less expensive than long-distance calls.

Local Content Server: See Content Delivery Network.

Local Loop: In telephony, the line used by the customer to reach the PSTN's central transport core.

Log File: A file that contains data on events.

Logical Link Control (LLC) Layer: The layer of functionality for the upper part of the data link layer, now largely ignored.

Logical Link Control Layer (LLC) Subheader: The header at the start of the data field that describes the type of packet contained in the data field.

Long Distance: A telephone call placed to a distance party; more expensive than a local call.

Long-Term Evolution (LTE) Advanced: Currently, all cellular carriers are planning to use a single transmission standard for 4G, at least initially. This is Long-Term Evolution (LTE) Advanced. Now that there is consensus on technology, 4G service is likely to move forward in a timelier manner. LTE is a slower introductory protocol.

Longest Match: The matching row that matches a packet's destination IP address to the greatest number of bits; chosen by a router when there are multiple matches.

Low Earth Orbit Satellite (LEO): A type of satellite used in mobile wireless transmission; orbits a few hundred miles or a few hundred kilometers above the earth.

LTE: See Long-Term Evolution.

MAC: See Media Access Control.

MAC Address: See Media Access Control.

Malware: Software that seeks to cause damage.

Malware Writers: Someone who creates malware; usually not illegal under freedom of speech.

MAN: See Metropolitan Area Network.

Managed Switch: A switch that has sufficient intelligence to be managed from a central computer (the Manager).

Managed Device: A device that needs to be administered, such as printers, hubs, switches, routers, application programs, user PCs, and other pieces of hardware and software.

Management Information Base (MIB): A specification that defines what objects can exist on each type of managed device and also the specific characteristics of each object; the actual database stored on a manager in SNMP. There are separate MIBs for different types of managed devices; both a schema and a database.

Manager: The central PC or more powerful computer that uses SNMP to collect information from many managed devices.

Mask: A 32-bit string beginning with a series of 1s and ending with a series of 0s; used by routing tables to interpret IP address part sizes. The 1s designate either the network part or the network plus software part.

Master–Slave: Form of transmission in which one host controls the transmission of another host.

Maximum Transmission Unit (MTU): The largest message that can pass through a single network.

Mbps: **1,000,000 bps.**

Media Access Control (MAC): The process of controlling when stations transmit; also, the lowest part of the data link layer, defining functionality specific to a particular LAN technology.

Media Gateway: A device that connects IP telephone networks to the ordinary public switched telephone network. Media gateways also convert between the signaling formats of the IP telephone system and the PSTN.

Medium Earth Orbit Satellite (MEO): A type of satellite used in mobile wireless transmission; orbits a few thousand miles or a few thousand kilometers above the earth.

Megabits per Second: Millions of bits per second.

Megahertz (MHz): One million hertz.

Member Server: In Active Directory, a server that is not a domain controller.

MEO: See Medium Earth Orbit Satellite.

Mesh Networking: A type of networking in which wireless devices route frames without the aid of wired LANs.

Mesh Topology: 1) A topology where there are many connections among switches or routers, so there are many alternative routes for messages to get from one end of the network to the other. 2) In network design, a topology that provides direct connections between many pair of sites.

Message: A discrete communication between hardware or software processes.

Message Integrity: The assurance that a message has not been changed en route; or if a message has been changed, the receiver can tell that it has.

Message Ordering: Controlling when one device in a pair may transmit.

Message Unit: Local telephone service in which a user is charged based on distance and duration.

Metered Service: A pay-as-you-go pricing model where a customer pays only for the service that he or she actually uses.

Metric: A number describing the desirability of a route represented by a certain row in a routing table.

Metric Prefix: In the metric system, a single letter (usually) that multiplies the base unit. For instance, in Mbps, the M stands for mega (million). So Mbps is 1 million bits per second. This is multiplied by the number before it. So 73.23 kbps is 73,230 bps without a metric prefix.

Metro Ethernet: Initial name for carrier Ethernet, which is the use of Ethernet for WAN or MAN transmission.

Metropolitan Area Network (MAN): A WAN that spans a single urban area.

MHz: See Megahertz.

MHz-km: Measure of modal bandwidth, a measure of multimode fiber quality.

MIB: See Management Information Base.

Micron: Unit of length. One millionth of a meter.

Microwave: Traditional point-to-point radio transmission system.

Microwave Repeater: Transmitter/receiver that extends the distance a microwave link can travel.

Millisecond (ms): The unit in which latency is measured.

Milliwatt (mW): One thousandth of a watt.

MIME: See Multipurpose Internet Mail Extensions.

MIMO: See Multiple Input/Multiple Output.

Minimum Permissions: The principle of giving each person only the permissions he or she needs to have to do his or her job.

Ministry of Telecommunications: A government-created regulatory body that oversees PTTs.

Mobile Code: Code that travels with a downloaded webpage from the webserver to the browser.

Mobile Phone: See Cellphone.

Mobile Telephone Switching Office (MTSO): A control center that connects cellular customers to one another and to wired telephone users, as well as overseeing all cellular calls (determining what to do when people move from one cell to another, including which cellsite should handle a caller when the caller wishes to place a call).

Modal Bandwidth: The measure of multimode fiber quality.

Modal Dispersion: The main propagation problem for optical fiber; dispersion in which the difference in the arrival times of various modes (permitted light rays) is too large, causing the light rays of adjacent pulses to overlap in their arrival times and rendering the signal unreadable.

Mode: An angle at which light rays are permitted to enter an optical fiber core.

Modem: A device that translates between digital computer signals and analog telephone line signals.

Momentary Traffic Peak: A surplus of traffic that briefly exceeds the network's capacity, happening only occasionally.

MPLS: See Multiprotocol Label Switching.

Ms: See Millisecond.

MTSO: See Mobile Telephone Switching Office.

MTU: See Maximum Transmission Unit.

Multi-User MIMO: A form of MIMO in which multiple users can send and receive in the same channel simultaneously.

Multimode Fiber: The most common type of fiber in LANs, wherein light rays in a pulse can enter a fairly thick core at multiple angles. Inexpensive but can transmit signals over sufficient distance for LAN usage.

Multipath Interference: Interference caused when a receiver receives two or more signals—a direct signal and one or more reflected signals. The multiple signals may interfere with one another.

Multiple Input/Multiple Output (MIMO): A radio transmission method that sends several signals simultaneously in a single radio channel.

Multiplexing: 1) Having the packets of many conversations share trunk lines; reduces trunk line cost. 2) The ability of a protocol to carry messages from multiple next-higher-layer protocols in a single communication session.

Multiplexes: Mixes together, typically to reduce cost through economies of scale.

Multiprotocol: Characterized by implementing many different protocols and products following different architectures.

Multiprotocol Label Switching (MPLS): A traffic management tool used by many ISPs.

mW: See Milliwatt.

Nanometer (nm): A length in the metric system; one billionth (1 times 10^9) of a meter. Abbreviated as nm; used to measure light waves near the visible area of the spectrum.

NAT: See Network Address Translation.

Near Field Communication (NFC): Form of radio transmission in which devices within about 4 cm (roughly 2 in.) can communicate peer-to-peer.

Network: In IP addressing, an organizational concept: a group of hosts, single networks, and routers owned by a single organization.

Network Address Translation (NAT): Converting an IP address into another IP address, usually at a border firewall; disguises a host's true IP address from sniffers. Allows more internal addresses to be used than an ISP supplies a firm with external addresses.

Network Core: The central part of the network.

Network Layer: In OSI, Layer 3; governs internetworking. OSI network layer standards are rarely used.

Network Management Agent (Agent): A piece of software on the managed device that communicates with the manager on behalf of the managed device.

Network Management Program (Manager): A program run by the network administrator on a central computer.

Network Mask: A mask that has 1s in the network part of an IP address and 0s in all other parts.

Network Operations Center (NOC): Central control room for the network.

Network Part: The part of an IP address that identifies the host's network on the Internet.

Network Printer: Printer that connects directly to a network port rather than to an individual computer.

Network Software: On a host computer, the software that manages the host's interaction with a network.

Network Standard: A rule of operation that governs the exchange of messages between two hardware or software processes.

Network Visibility: In network management, the ability to visualize what is happening inside the network in a way that helps manage the network.

Networked Application: An application that provides service over a network.

Next Header Field: In an IPv6 main or extension header, the field that specifies the next header's type or specifies that the payload follows the header.

Next-Hop Router: A router to which another router forwards a packet in order to get the packet a step closer to reaching its destination host.

NGFW: See Next-Generation Firewall.

Nm (nm): See Nanometer.

NOC: See Network Operations Center.

Node: A client, server, switch, router, or other type of device in a network.

Noise: Unwanted electrical energy in a wire; can add to the signal and make the signal unreadable.

Not Set: When a flag's field is given the value 0.

Object: In SNMP, an aspect of a managed device about which data is kept.

OC: See Optical Carrier.

Octet: A collection of 8 bits; same as a byte.

OFDM: See Orthogonal Frequency Division Multiplexing.

Omnidirectional Antenna: An antenna that transmits signals in all directions and receives incoming signals equally well from all directions.

One-to-One Connection: Transmission from one host to another. Unicasting.

One-Pair Voice-Grade (1PVG) UTP: The traditional telephone access lines to individual residences.

Open Shortest Path First (OSPF): Complex but highly scalable interior routing protocol.

Optical Carrier: In the Synchronous Optical Network (SONET) standard, a designator of a particular speed.

Optical Fiber: Cabling that sends signals as light pulses.

Optical Fiber Cord: A length of optical fiber.

Option: One of several possibilities that a user or technologist can select.

Organizational Unit: In directory servers, a subunit of the Organization node.

Orthogonal Frequency Division Multiplexing (OFDM): A form of spread spectrum transmission that divides each broadband channel into subcarriers and then transmits parts of each frame in each subcarrier.

OSI: The Reference Model of Open Systems Interconnection; the 7-layer network standards architecture created by ISO and ITU-T; dominant at the physical and data link layers, which govern transmission within single networks (LANs or WANs).

OSPF: See Open Shortest Path First.

Overprovisioning: To install much more capacity in switches and trunk links than will be needed most of the time, so that momentary traffic peaks will not cause problems.

Oversight: A collection of methods to ensure that policies have been implemented properly.

P2P: See Peer-to-Peer.

Packet: At layer 3, the basic unit of organization.

Packet Error Rate: The percentage of packets that are incorrect.

Packet Switching: The breaking of conversations into short messages (typically a few hundred bits long); allows multiplexing on trunk lines to reduce trunk line costs.

PAD Field: A field that the sender adds to an Ethernet frame if the data field is less than 46 octets long (the total length of the PAD plus data field must be exactly 46 octets long).

PAN: See Personal Area Network.

Parallel Transmission: A form of transmission that uses multiple wire pairs or other transmission media simultaneously to send a signal; increases transmission speed.

Pass Phrase: A series of words used to generate a key.

Passive Radio Frequency ID (RFID) Tags: Radio frequency ID tags that do not possess a power source. They are powered by the energy of the radio signal that reads them.

Password: A secret string of keyboard characters used to authenticate a supplicant.

Password Length: The number of characters in a password.

Patch: An addition to a program that will close a security vulnerability in that program.

Payload: 1) In security, a piece of code that can be executed by a virus or worm after it has spread to multiple machines. 2) In IPv6, all of the packet after the main packet header.

Payment Card Industry–Data Security Standard (PCI–DSS): Security standards for companies that accept credit card payments.

Payload Length Field: In IPv6 packets, a field that gives the length of everything following the main header, including subsidiary headers.

PBX: See Private Branch Exchange.

PCI–DSS: See Payment Card Industry–Data Security Standard.

Peer-to-Peer Architecture (P2P): The application architecture in which most or all of the work is done by cooperating user computers, such as desktop PCs. If servers are present at all, they serve only facilitating roles and do not control the processing.

Peering: For two Bluetooth devices to work together, they must first go through an initial handshaking stage called peering. This will require them to exchange information about themselves.

Permanent IP Address: An unchanging IP address; usually entered into a device manually, and normally used for servers so that clients can locate them.

Permission: A rule that determines what an account owner can do to a particular resource (file or directory).

Personal Area Network (PAN): A small wireless network used by a single person.

Personal Identification Number (PIN): A four- or six-digit number a cardholder types to authenticate himself or herself.

Personal Mode: Pre-shared Key Mode in WPA or 802.11i.

Phase Modulation: Modulation in which one wave serves as a reference wave or a carrier wave. Another wave varies its phase to represent one or more bits.

Phishing: Social engineering attack that uses an official-looking e-mail message or website.

Physical Layer: The standards layer that governs physical transmission between adjacent devices; OSI Layer 1.

Physical Link: A connection linking adjacent devices on a network.

Piconet: In Bluetooth, a personal area network with up to eight devices.

PIN: See Personal Identification Number.

Ping: Sending a message to another host and listening for a response to see if it is active.

Plan–Protect–Respond Cycle: The basic management cycle in which the three named stages are executed repeatedly.

Planning: In security, developing a broad security strategy that will be appropriate for a firm's security threats.

Plenum: Type of wiring with reduced toxic fumes. Required for runs through air-conditioning ducts and other critical airspaces (plenums).

POE: See Power over Ethernet.

Point of Presence (POP): 1) In cellular telephony, a site at which various carriers that provide telephone service are interconnected. 2) In PSDNs, a point of connection for user sites. There must be a private line between the site and the POP.

Point-to-Point Network: A single network that connects two devices directly with a single physical layer transmission link. In internets, often used to connect a pair of routers.

Point-to-Point Topology: A topology wherein two nodes are connected directly.

Point-to-Point Protocol (PPP): A protocol commonly used in point-to-point networks.

Policy: A broad statement that specifies what should be accomplished.

POP: See 1) Point of Presence. 2) Post Office Protocol.

Port: In a switch, a portal for incoming or outgoing wire or optical fiber cords. In software engineering, a famous researcher.

Port-Based Access Control: Another name for 802.1X.

Port Number: The field in TCP and UDP that tells the transport process what application process sent the data in the data field or should receive the data in the data field.

Post Office Protocol (POP): The most popular protocol used to download e-mail from an e-mail server to an e-mail client.

Potential Single Point of Takeover: In a system, a location which, if taken over by an attacker, would give the attacker complete or nearly complete control of the system.

Power over Ethernet (POE): A standard that can bring electrical power to RJ-45 wall jacks.

Preamble Field: The initial field in an Ethernet MAC frame; synchronizes the receiver's clock to the sender's clock.

Prefix Notation: A way of representing masks. Gives the number of initial 1s in the mask.

Premises: In telecommunications, a building or other physical area owned by a customer rather than by a carrier.

Pre-Shared Key (PSK): A mode of operation in WPA and 802.11i in which all stations and an access point share the same initial key.

Printer Sharing: A network service in which multiple users can share a printer over a network.

Priority: Preference given to latency-sensitive traffic, such as voice and video traffic, so that latency-sensitive traffic will go first if there is congestion.

Priority Level: The three-bit field used to give a frame one of eight priority levels from 000 (zero) to 111 (eight).

Private Branch Exchange (PBX): An internal telephone switch.

Private IP Address: An IP address that may be used only within a firm. Private IP addresses have three designated ranges: 10.x.x.x, 192.168.x.x, and 172.16.x.x through 172.31.x.x.

Private Key: A key that only the true party should know. Part of a public key–private key pair.

Probe Packet: A packet sent by an attacker to help the attacker understand a network and its hosts.

Project Portfolio: A selection of projects that the firm will implement during a plan's initial period.

Propagate: In signals, to travel.

Propagation Effects: Changes that take place as a signal propagates; if too large, will make the signal unreadable.

Propagation Vector: A method malware uses to move to a victim computer.

Property: A characteristic of an object.

Protecting: Implementing a security plan; the most time-consuming stage in the plan–protect–respond management cycle.

Protocol: Another name for standard.

Protocol Field: In IP, a field that designates the protocol of the message in the IP packet's data field.

Provable Attack Packet: A packet that is provably an attack packet.

Proximity Access Card: Access card that does not have to be inserted into or swiped through a reader; only close presence is necessary to be read.

PSDN: See Public Switched Data Network.

PSTN: See Public Switched Telephone Network.

PTT: See Public Telephone and Telegraph Authority.

Public IP Address: A range of IP addresses that may be used on the Internet, as opposed to a private IP address range, which may only be used within a firm.

Public Key: A key that is not kept secret. Part of a public key–private key pair.

Public Key Authentication: Authentication in which each user has a public key and a private key. Authentication depends on the applicant knowing the true party's private key; requires a digital certificate to give the true party's public key.

Public Key Encryption: Encryption in which each side has a public key and a private key, so there are four keys in total for bidirectional communication. The sender encrypts messages with the receiver's public key. The receiver, in turn, decrypts incoming messages with the receiver's own private key.

Public Key Infrastructure (PKI): A total system (infrastructure) for public key encryption.

Public Switched Data Network (PSDN): A carrier WAN that provides data transmission service. The customer only needs to connect to the PSDN by running one private line from each site to the PSDN carrier's nearest POP.

Public Switched Telephone Network (PSTN): The worldwide telephone network.

Public Telephone and Telegraph Authority (PTT): The title for the traditional monopoly telephone carrier in most countries.

Public Utilities Commission (PUC): In the United States, telecommunications regulatory agency at the state level.

PUC: See Public Utilities Commission.

QAM: See Quadrature Amplitude Modulation.

QoS: See Quality of Service.

QoS Parameters: See Quality-of-Service Parameters.

QPSK: See Quadrature Phase Shift Keying.

Quadrature Amplitude Modulation (QAM): Modulation technique that uses two carrier waves—a sine carrier wave and a cosine carrier wave. Each can vary in amplitude.

Quadrature Phase Shift Keying (QPSK): Modulation with four possible phases. Each of the four states represents two bits (00, 01, 10, and 11).

Quality of Service (QoS): Numerical service targets that must be met by networking staff.

Quality-of-Service (QoS) Parameters: A metric for a particular quality-of-service parameter such as speed, latency, or jitter.

Radio Frequency ID (RFID): A tag that can be read at a distance by a radio transmitter/receiver.

Radio Wave: An electromagnetic signal that carries useful information

RADIUS: A standard for central authentication server operation; the abbreviation is almost never spelled out.

Rapid Spanning Tree Protocol (RSTP): A version of the Spanning Tree Protocol that has faster convergence.

Rated Speed: The official standard speed of a technology.

RBOC: See Regional Bell Operating Company.

Real Time Protocol (RTP): The protocol that adds headers that contain sequence numbers to ensure that the UDP datagrams are placed in proper sequence and that they contain time stamps so that jitter can be eliminated.

Redundancy: Duplication of a hardware device in order to enhance reliability.

Regenerate: To recreate an original signal; done by each switch along a data link or on each router along a route before passing on an arriving frame or packet.

Regional Bell Operating Company (RBOC): One of the companies that was created to provide local

service when the Bell System (AT&T) was broken up in the early 1980s.

Relative Signal Strength Indicator (RSSI): Signifies the signal strength available to a wireless host, relative to the signal strengths of other access points.

Reliable: A protocol in which errors are corrected by resending lost or damaged messages.

Reliability: The likelihood that a system will work.

Remote Access VPN: Virtual private network that allows a remote host to communicate securely with a site.

Request for Comments: Internet Engineering Task Force Document created for comments; some are standards-track documents, and some are actual standards.

Request to Send: In 802.11 networks, a message sent to an access point when a station wishes to send and is able to send because of CSMA/CA. The station may send when it receives a clear-to-send message.

Request to Send/Clear to Send: A system that uses request-to-send and clear-to-send messages to control transmissions and avoid collisions in wireless transmission.

Request–Response Cycle: When one process sends another a request for service and the receiving process sends back a reply.

Reserved Capacity: Transmission or switching capacity reserved for a particular application. If the application does not use the reserved capacity, it is still not available for other applications.

Responding: In security, the act of stopping and repairing an attack.

Response: 1) A reaction to an incoming message. 2) Responding according to plan to security incidents.

Response Message: In Challenge–Response Authentication Protocols, the message that the applicant returns to the verifier.

Reusable Password: Password that is used repeatedly to get access.

RFC: See Request for Comment.

RFC 2822: The standard for e-mail bodies that are plaintext messages.

RFID: See Radio Frequency ID.

Right of Way: Permission to lay wires in public areas; given by government regulators to transmission carriers.

Risk Analysis: The process of balancing threats and protection costs.

RJ-45 Connector: The connector at the end of a UTP cord, which plugs into an RJ-45 jack.

RJ-45 Jack: The type of jack into which UTP cords RJ-45 connectors may plug.

Roaming: 1) In cellular telephony, the situation when a subscriber leaves a metropolitan cellular system and goes to another city or country. 2) In 802.11, when a wireless host travels from one access point to another.

Rogue Access Point: An unauthorized access point.

Root: 1) The level at the top of a DNS hierarchy, consisting of all domain names. 2) A super account on a Unix server that automatically has full permissions in every directory on the server.

Root DNS Server: One of 13 top-level servers in the Domain Name System (DNS).

Route: The path that a packet takes across an internet.

Router: A device that forwards packets within an internet. Routers connect two or more single networks (subnets).

Routing: 1) The forwarding of IP packets. 2) The exchange of routing protocol information through routing protocols.

Routing Protocol: A protocol used by routers to communicate in order to exchange routing table information.

RSSI: See Relative Signal Strength Indicator.

RSTP: See Rapid Spanning Tree Protocol.

RTP: See Real Time Protocol.

RTS: See Request to Send.

RTS/CTS: See Request to Send/Clear to Send.

SaaS: See Software as a Service.

SC Connector: A square optical fiber connector, recommended in the TIA/EIA-568 standard for use in new installations.

Scalability: The ability of a technology to handle growth well.

Scale: The ability to grow to sufficient size to meet an organization's needs and to do so in a way that is economical at larger sizes.

Scan: To examine frames, packets, or other entities.

Script: A group of commands written in a simplified programming language.

SDH: See Synchronous Digital Hierarchy.

SDN Controller: In software-defined networking, a server that sends forwarding rules to individual switches and routers based on the requirements of an SDN application. Without SDN, the control function is built into individual switches and routers.

Second-Level Domain: The third level of a DNS hierarchy, which usually specifies an organization (e.g., microsoft.com, hawaii.edu).

Secure Sockets Layer (SSL): The simplest VPN security standard to implement; later renamed Transport Layer Security. Provides a secure connection at the transport layer, protecting any applications above it that are SSL/TLS-aware.

Security Association (SAs): An agreement between two parties on the security methods and parameters they will use in their subsequent interactions.

Segment: In the Transmission Control Protocol, the name for a message at the transport layer.

Semantics: In message exchange, the meaning of each message.

Sequence Number Field: In TCP, a header field that tells a TCP segment's order among the multiple TCP segments sent by one side.

Serial Transmission: Ethernet transmission over a single pair in each direction.

Server Host: A host that provides services to other (client) hosts.

Service: In a service-oriented architecture (SOA), a service object provides services to calling programs.

Service Band: A subdivision of the frequency spectrum, dedicated to a specific service such as FM radio or cellular telephone service.

Service Level Agreement (SLA): A quality-of-service guarantee for throughput, availability, latency, error rate, and other matters.

Service Set identifier (SSID): On a wireless access point, the name of the network.

Session Initiation Protocol (SIP): Relatively simple signaling protocol for voice over IP.

Session Key: Symmetric key that is used only during a single communication session between two parties.

Set: 1) When a flag's field is given the value 1. 2) An SNMP command sent by the manager that tells the agent to change a parameter on the managed device.

SETI@home: A project from the Search for Extraterrestrial Intelligence (SETI), in which volunteers download SETI@home screen savers that are really programs. These programs do work for the SETI@ home server when the volunteer computer is idle. Processing ends when the user begins to do work.

Shadow Zone (Dead Spot): A location where a receiver cannot receive radio transmission, due to an obstruction blocking the direct path between sender and receiver.

Shared Internet Access: Access that allows two or more client PCs to use the Internet simultaneously, as if each was plugged directly into the broadband modem.

Signal: An information-carrying disturbance that propagates through a transmission medium.

Signal Bandwidth: The range of frequencies in a signal, determined by subtracting the lowest frequency from the highest frequency.

Single Network: A network using a single networking standard (technology), under the control of a single organization, and having a coordinated address space in each host has a unique address.

Signaling: In telephony, the controlling of calling, including setting up a path for a conversation through the transport core, maintaining and terminating the conversation path, collecting billing information, and handling other supervisory functions.

Signaling Gateway: The device that sets up conversations between parties, maintains these conversations, ends them, provides billing information, and does other work.

Signaling System 7 (SS7): Telephone signaling system in the United States.

Signal-to-Noise Ratio (SNR): The ratio of the signal strength to average noise strength; should be high in order for the signal to be effectively received.

Signing: Encrypting something with the sender's private key.

Simple Mail Transfer Protocol (SMTP): The protocol used to send a message to a user's outgoing mail host and from one mail host to another; requires a complex series of interactions between the sender and the receiver before and after mail delivery.

Simple Network Management Protocol (SNMP): The protocol that allows a general way to collect rich data from various managed devices in a network.

Single Point of Failure: When the failure in a single component of a system can cause a system to fail or be seriously degraded.

Single-Mode Fiber: Optical fiber whose core is so thin (usually 8.3 microns in diameter) that only a single mode can propagate, also the one traveling straight along the axis.

SIP: See Session Initiation Protocol.

Site-to-Site VPN: Virtual private network that secures all communication between two sites.

Site Survey: In wireless LANs, a radio survey to help determine where to place access points.

Skype: A P2P VoIP service that currently offers free calling among Skype customers over the Internet and reduced-costs calling to and from public switched telephone network customers.

Skype Login Server: A central server in the Skype network, managed directly by Skype.

SLA: See Service Level Agreement.

Sliding Window Protocol: Flow control protocol that tells a receiver how many more bytes it may transmit before receiving another acknowledgment, which will give a longer transmission window.

Slot: A very brief time period used in time division multiplexing; a subdivision of a frame. Carries one sample for one circuit.

Smart Access Point: An access point that has sufficient processing capacity to be managed directly.

Smart Cards: Credit or debit card that has an integrated circuit chip instead of (or in addition to) a magnetic stripe; more secure than a traditional magnetic stripe card.

Smartphone: Cellular telephone that offers many non telephony functions, such as internet access and running applications.

SMTP: See Simple Mail Transfer Protocol.

Sniffer Program: In security, a device that intercepts traffic to read it in order to find information useful to an attacker.

SNMP: See Simple Network Management Protocol.

Social Engineering: Tricking people into doing something to get around security protections.

Socket: The combination of an IP address and a port number, designating a specific connection to a specific application on a specific host. It is written as an IP address, a colon, and a port number, for instance, 128.171.17.13:80.

Software as a Service (SaaS): Service in which an application service provider supplies an application to customers on demand.

Software-defined networking: The replacement of the control function in individual switches and routers with a centralized control function; permits radical changes in network control functions to be implemented rapidly; permits new control functions to be deployed in all or part of the network.

Solid-Wire UTP: Type of UTP in which each of the eight wires really is a single solid wire.

SONET: See Synchronous Optical Network.

Spam: Unsolicited commercial e-mail.

Spawn: In virtualization, create a new copy of a virtual machine.

Spatial Streams: Radio signals in the same channel between two or more different antennas on access points and wireless hosts.

Spear-phishing attack: Attack in which a phishing mechanism is targeted at a particular individual. Contains information designed to reassure that individual that the message is legitimate, so that the individual will open an attachment.

SPI: See Stateful Packet Inspection.

Splitter: A device that a DSL user plugs into each telephone jack; the splitter separates the voice signal from the data signal so that they cannot interfere with each other.

Spread Spectrum Transmission: A type of radio transmission that takes the original signal and spreads the signal energy over a much broader channel than would be used in normal radio transmission; used in order to reduce propagation problems, not for security.

Spyware: Software that sits on a victim's machine and gathers information about the victim.

SS7: See Signaling System 7.

SSID: See Service Set ID.

SSL: See Secure Sockets Layer.

SSL/TLS: See Secure Sockets Layer and Transport Layer Security.

SSL/TLS-Aware: Modified to work with SSL/TLS.

ST Connector: A cylindrical optical fiber connector, sometimes called a bayonet connector because of the manner in which it pushes into an ST port and then twists to be locked in place.

ST Jack: Port for an ST connector.

Standard: A rule of operation that allows two hardware or software processes to work together. Standards normally govern the exchange of messages between two entities.

Standards Agency: An organization that creates and maintains standards.

Standards Architecture: A family of related standards that collectively allows an application program on one machine on an internet to communicate with another application program on another machine on the internet.

State: In digital physical layer signaling, one of the few line conditions that represent information.

Stateful Packet Inspection Firewall: A firewall whose default behavior is to allow all connections initiated by internal hosts but to block all connections initiated by external hosts. Only passes packets that are part of approved connections.

Stateful Packet Inspection: Firewall filtering mechanism that uses different filtering methods in different states of a conversation.

Static IP Address: An IP address that never changes.

Strain Relief: In a UTP connectorization, pressing the RJ-45 connector into the jacket of a UTP cord. This means that even if the cord is pulled, causing strain, the cord will not pull out of the connector.

Strand: In optical fiber, a core surrounded by a cladding. For two-way transmission, two optical fiber strands are needed.

Stranded-Wire UTP: Type of UTP in which each of the eight "wires" really is a collection of wire strands.

Stripping Tool: Tool for stripping the sheath off the end of a UTP cord.

Subcarrier: A channel that is itself a subdivision of a broadband channel, used to transmit frames in OFDM.

Subnet: A small network that is a subdivision of a large organization's network.

Subnet Mask: A mask with 1s in the network and subnet parts and 0s in the host part.

Subnet Part: The part of an IP address that specifies a particular subnet within a network.

Super Node: In Skype, a host node that takes on the work of signaling.

Supervisory Standard: A standard that used to keep a network or internet working.

Supplicant: The party trying to prove his or her identity.

Surreptitiously: Done without someone's knowledge, such as surreptitious face recognition scanning.

Switch: A device that forwards frames within a single network.

Switched Single Network: A single network that uses switches to route frames.

Switching Decision: When a frame arrives at a switch, the decision the switch makes to select a port to send the frame back out.

Switching Table: Table containing information used by a switch in switching decisions. At a minimum, contains rows that associate host addresses at Layer 2 with specific ports on the switch.

Symmetric: Speeds that are equal in both directions.

Symmetric Speed: A transmission link providing the same speed in both directions.

Symmetric Key Encryption: Family of encryption methods in which the two sides use the same key to encrypt messages to each other and to decrypt incoming messages. In bidirectional communication, only a single key is used.

SYN Bit: In TCP, a bit that is set to indicate that a TCP process wishes to or is willing to open a connection.

Synchronous Digital Hierarchy (SDH): In Europe, a hierarchy for leased lines faster than 50 Mbps; compatible by the Synchronous Optical Network standard used in North America.

Synchronous Optical Network (SONET): In North America, a hierarchy for leased lines faster than 50 Mbps; compatible by the Synchronous Digital Hierarchy standard used in Europe.

Syntax: In message exchange, how messages are organized.

T1 Leased Line: In the North American Digital Hierarchy, a leased line with a speed of 1.544 Mbps.

Tag: An indicator on an HTML file to show where the browser should render graphics files, when it should play audio files, and so forth.

Tag Field: One of the two fields added to an Ethernet MAC layer frame by the 802.1Q standard.

Tbps: Terabits per second—a thousand billions of bits per second.

TCP: See Transmission Control Protocol.

TCP Reset Segment: TCP segment in which the RST flag bit is set.

TCP Segment: A TCP message.

TCP/IP: The Internet Engineering Tasks Force's standards architecture; dominant above the data link layer.

TDM: See Time Division Multiplexing.

TDR: See Time Domain Reflectometry.

Telecommunications: The transmission of voice and video, as opposed to data.

Telecommunications Closet: The location on each floor of a building where cords coming up from the basement are connected to cords that span out horizontally to telephones and computers on that floor.

Terabits per Second: Transmission speed measured in multiples of 1,000,000,000,000 bps.

Terminal Crosstalk Interference: Crosstalk interference at the ends of a UTP cord, where wires are untwisted to fit into the connector. To control terminal crosstalk interference, wires should not be untwisted more than a half inch to fit into connectors.

Termination Equipment: Equipment that connects a site's internal telephone system to the local exchange carrier.

Terrestrial: Earth-bound transmissions.

Test Signals: Signal sent by a high-quality UTP tester through a UTP cord to check signal quality parameters.

Texting: In cellular telephony, the transmission of text messages.

Threat Environment: The threats that face the company.

Three-Party Call: A call in which three people can take part in a conversation.

Three-Step Handshake: A three-message exchange that opens a connection in TCP.

Throughput: The transmission speed that users *actually* get. Usually lower than a transmission system's rated speed.

Time Division Multiplexing (TDM): A technology used by telephone carriers to provide reserved capacity on trunk lines between switches. In TDM, time is first divided into frames, each of which are divided into slots; a circuit is given the same slot in every frame.

Time Domain Reflectometry (TDR): A testing system for UTP that can detect breaks in the wire.

Time to Live (TTL): The field added to a packet and given a value by a source host, usually between 64 and 128. Each router along the way decrements the TTL field by one. A router decrementing the TTL to zero will discard the packet; this prevents misaddressed packets from circulating endlessly among packet switches in search of their nonexistent destinations.

TLS: See Transport Layer Security.

Toll Call: Long-distance call pricing in which the price depends on distance and duration.

Toll-Free Numbers: Service in which anyone can call into a company, usually without being charged. Area codes are 800, 888, 877, 866, and 855.

Top-Level Domain: The second level of a DNS hierarchy, which categorizes the domain by organization type (e.g., .com, .net, .edu, .biz, .info) or by country (e.g., .uk, .ca, .ie, .au, .jp, .ch).

Topology: The physical organization of switches, routers, and other network devices; point-to-point, broadcast, mesh, switched, and so forth.

Tracker: In BitTorrent, a server that coordinates the file transfer.

Traffic Analysis: Analyzing patterns and requirements in transmission links within a network.

Traffic Class Field: An IPv6 field for specifying special handing for a packet.

Traffic Engineering: Designing and managing traffic on a network.

Traffic Shaping: Limiting access to a network based on type of traffic.

Trailer: The part of a message that comes after the data field.

Transceiver: A transmitter/receiver.

Transcode: In streaming video, to convert the program into a bit stream designed for a particular device and set of network conditions.

Transmission Control Protocol (TCP): The most common TCP/IP protocol at the transport layer. Connection-oriented and reliable.

Transparently: The ability to operate without the knowledge of another process; for example, IPsec protects transport layer and application layer traffic transparently; simplifies the operation of the process being supported transparently.

Transport: In telephony, transmission; taking voice signals from one subscriber's access line and delivering them to another customer's access line.

Transport Core: The switches and transmission lines that carry voice signals from one subscriber's access line and delivering them to another customer's access line.

Transport Layer: The layer that governs communication between two hosts; Layer 4 in both OSI and TCP/IP.

Transport Layer Security (TLS): The simplest VPN security standard to implement; originally named Secure Sockets Layer. Provides a secure connection at the transport layer, protecting any applications above it that are SSL/TLS-aware.

Transport Mode: One of IPsec's two modes of operation, in which the two computers that are communicating implement IPsec. Transport mode gives strong end-to-end security between the computers, but it requires IPsec configuration and a digital certificate on all machines.

Traps: The type of message that an agent sends if it detects a condition that it thinks the manager should know about.

Trojan Horse: A program that looks like an ordinary system file, but continues to exploit the user indefinitely.

True Party: In authentication, the person the supplicant says that he or she is.

Trunk Line: A transmission link that connects switches to other switches (or routers to other routers).

Trunking: See Link Aggregation.

TTL: See Time to Live.

Tunnel Mode: One of IPsec's two modes of operation, in which the IPsec connection extends only between IPsec gateways at the two sites. Tunnel mode provides no protection within sites, but it offers transparent security.

Twisted-Pair Copper Wiring: Wiring in which each pair's wires are twisted around each other several times per inch, reducing EMI.

Two-Factor Authentication: A type of authentication that requires two forms of credentials.

Two-Way Amplifier: In cable television, an amplifier that amplifies signals traveling in both directions.

U: See Unit.

UDP: See User Datagram Protocol.

UDP Checksum: Field in the UDP header that the receiver uses to check for errors. If the receiving transport process finds an error, it drops the UDP datagram.

UDP Length: Field in the UDP header that gives the length of the UDP data field in octets.

Unicasting: Transmission sent from one device to other device.

UNICODE: The standard that allows characters of all languages to be represented.

Unlicensed Radio Band: A radio band that does not require each station using it to have a license.

Unreliable: A protocol that does not provide error correction; error detection is not enough—there must also be the retransmission of lost or damaged messages; more efficient than reliable protocols, which provide error correction.

Unshielded Twisted Pair (UTP): A type of wiring in which each pair of wires is twisted around itself, usually several times per inch, to reduce the impact of external interference; cords may contain one, two, four, or more twisted pairs.

Uplink: In satellites, transmission from the Earth to a communication satellite.

User Datagram Protocol (UDP): Unreliable transport-layer protocol in TCP/IP.

Username: An alias that signifies the account that the account holder will be using.

UTP: See Unshielded Twisted Pair.

Verifier: The party requiring the supplicant to prove his or her identity.

Version: Field in an IP packet header that indicates whether the packet is an IPv4 or IPv6 packet.

Vertical Riser: Space between the floors of a building that telephone and data cabling go through to get to the building's upper floor.

Very Small Aperture Terminal (VSAT): Communication satellite earth station that has a small-diameter antenna.

Virtual Client: A of a client stored by a cloud provider. Real clients connected to the cloud are connected to the virtual machine for access to all of its resources. Different real clients will all see the same thing.

Virtual LAN (VLAN): A set of devices that can only communicate with each other.

Virtual Machine (VM): One of multiple logical machines in a real machine; to its users, it appears to be a real machine.

Virtual Private Network (VPN): A network that uses the Internet or a wireless network with added security for data transmission.

Virtualization: A process where the real computer's capacity is divided among a number of virtual machines.

Virus: A piece of executable code that attaches itself to programs or data files. When the program is executed or the data file opened, the virus spreads to other programs or data files.

VLAN: See Virtual LAN.

VM: See Virtual Machine.

Voice Mail: A service that allows people to leave a message if the user does not answer his or her phone.

Voice over IP (VoIP): The transmission of voice signals over an IP network.

Voice-Grade: Wire of a quality designed for transmitting voice signals in the PSTN.

VoIP: See Voice over IP.

VoIP Telephone: A telephone that has the electronics to encode voice for digital transmission and to handle packets over an IP internet.

VPN: See Virtual Private Network.

VSAT: See Very Small Aperture Terminal.

Vulnerability: A security weakness found in software.

Vulnerability-Specific Malware: Malware that is only effective if a device or program has a specific vulnerability.

Vulnerability Testing: Testing after protections have been configured, in which a company or a consultant attacks protections in the way a determined attacker would and notes which attacks that should have been stopped actually succeeded.

W3C: See World Wide Web Consortium.

WAN: See Wide Area Network.

War Driver: Person outside a company's walls who intercepts information to record publically available information about the company's wireless LAN, including SSID, signal strengths, and so forth; not illegal unless the person goes farther and becomes a drive-by hacker.

WATS: See Wide Area Telephone Service.

Wavelength: The physical distance between comparable points (e.g., from peak to peak) in successive cycles of a wave.

Webservice: The provision of World Wide Web service via the Hypertext Transfer Protocol (HTTP).

Well-Known Port Number: Standard port number of a major application that is usually (but not always) used. For example, the well-known TCP port number for HTTP is 80. Well-known port numbers range from 0 through 1023.

WEP: See Wired Equivalent Privacy.

Wide Area Network (WAN): A network that links different sites together.

Wide Area Telephone Service (WATS): Service that allows a company to place outgoing long-distance calls at per-minute prices lower than those of directly dialed calls.

Wi-Fi Alliance: Trade group created to create interoperability tests of 802.11 LANs; actually produced the WPA standard.

Wi-Fi Direct: Standard that permits direct transmission between two 802.11 devices without using an access point.

Wi-Fi Network: A network that follows 802.11 standards, with equipment that has been certified by the Wi-Fi Alliance.

Window Size Field: TCP header field that is used for flow control. It tells the station that receives the segment how many more octets that station may transmit before getting another acknowledgment message that will allow it to send more octets.

Wired Equivalent Privacy (WEP): A weak security mechanism for 802.11.

Wireless Access Point: Devices that control wireless clients and that bridge wireless clients to servers and routers on the firm's main wired LAN.

Wireless LAN (WLAN): A local area network that uses radio transmission instead of cabling to connect devices.

Wireless LAN Switch: An Ethernet switch to which multiple wireless access points connect; manages the access points.

Wireless Networking: Networking that uses radio transmission instead of wires to connect devices.

Wireless Protected Access (WPA): The 802.11 security method created as a stopgap between WEP and 802.11i.

Wireless Protected Access 2 (WPA2): Another name for 802.11 security.

Wireless Sniffer: Program that provides information about nearby access points and perhaps other wireless devices.

Wire-Speed Operation: The ability of a resource such as a firewall to operate properly even if incoming traffic is the maximum possible for each incoming port for the device. Important in firewalls because packets that cannot be processed will be dropped even if they are legitimate.

WLAN: See Wireless LAN.

World Wide Web Consortium: Consortium that sets World Wide Web standards, although the Internet Engineering Task Force creates many of these standards.

Workgroup Switch: A switch to which stations connect directly.

Working Group: A specific subgroup of the 802 Committee, in charge of developing a specific group of standards. For instance, the 802.3 Working Group creates Ethernet standards.

Worm: An attack program that propagates on its own by seeking out other computers, jumping to them, and installing itself.

Worst Case: In service level agreements, the worst service a customer will receive without the service

provider paying a penalty. The worst case for speed would be a certain *minimum* speed.

WPA: See Wireless Protected Access.

WPA2: See Wireless Protected Access 2.

X.25: The original PSDN standard. Relatively slow because it did error correction.

Zero-Day Attack: Attack that takes advantage of a vulnerability for which no patch or other workaround has been released.

INDEX

Page numbers in **bold** type indicate where terms are defined or characterized; page numbers in *italics* indicate tables or figures; page numbers with an "n" indicate a footnote.